D1232743

mazen
Oct. 2018

# SECRET SOLDIERS OF THE SECOND ARMY

**REGULATIONS OF**
**ROBERT A. FROST**
**MEMORIAL LIBRARY**
**Limestone, Maine**

Any person keeping a book from the Library more than two weeks shall be charged 5 cents per day for every day over that time.

Any person injuring a book belonging to the Library must pay such damage as is thought right by the Librarian. A person injuring a book shall not be allowed the use of the Library until such damage is paid.

IE A. CHAPMAN

authorHOUSE®

*AuthorHouse™*
*1663 Liberty Drive*
*Bloomington, IN 47403*
*www.authorhouse.com*
*Phone: 1-800-839-8640*

*© 2011 Leslie A. Chapman. All rights reserved.*

*No part of this book may be reproduced, stored in a retrieval system, or transmitted by any means without the written permission of the author.*

*First published by AuthorHouse 08/08/2011*

*ISBN: 978-1-4520-6768-1 (hc)*
*ISBN: 978-1-4520-6769-8 (sc)*
*ISBN: 978-1-4520-6770-4 (ebk)*

*Library of Congress Control Number: 2010934659*

*Printed in the United States of America*

*This book is printed on acid-free paper.*

*Because of the dynamic nature of the Internet, any Web addresses or links contained in this book may have changed since publication and may no longer be valid. The views expressed in this work are solely those of the author and do not necessarily reflect the views of the publisher, and the publisher hereby disclaims any responsibility for them.*

# PROLOGUE

I've sat silent for over 37 years, pondering over the many sights and experiences I've encountered over the course of my lifetime. I never thought or even contemplated the idea of setting down and revealing to the world, periods in my life as a member of one of the most Top Secret units operational during the Vietnam conflict.

Our Top Secret covert, classified intelligence-gathering missions were conducted in denied areas of South East Asia against an almost invisible elusive enemy in which we were exposing his hiding places, strength, assets and capabilities. All of our missions were considered suicidal due to the enemy size and their capabilities used against us, their geographical locations where we inserted, and the country in which we conducted those operations. We accepted the fact and boldly went forward knowing that we were out numbered, out manned, out gunned but we were steadfast in our resolve to infiltrate the areas that our enemy was attempting to deny us access.

Our casualty (wounded in action, WIA) death (killed in action, KIA) and missing in action (MIA) rates are historically documented at consistently above 100% at all times.

These WIA, KIA, and MIA figures were acceptable behind closed political doors in Washington, and condoned by the military chain-of-command within the Military Assistance Command Vietnam (MACV) structure.

What we few learned about our enemy and the intelligence we gained concerning that enemy could not be obtained by any other sources than to deploy us as sacrificial ponds in order to gain the intelligence necessary to save the many.

But, today here I set, dedicated in my resolve to lay before you my personnel Vietnam experiences and the experiences of some of the most gallantly brave soldiers that have brought me to this point in my life.

Within the past 37 years we've all been spell bound and emotionally captivated by Hollywood's attempts to provide us with the "real story" through films of how it really was in Vietnam. Through their graphic portrayals of Soldiers, Sailors, Airman and Marines participating in the Vietnam War who were uneducated, dope using, war mongering social losers who fought in the jungles of Vietnam.

The majority of their miserable visual attempts and miss-representation of who we really were and what we were doing to the public "what it was really like" is about 95% Bovine Feces. Hollywood can't or ever will be able to catch the true emotions we felt, the mental pressure and memories that we carry and the physical disfigurements and pain we experienced then and still carry today.

No man, book or movie will ever be able to demonstrate or reveal to the unknowing mind the feeling and emotions hidden by those, Soldiers, Sailors, Airman and Marines who lived it. However, some of Hollywood's documentaries concerning Vietnam have truly touched our hearts while others have tortured our innermost emotions and feelings.

The time has come to release those dark shadows of our past and bring forward the illusive and transparent ghost from the archives of the Top Secret, death missions, and human sacrificial missions ever undertaken in the History of the United States. These missions were undertaken and executed at great cost by the braves, self-sacrificing, freedom-loving men that have ever walked the face of this earth.

Today, many of the survivors from the Vietnam era are still questioned and queried concerning their comments or explanations of the intricacies and emotional ups and downs of combat. These inquisitions concerning Vietnam and how we felt and feel is raised from an inquisitive, questioning, hungry society for the truth.

Our youth and their naive thinking, think they are mentally equipped and prepared to receive the truth. They are expecting a pre-edited, pre-rehearsed flowery response. However, they surprisingly receive an angrily immediate response from the Veteran of "you really don't want to know, I don't want to talk about it or you haven't earned the right to know."

The negative response and answers the inquisitive mind seeks is never provided. So blinded by the facade that their mind begins to fantasize and mentally conjure up there own interpretation of the response they were looking for that they didn't get. They don't understand that we veteran's of the Vietnam era have had to hide our feeling and our stories because of the mental and at times physical persecution some of us have had to endure over the course of many years. So when a person today seeks the truth or asks the questions of "what was it like," we immediately go on the defensive prepared to protect our selves through silence.

However, now the youth of our country and some of those who protested against us during that period of time are ready and willing to hear the truth about us. Our society has now opened their eyes and see's the media today for what it unfortunately accomplished then. Now society is genuinely ready to listen and wants the uncut, un-flowered, unedited truth about Vietnam and the part that we played in it.

Many who heard the truth twenty years ago from us weren't prepared to hear or acknowledge the horrors we experienced. They wanted to hear fairy tales about the glory and victories of Vietnam, not anything about the blood, guts, death and maiming truth that we lived.

Today's youth is asking those sincere questions that were once taboo to the American people. "Tell us what it was about and what it was like." The youth of today is more curious, educated and open minded to what the truth really is and they are prepared to except it. Young people are now questioning their parents, teachers, and professors seeking the truth. No longer can or will the truth be held back from these inquisitive minds. They want conformation from those who were there to confirm or deny what is being relayed or taught in our educational institutions by our liberal left winged professional educators today.

They are no longer satisfied with a canned answer to their questions, they question what they see on television or what someone tells them through some type of media. They want to know the truth from the actual participants not the want-to-bee's or the great scholars who only know of Vietnam from books and articles they have studied from or researched, communicating their own interpretation of their research never really knowing, feeling or tasting the agony of war.

Today's inquisitive minds ask how does it feel to be out there in the deep jungle with all that constant stress and fear around you? Why did you go to Vietnam? How did the protesting about you being in Vietnam affect the war effort? Why were you treated so unjustly the way you were? What is Post-Traumatic Stress Syndrome? Did you ever kill anyone? How old were you when you went to Vietnam? How did the people there treat you? Why did all the people here in the United States treat you the way they did? Their questions are profound and information seeking.

It's hard for us to come to grips with these questions at times? Some of them are offensive when asked while others are stressful to answer. But now they are ready and deserve the answers to their questions.

For many years no one was interested in my feelings or what I went through. But now 37 years later, after we've hidden our stories, suppressed our pain, and suffering from the world for years. Now all of a sudden everyone wants to know and hear of our story of the Vietnam era.

It's ironic that some of those same people were protesters who lived during those times are now interested in knowing what the real story is. But, back then they were too busy protesting our presence in Vietnam, dodging the draft and publicly burning the American flag in defiance of our government and especially against us.

We were publically and openly chastised and hated by those protesting our presence in Vietnam. They were openly verbal concerning their feelings towards us. They took great joy and personal pleasure in screaming obscenities at us when we came home. The protesters thought that it was great sport for them to throw bags of dog and animal feces at us in and around airports to display their outward hatred and internal disgust towards us because we wore the uniform of the Armed Forces for our beloved United States of America.

I can recall overhearing those heroes's and heroin's of World War II and the Korean conflict Veterans often saying, "those boys who fought in Vietnam really didn't have it all that bad as we did." Or another expressed comment was "all those Vietnam Vet do is complain and try to get something for nothing from the government."

Don't misunderstand or read something into my personal comments about our predecessor military servicemen and women. For they were heroes during their time and still remembered as heroes by the thousands of Americans today. No matter what type of war or conflict a man or woman has taken part in, each veteran has his or her own stories or pain and despair. Each veteran has his owns personal feeling and pain that they must deal with secretly, silently and alone. Each has attempted to close and nail shut the door to that dark dreary place where we've hidden the horrible sights, deadly sounds and foul odors we no longer want to remember or ever again endure.

Most true combat veterans, if you can ever get them to talk to you about it will always refer to the funny and humorous time they had during the war. Or possibly about their best friends and buddies who were in the service with them. However, seldom if ever will they allow you to put them in a corner, revealing or even discussing openly with you, what it was like. For that dark closely guarded area in each of us is protected and tucked away in the deepest, darkest place we can cache it from appearing.

Some of us have it tucked so deep; we don't even refer to it or dare turn back the pages to remember any of it. The majority of us are proud of what we did during the Vietnam conflict in support of our government. Some veterans just want to blacken out that part of their lives as a bad chapter that we never want to read or have read again.

Now, enough time has passed and you're ready to hear and attempt to understand our story. It's important for the young people of today understand that those of us who went to Vietnam did so because we felt honored to represent our country. Some of us were drafted and served, while others of us volunteered for the Nam, having to prove something to himself or herself or someone. Either way we served as the laws of the land so dictated.

So with enduring personal resolve in our heart, our chests out and our heads held high we marched off like sheep to sloter. Defending our country as we were ordered to do, in a little backwards country called, South Vietnam. As in any war "Old men start wars and young men have to die fighting them."

Trying to explain to an outsider of our experiences in Vietnam is an almost impossible task. I can't even begin to explain to a now attentive audience what it was like, and them truly see or feel the emotions and agony I'm describing. I can verbalize the feeling that I felt but they will fall on deaf ears to those who have never experienced or undergone those feelings. I can attempt to put into words the real story only to be hampered by memories in a futile attempt to make you understand.

An analogy that I use to explain war to a young person or an inquiring person is a woman having a baby. A woman can explain in great detail the mental and physical anguish that they undergo when delivering a baby and us guys will stand there and say, "I know the feeling, or I understand." When in reality we have no concept. We know what pain is, we have all felt it, and we know how to convey it verbally but not the exact pain that a woman undergoes during childbirth.

But, on the other hand, you take that same woman who is attempting desperately to explain to a man what child birth is like to another knowledgeable woman having undergone the same pain and the inner feelings and understanding of one woman experience to another is clear as water. They immediately relate to every vivid and excruciating word and detail of the experience. They express the same pain and the understanding of that pain, and then together they share the compassion of the experience with one another.

We've all listened mesmerized, for countless hours to our fathers, mothers, grandparents, aunts and uncles tell us magnificent stories of victories, which were achieved during the Great War. Their very descriptive, mental picture of victory parades held in their honor for the returning victors and heroes. And the praise and admiration expressed publicly by all for their self-sacrifices and patriotism. Welcome home to open arms.

We never once overheard anyone discuss or even talk of a United States defeat its despair or humiliation we endured during that time. Because

America doesn't want to admit we lost, that would be to embarrassing. America loves a winner.

So as human nature dealt the cards. We the young men of the Vietnam era prepared graciously to go into battle with our heads held high. Only to return home to be greeted by an ungrateful nation that hated every single one of us for what we were ordered to do by our superiors and the laws of the land.

How do we tell a young person of today that war is not all that it's cracked up to be? People die, they're disabled mentally and physically, and they change mentally due to the horrifying trauma they have experienced, witnessed or endured.

I'll attempt with every ounce of my being, to convey to you some of my feeling and experiences. Hoping you'll understand how non-glorious war was, is, and will always be. I'll share with you some of the empty feeling most of us have been left with and live with daily. I'll present to you some of the bravest, unknown, unremembered men and their sacrifices they gave in our resolve in Vietnam.

Many of the details, explanations, words and descriptions you're about to read have never been shared until now. Our inter-most feeling we deal with then and now are going to be exposed for the first time to those of you outside of our protected circles.

Are you really ready for the truth? It's time for the real story to unfold, not a fairy tale that will start out with "Once upon a time i9n Vietnam," the real truth concerning the, "Secret Soldiers of the Second Army." Are you ready to be shocked? Are you ready to have tears well up in your eyes? Arc you prepared for the fear and pain your heart is about to stop for? Are your ready to learn of the United States Governmental Denied unit and the daring, ghostly missions of "Military Assistance Command Vietnam, Special Operations Group, Command and Control North (MACV-SOG-CCN)?"

Then let us begin.

# DEDICATION

These historical experiences, recollections, and writing are dedicated in memory of my most respected and beloved fallen comrades. Some of us were fortunate enough to have come home to an ungrateful nation while others died there in the hot, sweltering jungles having made the ultimate sacrifice for freedom with their lives. For we the Special Operations Soldiers or "Soldiers of the Second Army" daily put it all on the line in order that others may live.

Many of those brave sacrificial Green Berets lost their lives are but cherished memories of a dreadful past.

These writing are also dedicated to those of us who had the misfortune of surviving and returning home from Vietnam to a Nation filled with hatred and shame towards each of us. The majority of returnees were mentally maimed while other physically impaired. We returned to a nation that never once attempted to or wanted to understand our kind of war we fought. For us the shameful returning survivors carry the personal persecution, shame and retribution of American.

Furthermore I dedicate these memories of my past to my beloved wife and bride Jan, my children (Les, Lorie, Lisa, & Lenny), and to, my grand children and to the young of this great Nation. In hopes that you will see the sacrifices and truth of our war, its destructive power it shed on all Americans physically and mentally for decades to come.

Don't misinterpret or read into the message that will be delivered as hatred for or towards my country. For even today I would humbly and gratefully lay down my life to defend her against any foe. However, to each of you readers this book provides to each of you lesson learned from the actual examples that will be explicitly presented to you.

Young Americans, if you're called upon to defend this great nation and our way of life against aggression or oppression against any and all advisories, apply these proven techniques and examples in her defense.

Be bold and unyielding in her defense. Remain mentally and physically ruthless, as you stand ready to be intercept into the face of battle. Maintain tattooed within your spirit and sole the belief of our people that we shall prevail. Be swift in crushing the enemies of our country displaying no mercy or rendering any quarter. For you are now the carriers and caretakers of the sword of freedom and liberty.

However, be cautious and reserved in your motivation for war. Its ugly, unforgiving, physically and mentally demanding and will forever be embossed in your mind and conscious.

Beware if you've drawn the sword of freedom to take it into battle to prove yourself a man or to selfishly display your bravery and self glory for medals. For when its all over you'll try to answer the question or attempt to interpret the crucial question man has contemplated, searched for, analyzed and struggled to understand since time began. Why?

Go proudly if you're summoned, as you bear arms in our Armed Services, fighting our enemies. However, again evaluate yourself and mentally maintain the real reason why you are there and what you are doing. For when you dawn that shinning coat of armor for individual glory or self-recognition, the only glory you'll receive is pain, anguishing memories and indescribable haunting horror beyond human explanation.

Your now tarnished armor you once dawned will no longer shine with luster as it once did. It will be dark and gray with the blood of men. And your darkened and tarnished armor will be hard to put away and even heavier to carry.

Medals upon your chest and individual glory are simply material objects and false securities that all men can live without. Your honor, the honor or our Nation and the long lasting freedom and liberty for our people is your true rewards you seek.

We had a saying in Special Operations that went, "We gave up our today for your tomorrow." Take this day that we have given you and glorify our country through you honor, you courage in its defense and return with the dignity that you deserve.

"Greater love hath no man than this, that a man lay down his life for his friends."

Holy Bible John 15:13 Jesus speaking to the 12 Apostles

I'd Like to Have Two Armies

"One for display with lovely guns, tanks, little soldiers, staffs, distinguished and doddering Generals, and dear little Regimental Officers who would be deeply concerned over their General's bowel movements or their Colonel's piles; an Army that would be shown for a modest fee on every fairground in the country."

"The second Army would be the real one, composed entirely of young enthusiasts in camouflage uniforms, who would not be put on display, but from whom impossible mission would be demanded and to whom all sorts of tricks would be taught. That's the army in which I should like to fight

Author Unknown

"You've never lived until you've almost died.

For those who have fought for it,

Life has a special flavor the protected will never know."

Author Unknown

# THE TRUTH & NEED TO KNOW

All of the missions in this novel are true to the best of my knowledge. My personal missions will be followed at the end of each specific section with my personal awards and decoration received from the Department of the Army and or President of the United States.

Chapters 3-9 are true accounts presented to me by my best friend and brother of the sword Charles (Wes) F. Wesley who has passed away. During many conversations Wes told me of his exploits with his "A" Team. I can't remember the team designator Wes told me about so I have used a team that I ran a few missions with early during my first tour of service while in Vietnam.

That team is "A-104" Ha Than. I ran two missions with A-104 and knew most of the guys on the team so I have used their names within the text of the chapters as those with Wes. I do not profess or claim to have been on A-104, I only relate Wes's story to his year as an "A" team member. I mean no disrespect or dishonor to the true members of A-104, for they too were great and courageous warriors.

I will be substituting the word I, for that of Charles (Wes) F. Wesley in chapters 3-9, but in reality they were the true missions of Charles (Wes) F. Wesley. The remainder of the novel (A-101 Mai Loc, Hickory, and A Shau) will in fact be my missions and you will be able to distinguish between the others.

Those of us who have actually been there know the truth when we, feel it, hear it, read it, or for those of us who have lived it know it. We who have been there know what is truth and what is fiction by; the veterans silence when outsiders discuss the subject; we respond with confidence and trust when we know who has traveled the agonizing road of defeat labeled upon us by our fellow Americans and the mental misery and shame that has been tattooed on each of us; we immediately pick-put and recognize with disgust those braggers, and begets who are the want-a-be(s) and those who profess to have been there but never really did anything,

I leave the truth and interpretation of the truth within the following chapters up to you the reader. Names have been changed in some instances and the real names of some of America's Secret Soldiers of the Second Army are actual living or deceased persons. The stories of these unsung, unknown brave hero's who gave it their all should never be forgotten or their lives and accomplishments swept under the rug or lost in the shame of American history.

You the reader (Veterans) will know beyond a shadow of a doubt the truth when you read the contents of this book, because it will be accompanied with United States Department of the Army verification documentation. Those areas you are not sure of as being the truth or fiction, I leave up to you to determine within your own heart. My desires are these sacrifices given by these Secret Soldiers for our way of life and tremendous feats of valor and gallantry are never forgotten. You can place any name in place of the people who are mentioned here and you will have read the many deeds of each mans story who served within the Special Operations Command of America's Secret Soldiers of the Second Army in Vietnam.

# CHAPTER 1

I was only eighteen years old when I enlisted in the United States Army. Looking back, it seemed like the only exciting thing to do. I'd graduated from high school and had no desire to enroll in college. What could a university education provide that I couldn't earn myself? I couldn't stand the thought of wasting any more time.

You see, I was young and strong, and there was a war going on and I didn't want to let it pass me by. I yearned to be like my uncle who'd fought the Japanese in World War II, and to emulate my father who'd fought against Rommel, *The Desert Fox in Africa*. I wanted a chest full of medals and a massive collection of heroic stories that I'd be able to tell my children and grandchildren.

Most of all, I honestly wanted my family and my countrymen to be proud of me. I wanted them to be able to know from my actions that I had served my country faithfully, with genuine pride.

Filled with conviction, I sought out the local US Army Recruiting office and signed on the dotted line. Right on schedule, seven months later, I'd finished my basic and advanced training. I'd even completed my airborne instruction at Fort Benning, Georgia. Naturally, each of these achievements boosted my self-confidence and elevated my abilities; I took to the Army like a fish to water.

Not long after graduating airborne training, I was standing around joking with some friends near the Post Exchange in Fort Benning, when I noticed a ramrod straight, strack-looking Staff Sergeant walking toward our group. To say that he commanded respect would be an understatement; everything about him had "professional" written all over it. And, to top it off, he was wearing some sort of hat I'd never seen. At first, I assumed he was in another branch of the military or possibly from another country.

In an arrogant tone, I began questioning my friends, "What the hell is he supposed to be, and in what branch of service?"

Quickly, my friends encouraged me to shut my mouth and hope like hell he hadn't heard me. Naively, I asked again, "what in the hell are you talking about?" One of them revealed, "the guy you're making reference to is possibly one of the greatest fighting machines in the United States Army. Man, don't you know anything? He's a Green Beret!"

I was awestruck to say the least. What a proud, confident soldier he appeared to be. I was spellbound by his TW's and the way he fit his uniform, his radiating pride, cockiness and the way he carried himself, transfixed with envy I stood staring spell bound.

Leaning toward my friends, whose mouths were open in surprise, I whispered, "guys that is what I want to become: a Green Beret." Needless to say, they roared with laughter, quickly pointing out, "You don't have what it takes to become a Green Beret. Besides, you're too young." undaunted by their opposition, I sprinted to the on-base Special Forces Recruiter and informed him that I wanted to become a Green Beret.

Turns out, there were a few issues I had to overcome prior to being accepted into the ranks of the Special Forces. Since I was only 19 and a Private E2, I needed a waiver from the Department of the Army, giving exception to both my age and lack-of-rank.

So, as it goes in bureaucracies, I waited while the paperwork was submitted for approval. Every day I waited for word to come down from the Department of Army (DA) waiting for an answer one way or another was agonizing. Patience had never been one of my finer qualities, and 30 long days passed without any word from the higher-ups. I stayed on edge.

Finally, one day while I was on kitchen detail, I received word that I had been approved to take the battery of tests required to qualify for acceptance into the Special Forces Training Group. Nervously, full of doubt and lacking individual confidence, I took the physical fitness test, mental exams and evaluations, passing them all. Once again, I would have to play the waiting game while my test scores and requests for waivers filtered through the Department of the Army. Ultimately after forty-five days, word made its way down through military channels; I had been accepted to begin Special Forces Training at Fort Bragg, North Carolina.

My pride and arrogance was obvious as I paraded around the holding company area, boasting and strutting for all to see. I was to be the youngest soldier to have ever been accepted into the Special Forces program.

Looking back, I'm fairly sure my display of self-praise and tremendous ego made everyone a little sick to their stomachs.

I was reassigned to Fort Bragg, North Carolina. In May of 1967 I was assigned to B Company, Training Battalion, Special Forces Training Group. The focal point for all Special Forces training. Upon our arrival we were hustled inside a massive building for in processing and barracks assignment.

Not surprisingly, the paperwork took up most of the day. I literally filled out so many forms, that after a while, I didn't have a clue as to what I'd signed. Upon completion of in processing, the sergeant gathered us into formation outside with our duffle bags draped across our bodies.

I remember standing in that line, scanning the formation and realizing that guys from every military operational specialty were trying out for Special Forces. The maturity level encompassed both novice and journeyman, and a whole lot of in-betweens. As can be expected, my self-confidence and self-esteem was challenged as I mentally sized up my contemporaries.

Suddenly, the Sergeant First Class roars, "Class Attention." Everyone assumed ridged attention, awaiting his next command. From the corner of my eye, I caught sight of an extremely large man in the front of the formation. Without hesitation, he issued the second part of the command, "Right Face!" Of course we responded slowly, because our bags and equipment weighed us down. He then commanded, "Forward" hesitated momentarily then gave the command of execution "March," as he marched us to our barracks.

Upon arrival at our new home, he halted the formation, directed us to go inside, find our assigned rooms and bunks and get settled in. Once inside the barracks, everyone was friendly and more than willing to help with unfamiliar procedures.

The remainder of my first day involved a visual and mental evaluation of the people in my company. Naturally, everyone was older and had more stripes and military experience than I. They also appeared to be more mentally and physically prepared for the training we were about to undergo.

I made friends with a guy by the name of Mike Jones, a Sergeant E5 who already had one tour of Vietnam under his belt. He was exciting to be around and he immediately took me under his wing, promising to help me make it through the first phase of training.

Mike was 23 years old and came from your basic everyday family in Austin, Texas. Just like the state, he was a big guy; around six feet tall, extremely muscular and he drank like a fish. His political resolve was simple: God, Country and Killing North Vietnamese. Mike's face confirmed his acquaintance with mental anguish, pain and trouble. After he'd had a few drinks, he'd tell stories that made my skin crawl about Vietnam.

Maybe because we were roommates, or maybe out of some self-preserving admiration, I began slowly fashioning myself mentally and physically after him. In order to emulate Mike, I took on a constant facial expression of seriousness. Preaching to anyone who would listen, I professed to hate a group of people that I knew nothing about, or hadn't even seen.

Right then and there, I began to build a facade, like so many young men did before and will again. I was trying to be something I was not, mimicking someone else. What I could not realize then was this practice would have a price, and it would demand payment in full.

Mike consistently harped at me "You'd better learn right now that in this unit, if you don't keep your shit wired tight, someone will tighten it up for you." Deep down, I believed that there was some kind of truth to his ramblings, so I began to try and get my act together, or so I thought.

3:00 a.m. Monday – I lay sleeping in my bunk only to be awakened by a thundering noise, followed by brilliant lights surrounding me. The next thing I knew, my bunk had been turned over and I was face down on the cold cement floor. Sure enough, a huge man wearing a green beret stood over me screaming, "Get your fatigues and boots on and fall out for physical training.

Although I moved as fast as I could physically move, it wasn't fast enough. More of the towering men appeared and proceeded to throw all of our equipment and bedding out of the windows.

Having no idea where I was supposed to go in order to line up with my company, I ran downstairs and stood in the first formation I could find. I just found a spot and stood absolutely motionless. It was pitch black and none of us could see anyone else in the formation except the man on our right, left, front and rear. Instantly, a blinding flash of floodlights pierced the darkness from all directions, literally turning the night into day. We were all standing in formation like little tin soldiers while the big men who had so violently awakened us were going through the ranks.

All 10 of them were screaming simultaneously over and over ordering for everyone to get down into the front leaning rest position and "Start pushing Fort Bragg away." After they'd exhausted us with that drill, we were taught a new exercise that involved standing on your head, low crawling, elevating your feet on a tree and attempting to do pushups while your feet were elevated. This lasted for about 15 minutes before we were ordered back into formation. We then ran about half a mile down the road until we came to a big parade field where we formed up into the standard military P.T. formation, facing our instructor at open ranks.

We then began the most rigorous physical training program I had ever undertaken in my entire life. We did pushups until my arms felt like they were going to fall off. We did squats, high jumpers, body twists, trunk twisters and team/buddy exercises until the sun came up at 5:30 a.m.

As the lead P.T. instructor ordered the formation to close ranks, a sigh of relief began to come over us. We moved into a marching formation with instructors on all sides and began marching down the road.

From the left of the formation came the prepatory command, "Double Time" hesitating momentarily followed by the command of execution "March." The pace of the double time was similar to being shot out of a cannon. We began at a full run, which we all maintained for a while. However, as the pace continued to accelerate, I began to fall out. And, I wasn't the only one; the majority of the new students were just as unprepared for what was happening, as was I. We only ran three miles, but the pace matched that of Olympic runners.

When we returned to the barracks, we were introduced to the senior tactical advisor, Master Sergeant George. The first words out of his mouth were "Who wants to quit? Those who want to quit now move out into the barracks and get your gear then form back up to my left." That was it – no welcome, no pleasantries.

After I saw almost half of the company fall out, I began questioning my own sanity and high ideals of becoming a green beret. I began to wonder if I really had the intestinal and physical fortitude for this kind of training it was going to demand. *Did I have the right stuff?* As I watched one after another of the initial trainees head for the barracks, I remember thinking, *"I did not come this far to tuck my tail between my legs and run off just because the going is getting tough."*

The next two weeks were filled with this same kind of physical training twice a day. And then there were the nights? Oh, the nights were interesting full of fun and games, to say the least. It was common for the training instructors to come into the barracks at all hours and conduct footlocker drill.

For those unfamiliar with the term, it basically consisted of hoisting your fully loaded footlocker over your head and running in and out of the barracks until the training instructors became bored or tired. Footlocker fun could go on for a minimum of an hour, depending on how the cadre was feeling at that particular moment. Every day started with the Senior TAC out in front of our formation asking the same question, "Who wants to quit?" And every day, a few more guys would be outside the barracks with their gear, honestly confessing that this particular training was just too much for them.

As our numbers dwindled, the mental and physical abuse increased. In fact, the harassment never ended; the training instructors never let up. Someone was always in your face cursing, yelling, wailing, "You don't have what it takes." They were constantly begging you to quit, and to admit that you just didn't have the energy to hang in there. In an effort not to fold, we gave each of the tactical instructor's names, and started treating their harassment and insults as a continual game.

Phase One Training followed Hell Week, as it was known. This training segment encompassed tactical classes, hand-to-hand combat, map reading, negotiating terrain courses using your map and compass, survival techniques, Special Forces unconventional warfare concepts and the beginning of a lifelong study of guerrilla warfare. The initial training phase lasted for about six weeks.

Upon completion, you entered into Phase Two, your specialty training or Military Occupational Specialty. As a reward, the survivors of Hell Week and Phase One Training were moved to new barracks and received new TACs. Phase Two was a little calmer than the previous training, but not much.

This phase was the beginning of my weapons training at Fort Bragg. It was intense, demanding and extremely comprehensive training, lasting about nineteen more weeks. We learned every kind of foreign and domestic weapons system to include heavy weapons, i.e., 60 mortar, 81 mortar, 4.2mm mortar, target analysis, use of artillery and mortar plotting boards and associated ammunitions that accompanied each of the weapons systems.

Having successfully completed the Special Forces 11B/11C Weapons Course, I proudly received my Green Beret. Looking back, I wonder what kept me going and from where I drew my strength? I remembered that my Special Forces Training class started out with 33 people. My graduating class from the Weapons Course consisted of only 15 weapons men who were awarded their beret.

Upon graduation I was placed into a Special Forces line company. My new home was B Company, 7th Special Forces, Fort Bragg, North Carolina. Since I'd been promoted to Specialist E-4 upon graduation from training group, I was on top of the world. Upon entering the company orderly room, I asked a sergeant sitting behind a desk for directions to the Company Sergeant Majors office.

Without even raising his head from his desktop, he pointed to a door down the hall. Thanking him, I moved quickly to the office labeled Sergeant Major. I straighten my beret and uniform and knocked at the closed door only to be answered with a gruff response of "Get your ass in here." I opened the door and stood before an older man who was somewhat overweight.

For what seemed like five minutes, the Sergeant Major looked me up and down, never speaking, just looking at me. Finally, he spoke, "Stand at ease." I briskly snapped to. As he attended to something on his desk, he maintained his silence. I tried to determine what manner of man he was. The Sergeant Major must have been the first Special Forces soldier ever accepted into the unit because he appeared to be two days older than dirt. Deep lines were carved into his round face, telling of a bitter hard road to gain his knowledge and wisdom.

His appearance and speech were gruff, immediately letting you know who was in charge. As he began talking to me, it became obvious that I was the lowest ranking maggot in his company and he wasn't happy about it.

His expressed displeasure became evident when he said, "I don't know how you got this far, but if you don't perform and live up to the company's expectations of a well-rounded, trainable soldier, I am going to run you off."

He began to lecture me, saying, "You are a member of the most elite fighting force in the world today "boy". You are a trained killer of men and a freedom fighter for the oppressed people throughout the world. You are, and will be capable of killing a man 100 different ways. Your combat capabilities will be honed to a fine edge, far beyond that of any other soldiers within the United States Armed Forces."

He hesitated momentarily and seemed to mentally wander off into another world; a world where no one was allowed unless invited. I wondered what was going on. As he raised his head, our eyes met. He stared at me through piercing bloodshot blue eyes and then, like the whisper of the light wind, he softly spoke: "Son, you will more than likely die when you go to Vietnam. But, before you leave my company, I will personally see to it that you are prepared to meet the Viet Cong on his own ground and kick the living shit out of him." That was the end of our one-way conversation. The Sergeant Major spun swiftly around in his chair looking at the team status board that hung behind him to determine what team he was going to assign me to.

The board was broken down into seven specific columns, military operation specialties (MOSs) with names filling the board. One column was for the headquarters personnel and the other six lines or columns were the Special Forces "A" teams assigned to the company. He grease penciled my name in, assigning me to the Gabriel Demonstration Team, which performed the many and diverse capabilities of Special Forces for all high-ranking officials who came to Fort Bragg to see exactly what it was that made Special Forces so special.

Since I was the new team member, I was appointed the gopher for everything. However, I learned so many things that would keep a soldier alive and be a benefit to any team; like survival techniques, more hand-to-hand, weapons training, communications techniques and intelligence gathering.

I was a member of this team for about three months until orders came down from 7th Group Headquarters, re-assigning me to Signal Company to undergo communications training.

I learned to use clandestine communications techniques, becoming trained in Morse code or commonly referred to in Special Forces as C.W. The curriculum for communications training was clandestine antenna construction, radio and communications theory, frequency theory, operational deployment of Special Forces communications equipment and capability and classified communications. The primary thrust of the training was to send and receive code.

I listened and practiced code for hours on end, I actually began to dream in code. The testing for this particular training was long and stressful.

When final exam scores were posted, I could send and receive 17 groups per minute in code, a passing score.

I no sooner had finished communications training, when I reported back to the Orderly Room to go back to my team when once again the Sergeants Major didn't say a word to me he simply handed me orders to directing me to attend Cross Training as a Special Forces Medic.

For the next twenty-six weeks I was once again sitting on my butt, in a classroom and the war was passing me by.

During my cross training we started out with anatomy, physiology, drug therapy, current treatment diagnosis, patient history taking, how to take vitals and transcribe records. Once we had completed the first six weeks of that initial Special Forces medic indoctrination training we moved on to some more advance medic training which included more treatment and diagnosis, drug therapy, fluid therapy and additional anatomy and physiology and the beginning of minor surgery techniques.

At the completion of the third six weeks of training we were assigned to the Special Forces Dispensary for five week where we learned how to run and participate in sick call then we were sent to Womack Army Hospital there at Fort Bragg.

In the hospital we performed minor duties primarily as observers in most of the departments but occasionally we actually did work in the maternity ward, surgery ward, emergency room, laboratory department, orthopedic section, gastrointestinal and treatment facilities. All of this training was very important and most interesting. Now that I was being cross-trained as a Medic I wanted to learn more. When we received a patient in the hospital emergency room we went to work immediately insuring that the airway was clear, stop the bleeding, treating the person for shock and starting minor surgery if required. Always under the supervision and watchful eye of a Doctor, of course.

After completing another 26 weeks of training I had successfully completed the Special Forces cross-training course and I was awarded a additional MOS as a 91B Special Forces Medic. By this time, I was burned out on schools, feeling as though I was a professional student rather than a Special Forces Green Beret preparing to go to war. I'd been in training for almost the past two years and the closest thing to a war story I could tell was the number of weapons I could break down and reassemble.

Upon successful completion of the Medic Course I was taken out of B Company 7th Special Forces and reassigned to C Company 7th Special Forces. At last I was in a Special Forces line company no more schooling or just sitting on my butt. Finally, I was assigned to a team where everyone was a combat veteran. Being the only one without combat experience, I was mesmerized by their stories of fighting the Viet Cong that they told in the team room.

I couldn't get enough of their patriotism and bravery. Burning with envy, I longed to go to war. I was afraid the war would pass me by and I'd be unable to prove (to myself or anyone else) what I was really made of.

The great day finally came in August of 1968. My Sergeant Major presented me with my assignment orders to be assigned to the 5th Special Forces in Vietnam, with a report date of October 8, 1968. I left the orderly room on a cloud. Finally, it was my turn; I was going to go to war. My idea of war and its enduring glory would become a scar that I'd live with the rest of my life.

I was so filled with excitement that I don't know how I got to Group Headquarters. One second, I was in the orderly room and the next I was standing at the personnel sergeant's desk, trying to clear post.

When I got home that night to my beautiful wife Jan, I proudly told her about my assignment to Vietnam. But for some reason, she didn't share my joy. I was confused and somewhat angry. She was supposed to be more like me, hard and aggressive and prepared to do whatever was necessary for the war effort. Yet, I was seeing a completely different side of her, one that I had never been aware of. Her eyes reflected fear and uncertainty about our destiny together.

# CHAPTER 2

After finishing my out-processing, I set up my household in California so that my family would be secure while I was in Vietnam. Largely because of my intense focus on being a Special Forces soldier and my sincere belief that I could make a difference in the world, I gave no consideration to the sensitive side of my emotions nor anyone else. Nor did I dwell on my wife Jan and newborn son Les.

I had not yet admitted that I might never see them again. Quite simply, I pushed such thoughts from my mind and refused to acknowledge that there was a good possibility I wouldn't be able to see my son grow up. I never gave a thought to what his father figure might be if I failed to return from the jungles. None of these scenarios were allowed into my conscious realm until it was far too late.

A young man's foolish pride and vain desire for glory have blinded him since the beginning of time; I was no different; I had fallen prey to an egotistical illusion of grandeur. When I look back at how my actions affected my wife and child, I am ashamed that I was so selfish and narrow-minded, thinking only of myself and my dreams of glory. I've never exposed these feelings of regret and shame until now.

Many a time in Vietnam, I held a dying soldier in my arms or listened to a dying friend, pleading for me to swear before God, that I would tell his wife or his mother these exact words. "Tell my wife, I'm sorry for the way that this has turned out, and that I love her very much." Then, as the Man Upstairs called this brave soldier home, the young man would try desperately to grab the last breath of life, struggling with all of his strength, to no avail. Death came and carried him to a place where only soldiers go to wait, hopefully that is Heaven.

In 1968, I came to the realization that I was going to a place where death and pain were an everyday occurrence. In a little more than three weeks, I would be halfway around the world, and I might not return. Reality is a real bitch, when you finally recognize her; I was leaving everything I loved and everything that loved me.

For the first time in my life, I experienced terror and genuine fear. At times, the fear became intense enough to cause me to physically tremble. I loved my wife of two years very deeply, a kind of love that can only be shared between a man and woman. We had stumbled and struggled through hardships, and trotted and danced through joys, always physiologically and emotionally sharing our existence. Through our love, we were blessed with the birth of our son.

Although I had been unable to find words to adequately express my sense of pride while holding this innocent child close to my body, the wonder was overwhelming. I desperately wanted to convey my love and eternal best wishes for his future. Yet, as I gazed into his innocent, curious little eyes, all I could feel was pain. This pain pierced my heart and tore a hole in my soul.

I ended up continually second-guessing my decisions with questions like: "*Why have I put this death sentence on my family?*" "*What exactly was I thinking would happen after all of my training?*" Though my questions remained unanswered, the brave liberator-of-the-oppressed, the trained killer-of-man was brought to his knees, my heart was weeping like a child. Instead of crying because of physical pain, I secretly cried due to fear of the unknown and an overwhelming sense of never returning home. Strange the way home doesn't seem like a big deal until you think you might never see it again. At that point, it becomes monumental.

Suddenly, days seemed to pick up speed, flying by at an alarming rate. I tried desperately to hold on to time, willing it to slow down so that I might reset its pace. I tried like a madman to cram minutes into seconds, hours into minutes and days into hours, all to no avail. Time is its own boss and presses on, refusing to be controlled by anyone. The only thing I could do was hang- on to every precious minute.

I felt an overwhelming need to mend old wounds between friends, family and anyone else I might have offended in my youth. I began to honestly share my feelings, especially with those that I loved. Realizing that this might be my last chance, I bared my soul. I felt like my brothers began to see me in a different light as we turned back the pages of my life with them. We laughed as we reminisced about the mean tricks and practical jokes we had played on each other. We chuckled out loud about the most mundane of topics. And all of the while, I hoped they would remember me for my goodness and allow the bad memories to slide.

My sisters gave off quite another vibration. I could see the pain and fear they had for me because they didn't attempt to hide it. They wanted me to reassure them that I would indeed return home. There was no other option; I was their brother and there would be no other ending to the story. Most of my life, I'd believed my brothers to be athletically superior to me, and my sisters more studious and thoughtful than I could ever be. Now, the only thing I wanted to do was hold them in my arms before I left.

However, this wasn't the Special Forces way of doing things. And amazingly, my outward attitude had changed, giving the false impression of a hardened, unemotional response. I was Special Forces and my emotions were supposed to be suppressed. Even the most macho of males are unable to deceive one person, their mother. Mothers normally hold a special place within a man's heart, and my mom was no different. Time and again, she'd unselfishly demonstrated complete disregard for her personal well-being to cater to her children's needs.

As I looked into her eyes, I remembered how much I'd wanted to prove my worth to her. I wanted her to know that she'd raised a man who was willing to die for his country, the kind of son she'd be proud of. Looking back today, I don't know who I was trying to impress, because it wasn't her. Now that I have sons and daughters of my own who are old enough to go to war or send a loved one to war, I realize just a little of what my mother must have felt.

You see, I'm tremendously proud of my sons and daughters, and they don't ever have to prove anything to me or anyone else. The only person they must prove anything to is to themselves. I wonder how many times each of us has been a people pleaser instead of doing what we really knew was right or wanted to do?

Speaking as a parent, I honestly don't believe I could bear the hurt of losing one of my children. How would you fill the void of one of the most valuable thing in your life? What would you do to fill your hearts emptiness should one of your children suddenly be gone? Looking back, I realize the anguish my mother bravely endured. Because I didn't want anyone except my wife and son to accompany me to the airport, I said good-bye to my family at my mother's house.

Everyone was there: brothers, sisters, in-laws, nephews, nieces and friends. Emotions ran the gambit from laughter to outright sobbing. I spotted my mother standing off to the rear, tears streaming down her face, a horrible mixture of love and fear in her eyes.

As if orchestrated by an unseen maestro, everyone stepped aside, clearing a path to her. I moved ever so proudly to hold her, hugging her tightly and whispering into her ear, "I love you," as I tried to hold back the tears that suddenly filled my eyes. Still holding her tightly, we began to rock from side to side, just like she had rocked me as a child.

It was as if she was trying her best to remove my pain. As we slowly separated, she said ever so lovingly, "God will bring you home to me."

Rapidly, I moved directly to my car without looking back, where my beautiful little Jan and Les waited patiently. As I pulled the little Volkswagen beetle away from the curb, I could barely breathe. My throat was almost swollen shut, making it difficult to swallow; my heart was pounding and every muscle in my body quivered. While I kept up the facade of being cool as a cucumber, I was sobbing inside, dangerously close to breaking down. Somehow I didn't. Somehow, I managed to hold my emotions in check because the precious young woman who sat beside me holding our son, was quietly being torn apart inside.

Soldiers and their families were milling about everywhere inside the Los Angeles airport. Marines, Sailors and Airmen were all experiencing the same pain I felt, and so many of those young men would never return home. Never again would they be able to hold their wives or feel their sweet breath on their necks. In fact, within a few days, weeks or months, many of those young brides would have a bright shinning military vehicle drive up to their front yard. Two spit-and-polished officers would emerge with news that their husband, had died in the service of his country in Southeast Asia. And, that would be the end of their fairy-tale marriage.

As I sat with my arm around Jan and played with Les, a stabbing sensation pierced my stomach; the loudspeakers roared, "Now announcing the immediate boarding and departure of Flight 222, for Seattle-Tacoma, Washington." I met my wife's eyes and we realized our moment of heartbreak had arrived. Jan began to cry, sobbing, begging me not to board the plane, although she knew I couldn't stay.

I was a soldier and I was on my way to war. Feeling her stare at my back while I made my way to the door, I looked straight ahead, sure that if I turned around, I wouldn't board my plane. I could literally feel her heart breaking. All I could think about was *"You're Special Forces; you don't cry; you're hard; you're tough, you're the liberator of your country."* I waited until I was in my seat searing out the window of the airplane before tears flowed down my cheeks. I was unable to hold back my pain and sorrow.

# CHAPTER 3

One week later, I was in Cam Ranh Bay, South Vietnam completing my in-processing and attending briefing after briefing. Since my in-country assignment was Nah Trang, 5th Special Forces Group, it was mandatory that all newly assigned personnel receive additional jungle training on a nearby island. Here, we experienced the Clandestine Operations Course (COC); learned to call in air strikes, received additional patrol techniques, practiced ambush techniques, went through the quick-kill firing courses and small group tactics. Upon completion of our training on Hon Tra Island, we were sent back to the 5th Special Forces Operational Base (SFOB) and assigned to our respective Companies and Special Forces "A" camps.

My assignment was Company C, 5th Special Forces Group, Da Nang, A-104 Ha Than. Finally, I was going into the field, brimming with excitement, yet apprehensive about making the grade. Vietnam was a game of high-risk, calculated psychological factors; a war that involved wearing down the human mind, morals, individual constitutions, beliefs and character.

The mind is an extremely complicated and delicate apparatus, one that is easily influenced by trauma or perceived danger. With careful yet intricate manipulation the mind can be convinced to do just about anything because of fear, intimidation or coercion. Psychological warfare is devastating and can produce mass, rapid mood changes, as was the case in Vietnam. When the US first became involved in this conflict, it was widely perceived that we would defeat the ill-equipped, militarily inferior, technologically backward government of North Vietnam quickly and efficiently. However, we failed to plan for unorthodox enemy guerilla operations, the kind that butted heads with our high-tech, fast-moving modern forces–Gorilla Warfare, coupled with psychological operations.

All of the United States' previous conflicts and wars consisted of defined lines, territories and boundaries of enemy-held positions fighting against a uniformed enemy. Normally, we battled foes who were dressed in distinct uniforms for easy identification. However, Vietnam dealt us an entirely different deck of cards. There were no true enemy lines, the NVA wasn't always dressed in a unique uniform for clear recognition and they rarely grouped their forces into one location. Their refusal to fight with conventional warfare tactics inhibited the allied forces' chances of intercepting and engaging in the combat operations necessary to either eradicate them or completely eliminate them.

Extremely limited intelligence was available about the actions of the North Vietnamese Army (NVA), further reducing large-scale attacks against them; we were constantly scrambling to find him. This enemy, the NVA and Viet Cong was cunning and highly capable of delivering a crushing blow at the time and place of their choosing. Day in and day out, it became obvious that our enemy was almost ghostlike having the ability to disappear like cigarette smoke in the wind.

Repeated deadly experiences belied the fact that the jungle concealed an enemy who could deliver ground, grenade and bomb attacks at any time. And, their method of delivery had devastating results. We had no idea how many, where they came from, whether they were male or female, child or adult. We literally worked and trained with them during the day and fought them at night.

Imagine working beside a man who professes democracy during the day, yet actually condones and operates against you as a Viet Cong communist sympathizer at night. He plants booby traps and mines, lying in wait with an ambush to send you home in a body bag. Remember, psychological warfare is terror that toys with the mind through surprise attacks and continual fear. This kind of terrorism exists today with terrorists gunning people down in airports, bombing embassies, blowing airplanes out of the sky.

Terrorism is extremely upsetting, mild boggling causing you to constantly wonder if some group or person is preparing to play out some sick fantasy. How many Americans today are afraid, or at least hesitant about traveling to a foreign country for fear of high jacking or being blown out of the sky at 30,000 feet?

This is the kind of terror that constantly surrounded us day-in and day-out in Vietnam. Americans are largely creatures of habit, unconcerned with events that don't directly affect us. We are also normally not very observant and tend to accept things as they appear. As such, mental and physical adjustments are a burden to us. We don't usually distrust a fellow worker, nor do we suspect an allied soldier whom we've fought beside of being a guerrilla or subversive agitator.

Instead, we rationalize this kind of thought as being totally absurd. We convince ourselves that we're here to help free them from the evil communists, and we honestly believe that everyone will be better off in the end. We would never suspect a woman or child of wanting to send us home in a rubber bag. But we were wrong; the North Vietnamese sympathizers and Viet Cong were all around us, and were more than eager to take our lives away.

When I arrived in Vietnam in 1968, I was assigned to an "A" Detachment, (a 12-man, Special Forces, Green Beret team with all desired and required military occupational specialties; two communications men, two demolitions men, two medics, two intelligence men, two weapons men and two officers). I came to Camp A-104, Ha Tan, which was located in I Corp. Upon my arrival I was introduced to all of the Americans and to my Vietnamese Special Forces counterpart (LLDB, RVN) and was received with a high degree of suspicion. Everyone appeared to be silently asking them selves "Will he last or will he become another statistic?

An "A" Camp is unique in that it is part base camp, home for the indigenous personnel and part-fighting fortress. It is a fort, a safety retreat for local villagers, Vietnamese or Montagnards. All of these camps were built from the ground up. Viewing an "A" camp from the air some were designed to look like a star, having five distinct points. Normally, the points held automatic weapons which were designed to interlock or cross fire with each other. Other "A" camps were built triangular, rectangular or oval in shape. As such, they were built around or on prominent terrain features for easy recognition from the air. The camps building and bunkers were very plain; your basic corrugated tin, cement bunkers, trench lines, thousands of sand bags and miles and miles of barbed wire encircled the camp. There were no scenic pictures of plush mountain views on the walls nor were there any cultural photographs spread around.

Instead, the walls of the camp were lined with enemy situation maps, maps of suspected enemy locations and combat operations in planning stages. There were no windows to leisurely gaze out, only firing ports for our rifles. Quite plainly speaking, it was a battle camp simply in existence to seek out and destroy the communist aggressor.

The Special Forces "A" camp defense normally consisted of three perimeters. The outer perimeter was lined with barbed wire tangle foot wire with lots of beer and coke cans attached to it. The cans were hung on the barbed wire half filled with rocks so they would make noise if they were disturbed.

Between the first and second perimeter were numerous destructive antipersonnel devices, specifically geared toward maiming or killing men. Some of these included the precious claymore mines. A claymore mine was an antipersonnel mine with approximately 1200 BBs packed in a plastic substance inside, backed with 2 1/2 pounds of plastic explosive C-4. It could either be command detonated or booby-trapped. Also, within this perimeter were pungi stakes. Pungi stakes were normally 12- to 18-inch long bamboo sticks that had been sectioned off into four or more equally measured lengths. After being dried out by the blistering Vietnam sun, they were whittled down to a razor-sharp point.

To add insult to injury, the pungi stakes were then dipped in buffalo feces. Once a person had his skin pierced by the stakes, he not only had a hole in his body, but the fecal-dipped stake ensured an intense infection as well. Hopefully, if the perimeter was penetrated, the enemy would unknowingly hurl himself onto the stakes, resulting in his death or at least a secondary infection. Either way, he was out of the game. Pungi pits or various types and sized were used most effectively against American and all of the Allied forces.

Additionally, antipersonnel land mines were intermingled throughout the first and second perimeter, creating another line of defense. Some of the antipersonnel mines were the size of a tuna can and others were as large as a coffee can, with their primary purpose being to maim or kill. Uncharted mine fields are a tremendous psychological weapon and enemy deterrent when your enemy doesn't know where they are. While some of the antipersonnel mines were designed to simply take off a foot or a leg, others were designed to bounce up out of the ground and explode at hip level, effectively cutting your enemy in half. Still others would simply disintegrate a human being in an instant. If someone entered a minefield and failed to trip a mine himself, possibly someone to his left or right might trip one, the concussion or possibly his panic could cause him to move into another mine. Boom! Imagine the horror of knowing you're in a minefield, defenseless, unaware of what is below you or around you, and being unable to get out. Psychological trauma envelopes you. Without a doubt, you are now in what we called "a world of shit." Mines were a minus to both sides of the war.

Yet another means of camp defense was Fu-Gas, a Napalm stick to you skin type substance. The recipe is as follows; a 55-gallon drum, filled 3/4th full of regular diesel fuel mixed with M-2 fuel thickener. This combination formed jell-like glue that sticks to everything it comes into contact with. The drum is placed on its side and earth is dug out to make a place for it to lay, with approximately 10-20 pounds of C-4 plastic explosives placed behind it as a charge.

It works like this: fire has and always will be a great psychological weapon. When used against ground attacks, it normally ends the aggression quickly. First, you allow your enemy to get almost on top of the explosive. Then, you detonate the C-4, which in turn ignites the Fu-gas, throwing its lethal ingredients onto your enemy and inflicting massive casualties. Coupled with the rupturing of the 55-gallon closed container, the C-4 becomes a bursting, rolling ball of fire traveling at a high rate of speed horizontally across the ground and through the air, its contents sticking to everything it touches. If, by chance, your enemy is not physically hit by the Fu-gas itself, it will still take all of the oxygen out of his lungs, collapsing them. Therefore, you've reached the desired conclusion to the attack. The Fu-gas will burn anywhere from five to seven minutes before burning itself out.

The second and third protective perimeters were sandwiched with more destruction devices, claymore mines, bouncing Betty's, top poppers, antipersonnel mines, fu-gas and pungi stakes.

The final protective line contained intermingled, interlocking automatic weapons. Inside the inner perimeter were defensive bunkers, trench lines, mortar positions, heavy barreled .50 machine-guns, 105mm Howitzers, 57mm & 106mm recoilless rifles, M-16's, M-60 machine-guns, grenades and .45 caliber pistols. If this final protective line was ever breached by the enemy, you retreated as quickly as humanly possible to the command bunker and prepared for hand-to-hand combat or better known as close order knuckle drill.

An average "A" Camp consisted of between 300 to 500 indigenous Vietnamese or Montagnard soldiers with another 150-200 family members that lived within the confines of the camp. Normally, a camp was built near other Vietnamese and/or Montagnard villages so we could shelter them against massacre or black propaganda operations. Should the North Vietnamese Army decide to attack a camp, they would also hit the isolated, defenseless villages nearby. The Montagnard's or mountain Indians were basically at the mercy of a death machine who would kill everything in its path with absolutely no compassion or remorse.

One of the most feared psychological weapons was the mortar. A mortar is a high-angle, muzzle loaded weapon which varies in size and is similar to a cannon, except it doesn't have a blast when it is fired. Instead, the round exits the tube with no shell casing left; it is self-contained, self-charged and extremely deadly. The mortar is loaded and fired from the muzzle, once dropped it travels down the tube and strikes the firing pin. It then exits the tube with a deep thud, and is silent during its ascent and descent. If you're not near the tube, you would never hear it fired. Patrols have been moving through the jungles, when out of nowhere slithering down through the trees like pure evil, mortar rounds pound down on them bring a silent death on the wind.

The unheard, unseen flight of the mortar round is followed by a deafening, horrifying, blinding explosion. Even if you are not hit by the massive amount of flying fragments, you instinctively lunge for the ground, trying to get underneath mother earth. You lie perfectly still, trapped in your own mental hell, wondering where the mortar came from, how many rounds are still in the air and where the remaining silent killers will land?

# CHAPTER 4

As the inhabitants of Special Force camp, A-104, Ha Than were awakened at 0100 hours to sounds of distant muffled explosions and gunfire echoing through the jungle. Though not an uncommon occurrence, something was different this time.

The Americans, Vietnamese and Montagnards all felt the presence of a deadly evil off in the darkness. Everyone moved quickly toward their assigned defensive positions, anticipating a ground attack. We all knew what to do, where to go and which security position we were responsible for, having been mentally and physically conditioned to immediately respond with total control of our faculties.

Not only was total awareness and quick response vital to our health, anything less could result in one's demise. Therefore, we learned very quickly to sleep while subconsciously remaining alert to sounds around us. Our hearing became keen, sharp and catlike; we were always listening for familiar sounds announcing death from within the shadows. Our minds and bodies were consistently coiled, prepared to react and our physical agility rivaled that of a gymnast.

As the "A" Camp members scrambled to their fighting positions that night, we did so without even the illumination of the moon. While crossing the camp, every man was extremely cautious, knowing that it wasn't unheard of to run face-to-face into an enemy soldier. As soon as we'd reached our designated defensive position, we followed camp procedures and immediately reported to the Tactical Operations Center via the TA-312 (a hand-cranked telephone) pre-positioned at each fighting position. After all of the defensive positions were manned and reports rendered to the TOC, we began to participate in an all too familiar extended waiting game.

We stood ready, peering out from our firing points, desperately searching the darkness for movement. All the while, adrenaline rushed through our veins, sharpening our senses and heightening our awareness. From within the stillness, we detected the familiar thudding of our own friendly 81mm mortar, launching illumination rounds skyward. As the rounds ascended into the sky, we searched the heavens for their welcomed light.

Almost immediately, they burst, turning darkness into day. Our experienced mortar crew had expertly timed each illumination round to detonate just prior to the previous one burning out. As the mortar rounds slowly parachuted downward toward the earth, they provided 100 million candlepower light, assisting us with visual reconnaissance of the area.

Every eye scanned the barbed wire and the open areas out to their front. Round after mortar round was fired, maintaining a constant source of dreary artificial light. Minutes passed, but despite the illumination, we could only make out masses of gray barbed wire and empty fields of newly planted rice paddies to our front. We knew that just beyond those rice paddies, our enemies were observing our response collecting intelligence about our reaction to their disturbance. Alert camp defenders watched as the jungle was silhouetted by reddish-yellow fire, dancing over the trees off in the distance.

The faint report of automatic weapons and explosions could be heard in the direction of the fire. Bright green tracer rounds ricocheted off the hardened jungle surface, disappearing silently off into the void as their phosphorous elements burned out. From the security of our bunkers, we knew that the gunfire and explosions were about four to five kilometers away, in the direction of the friendly Montagnard village. Sympathetic to our cause, this village regularly supplied us with enemy intelligence and men for our camp.

Explosion after explosion flashed followed by muffled roars reverberating through the oppressively humid night. A slight pressure from the shock wave caused by the blasts could be felt within our bodies. Time and again distant bright flashes lit up the sky, followed by rapid pressure changes from the detonated explosions. We all knew that death rode on the wind. Evil and mayhem was running rampant off in the distant friendly Montagnard village.

Being young and eager to engage the enemy, I momentarily abandoned my defensive position and ran in the direction of the command bunker. Entering the doorway, I boldly announced, "let's go to the village and counterattack." Shocked that I had abandoned my position, the Team Commander, team sergeant, Intel sergeant and commo man stared at me in disbelief.

The team sergeant approached me first, placing his hand on my shoulder. Softly but sternly, he announced, "the NVA are staging this attack against the Montagnard village on purpose, hoping to draw us out into the jungle. You can't see those little bastards, but let me assure you, they are there, watching, waiting, hoping that we will make a fatal stupid mistake and come out after them."

He went on to say, "Chapman, this is not all fun and games, like you thought it would be when you were back in the world. Boy, this is real. During the night, Charlie owns the jungle. You never move in it during darkness. You wait until you can see. Don't forget, this is his neighborhood and he knows every square inch of it." I looked deep into the sergeant's eyes as he finished lecturing me. *"What kind of answer is that?"* I asked myself. Confused with his explanation and inexperienced I thought, "look at all the firepower we have, the number of personnel, not to mention the sheer combat experience." I was confused and disheartened by his explanation.

However, my inexperienced thought process would be corrected as soon as the morning sun arose. Without further delay, the wise team sergeant directed me to, "get my cherry little skinny ass back to my defensive position and stay there until ordered to do otherwise." I quickly made it back to my bunker line position without incident and proceeded to watch the light display and muffled explosions off in the distance. Eventually, the gunfire and explosions fell off into silence, but the raging fires continued to perform their demented eerie treetop dance.

As the sun slowly rose in the east, the fire began to disappear as the light from the morning sun took it place. In what seemed like the twinkling of an eye, the dancing light from the village fires was replaced by blackish-gray smoke, spiraling skyward. The jungle surrounding the camp lay silent and motionless. Unknown to me, preparations were well underway to send out an American-led reaction team to aid and assist the villagers.

A runner suddenly appeared from out of nowhere, directing me to report to the team sergeant in the TOC immediately. I was further instructed to gather my medical gear; I was finally being sent in. Diligently, I prepared my M-5 (combat medical bag) medical bag, taking everything I could possibly carry in it. Three Americans and a company-sized element of 100 Montagnards were preparing to head to the village.

We went about issuing ammunition, c-rations, grenades, claymores and additional supplies. Less than one hour after daybreak, the reaction force was assembled inside the inner perimeter, taking an accurate head count of all deploying personnel. As was secretively explained to me by the team sergeant, many of our own troops would not be in the camp for head count because more than likely; they were the very ones who had been in the jungle attacking that village alongside the VC.

The point element led the way out of the camp down the dusty red clay road, passing through the camp's defenses and barbed wire. Approximately five minutes later, the main body followed, until it too was outside the wire. Each and every man was on full alert and focused.

Newly planted rice paddies surrounded the camp, stretching a 1,000 meters in all directions; they're murky, black water-filled dikes nursing the life-giving rice that grew within. The paddies lay checker-boarded in all directions, broken only by the jungle's edge. As soon as the in-line reaction formation left camp leading out into the open, our combat formation took on an entirely different physical shape, instinctively forming an arrowhead and shaft configuration with security out on our flanks.

The lead element or point acted as the arrowhead and the main body formed the shaft. Flank security moved on either side of the shaft portion as we moved providing protection and early warnings should the enemy try and surprises us with a flaking ground attack or ambush. While maneuvering around the rice paddy dikes, I felt a flood of pride and superiority within me. I distinctly remember thinking that forces commanded by men like us were indestructible.

Approaching the edge of the jungle, the arrowhead formation began a slow methodical collapse, maneuvering back into a single column as we entered. The trees and bushes from the confines of the camp and bunker line looked to be of normal size, transformed into giant masses towering over us, thick enough to hide any number of enemy soldiers. When it finally came my turn to transverse the darkened labyrinth, I had to push and shove my way through, despite the fact that numerous men had already made their entrance at the same place.

It was like hitting a solid wall of green, brown and black decaying vegetation, with intertwined vines of every shape and size. We had to fight for every step. As I tried to negotiate the entanglements, I began to experience claustrophobia. The air was stagnant, stale and smelled of urine; there was no breeze flowing on the jungle floor nor was there any movement of the vegetation, only men's sweating bodies as they pushed against the stillness attempting to break a path.

The jungle was so thick that we could only see four or five men in front or behind. Still, we pressed forward through the bowels of the stench-ridden jungle toward our objective. The steady noises made by the reaction force as we moved helped to maintain our sanity. I tried in vain to look up through the trees to see the sky; it was impossible. The treetops were all matted together, completely encapsulating us.

Fighting for every inch of terrain, I began to experience breathing difficulties. The stagnant air, coupled with our extreme physical exhaustion began to cause profuse uncontrollable sweating, followed closely by dehydration. For that reason, water replacement was a must; we had to drink water at every opportunity. With time, your body would learn to cope with water deficiency. After what seemed like a lifetime of labored traveling, the jungle began to open slightly, exposing the edge of the village. The first thing I noticed was a grotesque smell, unlike anything I had ever experienced before. I can only describe it as a mixture of burning hair and something else that words can't describe.

I felt nausea rise in my stomach up my throat and fighting back the urge to vomit. Straight ahead, I could see the village, or what was left of it.

Under the direction of the American advisors, the reaction force began to tactically deploy left and right, maintaining cover and concealment of the jungle. Men automatically breaking left and right, moving into better positions to provide mutual fire support. Everyone was acutely aware of his individual and team responsibilities. We carefully maneuvered the first and second platoons to an online formation at the edge of the village, our hearts pounding as the stench permeated our bodies. Since I was the new, inexperienced American on his first operation, I was assigned to move with the team sergeant in a sweep of the village.

My heart was literally pounding out of my chest, to the point of embarrassment. My team sergeant kept looking over his shoulder at me and I was sure he could hear my heart beating. Paranoia and fear was getting the best of me, a feeling similar to the Confucius saying, "The fear of dying is worse than dying itself." The team sergeant in reality couldn't hear my heart, it was just my blood rushing through my body; he was just making sure I was keeping in line with everyone else.

Step by step, we moved closer to the edge of the smoldering village, all the while anticipating enemy gunfire at any moment. My mind began to run wild with images of hundreds of North Vietnamese soldiers hiding, waiting to engage us from the jungle, allowing us to get about half way through the open area before opening fire.

What was designed to be a well-coordinated, tactical exit from the jungle tree line turned out to be sporadic? One man left the jungle wall, then 10, and then 30. Finally, as if someone had rolled back the vegetation, the entire reaction force moved out into the open. I could hear the advancing men's fatigue pants rustling as they walked slowly forward. Simultaneously each of us staring at the smoke coming from within the village as it continued to rise from the ghostly frames of the black ash-ridden houches. Beads of sweat rolled down our faces, like faucets slowly dripping water. Images of enemy ambushes filled my head: snipers everywhere, mine fields and booby traps lacing the ground.

Although I tried to maintain my composure, my imagination ran wild, causing each step to become heavier, each heartbeat amplified, and each breath that I took to be more shallow than the last. The closer I got to the main portion of the village, the more I could see. And, what a sight it was: huts still smoldering; farm animals charred, dead, mangled, broken, decapitated and immersed in their own blood and organs. Wait a minute! Where were all of the people? Where were the children, the women?

Silence screamed at us! A dreadful stillness pervaded the village as the team sergeant raising his right hand high above his head signaled the assault formation to halt. We knelt as a unit, our frayed nerves demanding that we evacuate. Our extensive training overrode these primal emotions and we jerked to a halt, each taking a knee, every rifle pointed toward the village. The team sergeant gave the hand-and-arm signal for the point element to enter the village, quickly the small body of men were up and moving.

Long, heavy minutes passed. I felt naked and exposed down on one knee, out in the open. An eerie feeling began to overcome me: no doubt about it, something was drastically wrong here, but what? Abruptly, word came over the radio,

> Victor Zulu. Victor Zulu, this is Charlie Mike, over.
>
> Charlie Mike, this is Victor Zulu over
>
> Victor Zulu Come on in. You aren't going to believe this, over
>
> Charlie Mike, this is Victor Zulu, we're up and moving towards your location. Out

News of this atrocity would spread like a tidal wave through the countryside, gathering momentum as it was passed from person to person. Terror would be stamped into each mind, the kind of terror not easily erased.

The American and South Vietnamese Armies were consistently attempting to establish credibility with the local country people through civic-action programs. Our basic intent was to help make their lives easier, and hopefully encourage them to rally with us against the communists. As a result of their loyalty, we promised them protection from the communists. Yet, we had failed. Our pledge of protection lay crushed beyond any recoverable means; we were back at square one.

Responding like a well-oiled machine, the reaction force was up and moving once again. As the main body of the formation advanced into the village, the security element instinctively positioned automatic weapons to our flanks for support in case whatever hit this place was still present.

As we slowly made our way through the decimated village, I saw death and destruction everywhere. It was clear that all of the inhabitants were herded into the center of the hamlet having undergone brutal torture and execution. Since I'd never seen this degree of human disfigurement, I began to feel lightheaded and nauseated. I tried desperately not to vomit, but was unsuccessful. My stomach contents spewed forth uncontrollably. I fell to my hands and knees, dry heaving, my guts retching.

After that wave of sickness abated me, I temporarily regained my mental and physical stability. Although ashamed of failing to control my gag reflex, I was overwhelmingly appalled at the devastation and pure evil I was witnessing. The village chief and his entire family had been brought to the center of the village, where he had been beheaded. Evidently, his family had been forced to watch and afterward, they had each been executed with a single bullet to the back of their heads.

The remaining villagers were machine-gunned from close range. Bodies were lying on top of each other, arms and legs intertwined. Some were laying facedown in the dirt, while others had taken their last look skyward. It is difficult to describe the horrifically awful ways a human body can distort in its last few moments of life. The deceased Montagnard's lay motionless, their dark brown eyes half open as if staring off into infinity. Their facial muscles were drawn, bearing permanent witness to the severe pain and suffering they'd experienced as bullets tore through their bodies, blazing a path of destruction into their internal organs and leaving gaping exit wounds. Their lips were tightly drawn across their teeth, further attesting to extreme agony.

All I could do was ask myself, "*How could this kind of inhumane slaughter be inflicted among any race or nationality of people? What kind of individuals is capable of mass execution? Who are they? What kind of stuff are they made of?*"

We began an intense search through the stacks of bodies, desperately hoping to find someone with signs of life. Although noble, our search proved useless and futile. Every man and woman in the stack of bodies had long ago been robbed of their lives. As we picked through a pile of corpses, a Montagnard soldier came in search of me. Realization set in that we weren't serving any purpose by continuing to handle these dead bodies. So, we followed the frazzled soldier through the heart of the hamlet.

As we stepped out of the Western edge, we came face-to-face with the most hideous sight these eyes have ever seen. Children, or what had once been children, had been tied to poles and burned to death.

Their lifeless charred bodies hung limp, shrunken and almost unrecognizable as human. The North Vietnamese soldiers had doused them with diesel fuel and set them on fire while they were still alive. Tears flowed uncontrollably down my cheeks my heart was filled with anxiety and anger. The only thing these little ones had done was to be in the wrong place at the wrong time. Their poor little drawn-up bodies dangled lifeless from the poles; now nothing more than burned globs of meat.

Examining the ground around the children, I saw that the source of fire had been a jelly substance possibly a flame-thrower. As I moved closer to their charred remains, I noticed more of the jelly-like substance dripping from what had once been their elbows and what was left of their faces. Definitely, a jelled fuel had been used on these poor defenseless little children. The heat and flames must have been so intense that the flesh literally fell from their bones.

Again, the urge to vomit struck quick and I fell back down on my hands and knees. Because I had nothing in my system to expel, I went through the motions of dry heaving. After the convulsions subsided, I stood and became filled with rage. I began throwing my equipment in every direction, cursing the ground the communists walked upon and praying that God would allow me to avenge the deaths of these poor little children.

The team sergeant grabbed me from behind, slamming me to the ground. Caught totally off guard, I went down too fast to prepare for the impact. He stood over me shouting, "you get control of yourself, and face the fact that this is an everyday occurrence here. Keep what you've seen in mind the next time you come in contact with these bastards you kill um, as many as you can. Now get up off your ass, get control of your emotions and get these kids down off these poles."

Although unprepared for his reaction, in time, I too learned to become calloused to such horrendous sights. I snapped out of my emotional outburst and set about removing the charred little bodies from the stakes.

As we gingerly placed them into body bags, their little extremities separated from their bodies. The Montagnards started digging a huge, mass grave for the dead. One by one, we took the corpses to their unmarked gravesite and began placing them in, head to foot; 20, then 30, finally up to 80 people brutality murdered and placed in one mass grave.

While the main body of the reaction force was digging graves and putting bodies into bags, the point element began searching the edges of the dense jungle. I assumed they were looking for enemy personnel who might have been waiting to ambush. However, the team sergeant informed me that the V.C. had left long ago. The point element was searching for the young teenaged males and females of the village because they were physically unaccounted for. The search continued with no results. The V.C. had forcibly taken them into the jungle. Where they took them and what they did to them, only God knows. Their disappearance will always be a mystery; we never found a trace of them.

Communist propaganda leaflets were scattered around the village as a reminder of who was responsible for this travesty. The leaflets were written in Vietnamese and stated that, "The South Vietnamese and Imperialist Americans are directly responsible for what the Peoples Republic of North Vietnam had to do. This type of cleansing of the country will continue as long as there is such treason being committed."

Although primarily intended for us, this message was also meant to be seen by villagers throughout the district, especially the mercenary force within our camp. It was a clear warning to any Montagnard villagers who accepted food, medical treatment, farming equipment of other assistance from the American Special Forces. They could expect the same treatment as these villagers had received. Why would an army of self-proclaimed "freedom fighters" attack and kill defenseless civilians, including women and children, and then take all of the teenaged males and female's captive?

The answer: psychological warfare. With their mass inhumane executions and their complete destruction of the village, the V.C. had placed insurmountable fear and insecurity into the minds of the villagers throughout the area. In their primitive, easily manipulated minds, the villagers were at the mercy of the V.C. In reality, they had two enemies to contend with. First, were the Americans and the RVNs who threatened to confine them to military prisons and destroy their villages if they were sympathetic to the communists? Their second enemy was the NVA or VC who countered these threats with their own not-so-subtle promises.

For example, if the locals accepted gifts, aid or supported the imperialist American or South Vietnamese Army, the NVA would destroy everything in the village. It was a big game that both sides played well, using psychological advantage as it presented itself. The allied troops claimed they are there to serve and protect them against communism. The NVA claimed the opposite. Place yourself in their situation. As a simple villager, which side would you support? It is a little more complicated than it appears. Remember, the rural Vietnamese and Montagnards were in the middle. They were the pawns around which this deadly game was played.

Imagine yourself as a Vietnamese or Montagnard villager. Right or wrong, the NVA are able to come and go as they please during the hours of darkness, when the Americans, who've sworn to protect you are back in the confines of their camps. By accepting food, medical care, farming tools, cattle, money or liquor, you place yourself and your family in extreme danger.

The communist side of the coin goes like this: If you accept these gifts, share them with the NVA against the Americans and follow the wishes of the communist party, you can have the best of both worlds. And, you have a little more insurance that your family will not be slaughtered.

The rural, uneducated South Vietnamese mind is very basic; food, shelter and life are important to them. They are like children; the side that places the most fear in them is the group they will follow. Where would you stand; left, right or in the middle?

After hours of grueling body recovery, we finished burying all of the villagers in a simple mass grave. No markers, no names, no priests, no songs, no flowers. The only thing left of these people was their memory, held by the living.

The horrors of their executions were etched into our minds. Slowly, we assembled our mentally and physically-exhausted bodies to negotiate the rigors of the jungle for the return trip to the safety of the "A" camp. As we stood silently waiting for orders to move out, I felt an overwhelming emptiness inside my soul. Recalling the hideous devastation and grotesque obliteration of the villagers, I couldn't help but think about the futures of these people which have been denied them. *"What might have become of these people had they been allowed to live out their lives?"*

As we began our tedious retreat, almost every soldier looked back, silently confirming that this had not been a dream. War had raised its ugly head and we had experienced its horror firsthand. The beginning of our return trip wasn't as intense as before. Instead, we were largely oblivious to the heat and stench, recalling only the devastation we'd just encountered and trying to make sense out of it. Slowly, we began to remember where we were and what we were doing. I could feel my muscles tighten as awareness set in. We were traveling through the jungle and Charlie the owner and caretaker of this jungle could be out there waiting to inflict his handiwork upon us.

As the sun began to set, my anxiety level increased. After traveling for hours in the jungle shadows, my senses were peaked as I spotted a very small flicker of light up ahead. We were getting close to the edge of the jungle and back to the security of camp. I had to restrain my desire from breaking formation and sprinting out of the jungle into the open. Slowly we began to exit the pits of hell into the quasi-safety of the open air. Off in the distance lay the rice paddies and our beloved camp, if we could only get there in one piece.

We pressed on ever so carefully, refusing to let our guard down. Charlie had been known to hit large elements when they were midway between the jungle and the edge of camp. Relief began to wash over us, although anxiety was still high. At last, the gates of the camp swung open to allow us passage, while shutting out the evils of this hell-on-earth. The Americans who had stayed behind in camp ran to greet us with cold beers in their hands.

Prior to my arrival in Vietnam, I never drank. But, when that beer was placed in my hand, I gulped it down like a pro. The simple gesture of a friendly face meeting us was extremely appreciated. We all made a point of greeting a retuning group of Americans when it was our time to remain in camp greeting them with cold beers.

Our fellow soldiers took our rucks and weapons as if we'd been gone for weeks. In reality, we'd been away for little more than 14 hours. Once our reports and debriefings were complete, the camp sort of cocooned itself, as if needing rest and concealment. Some went to the team house, while others vanished into their bunkers seeking solitude. While in the privacy of my bunker, I tried to clean up. Regardless of how much soap and water I used, I was just as nasty, sweaty and sticky as when I came through the door. But, I felt clean. I tried to rest, staring blindly up at the ceiling at nothing in particular.

Realizing that I needed sleep, I attempted to will my mind to slow itself down and go to a more pleasurable place. That proved useless, as all I could do was visualize the death, dismemberment and inhumane sights I'd just witnessed. I saw every dead face, every contorted body, all of the charred lifeless remains of the children staked to poles, like some middle-aged barbaric war totem.

I tossed and turned, trying to erase the horrific images. My tired body demanded rest, but my subconscious was in control, and it wasn't about to sleep. Too much had happened.

I got up and went to the team house. Surprisingly, everyone who'd gone on the operation was there, silently staring into space. No one acknowledged my presence, each cradling an empty beer can. And so, I too joined the quiet drinking party for the remainder of the evening. We drank in silence until the morning sun shone through the door.

Without a word, I left the team house, moving in a world of my own, no cares, and no distraction, just a pleasant mental haze. Spotting one of the camp's observation towers, I decided to climb up the 30 feet and survey the countryside. A guard greeted me with "Morning Tung Si," meaning "Good Morning Sergeant," and I moved to the edge of the tower, peering off into the surrounding jungle.

What a magnificent sight, so green, lush and filled with natural resources. Next, I looked in the direction of what had yesterday been the vibrant Montagnard village, filled with animals, people and life. I had to reaffirm that it had indeed been reduced to death and destruction.

As I looked for signs of life in the surrounding area, I noticed a local farmer out in the rice paddies. He was dressed in their traditional wide brimmed straw hat, black pajama top and bottoms with the pant legs rolled up high above his knees. He was coaching his water buffalo into pulling the plow through the black mud. They worked as one well-synchronized unit, cooperating together ever so slowly, preparing the earth for a new crop of rice.

As my bloodshot eyes moved from him to the edge of the jungle, I watched a thick gray mist making its way up through the vegetation. Crawling out from the depths of the humid jungle floor, the mist dissipated as it reached the edges of the rice paddies. *"Birds,"* I thought, *"Where are the birds?"* Then it struck me; *"I have not seen nor heard a bird, since I arrived in Vietnam. Where are they?"* Given the abundance of natural resources and vegetation, I thought it only natural that God's creatures of flight would be everywhere. Yet, I never saw a single bird while I was in country.

# CHAPTER 5

Perched high upon one of the observation tower, I watched as the camp slowly came to life. Inside the safety of the bunker line, small fires boiled water for rice. Wondering what kind of day this would be, my eyes were drawn to the children. Without a care in the world, they scurried here and there, chasing each other, laughing and playing. This camp was the only security some of them had ever known. Like any other kids, they were interested in food, fun, exploring and getting into a little mischief.

My thoughts were interrupted as the senior medic called up to me, "hey, cherry boy, get your ass down here so you can learn what sick call is all about." As I descended from my perch in the observation tower I wondered how much longer I would be stuck with the nickname "cherry boy?" I'd been in camp and on team for a month now and this expression was getting old. What the heck I shook it off because I knew I had to take my lumps just like everyone else. It couldn't last forever.

Sick call was held in the medical bunker and was fairly routine. We treated colds, malaria, cuts and soldiers getting ready to go on operations. The majority of these Vietnamese soldiers tried to get assigned to bed rest, claiming all kinds of unknown ailments. Basically, they were trying their best to get out of going to the field and fighting the NVA. This same type of behavior had been going on for some time, and the American medics, the brightest our nation had to offer, caught onto their game fairly early, long before my arrival in Vietnam. As can be expected from intelligent, experienced and highly trained American medics, they had a variety of tricks up their sleeves. They were just waiting on the right patient to dispense their advanced medical treatment. With a major operation coming up in two days, I was about to learn how to turn the tables so that we could get all of the men we needed for battle.

The maligned soldiers came to us complaining of diarrhea and severe stomach cramps. Being sympathetic medics concerned with their health, we listened to their symptoms and then conducted a thorough examination; we pricked their fingers. We then make a smear of the bloodstain and placed it under a microscope to determine a diagnosis. Since nine times out of ten, there was nothing to be seen on the smear, we proceeded to beat them at their own game. Through the medical interpreter, we explained that they had a rare disease called malingeringitis.

However, they didn't have to worry because we had the right medicine to cure this dreaded ailment. Even the Vietnamese knew that pills came in multiple colors and shapes, and that they often had letters or emblems on them. So, when we dispensed pills, we were usually giving them nothing more than M&Ms.

Least we be judged too harshly, if a soldier was truly sick, we treated him with any and all of the medicines we had at our disposal. However, more often than not, we were required to find a solution for their habitual fear of fighting. And M&Ms were the cure-all drug.

In case you're wondering where we got M&Ms while in Vietnam, it was simple. When any of the Special Forces team members was sent back to the rear, he was instructed to buy as many bags of M&Ms as he could possibly purchase from the PX. Upon his return, he would surrender them to us and we would set about separating them by color. We'd then place 10 of the same color into small paper envelopes and seal them shut.

It was part of the game. If we did not stay ahead of them, they would stay ahead of us. Therefore, we had the cure for malingeringitis and dispensed the 10-pack prescription antidote freely, sincerely expressing assurance that the patient would feel better shortly. Again, when a camp refugee actually had a valid disease, we truly worked hard to cure them. As can be expected of a third-world country, disease is extremely prevalent in Vietnam. We treated many cases of malaria, dysentery, rabies from bat bites, jungle rot and other infections of every description.

These diseases, which at first seemed monumental, were in fact everyday occurrences and their treatment became commonplace. The number one medical emergency was infection. We had soldiers return from operations with wounds already in the secondary stages of severe infection. We worked frantically to clean the wounds and often injected enough penicillin into a single patient to cure the entire camp.

We were normally successful. However, once the infection had progressed beyond a certain point, we simply couldn't stop it. The only thing we could do was med-evac the patient to the Da Nang hospital where they normally underwent limb amputation. If the wound was in the trunk of the body, surgeons would perform erratic muscle removal. Vietnamese soldiers were not sent to American hospitals for treatment. They were sent to their own hospitals and, if surgery was required, it was performed by Vietnamese doctors.

What really hit home was when a local villager would bring in a little child that had fallen into a pig trap. Set primarily by the V.C. for American and Vietnamese soldiers. These pig traps were filled with pungi stakes, nail boards or broken glass that had been dipped in water buffalo feces, ensuring the spread of infection. When a child fell into a pig trap, time was of the essence. Children were repeatedly med-evaced to a hospital only to return missing a limb. After a while, you became numb to the sight, your feelings hardened and you accepted amputation as a way of life in Vietnam. Compassion for my fellow man slowly began to diminish and was replaced with an acceptance of fate "what will be, will be."

After three months in camp, I had become one of the boys. I ran combat operations with other Americans and was assigned my own Company of RVN soldiers, including my counterpart, a South Vietnamese Special Forces Lieutenant. They called themselves, "Loc Lam Doc Biet," Vietnamese Special Forces, or LLDB. But we had a different name for them. We arbitrarily changed the letters of the original meaning to, "Little Low Life Dirty Bastards." The Vietnamese officers, who were placed in charge (RVN LLDBs), were without scruples, morals or patriotism.

Each LLDB officer was given the supervisory task to maintain and ensure that his company was issued rations of rice, food, clothing and cigarettes.

It was commonplace for the LLDB to take 1/4 to 1/2 of their troops' rations and sell them on the black market for their own greed.

We frequently found Vietnamese soldiers hungry, without uniforms, smoking banana leaves instead of the cigarettes they were to be issued. It was maddening. But, all you could do was report our findings to the LLDB commander. And, what good did that do? The LLDB commander was getting half of the money from the black market sales. So, we started getting smart. We began to only issue seven days worth of supplies to the LLDB, upsetting their plans and curtailing their personal income. They said we didn't trust them; how right they were.

After we returned from operations, it was always a high-point of the debriefings to hear our fellow team member's adventures of working with their LLDB counterpart. Prior to deployments from the "A" Camp, intelligence reports told us the general location of the V.C. and/or NVA units who were moving through the area. Upon receiving Intel that large units were on the move, we would launch company-sized element to try and intercept them. Although travel was slow and tedious, in time you'd be in the general area of the suspected enemy location.

It was customary to ask our LLDB counterpart where he thought the VC was. This way, they wouldn't lose face with the men, yet all the while we knew where the movement of the bad guys really was. The LLDB Lieutenant would look at the map and try to convince you that he was tactically planning a move against the enemy. After studying the map for moments on end, he'd point in the general direction of where he believed the enemy to be. The entire time, we knew the enemy was in the opposite direction. The LLDB Lieutenants and officers were notorious for running away from combat, especially when it meant going against a hard-core NVA unit. As a result, we started changing our tactics.

When we were on operation, we'd occasionally ask our counterpart where he thought the enemy could be found. Once again in order not to loose face with the men, he would study the map. You could see what was going through his mind. He'd give the impression that he was truly trying to locate them, as he pondered his decision. Knowing all along that if he told you where they weren't, you'd go in the opposite direction and make contact with the enemy. The LLDB officer would ponder his decision for a long time and then tell you where he really thought they were, hoping once again that you would go in the opposite direction, away from them. Then, the LLDB officer would point to the map and say "V.C. there," where you already knew they were.

In turn, you'd say, "Okay, we go." The expression on his face when you took him at his word was worth the cat-and-mouse game you had to play. As soon as he realized that he had inadvertently led you to the enemy; an enemy he would actually have to fight, his eyes shot open, his jaw dropped and genuine shock registered on his face. Abruptly, he would begin to renegotiate, backpedal, anything to change your mind. Frantically, he'd blurt out, "Tung Si (Sergeant), I be wrong. V.C. be there, (pointing to another location on the map). I make mistake, we go that way."

I received great personal satisfaction and pleasure from watching these malfunctioning, noncombatant, perverted carpetbaggers cry like a rat eating onions. I often wondered if other Americans were having similar experiences with their LLDB counterparts. *Why didn't the US Military step in and resolve the issue or simply remove them?* The reason: politics. You see, the US was systematically trying to prepare the South Vietnamese Army for a slow transition from an American-led force to a Vietnamese-led force. Consequently, the LLDB were gradually supposed to accept full responsibility and the role of leadership, resulting in them taking their own actions against the communist aggressors.

In short, having been trained and assisted by the US Military, they were supposed to rise to the challenge and actually fight for their own country themselves. The US Military could then fall back into the role of advisors, instead of combat operations directors. Such was the plan. U.S. Military Command Vietnam, repeatedly made excuses for them. They'd say things like, "they will eventually come around to take over your capacity as combat operations leader. When they see and learn how effective you are, they will model themselves after you."

This was such a load of crap. The only people they modeled themselves after were thieves, liars and cowards. Honor and integrity had no place in their daily lives. With that, every rule has an exception. Almost always, a camp had at least one, sometimes two LLDB Officers whom you could trust. These rare individuals were more than capable of demonstrating quality leadership and aggressive combat tactics. When these highly motivated Vietnamese officers were given a mission to seek out and destroy the enemy, they did so aggressively and relentlessly.

Because of their enthusiasm, these topnotch soldiers could be hard to control during combat operations. Once they made contact with the enemy, most of them didn't want to let go. I've seen them get into firefights with the NVA or VC that lasted for days, never giving the enemy a chance to slip away. While this kind of determination was commendable, certain conditions called for less aggression. Jungle combat often dictated that you not pressure the enemy excessively because they were notorious for sacrificing a few soldiers to give the false impression that they were on the run. Then, without warning, you'd be in the center of an ambush where you'd not only have casualties from enemy fire but friendly fire would be a problem as well. Repeatedly, large company-sized units chased the NVA or VC to their own destruction.

An enemy-initiated ambush was common in Vietnam, and a most-dreaded one to be caught in. The sheer terror and mayhem it produces explains why it has been used throughout history.

Ambushes can be employed in small well foliated areas as well as larger semi-foliated areas, depending upon the terrain and other critical parameters, they don't require an overabundance of manpower to produce high rates of casualties. It all depends upon what strategic outcome is desired.

There are many types of ambush including: demolition, mechanical, a combination of the two, a standard claymore mine, grenade/automatic weapon version. The shapes and types of ambushes differ as well, featuring the area, "L" shaped, linear and improvised or hasty ambush. This particular tactic is executed in order to destroy a unit, capture prisoners or slowing a fast-moving advance of enemy troops.

Originally used as a harassment tactic, this method of battle is meant to instill fear or used as a hit-and-run guerilla maneuver. Numerous physiological factors occur prior to, during and after an ambush. By definition, this tactical maneuver allows an unsuspecting enemy to enter its kill zone and on signal, concentrate all firepower on the humans caught within the trap.

Charlie was a master of the ambush; he had the patience, discipline, cunning and ability to brilliantly execute these mass-casualty assaults against American military units. It has been documented that they have laid patiently waiting for days in order to inflict their punishment on an unsuspecting allied unit that enters into their kill zone. When it came to ambushes, Charlie was a master at the technique.

# CHAPTER 6

December of 1969 brought orders for Special Forces detachments A-104 Ha Thanh and A-107 Tra Bong to conduct a battalion-sized combat operation in the Quang Ngai Provence, I Corps. "A" Team A-104 was to be moved by UH-1 helicopter to our area of operation, where we'd move independently as two reinforced company elements. Plainly stated, we were to search out and destroy the 352nd NVA Infantry regiment.

The first team (A-104 or A-107) to locate the enemy was to maintain contact with the enemy, then coordinate with their sister-unit and formulate a plan of attack allowing both companies to close in and destroy the NVA regiment.

Team A-104 was to move along the western ridgeline, while Team A-107 traveled the eastern valley ridgeline. The first unit coming in contact with the enemy was to maintain contact and push the NVA forces into the direction of the other American detachment acting as a blocking force.

The unit failing to make initial contact would be fed communications and intelligence on enemy movement so they could act as a blocking agent for the team doing the pushing. A reaction force or "Mike Force," out of Company C, 5th Special Forces, Da Nang was alerted and on standby. If called, they were to aid and assist either of the two operational companies. Although we had no way of knowing it at the time, this particular joint operation would change the attitudes, mental out look on life and lives of many.

Equipment, ammunition, rations, medical supplies and intelligence reports arrived at each "A" Camp in preparation for the mission. This

45

was the first time American Special Forces units were being deployed in a semi-conventional combat role. Normally, Special Forces conducted guerrilla operations, clandestine operations, ambushes and small-scale search-and-destroy missions on enemy units within their own area of operations.

Since this was my first time participating in a full-scale combat operation against a suspected hard-core NVA regiment, I was wired. My head was filled with dreams of being decorated for heroism and valor, visions of killing and capturing huge numbers of communist troops and images of other battle-related fantasies. After months of waiting, searching the jungle for the elusive enemy and constantly coming up empty-handed, my well-trained, combat-seasoned Special Forces "A" camp company was about to trample this inferior foe; or so I thought.

While in the confines of the team room, I studied my map of our area of responsibility like a computer tech pores over his system schematic. I memorized everything about the area of operation, having visualized each ridgeline, creek, hill and possible landing zone for miles around. With great attention to detail, I painstakingly drew target and reference overlays for artillery and mortar support, just in case they were needed. I relentlessly planned; taking into account everything I'd been taught. In fact, I was positive I hadn't overlooked anything, until I attended the commander's operations briefing in the TOC. Turns out, most of what I'd drawn up was backward or even irrelevant.

My mind was racing trying to digest all of the pertinent information during the briefing. After the fact-filled brief-back, everyone moved to their respective companies where we began checking equipment, personnel, arms and ammunition, making sure everything was in good working order and operationally ready. We checked and rechecked until the approaching helicopters could be heard. As we received orders to move into transport position, company commanders began leading their units out of the camp, down the road to the dusty hard red clay airstrip that lay outside the camps defenses.

Two Americans and a reserve company were left behind to maintain camp defenses during our absence. I haphazardly assumed position in the forward movement, although an overwhelming sense of being unprepared rushed through my veins.

I began to question my leadership abilities: *"How would I perform in combat, standing toe-to-toe with a hardcore NVA regiment? Would I make the right tactical decisions? Would I have the courage to perform my duty properly or would I run like a coward when the bullets began to fly? Could I really be counted on when the team needed me?"* And, most importantly, *"Would I ever see this camp or my wife and son again?"* All of these questions swirled around in my brain, bombarding my subconscious. I even began chastising myself for not telling my wife that I loved her more often. I had strong feeling that my artificial machismo and hyped-up heroism would some day be my downfall.

The team sergeant slapped me on the back, refocusing my attention to matters at hand. Struggling to be heard over the noise of the rotating blades, he shouted, "Get your head out of your ass and load your people." Jolted back to reality, I ran from chopper to chopper, receiving a "thumbs-up" signal from my indigenous platoon leaders. Satisfied that everything had been loaded, I climbed in Chopper number two and picked up the headset to listen to the lead pilot's communications.

The sun-blistered airstrip was bone dry and hot as the rotating blades from the helicopters whipped up a solid wall of red breath taking dust. On cue from Chopper number one communication with the trailing helicopters, the helicopter formation began running up their turbine engines for take-off. We could feel them picking up torque as vibrations shuddered from the floors of the big birds. With masterful hands, the young pilot skillfully lifted his skids off the airstrip and momentarily hovered, waiting for the lead aircraft to begin his climb into the sky.

My position within the flight formation provided a view of the lead ship gracefully nosing over, ever so carefully gaining ground speed as the blades continued to grab the air and lift the chopper skyward. The other helicopters followed suit and within seconds, we were airborne. Upon reaching 1,000 feet AGL, all of the aircraft began to turn toward the Northwest. My gaze spanned from the lead ship to the rearmost vessel of our flying armada. 20 helicopters were loaded for bear, their deadly cargo of combat soldiers and weapons of war packed into the bellies of these mighty workhorses.

Four sets of Cobra gunships flew off to our left and right flanks in support of the insertion. Slowly, they dispersed evenly throughout the flight formation and accompanied us, as we would quickly close the distance on our area of operation. I could see the 17-pound high explosive rockets protruding from the Cobras rocket pods. Each gunship carried four pods of rockets, two on each side of the chopper. The more experienced pilot sat in the rear, while the weapons officer or gunner occupied the front. What a tremendous display of military power; these war chariots were breathtaking and inspirational, giving me inner strength.

The crew chief leaned toward me from his side-seat position and tapped me on the shoulder, instructing me to plug in my radio headset. Immediately following directions, I was amazed at the amount of chatter that was being coordinated between helicopters. It was difficult to understand what was going on and who was talking to whom. The pilot directed me to dial into channel one so we could talk more about the mission. He informed me that we were 10 minutes out and I asked if there were any last minute intelligence updates. Replying in the negative, he announced that he was switching back to channel three. The channel change brought us back into the middle of an insert briefing as the Forward Air Controller (FAC) gave instructions to the gunships and troop carriers, reaffirming their responsibilities during insertion.

The FAC would direct all aircraft during the airmobile operations. As he talked to the gunships, I couldn't help but notice the similarity to that of a police dispatcher during a bank robbery. It was difficult to interpret the conversation and hard to keep up with due to the speed of response and directive communications being passed back and forth between the pilots. I frantically tried to follow the conversation and soon it slowly began to fall into place:

> Gunship Lead, this is FAC 174. Over
>
> FAC 174, this is Gun Lead. Over
>
> Roger babe, I see four sets of guns, what are you carrying? Over.

FAC 174, this is gun lead we all have four pods of 17-pound HE rockets, fully loaded 40 Mike Mike cannon, and maxed out 7.62 mini gun, how copy? Over.

Gun Lead, this is FAC 174, good copy.

Break, Break (changing communications with another group or persons)

Slick Lead, this is FAC 174. Over.

FAC 174, this is Slick Lead. Over.

Roger Lead, how many PAC's are your carrying per bird? Over

FAC 174, this is Slick Lead, we're carrying six apiece, with three more deliveries today. Over

Roger Lead, Good copy. Over.

Gun Lead and Slick Lead, this is FAC 174. We will be making a North-South insert. I'll mark the landing zone (LZ) with white smoke. Gun Lead, you escort Slick Lead in on his 9 o'clock. Gun 2, you pull drag on Bird 5 at his 3 o'clock, how copy? Over.

FAC 174, this is Gun Lead, good copy. Over.

Break, Break.

Guns 3 and 4, this is FAC 174. You tag up likewise with Birds 6 through 12, how copy? Over.

FAC 174 this is Gun 3, roger tagging up with Slicks 6 through 12. Over.

Guns 5 and 6, this is FAC 174. You tag up likewise with Birds 13 through 20, how copy? Over.

FAC 174 this is Gun 5, roger tagging up with Slicks 13 through 12. Over.

Guns 7 and 8, this is FAC 174. You stay high and dry and wait for my directives to support. How copy? Over

FAC 174, this is Gun 7, high and dry. Over.

Slicks 1 thru 20 this is FAC 174, go into a right orbit at this time. Over

FAC 174, this is Slick Lead, ships 1 through 20, orbiting now. Over

Slick Lead; give me an up when all your chicks are in orbit. Over

FAC 174, this is Slick Lead, will call you back when in orbit. Over

Guns, this is FAC 174, you ready for insert? Over

FAC 174, we're up. Over

FAC 174, this is Slick Lead, all slicks are in right orbit at this time standing by Over.

Gun Lead and Slick Lead this is FAC 174 OK guys let's take it to them and make it happen.

Guns, this is FAC 174 pick up your birds. Over

Slick Lead, this is FAC 174, break orbit and have your chicks follow you in. Over.

FAC 174, roger, breaking-orbit at this time. Over

All leads, this is FAC 174. I'm rolling in for a Mark, Mark do you have a good tally on this silver bird? Over

Roger, FAC 174, this is Slick Lead and Gun Lead got an eyeball on you at this time. Over

Gun Lead and Slick Lead, I'm rolling in hot, watch for smoke then identify. Over

From inside my chopper, I could see the FAC pilot in the OV-10 make an abrupt left-wing-down, right-wing-up maneuver to align his aircraft into a more suitable position to mark the landing zone. Simultaneously, the troop helicopters and Cobra gunships broke out of their pre-directed right orbits and began to assume the appropriate high-speed insert line up. The gunships broke their formation off first, staggering themselves throughout the air mobile combat formation. While leading us in, the FAC pilot suddenly announced, "I'm going in hot."

The OV-10 Bronco aircraft quickly executed another barrel role, banking hard to his left to align himself with his target. The rest of the helicopters mimicked the FAC pilot's hard turn, minus the barrel role. Quickly, they aligned their flight formation to maintain a visual on the FAC pilot as he dove his OV-10 toward the landing zone. As I watched this surreal aerial ballet, I noticed our crew chief take his chicken plate from his chest, which protected his chest from bullets and shove it beneath his butt. I remember wondering why, but didn't dwell on it because communications had started up again:

Mark, Mark.

FAC 174, this is Gun Lead, I got a good tally on your mark, and I see white smoke. How copy? Over

Gun Lead, this is FAC 174, that's a good copy. Over

Slick Lead, this is FAC 174, take your bird to the north end of the LZ and put down there, approximately 50 meters south of the tree line. Over

FAC 174, this is Slick Lead, good copy. Over

Trailing slicks, this is FAC 174, take your directives from Slick Lead and separate yourselves 50 meters from tail to nose on the ground. How copy. Over?

FAC 174, this is Slick Lead, good copy, over

Slick Lead, this is FAC 174, I'm going high and dry. You've got the helm good buddy. Good luck. Out

Roger, Roger FAC 174, thank you much. Over

Break, Break

Gun Lead, this is Slick Lead, cover my ass, I'm one minute out. Over

Roger that Slick Lead, all guns and rockets are ready. I'm on you like stink on shit. Over

All slicks, this is Slick Lead, come in hot, stay close, drop your PACs, come up, break right, reform over Eagles Beak. How copy. Over?

Roger.

Slick 2, watch my lead, all slick gunners lock and load, and cover our flanks.

This is Slick Lead; I'm one mile out and closing.

I'm half a mile out.

I'm 500 meters out.

I'm flaring now, stay close.

My heart pounded as I slowly slid my legs out the door of the helicopter, my butt barely making contact with the floor of the chopper. The wind from the rapidly descending chopper pressed my fatigues hard against my body. As I looked out the right side of the aircraft the wind pressed against my face rippling my skin and distorting my face. As the edge of the jungle began to appear less vegetated, I instinctively climbed out of the door my total weight on the skids, hanging onto the frame of the helicopter with my left hand. One at a time, my Little People mimicked my actions, hanging their legs out of the doors then climbing out.

As we flew over the lush treetops, the entire invasion force stood exposed outside of their respective choppers, everyone looking for signs of enemy personnel. Instantly, the thick green jungle disappeared, and we were over an open field of elephant grass. Violently pitching nose up and tail down, the chopper gracefully tried to stop its forward movement in mid air. As the aircraft leveled, I saw Slick Lead flaring hard below and in front of us to get into position so his troops could exit. Suddenly, an earth-shattering roar sounded. As Slick Lead made its final approach into the LZ, the treetops exploded, filling the sky with grayish-black smoke. For a fraction of a second, the doomed chopper appeared to hang suspended in mid air before bursting into flames then smashing skids-first violently into the ground.

We in the trail helicopters were in shock as we watched the entire command group disintegrate in the violent explosion. The chopper's rotor blades shot off in different directions, as it hit the ground with a thud, followed by a blinding fireball bursting toward the heavens. I watched body parts blow in every direction, with pieces of aircraft being hurled alongside arms and legs.

Long before we had planned this mission, the NVA or VC had anticipated a futuristic helicopter insert on this particular landing zone. They'd booby-trapped the tree-tops with large Chi-Com claymores and shrewdly positioned the mines so that each was facing in, toward each other, providing a deadly phalanx for unsuspecting helicopters. An x-shaped tripwire was laid across the northern end of the LZ, approximately 30-feet off the ground in order to deny enemy aircraft access to the area. A claymore mine was located at the base of each leg of the "X" facing in toward the center. Once the tripwires were hit by the downward pressure of the helicopter, the mines were designed to go off in unison, bringing down the unsuspecting aircraft.

Confusion, shock and surprise impacted the trailing insert aircraft; they too were on short final into the LZ, about to deliver their personnel to the same location and possibly an identical fate. Yet they pressed forward, Slick 2 instantly taking command, exactly as they had been trained to do. Slick 2's pilot immediately reiterated the last order given by Slick Lead, directing all aircraft to continue the insert mission into the LZ, deliver their personnel and follow the last command.

Uncontrollable fear flooded our minds. Under stress, the brain can recall and evaluate thousands of bits of information in a fraction of a second. *"Were we going to be disintegrated in midair or would we meet death in a more terrifying way?"* Regardless of their inner fears, those brave pilots and soldiers pressed on. The gunships started firing rockets, 40MM grenades and mini-gun fire into the landing zone's surrounding tree line.

My helicopter abruptly reared up, nose high, like a horse that has decided to stand on its rear haunches. Quickly, the helicopter nosed his aircraft over leveling out about 10 feet off the ground hovering, waiting for us to dismount. Leaping vigorously from the chopper, I mistakenly anticipated the ground to be directly under my feet, about two to three feet below the top of the elephant grass. From the air, the mass of sharp elephant grass appeared to be about three or four feet high; in reality it was closer to 10 feet.

I hit the ground with a thud, the air temporarily knocked out of me. We were loaded down heavier than normal. My rucksack was filled with ammo, medical supplies, normal packing items and load-bearing equipment, and it was all strapped around my waist and shoulders. The impact immediately shot intense pain through my legs and into my hips. I lay helplessly sprawled face down in the thick elephant grass, gasping for air. With Cobra gunfire going off in all directions around me, I knew I had to get to a more secure position in a hurry.

By some stroke of divine luck, I was able to get to my feet and began to move. The elephant grass sliced through my fatigues like hundreds of tiny razor blades. As a result, my face, arms, hands and other exposed skin was bleeding with paper-thin cuts. Intense heat and smoke from the burning helicopter combined with stagnant, humid air trapped in the elephant grass adding to my overall discomfort. Slowly I headed off in the direction of the downed chopper to render assistance to survivors. Although the thickness of the grass made for extremely limited vision, the smell of burning flesh filled my nostrils. My fight to break away from the clutches of the elephant grass and stifling thick smoke began to psychologically overwhelm me. The lack of air and the sweat running down my face was almost more that I could endure. Desperately, I fought my way through. The more I moved, the more I felt entrapped.

After what felt like hours of frustration, I emerged facing a wall of burning elephant grass, only to realize that I had to quickly retreat. I couldn't stay there. This is when I began to panic. As I frantically tried to break out of the maze of blinding, burning vegetation, helicopters were still in the process of delivering the second lift of personnel. The gunships continued to fire rockets in all directions at an enemy that had yet to show himself.

On the verge of mentally cracking, I escaped from the razor-edged grass into the arms of the lush green jungle. The last wave of personnel was trying to assist the disoriented, confused and exhausted soldiers throughout the landing zone. Everyone was haphazardly spread throughout the elephant grass and along the edges of the jungle. Some kind of order had be established and quickly. Commands were shouted and a head-count was quickly taken.

Communications were set up with the FAC, telling him about the fiasco with the initial insert package. The FAC advised the company commander that from what he could see, Slick Lead was completely destroyed with no survivors. FAC 174 asked if we were taking hostile fire. In our concern over the downed helicopter, survivors and getting out of the burning elephant grass, we hadn't had time to think about enemy fire. Due to the hurling winds from the helicopters, the fire on the LZ spread rapidly in every direction, bellowing smoke and engulfing the jungle floor in a blinding grayish haze. The FAC informed us that the entire LZ was burning and consequently, the remainder of the insert package would be delayed. No estimated time was given by the FAC for the rest of the combat force to join us.

The team commander had been killed on Slick Lead, and because of the way we had broken down during the insert formation, I was now in charge until the Executive Officer or Team Sergeant arrived. I attempted in vain to gain control of the situation. The harder I tried, the more dispersed everything became. My thoughts kept returning to a missing part of the equation: *"Why hadn't the Team Sergeant made commo with me yet?"* I almost panicked, thinking I might be the only American on the ground that was still alive, unsure of the fate of the others and feeling additional responsibility for forming up the company, I began securing the landing zone until the rest of A-104 Team could be inserted.

I established radio communications with the majority of the first insertion group of Vietnamese LLDB commanders on the ground, waiting and hoping someone with more experience would arrive soon. Like me, the LLDBs were wandering aimlessly along the edge of the jungle, slowly making their way to the pre-coordinated rally point. Off in the distance, a figure began to materialize out of the smoke. I thanked God when I saw that it was the Team Sergeant boldly walking toward us.

Sidestepping my defensive perimeter, I ran and embraced him with the enthusiasm and gratitude of a child hugging his father after a long absence. More than a little surprised by my enthusiastic embrace,

Little Joe, looked at me like I was crazy, asking, "Chapman, what the fuck is wrong with you, you gone queer on me or something?" I wasn't embarrassed or ashamed at all; I was just ecstatic to see him, happy that he was still alive and about to take charge of this goat roping I had attempted to form.

Without delay and with complete authority, Little Joe brought order to the dispersed unit in seconds. I felt like I was watching a master craftsman as he methodically whipped our small group back into shape. He ordered security out to our flanks, placed listening-post positions far enough away from the perimeter to detect any enemy infiltration, and set up a solid defensive perimeter within a matter of moments. Order had been restored and we were all thankful.

With the insert helicopters returning for the next round of troops, the explosions from the friendly Cobras abated and the jungle returned to its normal silence. The only sounds came from the landing zone as it crackled and smoldered, emitting gray smoke for hours. The FAC informed the Team Sergeant that it was impossible to insert the remainder of the unit until the LZ had burned itself out. Accordingly, they would attempt a reinsertion at first light tomorrow. FAC 174 also reported that our sister unit, A-107 had been successfully inserted without incident and was moving to the target area as scheduled. Those facts reported, the FAC departed the sky overhead and we were left to wait it out. No sooner had I begun to prepare my company's night defensive perimeter when word came by a runner that we were moving to a new location.

It didn't make sense to me. "We had a good perimeter set up now; it would be getting dark soon, and we had no problems to speak of. So, why the hell were we moving?" Within minutes, all unit commanders converged on the Team Sergeant's location. Little Joe informed everyone that we would move approximately 500 meters north, deeper into the jungle and farther away from the burning LZ to reestablish our defensive perimeter. Each commander grouped his unit into traveling formation and waited for the command to move out.

Since the vegetation wasn't as thick in this area, we were able to easily move away from the LZ. We made good time, relocating 500 meters north and setting up our defensive perimeter again. Our orders were simple: no fires, no smoking, no talking; just set up company early-warning defenses, including tripwires with ground flares and command-detonated claymore mines.

Darkness quickly fell around us. At first, we tried to look for signs of movement in the twilight, until we realized this wouldn't work here. Instead, we had to rely on sound, touch, smell and intuition as well. Movement within our unit ceased. Men lay motionless for hours. Although we weren't moving a muscle, our nerves were on full alert, focusing on the surrounding darkness and its possible dangers.

Slowly, the night wore on, uneventfully at first. However, it wasn't long before we heard what sounded like a whip cracking. Air molecules snapping back together announced communist rockets and mortars in flight, impacting the abandoned landing zone and surrounding area. Everyone within the defensive perimeter was on intense alert and prepared for battle. But nothing came. The rockets and mortars continued to be launched from an unknown location, impacting the abandoned landing zone. No one within our defensive formation was hit or injured by the surprise attack.

As if a light bulb suddenly switched on in my mind, I clearly understood why our wise, experienced Team Sergeant had ordered us to move deeper into the jungle. Had he left us where we were, our original defensive formation was we would have taken mass casualties from this heavy barrage of NVA rockets and mortars. Obviously, the North Vietnamese had assumed our defensive perimeter was on the edge of the landing zone. I would later learn that this NVA tactic had been successfully used against American troops deployed in the field, often triggering the defenders to fire blindly in all directions, resulting in friendly fire casualties as well.

But not this time; this time our enemy had been outsmarted by our well seasoned combat Team Sergeant, Little Joe. In just a few hours, the sun would bring a new and deadly day.

Far off in the distance we could hear the distant humming of the Forward Air Controller's OV-10 engines as he circled above us, advising our Team Sergeant of the situation from his vantage point. Yesterday's fire had burned itself out during the night, leaving only sporadic smoldering ashes still visible on the landing zone. The FAC also reported that the remainder of our unit was inbound to our location. Little Joe ordered us to secure all of our anti-intrusion devices, claymore mines and prepare to move back to our original perimeter.

As soon as we made our way back to the previous day's defensive perimeter, we were shocked by the devastation the NVA mortars and rockets had caused. The ground and surrounding vegetation bore the scars of war. It was as if a huge lawn mower had cleared out the underbrush, leaving only impact craters and black charred areas on the ground. The hot bursting metal had indiscriminately cut down all the vegetation in its path. Again silently, I thanked God for our seasoned Team Sergeant who knew the way his enemy thought and used that knowledge to shield us.

As sounds of helicopters broke through the silence of the jungle, communication was once again established by the ground commander with the Forward Air Controller orbiting directly overhead. Within a matter of minutes, the second part of our task force was safely on the ground. Insertion of men and equipment continued until approximately 1000 hours. After the entire combat force was present and accounted for, the seasoned Executive Officer, second in the chain-of-command, took charge. We began our search-and-destroy mission a day behind schedule. With everyone still on high alert, we started our northward trek along the ridgeline.

The first day proved uneventful with the exception of a case of heat exhaustion, and the excitement of a huge boar hog trotting through our formation. The extreme heat made our movement slow and tiring, yet we continued until 6:00 pm (1800 hours), when the Executive Officer ordered us to set up our overnight position. Prior to darkness, we executed the same tactic as the previous evening, pulling up and moving the entire group of combatants about 300-400 meters deeper into the jungle. This brilliant tactic had saved us before and we were banking on it doing the same tonight.

The standard rest-overnight (RON) procedures were performed: claymore mines out, listening posts out, automatic weapons deployed on primary avenues of enemy approach, dead spaces covered by claymores and M-79 grenade launchers. The night slowly passed without incident;

no enemy movement, no sounds, no surprises except the slow rising of the morning sun.

Three more grueling days were spent humping through the jungle, searching for an elusive enemy. We combed the target area, looking for some evidence of the NVA stronghold. Again we were finding nothing of our enemy no trace at all. Still we pressed on searching for ghosts all the while, the terrain became more and more rugged and difficult to get negotiate, with undergrowth becoming noticeably denser with each step we took. Leaches and mosquitoes grew in size and aggression. In order to conserve energy we rotated positions from point to flank on a daily basis. Everyone dreaded pulling point. Every time it was our turn, it seemed like you aged a few years; I know I did. Point position required you to be far out in front of the lead element and main body of men.

Because point elements for American forces were extended almost beyond reach of support, Charlie was notorious for ambushing the point element with Chi Com claymores or hit-and-run operations. When these ambushes were properly executed, the point element had little to no chance of surviving. Point men were also required to try and spot booby traps planted by the Vet Cong. One example of such an entrapment device is the pig trap. The normal pig trap was a hole filled with punji stakes nail boards or glass ment to shred your calf muscles like hamburger if you had the misfortune of fall into one of them.

Another common booby trap was known as the Malaysian Gate. This deadly instrument was a simple tree limb that had been bent to act as a whip when released, deploying about chest high. When tripped by an unsuspecting prey, the tree limb would whip back to its original growth position, impaling its sharpened stake into a chest cavity, groin or thigh of the individual who tripped it. Being hit with the bent tree limb wasn't bad it was the razor sharp spikes attached to the limb that was the killer. Originally utilized for snaring wild animals, Malaysian gates were now used for killing and maiming the unsuspecting targets or men.

By the morning of the fourth day, the majority of the combat force was beginning to lose mission focus. With overwhelming monotony, we trudged through the smoldering heat, placing one foot in front of the other until we became unobservant of our surroundings.

Without warning, the jungle came to life with automatic weapons fire and deafening explosions. We responded with suppressive fire as quickly as possible, unsure about what was happening.

About 100 yards ahead, the point element had run into something big. Reaching for the radio operator beside me, I grasped the headset, listening for commands from the Executive Officer. His commands never came though because he'd been with the point element and walked head first into a complex of camouflaged bunkers, with interlocking enemy automatic weapons and B-40 rockets. They couldn't have known what hit them; one minute silence, next the roar of death. Casualties were too numerous to estimate and the enemy's fire was so intense that supporting elements couldn't even move forward to reinforce them. All we knew was that we'd run into a heavy concentration of enemy soldiers and they were out in front of us.

Little Joe directed me to execute a flanking maneuver. Responding without question, I moved my unit as quickly as possible through the dense jungle. While my troops fought their way through the thick vegetation, attempting to deploy to the right flank, heavy automatic weapons fire, explosions and general chaos intensified to our left front. With a blinding flash and the blink-of-an eye, I was hurled through the air like a dirty dishrag. I felt myself crash to the ground with a heavy thud, followed by immediate numbness all over my body. My ears were ringing, completely obscuring the sounds of war; my nose and eyes were pouring blood from the concussion of the explosive round; someone ahead had tripped a booby trap.

As I slowly regained my senses, pain shot through my body. I could neither move, nor lessen the ringing in my ears and I was only barely able to make out sustained gunfire forward and off to the left. All I could think was, *"Who was left?"* and *"How badly am I injured?"* While enemy bullets thrashed around the jungle, I slowly rolled onto my stomach rising up to my hands and knees. About 10 feet in front of me, I spotted the lower quadrant of something that had once been a human. The top of the body, from the armpits up was gone and smoke from the rocket or bobby trap explosive ignition rose from the severed torso.

With my head still fixed on the smoking mass, my eyes swept to my right front. There lay more mangled bodies without arms, legs, faces, hands or feet. Semi-nauseated and attempting to regain self-confidence, I let my head fall limply to the ground, cradling it in my arms. Rolling over onto my back, I began a physical search of my own body, making sure everything was where it was supposed to be. The search ended with blood all over me, but it wasn't my blood.

Suddenly, I felt something hot poking into my lower back. Rolling over, I spotted a soldier's M16 rifle, hands still grasping the weapon. Horrified, I scrambled away on my hands and knees and crawled upon the body of the soldier who'd once held the M16. Panic immediately overtook me and I became disoriented. I didn't know which end was up; I didn't know which way to run. Weapon fire and explosions added to my confusion. Nothing was alive around me. I began to crawl faster, like a wounded animal. I must have crawled on my hands and knees for about 50 meters when I ran into the remainder of my company.

My interpreter jumped on me and began screaming, "Trung Si, Trung Si." Mike, the senior medic was kneeling directly over me, providing calming reassurance, "its okay Chapman, its okay. You're all right. Are you hit?" My expression of horror was apparently flashing like a neon sign. Suddenly, everything started to come back into some perspective and I looked Mike in the eyes and said, "Booby traps, everywhere to our front." Mike searched my body for wounds, as I continued to ramble. All he could find were small fragment wounds, nothing worth worrying about.

Still dazed, I grabbed his arm and screamed, "damn-it, didn't you hear me, there are booby traps up there." Mike leaned over me, close to my ear and said, "you dumb shit, you were ambushed with B-40 rockets don't you remember? You've been out of it for two hours now. We've been looking all over for you. We are getting the living shit kicked out of us everywhere we turn." It was all crazy and confusing; what I thought were a couple of minutes turned out to be a couple of hours. I'd been knocked out by the concussion of the RPG/B-40s and had obviously lain helplessly in the jungle for quite some time. Mike explained that the NVA had set up a linear ambush against our flanking maneuvers, and I'd walked right into it.

My first platoon, the one I was trying to flank the enemy with, had been decimated by the 30 or so B-40 rockets and automatic weapons fire. Mike continued, "everyone thought you'd bought the farm. Your second and third platoons are scattered all around here, setting up defensive fighting positions." Now, I was thoroughly confused. First, I was unconscious for more than two hours and now we're setting up a defensive position? What was going on? In a semi-controlled voice, Mike blurted out our status: "Chapman, you twit, we are surrounded by the NVA. Hopefully the reaction force from Da Nang will come and bail us out. It doesn't look good. 'A' company has lost the entire First platoon and part of the Second. We've sustained the majority of the casualties. 'C' company is somewhere in the center of the bunker complex. I think they are all dead. Other than that, we're doing wonderful, just fucking wonderful."

As I began to regain my scruples, I asked Mike, "how many dead do we have?" He replied, "man, there are bodies stacked up like cord wood, everywhere." Desperately in need of more info, I asked how many Americans had been killed. He replied, "Three that I know of."

When I asked where the others were, Mike said he didn't know. "The last I saw of Little Joe, he was moving forward to the XO's position to see what in the hell we had run into. Galiger, the demolitions man, was right behind the team daddy and Rudolpho, the Assistant Intelligence Sergeant." Just then, we heard a crashing noise to our front. Everyone turned; weapons pointed in that general direction when Little Joe, Rudolpho and Galiger appeared through the trees. They were completely drenched in blood and were being trailed by the remainder of the three companies, about 100 men total.

As soon as he entered the perimeter, Little Joe began barking orders. Turning to us, he bellowed, "are either of you hit? If not, you two assholes knock off the social bullshit and tend to our wounded. Don't worry about accounting for the dead just take care of the living. Rudolpho, you take what's left of your company you have the responsibility for the downhill slope. Galiger, you have the right flank. This natural cliff on our left flank will take care of itself. I'll take the high ground with my people." We all scrambled to accomplish our tasks, placing claymores and striping the dead of their ammunition.

As medic, I moved from one man to another, trying to determine who was worse performing triage as I went. We had every kind of wound imaginable, from blown off fingers to sucking chest wounds. No one had been spared; we all had a hole in us somewhere. Our defensive perimeter began to take shape just as Mike and I ran out of medical supplies. We had no fluid replacement, no morphine and no bandages. So, we resorted to striping the dead of their field dressing kits. It seemed like the more I tried to assist the wounded, the more extreme the wounds.

Many of the injured soldiers had crawled back to the defensive perimeter on sheer willpower, only to die moments later drenched in their own blood. We maintained a frantic pace of medical treatment for hours before we learned that the reaction force couldn't get inserted close enough to be of immediate assistance. Instead, they were being inserted about five kilometers south. Things turned sour real quickly. Here we were: surrounded by enemy, dead and wounded everywhere, running out of ammunition and medical supplies, the reaction force unable to come in on top of us to assist. And, quite frankly, we were inches from being captured if we didn't get some help soon.

Having avoided contact with the enemy, our sister team was about 10 kilometers to the north, while the reaction force was five kilometers south and, shortly, the sun would be making its downward swing, bringing night's dreaded darkness. Silence encompassed us, as every eye and ear attempted to detect the slightest noise or movement. As the jungle floor took on more shadows, our senses became increasingly astute. Little Joe had set up the command element in the middle of the perimeter.

From my defensive position, I heard him talking on the radio ever so faintly. I felt anxious. I had to know what was going on, to know if help would come, and from where and when? Impatience got the best of me; I left my defensive position and crawled over to Little Joe's position. As I approached, he paused, straining to see in the darkness who it was moving towards him. A brief moment passed before his intern came to meet me in the dark.

In a voice soft and stern, he asked, "what in the hell are you doing here?" I tried to explain my need to know who we were making contact with. At that point, his voice changed dramatically. I will never forget his words, or the manner in which they were spoken: "Boy, I do not know what you think this is nor where you think you are, but we are about to get the living shit kicked out of us. You move your scrawny little ass from your defensive position again without me telling you to move and I'll personally blow your fucking head off. Now, get back to your position and people. And, do it now!"

Whoa! There was no doubt in my young mind, that he was willing and capable of carrying out his threat. So, as directed I crawled back to my position, tail between my legs and did it pronto.

As time passed, I learned that times of crisis don't allow for explanations of actions or tones of voices. Back in my defensive position, I thought about the day's events, while maintaining a high level of awareness to my area of responsibility. Suddenly, I heard a propeller-driven plane flying overhead. My sector of the perimeter began to move about restlessly. In an effort to quiet them, I tried to bring their attention back to the issue at hand – possible enemy positions to our front.

Meanwhile, the airplane overhead continued to orbit. *What was it? Resupplies?* We had no drop zone party out. Heck, we didn't even have a drop zone prepared to receive resupplies. Silently Little Joe suddenly appeared from out of the darkness and whispered, "no matter what happens, you stay down and stay low. Do not, I repeat, do not stand up or move about. Stinger is on station and will be with us all night." "What is Stinger?" I questioned. Little Joe replied, "It's a gunship, cherry. Just lay back and get ready for all hell to break lose."

The plane circled overhead for hours. All the while, I kept wondering what the hell Stinger was about? Then, rearward and to the north of our perimeter came an explosion. It was a claymore mine. My heart jumped into my throat, my mind racing and my body began shaking. Enemy gunfire was going into our perimeter and friendly fire was going out.

Agonizing screams filled the air friend or foe was yet to be determined. Outgoing fire increased, flares screeching off into the sky in all different directions, but we couldn't see anything. I heard Galiger yell, "Ground Attack!" But, I still couldn't see anything. Trying to maintain my composure, I ordered my Little People to stay alert and watch their front. I continued, "don't fire at anything unless you have a definite target." I had been taught a long time ago that Charlie would sacrifice his troops by probing your perimeter to see where your weaknesses lay. Then, he would mount a full-scale ground attack against the weak spot in an attempt to break through into the inner perimeter.

The entire time we were carrying on our ground fight the mysterious humming from the airplane above signaled its orbit. Then, a long, loud belching sound rang out from the night sky above. Instinctively, I looked up to see a spectacle that has stayed with me ever since. A bright red wavy stream of tracers was plummeting rapidly toward Earth. The savage fury with which the rounds were hitting the ground was visually and audibly breathtaking. Although I couldn't see what the mighty stream of tracers was hitting, I could tell the fire was coming from this thing they called Stinger. As the tracers penetrated the triple canopy of the trees, the jungle came to life with screams of pain and ensuing confusion. Our enemies were experiencing firsthand the firepower of the dark demon from the sky; the one we knew affection ally as Stinger. Long live Stinger!

Tree limbs cracked, as the 7.62 millimeter projectiles, crashed to the ground. Vegetation fell lifeless to the jungle floor; tracers impacted everywhere, ricochets from mini gun cannons bounced around on the ground. Death screamed loudly-reverberating pain and agony as enemy soldiers were being bombarded with a vengeance.

Even those new to battle, like me, could tell that panic had overtaken our enemy. Stinger belched his rage of death for about 15 seconds stopping as quickly as it had begun. Still circling so that his deadly presence could be known, Stinger continued to hover above. Three more times during the night, Stinger raged his dragon-like roar of death upon the North Vietnamese Army. After the third probe, the area of destruction only emitted silence. A strange chill came over me. It made no sense: here I was in Vietnam, 85 degrees, yet I was as cold as if I were in Montana in winter. When you sweat all day in the blazing sun, you eventually chill during the evening, especially after being drenched in blood and sweat. That was my excuse. Truth was my emotions were dealing with the death that surrounded me, and the fact that mine could be close at hand. I was shaking with fear and emotional distress. Gradually, the sun began to rise.

One of the most dangerous times to prepare for during combat is first light. Every person within the defensive perimeter was at-the-ready, anticipating a ground attack, but nothing came. 4:30 am (0430 hours) then 5:00 am (0500 hours) – time crept by while we waited with our weapons ready. Nothing came. *"What were they waiting for?"* As sunlight forced its way into the jungle, Little Joe strode through the undergrowth, looking like the larger-than-life combat hero he was. I could see his mental exhaustion although I'd find out the details later. It turns out, our Team Sergeant had suffered frag wounds during the night, but true to his warrior nature, he'd refused to allow anyone to know. Instead of compromising our mental well being, he'd maintained his leadership with the dignity of a hero.

All night, he'd moved around the perimeter directing our defensive positions, as well as fire support from Stinger. Little Joe sat down, looking old and weary while I began to treat his wounds. He'd been hit in the forearm, cheek and shoulder. While none of his injuries were serious, they all had the potential of developing into something bad if unattended. The most severe wound was a half-inch laceration going through his cheek, penetrating his mouth. A metal particle had passed through his cheek with enough velocity to knock out two teeth. In an attempt to make him feel better, I asked if he thought the tooth fairy might pay him a visit. He gruffly replied "Knock off the grab ass and put some gauze in the holes."

I patched him up with what little we had left and he thanked me. As he started back toward the command position, he told us that our sister company and the reaction force would be arriving by 0800 hours. He continued by saying, "it's going to get worse from here on out boys. We have done what we set out to do. We have confirmed the presence of the enemy, and we have him right where we want him, surrounded from the inside." I personally failed to see the humor in his statement. As quickly as he'd appeared, he was gone. As time passed, our wounded became restless because we had no morphine to relieve their pain. Everyone knew our supplies were dwindling.

I thought about the massive quantities of ammo and weaponry we'd brought into this hell hole and wondered how much we had left? *"How long would it be before we ran out?"* Heck, I'd been unconscious for two hours the previous day, yet the rest of the companies had steadily fought off the NVA regiment, expending massive amounts of ammo and medical supplies. According to Mike, if we didn't get help soon, we were going to have to whip out our LHRs and BFRs.

Having never heard of these military acronyms, I inquired further. He looked at me and shook his head in disbelief saying, "you dumb shit, these are old terms Special Forces use when it really gets bad. It's a joke that we've been using for years. When everything looks grim and without hope, LHR stands for Long Handled Razors and BRF represents Big Fucking Rocks." I was overtaken with laughter, having to place my hat over my mouth to muffle the sounds. I laughed uncontrollably. Looking back, it was most likely a way to release tension because I could not stop laughing. And the funny part of it was, I was the only one laughing.

Little Joe peered through the vegetation and said, "Knock off the noise and grab ass, you two quick fucking around." Mike and I looked at each other, exchanging smiles as Little Joe disappeared back into the jungle. Within minutes, Little Joe crashed back into our sector of the defensive perimeter. Instinctively swinging around, I peered into the foliage asking, "what's going on TOP?" He replied, "shut up and listen." I turned my head into the direction that best served my hearing. Leaning over me, speaking with quiet intensity, Little Joe did his best to clarify the situation, "the reaction force is about 300 meters down the hill. Tell your Little People what's going on so they don't fire them up."

I scurried away, relaying the message to my sector of the perimeter. Everyone was trying their dead-level best to see through the jungle, as if we all had x-ray vision. Minutes passed while we absorbed various noises off in the distance. Anxiety ran high. *Who was responsible for this movement to our front? Was it the enemy or our brothers?*

Spotting what I knew to be human movement, I cautiously and deliberately raised my M-16 and willed myself to remain calm. I saw one figure, then another. No question about it, this was our reaction force. They were wearing distinctive scarves around their necks, differentiating them from other Special Forces units. Red and yellow checkered scarves, what glorious colors. Their arrival was exhilarating and a real morale boost to the entire company. They gave us hope. Awaiting clearance to penetrate our perimeter, a member of the reaction force recognized Little Joe. Our Team Sergeant gave him a quick status check. In no time, the reaction force leader and his Montagnard counterpart were kneeling beside Little Joe and I. Slowly and cautiously, the remainder of the force relented their jungle concealment to pass through our check point. Every single soldier passed in front of Little Joe, the Mike Force Commander and his Montagnard counterpart, looking into each other's eyes. This was done to ensure that they hadn't picked up an infiltrator in deep-cover mode.

# CHAPTER 7

Loaded with desperately needed medical supplies, the Mike Force medics used everything they had to help us care for our wounded. They were astounded at the number of casualties we'd sustained. Although we hadn't met previously, we bonded immediately working side-by-side.

The jungle's extreme heat caused the dead bodies to begin to swell, distorting the majority of all human recognizable features. Basically, we were just tagging them "John Doe" and placing them into body bags. Because well over half of our company had been in the kill zone, many of the dead were still unaccounted for. We were also unable to give any assistance to those unfortunate soldiers who still lay wounded in the middle of the kill zone. Many of these men could have been saved had they received medical attention. Instead, the NVA used them as bait against us. The enemy had skillfully anticipated our every move; when we tried to flank their forces, we encountered booby traps or automatic weapon fire. We were constantly forced to deviate from our plans and tactics.

Most importantly, the enemy troops were extremely familiar with the American moral obligation to our fellow soldiers. They knew we would attempt to recover the fallen from the battlefield. Therefore, they waited patiently for any overzealous American or indigenous soldiers to try and recover their dead or dying comrades. As soon as any attempts to recover a body began, Charlie deployed maximum firepower on them, rendering even more casualties.

In planning and preparation for destroying the entrenched enemy, our Team Sergeant and the Commander of the Mike Force summoned all

Americans, LLDBs our Montagnard counterparts and interpreters to the center of the perimeter, where we listened attentively to our responsibilities. They informed us that resupply choppers were on the way with beans, bullets and medical supplies. They were going to kick out the supplies to us down through the trees. Our sister unit, A-107 lay waiting for us to make our move on the back side of the ridge, approximately 200 meters below the opposite side of the hill's crest.

Additionally, we were to be supported by F-4s and A-6 fighter planes. These Air Force and Navy jets would conduct air strikes on the enemy's positions using Snake and Nap, (Cluster Bomb Units and Napalm). On H-Hour, the fast-movers would make numerous destructive passes, while two sets of orbiting Cobra Gunships stayed high and dry, awaiting orders from the ground commander for further assistance.

Once the fighter planes had peppered the target area with deadly ordnance, the Mike Force would begin their attack from the left and right flanks, and A-104 would conduct a frontal assault on the bunker complex. At the same time of the initial attack, our sister unit A-107 would press hard up the back side of the hill, taking the ridgeline above the enemy and routing him out down to us. With all units attacking simultaneously from four different directions, we were sure to deliver an unexpected and devastating blow to the enemy.

Watches were synchronized, radio frequencies and call signs reconfirmed. Medics were distributed throughout the attacking units and a chain-of-command was established. Once the operations order was complete and questions were entertained for clarification, we were dispersed back to our appropriate units and locations to prepare for battle. About 20 minutes passed, during which time I briefed my LLDB counterpart on our duties during the assault and the inbound resupply aircraft. I hadn't gotten the words out of my mouth when high above us hovered the resupply helicopters.

Little Joe popped smoke so the helicopters could locate us as he guided them into our defensive position. High above the resupply choppers lurked two sets of Cobra gunships, providing cover fire if required. While on short final into our position, the resupply birds began taking heavy automatic weapons fire from camouflaged NVA bunker positions just above us. The Cobra gunships immediately responded by laying down suppression fire. From our hidden vantage point, we could see the Cobras making their steep nose-first descent, and hearing the familiar rattles and belches as the mini-guns hurled 2,000 rounds a minute at lucrative targets of opportunity.

The resupply choppers hovered while the intensity of enemy fire increased dramatically. Still, the brave pilots held fast, continuing to deliver our supplies. Green tracers from NVA weapons soared indiscriminately through the air. How the tracers failed to hit the hovering birds is still beyond me. Time after time, the shark-faced Cobras dove in, spewing their deadly venom, blistering the hillside with mini-guns, rockets and cannons.

I was so enthralled with the display of firepower, I didn't pay attention to the supplies that were being dropped until cases of ammunition, grenades, chow, medical supplies, demolitions, rockets and body bags began crashing down around us. No one moved toward the supplies for fear of being struck by one of the heavy wooden or metal boxes. As quickly as one chopper arrived and kicked out its supplies, another took its place. All the while the resupply mission was underway; the Cobras continued to lay down suppressive fire for the workhorses of the Vietnam War.

As the last helicopter departed, silence returned over the jungle. Abruptly orders rang out from the Team Sergeants interpreter to the Little People; every third man was to gather the supplies and bring them to the center of the perimeter. As if rehearsed, the Montagnards and Vietnamese grabbed the crates and brought them in to the center of the perimeter where they were broken down and distributed amongst the assault forces. We carefully and methodically reloaded our magazines, replenished and secured hand grenades to our load bearing equipment and made a final check to make sure we had everything we needed for battle.

In the calm before the storm, these gallant men silently made peace with their God, mentally preparing to face death, yet hoping to cheat it one more time. Faces were void of expression men were praying, eyes closed, heads bowed, lips slightly moving as they prayed; humble warriors asking for peace and security. Beads of sweat were visible on each brow as they willed themselves to stare down the hooded black reaper of death. I wondered where these men came from and what possessed them to walk into the probability of death, day in and day out?

I prayed for myself and for all of the men with me, asking that we could return alive from this perilous mission. I prayed that God would spare my meager life and allow me to see my wife and child again. I prayed that God would shield each of us from the agony of death and the horror of this ordeal. I prayed that He would lead us into combat as brave men, allowing us to be victorious in our quest to liberate this small patch of ground from the oppressor. I believed with all of my heart that God would deliver each of us this day.

Suddenly, out of nowhere, my confidence was jarred as I experienced a sudden flashback of the last few days' combat experiences, chilling me to the bone. I began to shake and pray even more intensely, begging God to take me away from this hellhole. Slowly dropping my head so the others wouldn't see, tears of fear rolled down my cheeks.

With full authority and without a trace of reservation, Little Joe commanded us to move to our respective attack positions. I was so physically and mentally consumed with fear that I almost lost it right then and there. My legs felt like rubber and I had to force myself to place one foot in front of the other to the jump off point. The only way I got past the panic was to constantly remind myself that there was no choice except to face the fear. Fear is death, and if you let it overtake you, you will surely die.

I will never quite understand how, but I regained my inner strength and a burst of energy along with it. Adrenaline flowed through my veins as I directed my unit to follow me to the lower edge of the clearing so we could face upward into the darkened bunker complex. Minutes passed before the other units radioed that they to were in position ready for the order to attack. Having moved out earlier, the Reaction Force was silently observing the enemy while waiting for the A-104 to initiate the attack. On the opposite side of the ridge, A-107 had stealth fully moved up almost to the crest of the hill.

As all units lay in silence, I stared into the darkened firing ports of the bunkers directly in front of me. They looked haunted. Void of sound or movement, like ghostly scorched pyramids jutting out of the earth. Then came the squelch from the radio;

> Victor Tango, Victor Tango this is Gun Fighter 121. Over.

> Little Joe answered

> Gun Fighter 121, this is Victor Tango. Over

> Victor Tango, I have two sets of fast movers loaded with snake and nap. Where do you want it, over?

> Gun Fighter 121, this is Victor Tango I'll mark my location with smoke and direct you to the target, over.

> Roger, Victor Tango, this is Gun Fighter 121 standing by. I have an eyeball on the general area, over.

> Gun Fighter 121, this is Victor Tango smokes out, identify. Over.

> Roger Victor Tango, this is Gun Fighter 121, I see yellow smoke. Over.

> That a good copy, Gun Fighter 121 from my smoke, two hundred meters north, up the hill, bunker complex, troops with automatic weapons and B-40 rockets. Also five hundred meters from my position due west maneuvering northward is a large friendly element on the backside of mountain. How copy?

> Roger, Victor Tango that's a good copy, this is Gun Fighter 121 understand that there are friendlies two hundred meters due west of your position, moving north, a large friendly element on the reverse side of mountain, over?

> That's a good copy, Gun Fighter 121, over.

> Victor Tango, this is Gun Fighter 121 we'll be making a southwest to northeast run, with the nap. Then we'll return with our snake making a southeast to northwest

run. We'll alternate each pass to confuse them. How copy, over?

Gun Fighter 121, this is Victor Tango good copy, over.

Victor Tango, this is Gun Fighter 121, am I cleared in hot, over?

Gun Fighter 121, this is Victor Tango you're cleared in hot. Fire um up, over.

Little Joe quickly radioed each unit that the fast movers were coming in hot, and instructed everyone to stay low. I quickly moved to a better vantage point to watch the air-to-ground attack being provided by the Air Force and Navy. I could hear the F-4's jet engines howling, coming in fast from our rear. I rolled over onto my back and watched the F-4 drop cans of napalm, high in the air behind our position. "Oh my God, they're short," I screamed. My heart jumped into my throat and I froze, staring horrified at the canisters of napalm that rapidly fell in our direction.

My mind was stammering, not knowing if I should run or stay where I was. I watched in horror, as the canisters of napalm appeared to be rolling backward in the air, as they continued to make their deadly descent. I nervously stared intently, as they descended lower and lower, passing overhead with a deep air sucking noise. As I quickly rolled back over onto my stomach, they impacted the ground. A thunderous sucking roar and a wave of fire engulfed many of the bunkers. "Damn, what a sight!

The second F-4 rolled in with what appeared to be little silver balls falling from beneath his wings. However, these were no ordinary little silver balls; they were CBUs, better known as Cluster Bomb Units. They hammered their way down through the trees, exploding so rapidly it sounded like thousands of grenades going off at the same time. Cracks and snaps filled the air with flying metal particles searching for flesh to penetrate. Again and again, the F-4s and A-6's repeated their on slot of attacks using napalm and CBUs. The roar of the fiery napalm and the cracking of the Cluster Bomb Units impacting their targets, brought courage and hope that these strikes would weaken our enemy into submission.

The bunker complex to our front was totally engulfed in smoke and fire. I could only think, "*How could anything live after such an attack?*" As quickly as the F-4 and A-6 attack had begun, it ended. Silence returned to the area, with the exception of the occasional delayed cluster bomb explosion. Having vacated the general vicinity, the F-4 Lead, Gun Fighter 121 was reporting back to Victor Tango, asking if there was anything else they could do. Once again, the radio squelched:

Victor Tango, this is Gun Fighter 121, over.

Gun Fighter 121, this is Victor Tango, over.

Victor Tango, this is Gun Fighter 121, ah roger babe, we are Winchester, minus our 20 Mike, Mike. Do you require any further assistance at this time? Over

Gun Fighter 121, this is Victor Tango, thanks old buddy I think we'll give it a go from here. Thanks much, over.

Victor Tango, this is Gun Fighter Lead with three chicks heading home. Also Victor Tango, FAC 232 states he has three sets of Cobras headed your way in about two minutes, over.

No sooner had the fast-mover pilot made this announcement than Cobra Lead made radio contact with Little Joe.

Victor Tango, this is Gun 1 with 5 other guns in trail, awaiting your orders, over.

Gun 1, this is Victor Tango I would like you to stay high and dry until I call for you, how copy?

Victor Tango, this is Gun 1, high and dry and standing by over.

Roger that Gun 1 this is Victor Tango out.

Little Joe replacing the PRC-77 handset back in his rucksack quickly moved from behind a fallen tree with the red handled flare he'd use to initiate our attack. As he reached his position, he drew the device high above his head, removing the protective striker from the canister and replacing it on the underside of the flare. With a vigorous downward motion, he slammed the primer to the ground, shooting the red star cluster flare into the air. As soon as the hiss from the flare bolted skyward, assaulters were up and began moving forward, advancing in formation, troops abreast, weapons pointed uphill, locked and loaded in the direction of the bunkers.

The flanking M-60 machine-guns immediately spit out supporting fire onto the bunker line, encouraging us to continue forward. We slowly left the security of the tree line and the sparse hip-high undergrowth that had been spared from the fiery napalm. All the while, the darkened firing ports of the bunkers maintained their eerie silence. Inch by treacherous inch, we closed in on the pyramid-like bunkers. When we broke into the clearing, I became sick to my stomach.

Onward we marched, the entire assault force now out in the open. As much as I'd cursed the jungle's heat and bugs, I would have graciously accepted her shelter instead of this open-air death march. Blood crashed violently through my veins and my breathing became almost nonexistent. My palms were so clammy, I was afraid I'd drop my weapon. Nervous sweat, combined with the jungle's heat and the smells of burnt napalm as the perspirations flowed down my face, dripping into my eyes, burning and obscuring my vision. I repeatedly wiped at my face with my sleeve. My rucksack and load-bearing equipment began to feel heavier. It was as though I was moving in slow motion, while everything around me rushed by.

In a coordinated assault, it is vital that everyone maintain there interval spacing and line-of-movement. The line of assault must also be maintained to the left and right flanks, so no one will be too far ahead or behind. During assault operations, men have been known to develop tunnel vision on the targets to their front, excluding their left and right lines of march. Many times, this causes them to pass directly into friendly firing lanes. I nervously glanced repeatedly to my left and right, ensuring I was still on-line with the main body of the assault element. Horror and blank stares radiated from men stumbling up hill towards the unknown.

The gunships began to descend to provide a quick response if needed. Still, no movement from the bunkers, no sign of life, nor dead bodies from the previous day's fighting. *Where were the dead bodies? They should have been strewn everywhere.* The lack of enemy gunfire was so loud, it was deafening. I was within 10 feet of one of the firing ports before I received the stench and smell of burning flesh. The smoldering slope of the hill was covered with jelly-like napalm residue and the lush green foliage that had once dominated the hillside was gone. The mighty teakwood trees were now barren, burned black by the manifestations of war.

It felt like we were moving within the reels of a black and white movie. I cautiously passed by the left side of the first bunker line, bending slowly at the waist and peering into the charred firing port. I couldn't see anything, just darkness. Continuing my visual sweep, I was stunned to find the number of bunkers to our front ran endlessly up hill; row after row of enemy bunkers embedded into the hillside. We were right in the middle of a hornet's nest. The mental stress was almost unbelievable. I looked over my left shoulder at our fourteen year old Baby-Son, the youngest member of our Little People. His eyes were filled with confusion and fear. Like the rest of us, he had no idea what he was facing.

Catching his glance, I nodded my head up and down as a silent gesture of encouragement to him. Our eyes locked together. Just then, I heard the dreaded fizzing of a B-40 self-propelled rocket taking flight. Before we were able to dive to the ground, I was drenched with blood and pieces of flesh. Instinctively, I looked for Baby-Son; all that I could see was a cloud of gray smoke where he'd been.

Enemy-driven B-40 rockets and automatic weapons exploded with defiance all around me. Our left and right flank M-60 machine gunners responded, spewing red tracers impacting upon their targets. Friendly 7.62 machine gun bullets began ricocheting off the ground then taking flight off into the sky disappearing helplessly off into the void of the heavens. While friendly fire passed over our heads, the NVA answered with green tracer rounds from their Russian-made RPD, 7.62 light machine guns. In a test of the fittest and most accurate, a barrage of red and green tracers shared the sky a duel of firepower and resolve ensued.

Once the gunners from each side had shown their muscle, they turned their attention back to the advancing soldiers, scurrying like rats in a desperate searching for cover. The once silent bunker line was no longer quiet. Enemy fire picked up noticeably in intensity and accuracy.

I began to fire blindly, burning up rounds and searching for a better fighting position. Meanwhile, the demented dance of red and green tracers accelerated. Led by the American force, assaulters dropped their rucksacks in place and began a suicide charge straight up the hillside into the bunker line. Speed and violence-of-the-attack was the most important part of any assault. The more firepower and violence we could shove down their throats, the better our chances of success were.

I began making quick, deliberate rushes, trying to gain ground and find better cover. The combat rush, taught during basic training was a lifesaver. Spotting a mound of dirt that was the perfect size for me to hide behind, I began repeating the mantra we'd learned while perfecting the combat rush: "I'm up, I'm seen, I'm down." Over and over again, I repeated it as I mentally rehearsed my movement toward the dirt mound. With a burst of energy, the source of which I'm still unsure, I was up and moving, "I'm up, I'm seen, I'm down." With a combination of jagged forward movement and desperate diving motions, I landed with a thud behind an embankment, as the enemy fire intensified.

Rounds from an RPD struck the mound of dirt I was using for cover. That's when I realized that the pile of dirt I was hiding behind wasn't what it seemed to be. As rounds penetrated the darkened mass, I heard a slight hissing sound, similar to a gas heater just before it ignites.

This unsettling sound was followed by a nauseating odor. The smell was hideous, an ungodly mixture of burning flesh, rotten human tissue and gunpowder. The charred mound I had chosen wasn't dirt at all. It was a dead man's burned body. The unrecognizable charred remains of what had once been a human being was now my shelter against enemy automatic weapons fire. Reacting out of sheer horror and a need to escape the odor and substance of the dead remains, I was up and frantically moving forward before I realized what I'd done.

To my immediate front, about two steps away, lay the remains of a fallen tree. Silently chanting to myself as I lay behind the deflating body, "I'm up, I'm seen, I'm down," I made a desperate lunge for the fallen tree. I am a living testament to the fact that even under stress; you still remember your training.

From behind the fallen tree, I could see that the bunker complex had been built to resemble an amphitheater. The low silhouetted bunkers lay in a semicircle, one behind the other, offset to the left and right so that the shooters would have unobstructed fields of fire and be able to mutually assist and support each other. Each bunker had three firing ports, one to the front about a foot high off the jungle floor and two feet across, with evenly spaced side ports. Although I couldn't see faces inside the bunkers, their muzzle flashes were proof of the existence of NVA soldiers.

Enemy fire became more effective as advancing troops climbed closer to the bunkers. Sweat streamed down our bodies as the attackers crawled and clawed their way up the hill, showing signs of fatigue and anxiety. Wounded and dead bodies lie scattered in every direction. Crying and screaming men, writhing in pain intermixed with the sounds of war. The enemy was effectively mounting more casualties by the minute.

I saw movement out of the corner of my eye and rapidly rolled onto my back, weapon ready to fire. There, crouching as low as possible were three of our Little People rushing toward my position. Even as enemy bullets were zinging by their heads, they continued to advance. Suddenly, as if halted by an invisible wall, all three were jarred violently to a stop.

One fell to his knees, momentarily able to support himself. He looked at me with a mortal wound to his head and fell limply to one side, dead almost instantly. The other two young soldiers stood motionless for a moment and were then thrown back down the hill, sprawling coming to a halt into a twisted display of death. Everywhere I looked, men were charging headlong into intense enemy fire, advancing past each row of bunkers and hurling grenades into them as they passed. Higher and higher they climbed, only to be greeted by another row of bunkers.

Men continued to fall dead, or wounded, trying to hide from the fury. I had to advance as well, leaving the concealment of the fallen tree I hid behind. As enemy fire spewed all around, I crawled to the edge of an open depression in the terrain at the end of a massive tree trunk and peered around its jagged edge. To my right, about 10 meters up, I spotted another slight indention in the earth from which I could get cover and lob a grenade into one of the bunkers.

Momentarily waiting for a lull in the firing, I brought my right leg up as high as possible in preparation to move. My hands were directly under my shoulders, and my CAR-15 was grasped tightly in my right hand. With a forward pushing motion from my coiled leg, I hurled myself towards my next cover position. As I lunged for the shelter of the earth, I noticed the ground was still hot from napalm.

My new position afforded plenty of cover from the hail of enemy fire. I was about 10 feet to the left front of the bunker, when an AK-47 rifle round cracked through the air. Surprised, I jerked by head back down to the jungle floor, rolled onto my back and reached for my M-26 fragmentation grenade. I placed the grenade close to my chest, making sure to keep a tight grip on the spoon, pulling the pin and rolling back to my stomach to reconfirm my target's position. With a hefty thrust, I threw the grenade toward the bunker. It bounced once in front of the firing port and rolled inside. A second passed before a muffled explosion erupted from within the bunker. Without hesitation, I rushed into the direction of the smoking bunker, placing my back against its exterior wall before entering.

I secured another grenade, pulled the pin and tossed it in. Again, a roar followed the grenade's detonation. Moving with utmost speed, I entered the bunker and sprayed a complete 5.56mm magazine in one sweeping motion across the room. Three dead and mangled enemy soldiers lay inside the bunker. I got the hell out of that place and fast. Looking over the roofline of the bunker, I spotted four more identical fortifications with muzzle flashes spewing from each. At that instant, an earth-shattering explosion ripped somewhere high above us, along the crest line of the hill.

The intensity of this particular explosion was far greater than the other weapon fire and explosions from within our fire fight. The concussion hurled me back into the bunker I'd just blown up. Frantically, I picked myself up off the pile of dead enemy soldiers. Blood, pieces of human tissue and bone fragments on the floor of the bunker caused me to slip and fall as I tried to stand. A tremendous volley of automatic weapons fire and grenades rained down on the upper bunker line. From what I could see, A-107 was now in command of the top of the hill, attacking the bunker complex from the top.

Finally, a ray of hope; we might be able to bring this battle to an end after all and destroy these maggots in the process. Having obliterated the first bunker line, A-107 pressed hard on the second when the dug-in NVA soldiers started running out of the confines of the bunkers in all directions.

I rallied a couple of squads, and moved off to the right flank of the next bunker line. The once-savagely aggressive enemy was now in full retreat. Our group moved toward the jungle for a few meters and then upward, gaining ground each time. Unknown to me, Little Joe has observed my flanking maneuver and knew exactly what I was trying to accomplish. He responded quickly by ordering three other squads to move off to the left flank of the bunkers and ambush the fleeing NVA soldiers. Once again, the wise Team Sergeant had anticipated the enemy's tactics.

I directed my men to move forward to each row of bunkers; first bunker line, five men in position; second bunker line, another five men in place. Prior to reaching the last bunker line, I saw two NVA soldiers running down the hill toward me, obviously unaware of our presence. I knelt, patiently waiting for them to close in on me, and fired an entire burst of 5.56mm at them from pointblank range. Their faces registered surprise and trauma as their bodies absorbed the rounds and fell helplessly to the ground. I ended their lives with the simple retraction of my index finger; death was instantaneous.

Positioning ourselves for the final push, men continued to drop off at the remaining bunkers. Reaching my flank position, I noticed movement high and to the front. Since I only had two men with me, we couldn't offer much resistance if the enemy force was a large force. However, we had the element of surprise on our side. Lying low, we heard men rushing down the hill. Our line-of-sight leading up the hill was obscured by the smoke that still lingered from the battle. Louder and louder came the sounds of men thrashing and falling, running at full speed. It sounded like 20 or 30 enemy soldiers headed our way.

My squad nodded in reassurance with sweat streaming down their faces as they drew closer. I checked my weapon again and thought, *"Okay, let's get it done!"* Over the thunder of approaching soldiers, I heard someone yelling in English. In desperation, I screamed, "A-104?" No answer. I yelled again, "Special Forces A-104?" This time, a reply came, "Special Forces, A-107." My heart jumped with relief as I moved toward the source. Approaching where I thought they would be, I yelled again, "Where are you?" Without warning, I was jerked off my feet and slammed to the ground. The American next to me said, ever-so-softly, "If you keep having diarrhea of the mouth, we're all going to die."

He introduced himself as Sergeant Johnson, from A107. I told him who I was and what we were trying to do. He replied, "Yeah, we saw the same thing from up top and decided to give you guys some help." Sergeant Johnson had already positioned 10 men per bunker line in four other positions above us. I was sure that we were at the last row of bunkers, when the sergeant informed me there were more above us. I could only glare at him in surprise. Noting my shocked expression, he replied, "Yeah, there are bunkers all over this damn hill."

I reached for my canteen, finding that all of the water had leaked out of the two holes that had been shot in it. As I drank from Sergeant Johnson's canteen, he leaned toward me, saying, "You're lucky it was your canteen and not your ass." *"No kidding,"* I thought to myself. I told Johnson I was going down about 30 meters and continue the attack. He acknowledged my plan and I hurriedly joined my troops. When I was about half way between my troops and Johnson, I heard screaming from my rear, exploding grenades, law rockets being fired and American-led troops emerging from the tree line landing in the bunkers above.

Without hesitation, I began to attack, with my troops down to my left with Johnson's people above me. The fighting was savage and relentless, the fury of the attack built with intensity. Methodically we began our advance from bunker to bunker, blowing the enemy soldiers up with grenades, white phosphorous and gunfire. NVA soldiers were fleeing their strongholds with no place to go. The soldiers who were out of our weapons' range were heading toward the tree line and disappearing into the undergrowth. Suddenly, a roar filled the jungle. Friendly fire picked up, catching the retreating NVA soldiers in an ambush.

American machine-gunners who'd supported us earlier had now sealed off the enemy's retreat, laying down a sheet of bullets from which there was no escape. The firing intensity increased, bullets spewing forth repeatedly, yet finally dwindling into sporadic shots as enemy soldiers were destroyed.

We obliterated bunker after bunker, waging war for another hour. Since our ammunition was low, we took weapons from dead soldiers, regardless of their nationality and pressed forward. Our battle raged into a frenzy ending with isolated savage hand-to-hand combat. Finally, we had defeated our foe. Combat-weary soldiers moved to the edges of the jungle, taking up security positions. Everyone lay perfectly still, trying to pinpoint any movement or noise. The only thing we heard was moans and groans from the wounded.

Who should come walking up the hill through the smoke and haze but Little Joe? He'd been hit again and a medic was attempting to render him aid. True to his nature, our tough Team Sergeant would have nothing done to him self until the perimeter was set up and secure. Little Joe gestured at me, "Chapman, get your head out of your ass and account for your people, and don't forget to set up your defensive perimeter, redistribute ammunition and take care of your wounded." Slowly, I forced my battle-fatigued body to move. I could tell my adrenaline levels were returning to normal. I began to set up defensive positions, moving from man to man, trying to determine our losses and see who was wounded and how badly and/or dead.

With my interpreter's assistance, I began to re-position what was left of our company. We formed a skirmish line, two men per position. After a head count, I realized that what had started out as a Montagnard company of 130 had dwindled to 82 men. Although discouraging, I reasoned that during the two-day fight and our intermixing of the Special Forces teams, some of my men could be in another group. The men in my company were exhausted, weary and mentally drained from the fierce combat operation we'd been through. I directed the Montagnard leaders to have every other man go down the hill to recover our rucksacks.

Someone was calling my name from the center of the perimeter. Shuffling into that direction, I came upon two badly wounded Americans and immediately looked at each to determine which one was in the most danger of death. The first soldier had been hit in the leg and shoulder with AK-47 fire and had numerous superficial scrap metal wounds to the face. The second American had been hit in the chest with small arms fire and was propped up against a log. He sat motionless, looking off into space no eye movement, no symptoms of pain, and no facial expressions. He just sat staring off into the nothingness of the terrain.

As I knelt beside him, watching for movement, a second medic arrived and began tending to the soldier who was less critical. Talking softly to the severely wounded young man, I slowly inserted the intravenous needle into his arm. Ever so calmly, he rolled his head toward me, whispering, "Doc, don't waste your time. It doesn't hurt anymore." As I looked into his eyes, tears of sorrow and fear rolled down his cheeks. Leaning over to him, my lips close to his ear, I tried to encourage him, "Hey babe, hang in there. We've got you squared away. Med-a-vac's are on the way. You're going back to the world, just stay with me."

I focused intensely on his wounds, frantically working to stabilize him, trying with all my might to save his life. All the while he continued to stare up at the sky, as though trying to see as much as he could. He knew his time was short. Abruptly, his limp hands grabbed at his chest in a quick, jerking motion. With a vigorous movement, he rose to a full upright sitting position and began to make gasping, grunting sounds. As suddenly as he sat up, he lay back down against the fallen tree. I checked his carotid artery; there was nothing. Hoping against hope that I could save him, I pulled him down onto a semi-flat surface. With his eye lids half closed and the face of death settling in, I straddled his blood covered body and began giving him heart compressions, screaming for the other medic to assist.

He attempted to breath for the soldier, but it was too late. The young American soldier had gone into chain strokes, better known as the death rattle. Although I'd heard of it, I'd never witnessed it until now. Oblivious to my surroundings, I worked harder, pushing his bullet-ridden chest, trying to force his heart to pump. Dark black mucous-colored blood poured from the side of his mouth. His lungs were full of blood and who knows what else. The senior medic pulled me off, sternly ordering, "It's over; let him go." I sat silently staring at the patient, my eyes darting from his wounds to his face and back. His involuntary motor nerves were still reacting. Even though he was dead, his body was gasping for air. The deadly sounds that came from his throat are still etched in my mind.

Gasping and rasping vocal noises of air trying to fill a dead man's lungs. Moments passed and it was over. All movement from the body of the young, once-vigorous American soldier ceased. A single tear ran down the side of his face, swallowed up by the South Vietnamese jungle floor. Every witness was silent, realizing that we had no control over the moment that death comes to call. We all stared at the dead soldier, and thanked God that it wasn't us. I still carry the vision of a lone soldier, dying far away from home, without loved ones to comfort him during his last seconds on Earth. A harsh burst of orders echoed through the jungle as Little Joe commanded, "All right men, he's dead. You're alive and there is nothing more we can do for him. The wounded are still alive. Now, move your asses and do what you get paid to do."

Master Sergeant Williams, put a poncho over the man's body, to hide him from view. But, the sights and sounds of the soldier's last moments were still fresh in my mind. Reluctantly, I began treating the other wounded soldier, all the while reliving the sights and sounds of the death rattle. I couldn't get the dying soldiers face out of my mind. As I dressed wounds, I began to think about the future. I wondered if anyone really cared that we were fighting and dying over here. I wondered if anyone would remember this dead American boy except for his family and us. Or, would this young soldier's death be just another statistic that a war protester could manipulate without caring one way or the other?

Larger questions followed: what about these people who were protesting the war? Would they become lawmakers and policy generators of the future of America? Would they forget about the thousands of us who sacrificed everything to follow the laws of our land? Were we simply going to be a black mark in our nation's history one to which they would publicly announce gratitude and admiration for service, while secretly selling us down the river for their own gain? Everyone who pays for freedom with their lives must be remembered.

Their names need to be etched on a wall of heroes, never to be forgotten or slighted. But, just so happened, our political leaders never had a son in Nam, much less fighting for our freedom. That's one reason they are so quick to cast us aside with mere words and B.S. regrets.

It was now late afternoon and the med-a-vac helicopters had begun evacuation of the wounded. The dead would be the last to be extracted, for they no longer held priority. The evacuation choppers came in one after the other, until all of the wounded were on their way back to Da Nang. The next few trips would be the removal of the dead from the battlefield. Upon their arrival back in Da Nang, the dead soldiers would be sent to formaldehyde village, where they would be put into their own little boxes.

Since med-a-vac choppers were one of Charlie's favorite targets, we remained on high alert. Again, this was physiological warfare. If they could bring a med-a-vac helicopter down with wounded aboard, we would have to wrestle with that tragedy as well.

# CHAPTER 8

Transporting of the dead and wounded continued for the remainder of the day. After the last helicopter made its way out, we all stood motionless in the middle of the extraction zone. Combat-weary warriors with grimy faces bloodshot eyes; physically and mentally-impaired men stared off in the direction of the departing helicopters flight, waiting for our time to leave this Godforsaken place.

Slowly and methodically, one-by-one we returned to our defensive perimeter to await our own extraction. Demolition teams placed explosive charges throughout the bunkers that hadn't already been destroyed, as was standard procedure. We all knew it would only be a matter of time before we were back on this same piece of terrain, waging war again. Nothing was ever maintained or kept after a battle in Vietnam; we simply held real estate for a short period of time and then gave it back. Then we'd rush off into another portion of jungle, search for each other, fight it out and die there. So, the train of thought was once we had destroyed our adversary, we could at least wreck his battle emplacements. Within a matter of days, Charlie would be right back here in this battle raged land rebuilding. At least, he'd have to work for another victory.

Shortly, the charges were all in positioned and primed for activation after the last lift of troops was ready to be extracted. We waited for hours with only the occasional squelch from the radio breaking the silence. Finally, we heard the familiar monotone voice of the FAC notifying the ground commander that the choppers were five minutes out. We could hear the distant UH-1 helicopter blades, signaling our imminent lift off. By now, extreme battle fatigue had set in and was evident as I look into the emptiness of each man's face. Although I was totally exhausted and wanted sleep, my mind refused to rest. Instead, my sub-conscience screamed over and over again, *"Why?"*

Although thick vegetation prevented us from seeing them, the ear-piercing whirling and popping of the helicopter blades dulled my hearing. While we waited for our extraction the noise from the choppers would get louder and louder with each second that passed as they continued there approach, but the thickness of the jungle wouldn't allow you to see them until they were almost touching the ground in front of you.

The ground commander ordered us to break down into six-man extraction loads. My company was designated to blow the bunkers, which meant we would be the last to leave this hellhole. I found it peculiarly odd that I was to maintain the perimeter while the remainder of the company was extracted. Normally this duty was assigned to a more experienced, combat-seasoned soldier. It was my responsibility to maintain security on the perimeter until the last extraction helicopters were on short final back into our position. Then, I was to direct the demolitions sergeants to activate the charges and, as quickly as possible, get the remainder of the stay-behind personnel loaded into the helicopters and airborne before the charges detonated.

It was always a rush when the helicopters came in to extract the troops. Charlie was out there somewhere and would wait until the last bird was loaded then bring in his mortar and B-40 rocket attack. The NVA always wanted a hit because it relayed a physiological message to the previously extracted troops: "When you think you have beaten us, look over your shoulder. We're ghosts in the shadows who strike when least expected."

Marking smoke was out and the choppers were making their last-minute adjustments, the lead helicopter coming in right on top of the yellow smoke. Like geese coming to water, ten choppers landed on the ground, blades turning, debris being hurled in every direction, men running or limping to their respective chalks, loading quickly so they could get airborne. Every time one of the mighty birds brought their mighty engines to take off, my heart pounded in anticipation of a mortar or rocket impacting one of the remaining choppers. Each successful liftoff meant there were fewer defenders on the ground, should an attack be waged. Although I continued to mentally forecast disaster, the jungle maintained its silence. As I watched the last helicopter rise off the scorched jungle floor, it was as if my body remained on the ground and my spirit lifted into the sky.

I was left in the jungle with my small, extremely fatigued force, desperately waiting for the return of the extraction helicopters. My imagination ran wild: *"What if Charlie was waiting for the last chopper to leave before attacking us?"* We wouldn't be able to defend ourselves and/or maintain the security of the landing zone. I quickly abandoned my foolish notions about fighting an inferior enemy. Our recent battles had proven that this enemy was indeed a formidable force, determined to accomplish his goals regardless of the cost. Internally, I acknowledged my respect for him, and at the same time, my hatred for his existence grew immensely.

The high pitch noises from the helicopter blades began to be replaced by the steady humming of the FAC returning to our location, circling high above us just boring holes in the sky. Thank God, we were not entirely alone. Occasionally one of the gunships would make a fake gun run down the center of the landing zone to try and draw enemy fire. Still, the jungle maintained its eerie silence. The FAC informed me that our extraction birds were on their way back and I should get my people ready. Looking around, I realized that an hour had passed during my mental wandering. Had I fallen asleep or was I so mentally fatigued that I lost track of time? Regardless of the excuse, it wasn't the right one.

I began moving around the perimeter, alerting my troops to the arrival of the choppers. I contacted the demo team by radio and directed them to standby. From my vantage point, I could see Americans scurrying around, moving to their preset charges, waiting for my final orders to light the fuses. I was to signal the ignition of all of the demo charges simultaneously by firing a white star cluster into the air when the helicopters were in their short final. This would allow the demo team enough time to light the charges and run down hill to load into the awaiting choppers.

I informed the FAC of my intentions with the white star parachute flare. He acknowledged that he would inform the extracting helicopters so they would be prepared for the star cluster as it made its way into the sky. I didn't want the helicopters, FAC and/or gunships to think they were taking ground fire on short final and abort the extraction, or have the gunships roll in hot and fire us up with mini-guns and rockets. As soon as I saw the lead helicopter come over the tree line to begin his final approach, I notified the Forward Air Controller once again, reminding him that I was going to ignite and fire off the white star cluster. Acknowledging my transmission, he passed it onto the helicopters.

I pulled the parachute flare from my fatigue pant pocket, removed the safety cover and striker combination unit, reversed it into the firing end of the parachute flare and hit it firmly on the ground, resulting in an immediate hissing as the white star flare propelled itself from the canister into the sky with the speed of a bullet. Within seconds after firing the hand flare, I could see men running down the hillside to my position. They had armed the demolition charges and were making their way down to the landing zone, trying to put as much distance between themselves and the charges as possible. As the last man passed my position, I sprinted to an awaiting chopper and threw myself into its belly, immediately feeling the workhorse begin to torque up its engines.

Within seconds, we felt the familiar nose-over sensation of the helicopter gaining altitude and ground speed as it leapt skyward. Relief swept over me as I realized that I was at last leaving this bloodstained piece of dirt. As I situated myself on the floor of the slick, I glanced out the door and saw the jungle passing underneath me with great speed. Quickly I reached into my load-bearing equipment, pulled out a smoke canister and threw it out the door of the chopper. This signaled to all of the aircraft that the last of the friendlies were out and the landing zone was clear.

Within seconds, we had gained enough altitude to avoid enemy ground fire, thus we began to circle high above the bunker complex. All eyes were focused on the ground anxiously awaiting the demolition charges to detonate, which would bring total destruction to the complex of bunkers we'd just paid such a high price for. We didn't have long to wait. As we began to circle, a gigantic explosion erupted with such force it literally pushed the air away, causing a white circular visible shock wave flashing across the jungle floor.

Everyone in the chopper grinned with accomplishment. Our smiles were soon replaced with the solemn faces of men returning from war, thankful to be alive. After confirmation of the destruction of the enemy bunkers, the lead helicopter ordered all slicks to form into their right echelon flight formation and return to the camp. High above that bloody battlefield in Vietnam, my feelings and attitude of life began to change. Having survived while so many young men had been atrociously wounded and viciously killed right in front me was having a spiritual and sole altering effect.

Deep down within my soul, I knew that I was undergoing a mental transformation, one that thousands of soldiers who served in Vietnam experienced. I could only ask myself, *"What was happening to me? Why was I not more grateful for being spared from death? Why wasn't I feeling more sorrow for the men who had died in the past few days?"* Life's meaning was slowly beginning to dull. My concern for fair play, honesty, loyalty to God, country and family was turning into a mental mirage.

As time passed in this valley of death, moral issues that had been pounded into our brains since childhood would be quickly be substituted for loyalty to oneself, your own abilities, our weapon and our intimate relationship with a few chosen comrades. Anything outside of that circle seemed meaningless and unimportant. My relationship with my family and friends back in the world would become a facade. The door to my previous sheltered life was beginning to close and for most of us, would never open again. My attitude toward life was warping and beginning to be disfigured, making it difficult to distinguish between good and bad, right and wrong, evil and Godly. Mental scars of killing would create a desire to kill again and continue to wear the armor or war.

The world had changed from pride and patriotism to hate and revenge. I wanted to kill, maim and destroy as many of those slanty-eyed bastards as I could before they could destroy me. This enemy of my country had become my own personal nemesis. My hatred fueled rage and vice versa, a never-ending circle of mental and physical violence. I was the keeper of my own fate. I was crossing over from a fun-loving, caring, emotional kid, into a hideous, revengeful, drunken, killer, born of battle. I was reverting to the primitive times where strength and non- emotional, self-reliance was the apex of life.

# CHAPTER 9

Motioning for me to put my headset on, the pilot tuned into Armed Forces Radio so we could all listen to some music as we flew back to camp. Some of my fondest and most remorseful memories will forever be associated with music and artists from this time in my life. For most of us in Vietnam, these artists and songs would inspire our memories while at the same time recall misery and pain we endured. We would place a song with a certain period of time from which we would resurrect a memory only we could relate to. The fans of country music had "Mamma Tried" by Merle Haggard; the rock and rollers had "Maggie Mae" by Rod Stewart or "Bad Moon Rising" by Cretans Clearwater Revival; the Motown fans had a number of hits from the Temptations, Jackson Five and Four Tops, groups that were sweeping the nation, back in the world.

Although everyone had a particular song they related to, probably the most universal was Peter, Paul and Mary's "Leaving on a Jet Plane." Every jukebox in Vietnam played this song again and again. The music ended as quickly as it had started up as we began our descent back onto the "A" camps red dirt covered airstrip. It felt good knowing we were close to what we called home. As soon as the skids hit the ground, we disembarked into a dusty haze of red colored dirt, kicked up by the chopper blades. The ground was hard as cement because it had been a long time since moisture had fallen on it. But, that would change very soon. Within a matter of weeks, the monsoon rains would engulf this entire area and we would be praying for just a small patch of dry land to stand on.

Strolling up toward camp, our heads down and senses dulled, we began to hear sounds that accompany death notices. Already, wives whose husbands and sons had been killed during this operation were screaming and hurling themselves to the ground in mental anguish, heart-wrenching tears streaming down their faces. Some sat catatonic on top of the bunkers staring off into space, slowly rocking back and forth with shock and disbelief that their loved ones were actually gone. Children from the camp ran past us off in the direction of the airstrip, hoping that their fathers were among those returning alive. Many of these kids would make a mournful and tearful return trip back to the camp, mentally devastated, their world forever altered.

Upon arriving at the team house, I was greeted by the "C" Team Commander and Sergeant Major. Lieutenant Colonel Shackelton the "C" Company commander, a veteran of three tours in Vietnam and a giant of a man, extending his hand to me as I passed through the door. He stood well over six feet, six inches tall, weighed about 240 pounds and was in perfect physical shape, with broad shoulders. As his hand grasped mine, I could feel the power within him.

Sergeant Major "Rod" Rodriguez also extended his hand in a welcoming gesture. Sergeant Major Rod was serving his fifth tour in Vietnam. In contrast to the colonel, he was an average-sized man with brown skin common to those of Latin descent. His eyes revealed wisdom and experience in dealing with people and understanding what they do and why they do it. Sergeant Major Rod's only comments to me were, "good job," and "it sure sounds like you guys gave them a good ass kicking to me." The Sergeant Major had every award and decoration that an enlisted man could have except the Medal of Honor. His combat experience and ability to lead men extended back to the early portion of the Korean conflict.

All of the Americans who returned from the operation were required to attend a debriefing in the Tactical Operations Center. Prior to going to the TOC, I went to my room to dump off my rucksack and grab a cold beer. I painfully unloaded my ruck, rifle and load bearing equipment, aware that I was beginning to ache tremendously. Grabbing a six-pack of rusted Schlitz beer cans from the fridge, I noticed a stack of mail stacked up on my footlocker, but decided to read it later.

Slowly the Americans began entering the Tactical Operations Center, quietly drinking beer while waiting for the debriefing to begin. Finally, LTC Shackelton told us how proud he was of us, adding that it was an honor serving with men of our caliber. While his praise didn't begin to ease the horror of our recent experience, at least he'd personally made the effort to greet us upon our return. The debriefing took about four hours and covered every conceivable aspect of the operation. Recommendations for awards and decorations were given. I was getting a purple heart and a bronze star with "V" for valor. For what, I don't know.

After all the paperwork was complete, we were dismissed. I went to the team house to finish my last two beers and get some hot chow. Half an hour later, I was in my hooch and decided to clean up before I went to bed. Heck, it had been 7 days since I'd washed up. Before I headed to our makeshift shower, I sat down on my bunk. And, I was toast. It wasn't uncommon for men to return from a combat mission believing to be in control of them selves, only to find that when they stopped for a short period of time, the adrenaline rush they'd been thriving on for days emptied out much quicker than expected.

Subconsciously, I heard someone calling my name, yet I couldn't respond. Next, I felt something hitting the bottom of my boot. Springing to my feet, I came face-to-face with the communications man, John Fetler. My fists were drawn and I was staring at him through glassy wild eyes. Immediately realizing that he'd startled me awake, Mike raised his hands in a quick defensive posture saying, "hey man, be cool. I'm sorry, I came in too quickly." I responded angrily, "man don't bust in here like that, I could have blown your ass away." He just laughed and replied, "I'm cool." He informed me that Little Joe wanted a team meeting because some new guys had arrived about two hours ago.

My head was still foggy from the sleep, I asked Mike what time it was and how long I had slept. He laughed and said, "its 1000 hours, Thursday morning man. You have been cutting some heavy zees. We could have been under a mortar attack and you wouldn't have known the difference." He was right. I had slept for 16 hours continuously.

Slowing moving out of my hooch, we walked toward the team house, with Mike never shutting his mouth. Like me, this was his first tour in

Nam, but he hadn't gone on an operation yet. Instead, he'd been held at camp to maintain the communications systems until we got another commo man. Having been assigned to the team almost three months ago, Mike was biting at the bit to get into the action. Mike was a slender young fellow, whose height didn't match his weight; he looked like a beanpole with fingers and feet. He wore black horned-rimmed, military-issued glasses, and his youthfulness beamed like a flare in the night.

Mike would later be assigned to The Projects with me, and save my life. But right now, he was a pain-in-the-ass, talking constantly; never saying anything of importance, just rambling. As we entered the team house, I told him to shut up. He just laughed and kept talking. Finally, he confessed that he was excited that three new guys were here so that he'd no longer be referred to as the "cherry boy" on the team. Sharing in his excitement at the arrival of the new guys, I let him ramble on, put my arm around his shoulder and pretended to listen.

As we entered the team house, I saw three new faces that would serve as replacements for the three Americans killed only days before. Crossing the room to retrieve a cold beer, I looked their way and sat at the center table directly across from them. Little Joe began the introductions. First there was Sergeant E-5 Gilbert Haines, a young brown-haired fellow trained at Fort Bragg of course to be our light weapons sergeant. Haines was 22-years old and a small figure of a man; but he would prove to be invaluable to the team in the days to come.

The second guy, Staff Sergeant Jim Perkins was a veteran of one previous tour with the 101st Airborne Division. He glared at everyone around the room as Little Joe spoke. Perkins was about 5 feet 11 inches tall, normal build, 26-years old, and his hair was almost entirely gray. Jim's specialty was demolitions. He seemed to have a chip on his shoulder from the very beginning; but that would soon disappear, or he would.

The final replacement Sergeant Jerry Walds was a hyper 22-year old kid. That would die on his first operation because he panicked under fire. As he gazed around the room, he looked worried, almost jumpy within his own skin. I thought to myself, *"He'll be dead within a month."* And he was.

Little Joe's second announcement was shocking and caught all of us off guard. The "C" team commander had briefed him yesterday about MACV's directive to begin the turn over of the "A" camp to the Vietnamese. He continued, "men!, all the Special Forces "A" camps in I Corps will begin to be turned over to the L.L.D.B. as soon as possible. This order is directly from the President of The United States and confirmed by Group Headquarters in Nha Trang." Our camp "A-104," is to be one of the first to be turned over to those slanty-eyed bastards. Little Joe explained that the turn over would commence immediately and would take from three to six months for completion of the turnover. Everyone stared in disbelief. We were surprised and angry at the same time that the American government was going to turn over our camps to the Vietnamese Special Forces who were known black marketer's, and would eventually screw over their own people for self advancement and greed.

How could the United States turn over a smooth running, well equipped "A" camp to such a group of losers? We all knew that within 30 days of the changeover, every piece of equipment within the camp would either be on the black market or in-operable due to poor care and maintenance. There would be no more active combat operations run against the VC. These guys were not capable of running any type of operations, nor would they have a desire or intestinal fortitude to close with and destroy the enemy of their country.

I couldn't believe it, I was in total shock. How many Americans had entered into this jungle hell, constructed an operational combat base sacrificed their lives, only to turn it over to these little low-life dirty bastards?

Little Joe's news was not taken well and the old timers of the camp began protesting, but their objections fell on deaf ears. The order had come from Military Command Vietnam, Headquarters and there was no changing it. Little Joe could sense the tension in the room.

Slowly he moved into the center of the team house, the prestigious Team Sergeant yelled, "At ease!" Every eye was on him, for he was well respected among the troops. Speaking softly at first, Little Joe's intensity began to build as he spoke the following enlightenment: "All right, you sniveling assholes. We got our orders from the Commander to close this son-of-a-bitch down, and that is exactly what we are going to do. This camp will be turned over to the L.L.D.B. (Vietnamese Special Forces), within six months. We will support this order, whether you like it or not, end of conversation. and it's nonnegotiable. Anyone having any further problems with the order will deal directly with me. Any questions, comments, or concerns, speak now or forever hold your peace?" The room lay silent. Everyone was either staring off angry into the distance or directly at Little Joe.

Turning to me, Little Joe said, "At about 1500 hours today, the "C" team is sending out the assistant S-3 officer to act as the Team Leader until we get a new one in from the States. Take care of him and give him the old man's hooch." A few comments were made by a few of the team members about training another officer when Little Joe went off again, "Can that bull shit. You are noncommissioned officers and it is your duty and responsibility to train the officers of the United States Army. The next one who says something stupid will take a little walk around the perimeter with me as we discuss it further."

No one needed an interpreter to understand what that meant. As usual, Little Joe was right. The junior and senior Noncommissioned Corps trained their subordinates, peers and superiors since the inception of the corps itself. Many good officers have been trained by NCOs to go on to be great leaders of men. And vise versa, many officers have trained NCOs to go on to be great trainers also. No matter what the level, leadership has to be learned, trained and utilized in order to function properly. Moving toward the door, Little Joe asked, "Are there any more questions about the orders for Vietnamization?" He waited momentarily and stated plainly, "your individual reassignment orders should be here within 30 to 90 days, now quit your belly aching and let's get the job done."

Motioning to the three new replacements, Little Joe instructed them to follow him to the Tactical Operations Center where he would assign them houches, duties and responsibilities. They quickly rose to their feet and left with Little Joe. The remainder of the team shook our heads disgusted at what we had heard, cursing under our breath then departed the team room angry and quit plainly pissed-off. The only question that remained was, "If they are turning all of the "A" camps over, where are they going to reassign us?"

The only other Special Forces operations were the Projects. These Projects, or Special Operations as they were later called, were such projects as Delta, Phoenix and Military Assistance Command Vietnam the Studies and Observations Group (MAC-SOG). These special organizations were doing some heavy-duty sneaky pete deep penetration, cross border operations consequently, they survival rations were bad at best. Rumor had it that they sustained a minimum of 75% dead and 120% casualties, day in and day out. Why worry about it now? I only had three months left in country.

Something down deep within my sole was really beginning to bother me: outwardly I talked like I wanted to go home, yet something inside me wanted to stay. I couldn't explain it then, but I can now. I had begun to like this adventure, the intrigue and danger of combat operations against another human being. I enjoyed the chase, the natural high of combat, but most of all, I enjoyed the killing. *What had I turned into? What was going on inside of me? Why did I want revenge so badly? What had happened to my concept of life?* I was losing my value for human life and my feelings were rapidly diminishing. Simultaneously I was beginning to believe that my destiny was already determined. I was sent here as an avenger to kill as many of the enemy as I could.

My ego was at an all-time high and I was beginning to believe I had become invincible. This false image of myself would eventually be my mental and physical destruction. In the near future, I would be brought to my knees, hard, fast and furious. Another ego driving factor was that friends and even people I didn't know were beginning to talk about my exploits. Some were turning minor combat actions into something you would only see in Hollywood, and I liked it. I began to feed upon stories of my combat heroics even though the majority of them were not true. It was the beginning of continuous life-long lies and the bad part of it was I began to believe how great I was and how glorious it was to force my enemy to give up his life, instead of me giving up mine.

After stomping out of the team house I wandered around the compound, immune to the crying survivors, barely noticing the women and children wearing black armbands signifying a lost loved one. With all of the fighting and dying we had seen or caused, we no longer had compassion for the dead or the personal loss of others. We just equated dying, as "It was their time to go."

Youth and combat has such a single dimensional view of life. What we failed to realize about the Vietnamese people was that they had been at war with so many different countries for so many years, until fighting and dying was all some of them knew. Silence was everywhere. Soldiers who had returned from battle were resting or in some discrete location trying to make head and tails out of it all.

The dependents of the Montagnard and Vietnam's men who hadn't died were going about their daily work routines. As I passed some of the inhabitants, I wondered when they were left to defend their home land on their own, without American support, how many of them were going to die or be put into rehabilitation camps. Chills ran up my spine as I thought about the fractured future of these people when the South Vietnamese military took control.

Each passing day saw the camp's attitude slowly began to improve. People were gradually getting back to hard work. For through hard labor, their minds were able to stray from anger, numbness and sorrow. Time and activity tends to dissipate pain. The camp turnover was in full swing within a matter of weeks. "A-104" Ha Than was one of the first to be turned over to the Vietnamese. We were daily taking an inventory of equipment, rations, medical supplies, weapons and ammunition held within the confines of the camp. We Americans were diligently accounting for everything that wasn't nailed down, and the Vietnamese L.L.D.B. were anxiously awaiting our departure so they could use the treasure for their own personal gain.

It was also apparent that some of the troops, especially the Montagnards were gradually disappearing from the camp. One day, five were gone; then twenty, then fifty. By the time the camp was officially turned over to the Vietnamese, all of the Montagnards would be gone. They could see the handwriting on the wall; their fate was a deadly combination of threats: both from the South and North Vietnamese who hated them, and would do anything to exterminate them. Their persecution and ethnic cleansing by the North Vietnamese in following years would be devastating and intolerable.

Reassignment orders were filtering down, with everyone getting different duty stations. I received orders to report to Military Assistance Command Vietnam, Studies and Observation Group (Special Operations), Command and Control North, based out of Da Nang. Of all the possible assignments, I got MACV-SOG-CCN. At first, fleeting images of my death and capture ran through my mind. That is until my ego stepped in, bringing self-glorification, adventure and prestige along with it. Within moments, I was bragging that I was going to Special Operations.

Little did I know I was setting myself up for a great facade? Especially when you are young and inexperienced, your mind tends to fixate on extravagant wishes and dreams, while the reality of what will be involved eludes you. In my quest for grandeur and hero status, I had no conception of the horrors that would be imprinted into my memory; horrors from which there is no escape and no reprieve, it's something you live and die with.

Suddenly, my thoughts turned to my wife who was waiting for my return. Jan had been patiently waiting, taking care of our son Les and beautiful little daughter Lorie. But, I wasn't ready to come back to the world, settle down and do normal things that boring people did. How was I going to tell my wife that I had voluntarily extended my tour in Vietnam to go to a top-secret organization with a mortality rate of 75%? How could I pull this one off without telling her the truth?

It boiled down to flat out lying. I had the administrative sergeant type a memorandum to my wife, explaining that I had been militarily classified as operationally essential by the government, and had been involuntarily extended in Vietnam for another year. With any luck it would work. This was the beginning of my deceitful nature; this was where I started to place mistrust in my wife's heart towards me; a habit that would go on for years. And I wasn't the only one deceiving their loved ones. Many would play this trick on their families. But, low life tricks don't go without payment.

Some of our deceitfulness would result in divorce or an occasional suicide, while others would go through alcoholic therapy and a few would turn to addicting drugs. Deception was par-for-the course for the majority of the Special Operations soldiers who survived. For days, I mentally developed this lie that I would be telling to the one I loved most in the world. Prior to coming to Vietnam, we had a relationship based on 100% truth, honesty and trust. And now, a year after I had arrived, I blew all of that away with one single lie for my own self- gratification and greed.

I didn't dwell on it. My morals and virtues were diminishing on a daily basis anyway, rapidly marching toward oblivion. In order to back up my story about being involuntarily extended, I wrote letters to my wife complaining about the possibly of being kept here. I played my part marvelously, cursing the government, telling her how much I missed her. I could have been a television soap scriptwriter.

The day arrived for me to depart the "A" camp and fly about an hour away back to the "C" Team in Da Nang. I had to clear the company and then report to my new home, Command and Control North, the most feared assignment in all of Special Forces. My excitement was tempered by the realization that once again, I would have to prove myself and play the stupid game of trying to fit in. For the past few days, I'd been listening to Little Joe tell me, "if you survive CCN, your ticket in the Army will be punched all the way to the top." In other words, the unit was so small, so top secret that it was known and recognized by all branches of the military up to the President of the United States.

After a soldier completed a tour with Special Projects and lived to tell about it, he was considered a master of combat and a legend in military circles. I immediately imagined medals, glory, prestige, becoming a legend in Special Forces and having a reputation that would precede me into the civilian world. While all of these macho ideals would be great for a while, eventually they would lead me to a 10-year period of living a lie.

As I departed the team house with all the team present, I told Little Joe how much I appreciated him being my Team Sergeant. He replied, "if I had known you were going to Special Operations, I would have trained you even more." He went on to say that he had been in Special Operations SIGMA, OMEGA and WHITE STAR, three well-known intelligence-gathering units formed in the early 60's. He told me in a sincere and authoritative tone, "Don't let this hoopla and Special Operations bullshit go to your head. Just do your job while you are there. Don't try and understand it because it is an animal all unto itself. And, for God's sake, don't lose yourself in it."

We shook hands and he wished me luck. I could tell that he was feeling choked up at having to say good-bye to his troops. As he walked away, his comments penetrated my innermost self, and I began to have second thoughts. I respected Little Joe and his wisdom, but it was too late now, I had committed.

While I waited for the helicopter to take me to Da Nang, I sat on the bunker and captured last minute memories of the camp and the surrounding area. I could see smoke from the cooking pots of the Vietnamese and what few Montagnard mamma sons were left, the thatched roofs of their houses and people moving up and down the village paths. Smells of the camp filled my nostrils and aromas embedded themselves into my memory. Out in the distance, a farmer pain staking plowed his rice paddies with a water buffalo, preparing for the rains to fill its banks. My attention was drawn to a group of children playing at the edge of the camp's concertina wire these kids thought the world was a playground, while not more than 10 feet away from them lay mines intended to maim and kill. I wondered how these children would have liked American parks with swings, slides, merry-go-rounds and monkey bars. Sadly, they would never experience such places. Mike Fetler shouting, "choppers inbound, get your shit together and put it in the jeep", interrupted my daydreaming. I quickly loaded my gear with the help from the other team members. I couldn't tell them I was sorry to leave them or that I would miss them. Instead, I gave the old mundane "I never say good-bye because its forever, so I'll just say, see you down the road." We shook hands, did a little joking around and I was on my way down to the airstrip.

I jumped out of the front seat of the jeep, grabbing my weapon, load bearing equipment and rucksack, and loaded my gear inside the now awaiting helicopter. When I returned to the jeep for my footlockers, there was my entire team behind the jeep looking at me. Without hesitation, they gave me a hand with my additional heavy load. Once again, they were just mysteriously staring at me. I couldn't think of anything clever to say so I waved and boarded the chopper, my eyes on the ground. As I sat in the troop seat of the chopper, I saw the team speed away off in the direction of the camp. I was somewhat puzzled at their eagerness to depart, but thought maybe they didn't want to get beat up by the dust during lift off.

The pilot rapidly gained speed and altitude, and then surprisingly with the utmost of precision, pushed his left rudder pedal to the floor, executing a 180-degree turn back into the direction of the camp. The copilot turned in his seat and motioned for me to look out of the aircraft. I did as directed. As we passed the camp about 20 feet off the ground, I saw what they were so anxious for me to see. Every one of the Americans were standing in line on top of the bunkers with their pants down, facing away from us, bent over at the waist. Eight white butts mooning me as I had my last view of the camp. What better send off could a guy ask for? I laughed hysterically, and so did everyone on the helicopter. As I sat there feeling the cool air rush through the open doors I hoped the new guys at CNN were as good as this wild bunch I'd just left.

From a distance, the coastal city of Da Nang looked like one you'd see in the United States. However, as we drew closer, its beauty rapidly faded. Da Nang was nothing more than a slum-ridden metropolis of poor people thriving off of bars, GIs, hookers, black marketing, drug trafficking and a stronghold of United Nations branches of service.

My attention was drawn to the South China Sea for on the coastline lay "C" Company or as we referred to it as the "C" team. As we gradually descended, I could see the 95th Evacuation hospital and MAG-16 (Marine Air Group #16) off to my right. On the other side of the helicopter lay the POW camp and below Marble Mountain was Command and Control North (CNN), my soon-to-be new home. Looking again, the "C" team's helicopter pad was immediately to our front, along with rows of American houches, the club, and mess hall and adjoining Mike Force compound. These units of Mike Force were also transitioning to Vietnamization.

As the chopper slowly and lightly touched down, I climbed out, pulling everything that belonged to me a safe distance away from the helicopter so the bird could return to its home base. With my weapon in hand and my load bearing equipment on my shoulder I walked up the gravel road to the company orderly room where I reported to Sergeant Major Rodriguez. He assigned me temporary transit quarters while I cleared the Company during the next few days. He also sent a Vietnamese Private down to the chopper pad to retrieve my footlockers and personal belongings.

My hooch was nice. It had a bed with a mattress that wasn't mildewed, a screen over the windows, a door that locked and a fan at the foot of my bunk on a stool. The mattress was "S" rolled, so I just plopped myself down and lay against the mattress on top of the bed springs and fell asleep. As soon as I awoke, I went to the club to see who was here. As I entered, the "C" team club the members were busy pouring as many beers and drinks into their bodies as humanly possible. A few of them looked up, but the majority just kept drinking talking among them selves.

Old Goliath, the company mascot dog had already drank his Crown Royal and had passed out in the corner of the club, lying on his back, his feet skyward. At the far end of the bar sat the "C" team senior medic, Sergeant First Class Ed Fossit. He ordered me a cold beer from the barmaid and waved for me to join him. Ed extended his hand and said, "I heard you were on your way to CCN." Ed having been a Special Forces Medic for over 10 plus years, he enjoyed himself to the fullest when it was time to party. However, when it was time to perform his medical duties, he was a master tradesman.

Ed had been a chase medic, or dust off medic in another Special Operations unit known as Delta. He'd scene some pretty hairy combat action, had been wounded numerous times and was highly regarded within military circles. He was constantly trying to get reassigned back into the Special Operations units, but was continually denied because of his medical expertise, rank and teaching abilities. While we were discussing what responsibilities I might be performing at CCN, Pork Chop, the Mess Sergeant came through the door. A monster of a man, Pork Chop was about 5'10" tall and weighed about 300 pounds. His face looked like a bulldog, chins bobbing under his mouth and fatigues stretched to their maximum expansion in order to retain his body.

Pork Chop immediately requested Ed to inspect some meat he'd just received. Ed agreed, especially if we could have a couple of sandwiches in payment, Pork Chop agreed.

It didn't take Ed long to evaluate the beef. He turned to Pork Chop and told him to dispose of it, because it was spoiled. Pork Chop became enraged, not at Ed, but at his so-called buddies on the receiving docks who'd given him bad meat in the first place. Pork Chop didn't look much like a soldier, but he took great pride in the chow he served the troops. It was amazing to me how he was allowed to stay in the Army as overweight as he was. Except that he was the best Mess Sergeant the "C" team ever had. He was also a wheeler-dealer, with connections on the supply docks for any type of food available in Vietnam. He had access to steaks, lobster, fresh fish, fresh fruit, real milk, real eggs and fresh vegetables. Everyone in this part of Vietnam knew of his exploits as a-scrounge and a great Mess Hall Sergeant.

After Pork Chop had calmed down about his rotten beef, he made Ed and I two sandwiches that would have fed four men. Since I'd been to an "A" camp for nine months, fresh bread, lettuce, meat and mayonnaise were like a banquet fit for a king. Finishing only half of the fine meal, we adjourned back to the club for some serious drinking. We drank and laughed for hours until the club manager threw us out. Then, we staggered over to Pork Chop's hooch to drink all of his booze until the sun came up. Finally totally inebriated and staggering drunk, I returned to my hooch and passed out on the bedsprings of my bunk. When I woke up, hours later, my head felt like it was exploding. I took some aspirins, layback down and fell asleep once again. At about three in the afternoon, I awoke, thinking that I might live.

# CHAPTER 10

I was dressing slowly nursing a hangover when Ed came through the door carrying an M-5 medical bag. With a big grin on his face and a look of mischief in his eyes, he pulled out two cold beers. Alcohol of any kind was the last thing my system needed after last night's binge. But I thought, "*What the hell*," and we started up where we'd left off six hours ago. I will admit, the first beer was difficult to get down, but once that was accomplished, I felt better. In fact, I began to feel good. This kind of irrational thinking and drinking is normally a huge caution sign. But to me, it was a way to fit in and a way of life here in Vietnam.

I was beginning to develop the ability to drink anytime, any place and under any circumstances, a ritual that would plague me for years to come. Little did any of us realize that the road we were traveling led to an extremely shaky path? For many Vietnam veterans, this lifestyle, the drinking would turn into a huge physical and mental detriment. Some would die in their own vomit; others would travel the hard road of denial and obsession with the mind-altering, yet legal drug.

I'd finished three beers when Ed informed me he had to get to the dispensary and run sick call. We agreed to meet each other later at the club. I dressed in clean jungle fatigues and headed to the orderly room to get my clearance papers. After receiving the single sheet of paper, I began clearing the majority of the company and headed to the Mess Hall. Since it was early, the hired hands were eating their meal before cooking dinner.

I went in search of Ed and found him on the same bar stool he'd sat at the night before. I joined him for drinks and before long, we were deep into the alcohol, trying our best to solve the world's demise and coming up short.

Without warning, the club door slammed open, hitting the opposite wall with a thud. A runner from the command bunker stepped in yelling, "A-101 Mai Loc" is under heavy ground attack. They've sustained numerous casualties and have lots of dead. All personnel are to report to their respective sections and prepare to support the mission. All medics are to report to the command bunker immediately." Ed and I slammed our beers down and ran to the bunker. The Company Doctor, and "C" Team Commander with a complement of supporting staff were listening attentively to the radio communications coming from A-101 Mai Loc.

From the commo man's report, "Heavy ground fighting was under way. The attack was unexpected and was initiated from inside the compound. There was no daylight left when the attack started and not much time to prepare for a night defense." The commo Sergeant went on to say, "It's unknown at this time if we can hold out until the Mike Force arrives" Every time the commo man keyed the handset, we heard automatic weapons firing, grenades and explosions detonating in the background.

Mai Loc was the northernmost "A" camp in Vietnam. It had been overrun many times and had always been reconstructed because of its strategic location. The surrounding area was sparsely vegetated. The NVA never ceased to amaze me with their ability to mount a large-scale military assault, with equipment and personnel without being seen or detected. Even more astounding was the facts that, more than likely, Charlie had rehearsed this very attack more than once, literally walking through every phase. It was common knowledge that the NVA rehearsed on scale models in their base camps then conducted dry runs on their actual targets prior to their attacks.

During their rehearsals on the target, the VC would crawl up to the camp or field fortification during the hours of darkness, lie there and then crawl away. They would rehearse this over and over again until it was rehearsed perfectly. The VC also had a specialized terrifying group called "sappers," or better known as suicide troops. They were primarily deployed to get inside the friendly perimeter and blowholes in the wire, or take out vital targets during a ground attack.

Prior to any sapper mission, the sappers applied a-thick grease to their entire bodies, resulting in a form of camouflage and acting as a sealant to wounds as they made their way through the barbed wire. While performing his infiltration duties, a sapper wore tight-fitting black under shorts and an improvised utility belts which held numerous metal "S" hooks, used to pick up the bottom strain of coiled concertina wire then attach it to the top strain, providing him with a crawl space.

As he methodically traveled through the minefields and barbed wire entanglements, he drug behind him attached to his leg by means of rope or vines a satchel charge (explosives). He would drag this charge with him as he negotiated the friendly perimeter obstacles. Since they were attached to his leg, his hands were free to make his way through the impediments. Sappers were highly trained, extremely motivated and ready to sacrifice themselves for the cause. Their willingness to die made them extremely dangerous, both physically and physiologically. When an allied military unit believed they had sappers inside the wire, the level of fear went through the roof. Fear causes men to overreact and make mistakes. When sappers were thought to be present, every available firearm was brought to bear on the general area of concern.

An "A" camp couldn't afford to have sappers inside the perimeter because of their determination to destroy everything in their paths. This was exactly what happened at Mai Loc. First reports were that "A-101" was receiving heavy enemy ground and mortar fire, and the initial attack came from sappers having infiltrated the compound and initially destroying the camp's Tactical Operation Center, medical bunker and part of the communications bunker. Charlie had done his homework; he'd destroyed all of the major fortification and control areas that might hinder his mission. However, he'd neglected to neutralize the backup communications system, the one the survivors were now using to communicate back to the "C-Team" with.

We all listened attentively to every word being transmitted. The radio operator was asking for air support, a Mike Force night insertion and medical assistance anything just give us some help. The fear radiating from his voice needed no interpretation; their situation was critical. Each time he keyed his handset, we heard gunfire and explosions. There is nothing quite like the helpless feeling one feels while listening to a man who is about to die begging for help. All you can do is hope they can turn the tide. Situations like this invariably didn't normally allow for to many survivors if any.

Every eye in the Tactical Operations Center was on LTC Shackelton waiting for his decision. We hoped he'd give the command to assist the "A" camp. But, he too could only stare at the radio, trying to comprehend the gravity of the situation. He studiously listened while referring to and studied the situation map of "A-101" mentally preparing a support plan.

Each time the voice on the other end of the radio made contact, it screamed, "Just help us!" Finally, LTC Shackelton turned to us and ordered, "Put the Mike Force on alert and tell them to gear up. Have them prepare all three-strike companies. Doc, get all of your medics together and the necessary equipment. You'll accompany the Mike Force in at first light." LTC Shackelton went on, "Men, I don't think there will be much left when the sun comes up. I want all commanders, you too Doc, to get your people ready and return here at 0240 hours for the operations order to retake A-101."

We all scrambled from the room, knowing full well that men were dying and we were their only hope. Everyone sprang into action. The operations officer called the 5th Special Forces Group Headquarters in Nha Trang to report the situation. In turn, he directed our Air Force Liaison officer to contact Moon Beam (Airborne C-130 control aircraft) and request immediate night air support over Mai Loc.

The assistant operations officer was simultaneously on the horn contacting the 101st Airborne Division's aviation unit, requesting 40 helicopters to insert the Mike Force at first light. The aviation support was to arrive at MAG-16 fully fueled, blades turning no later than 0500 hours.

The TOC Operations Sergeant pulled the classified combat orders from the safe. These orders had been prepared prior, to any "A" camp construction, marking all of the landing zones, escape and evasion routes and rallying points to be used in the event the camp was overrun. The combat folder was extremely detailed, taking into account every contingency. Once opened, the folder's contents were distributed among the staff to help coordinate their areas of responsibility.

The Mike Force commander left the TOC to brief his company commanders on the upcoming mission. This specific group would be inserting around 200 seasoned combat troops into pre-designated landing zones in close proximity of Mai Loc. The Mike Force was well trained; combat seasoned and constantly rehearsed such rescue combat actions on desktop scenarios and at time real mission. If they had rehearsed on actual locations, it would have enabled Charlie to counter their tactics.

Likewise, the medical section was busy preparing equipment and supplies. Each medic would insert with two M-5 bags, one on his back and the other in his hand that wasn't holding his rifle. The doctor would carry more extensive medical equipment, in case he had to perform emergency surgery in the field. All of the medical personnel were carrying injectable drugs like morphine, benadryl, atropine, lidocaine, demerol and epinephrine, including lots of fluid replacement bags. Bandaging material was a must and lots of it. Doctor Philips had broken us down into different segments to be infiltrated into the ranks of the Mike Force. I was to go with the Mike Forces "A" Company.

Upon my arrival to "A" Company, I reported to Sergeant First Class Daley, a crusty old cuss who'd served six tours in Special Forces in Vietnam. Although only 35-years of age, Sergeant First Class Daley looked twice that age. He had been awarded the Purple Heart eight times and the Silver Star four times, along with other assorted metals for bravery. I was completely confident with his leadership because he was intelligent, tactful and resourceful. His Little People loved him dearly. Being the power company of the Mike Force, Daley's people were always out front when enemy contact was imminent.

The Mike Force Commander, Major Ellis requested all Americans to be in the Mess Hall not later than 0240 hours. With load-bearing equipment and weapons in hand ready to receive the field order. I followed Daley to the briefing. On our way, he asked me if I had seen combat yet? I responded by telling him that I'd just returned from "A-104" Ha Than and was being reassigned to CCN. He responded, "I guess I don't have to tell you to keep your ass down, from what I heard about your operation a couple of months ago." I nodded in agreement. The American leadership that were going to take back "A-101" were milling around in the Mess Hall, talking, laughing and joking around with one another to relieve stress. A loud voice rang out from the rear of the open-air building, "Gentlemen, The Commander."

We all sprang to attention as the old man (LTC Shackelton) led the way into the room, followed by the S-1 (Administrative Officer), S-2 (Intelligence Officer), S-3 (Operations Officer), S-4 (Supply Officer), Communications Officer and the Company's Sergeant Major. The Commander began by remorsefully stating, "Gentlemen, "A-101" Mai Loc has been overrun by the NVA at 0145 hours. Our mission is to regain control of the camp and reestablish ownership. We have eight confirmed American dead and the casualty reports are still coming in. The whereabouts of the other four Americans is unknown at this time. Hopefully they are in their E&E (Escape and Evasion) Plan. The Operations Officer will now brief you on our plan of action followed by the other staff section with the remainder of the five paragraph field order."

The report that LTC Shackelton gave us was a hard pill to swallow. A sense of rage filled the room as we carefully listened and took notes on the operations orders. By the time all of the staff had rendered their portions of the field order, everyone knew who was doing what and how it would be done. The Commander's closing comments were brief and to the point,"Go out there using your heads, not your emotions. I know you are pissed off and want to kick some ass, but you are soldiers and I expect each of you to conduct this operation with intelligence and sound judgment. Good luck and good hunting."

At 0430 hours, the Mike Force's "A" Company loaded fifteen 2 1/2 ton trucks and drove towards MAG-16. The trip was short and quick; we were unloading in less than five minutes. Within half an hour, the entire Mike Force was on the airstrip waiting for the choppers. I lay with my back on the ground my head on my M-5 bag, looking up at millions of twinkling stars illuminating the sky. There were so many of them so concentrated it was difficult to locate the Big Dipper. We heard humming off in the distance as the helicopters closed in on our location.

Once all the helicopters were on the ground we began loading as soon as their skids touched the tarmac. SFC Daley was leading the assault, riding in the first helicopter. He directed me to ride in chopper number five.

Within seconds, "A" company was completely loaded and ready to go. SFC Daley told me to stay on the headset in case we needed to communicate. Company "A" was given the most difficult part of the mission. We were to deploy the first and second platoons to the South of "A-101" while the third and fourth platoons landed on the northern perimeter of the camp. "B" Company was to secure the eastern ridgeline 500 meters from Mai Loc. Company "C" would secure and act as a blocking force for "B" Company when they began their push. If everything worked as planned, "A" Company would retake the camp; "B" Company would push the NVA into the waiting arms of "C" Company, who would kill everyone that came their way.

Our combat armada flew low-level up the coastline of Quang Tri, so we could land; take on additional fuel and head to Mai Loc. It felt good to be conducting a full-blown assault against the NVA. For as many search-and-destroy missions that were conducted in Vietnam, lots of them turned into a 15-30 day walk in the jungle. Maybe this would be different. Maybe we could make a dent, catch them out in the open and deal with them our way. I was anxious, excited and scared at the same time. Radio chatter over the radios was filled with coordination and directives. Within minutes, the aircraft began landing to take on fuel. I could hear the Forward Air Controller giving the helicopters a sketchy update. It was still dark and no one could see the ground clearly enough to make out anything yet.

The sun slowly began to peak over the horizon, unveiling a picturesque morning. I was at ease with myself. For a short period of time, I temporarily removed myself from the war and it felt wonderful. Two sets of Cobra gunships abruptly appeared out of the left and right doors of the chopper to escort the lead slicks on the insertion. Other gunships formed up on the flanks of the other helicopters in our flying armada. Obviously, they were "B" and "C" companies breaking away from the formation, heading to their respective landing zones. We were getting close.

Smoke could be seen rising off the horizon as the gunships began to slowly pull ahead of the slow-flying UH-1 assault birds. As I watched the horizon, I heard Daley exclaim, "Holy shit, what the hell hit this place?"

We came in fast and low over the camp looking out the doors of the helicopter and saw that the entire camp had been leveled; not one above ground structure was left standing. Portions of disfigured corrugated tin lay everywhere, parts of buildings and people lay motionless in every direction, bodies contorted almost beyond recognition. Smoke bellowed skyward and nothing moved, inside or outside the camp.

As soon as we touched down, everyone scampered out and assumed a security position around our chopper. No fire was being taken anywhere form inside the camp or the surrounding areas. *Was this going to be another ambush? What was going on?*

As the helicopters departed, we lay still, weapons pointed like a phalanx, eyes searching left and right, finding nothing. Daley ordered us to move out as he and the first platoon maneuvered toward the camp's entrance, or where it had once been. There was no longer an arched entry, only two splintered poles sticking out of the ground. Second platoon had four M-60 machine-guns trained on the flanks of the advancing Mike Force soldiers. Still no enemy fire every individual's nerves were on edge. With sweat running down our faces, we tried to prepare for what surely must be coming. The third and fourth platoons from "A" Company were deployed online, prepared to advance when ordered to do so by Sergeant First Class Daley. Still no enemy fire.

The camp was littered with bodies of disfigured civilians and CIDG. From the way their bodies were laying as they met death, it appeared they were in on the NVA's attack. *Why had they participated in the attack? Why had they turned on the American "A" Camp? Something was wrong here, but what?* SFC Daley and the first platoon were well within the confines of the camp perimeter, performed a picture-perfect search and advance. Each man used short concise rushes, slowly taking ground as he moved, always covered by a fellow soldier. For a full five minutes, Daley and his platoon moved beyond our line-of-sight. Then, a runner sprinted down the hill, screaming, "Boc Si, Boc Si." I was on my feet, when I felt four other soldiers moving in on my left and right in tandem with me. Unknown to me, Daley had assigned them to me as my bodyguards, and they were under strict orders to protect me or pay dearly. As I sprinted up the incline hill leading into the camp, I tried to maintain my focus, but it was almost impossible because of the incomprehensible amount of body parts strewn around. Concrete bunkers had been utterly destroyed turned to powder, leaving holes in the ground; metal and debris was scattered around like paper. What had once been a formidable stronghold was now rubble, cradling the aftermath of war. The place looked like a junkyard.

As I penetrated the inner perimeter, I saw Daley standing alone in the open, cursing and shouting orders to his little people. He turned toward me with tears in his eyes; he was outraged. Dead people lay all around him, yet he had no enemy to fight in which to take out his rage. I ran over to him and asked where he wanted me. He didn't speak he could only point. I turned and saw eight Americans lying face down, shoulder to shoulder in a straight line. Every one of them had been shot in the back of the head. As I reached for the first American to see if he was alive, Daley screamed, "Stop!" In my shock, I had forgotten that Charlie often bobby trapped the dead, using them as one last means of psychological tools in their sick warfare.

The Little People attached ropes to the soldiers' feet and dragged them backward about five feet. Satisfied Daley and myself that they were not bobby trapped, I turned over the first man. Most of his chest and groin area was missing, probably from some kind of blast.

I continued on my sickening mission of turning each of them over, discovering that they had all been fatally wounded prior to being placed here and receiving a final bullet to the head. Looking up at Daley, I told him there was nothing we could do for them. He just glared at me, replying, "Of course you can't do anything for them. They have been dead for hours. Charlie did this as an insult to them, to us and to everyone who would see them." I didn't respond; I simply dropped my head and looked at the bloodstained ground. The Mike Force communications man handed Dally the handset so he could report to the Mike Force Commander, Daley with anger in his tone informed the commander to "come on in, Charlie's gone and all he left behind are the dead."

Within moments, the remainder of the Mike Force "B & C" companies were inside the wire and providing security around the surrounding areas of what was once a thriving living camp. The other medics and I scurried around the camp seeing if anyone might still be alive in this hell hole. As we crept down what was left of the concrete hall leading to the command bunker, Tactical Operations Center and communications bunker, the smell of burned gunpowder was stifling. We moved with extreme caution, attempting to locate and avoid trip wires and/or bobby traps.

The communications bunker was littered with body parts and almost everything had been disintegrated in the blast. The radio room was gutted and not one single radio part remained. I stared at the floor only to see a jungle boot sitting upright, with the foot still in it. A closer look revealed a single dog tag attached to the bottom-most lace. I picked up the boot and foot and placed it in the hall so that I could account for its identity later. In continuing my search, I even found dead rats; nothing had survived this attack. As I emerged from the bunker, Dally saw that I was carrying the boot with the foot in it. Angrily, he ordered me, "Come on Doc, quit fucking around and just put it in a body bag." I reminded him that we'd better get all of these body parts into bags before the sun caused them all to bloat.

At 1200 hours, LTC Shackelton and staff arrived on site to access the damage. The Commander walked around the camp with his right hand over his mouth and his left hand on his hip, occasionally kicking the ground. Like the rest of us, he was most likely wondering how much this piece of terrain had cost in terms of human life. All of the Americans had been accounted for except for the team's Executive Officer and the Junior Medic. An extensive search was being conducted to locate them alive or their bodies. They had either been captured or escaped. It was impossible to determine how many Montagnards and Vietnamese's were missing because the only records for them were payroll documents, and these were in Da Nang.

Every Special Force "A" Camp had an escape and evasion route, known only to the Americans. LTC Shackelton ordered a helicopter to fly the E&E route hoping to locate survivors. He also ordered "B" Company to travel the route for five days straight. If they didn't find anyone, they would be picked up by helicopter, but not before they gave it their best. The American dead were carried to a makeshift-landing zone to be extracted back to Graves Registration in Da Nang.

Two platoons from Company "A" were to set up defensive positions within the camp and the other two platoons were to continue searching the area for survivors while beginning the cleanup. Company "C" minus one platoon, held accountability for the dead, set up external defenses and placed out observation and listening posts in every direction. For the next two weeks, this would be our home. Each company went about its assigned duties with caution and expertise. Much care was taken to look for and disarm booby traps. Realistically, it would be months before this camp was restored to complete operational capabilities.

Resupply helicopters began arriving, bringing rations, body bags, medical supplies, communications equipment, ammunition and building materials. Chopper after chopper brought materials and not one single survivor was found in the camp. The body recovery platoon placed corpses of indigenous defenders in to body bags, row after row. It was sickening to see all of those bags and realize what lay inside.

Night crept into the war-torn camp. Although we were more than weary, we began preparing for an enemy attack. Fires were not allowed and everyone was on 50% alert status; one man could sleep while the other stood guard. Tension was high as we prepared for an attack that never came. A C-119 Stinger gunship circled high above us all night. His presence, while comforting to us, served as a reminder to Charlie that he was ready to attack anyone who threatened us.

Morning finally came, bringing with it hope and light. As soon as I awoke, I made coffee for SFC Daley, who'd stayed up all night, moving about the perimeter. Since I'd been allowed to rest, I saw the fatigue in Daley's face and knew it was starting to overpower him. I suggested he lie down under the hooch and catch a few winks. At first, he wouldn't hear of it. But, as he sat and drank a few sips of hot coffee from the canteen cup he realized I was right. He slowly crawled under the corrugated tin shelter and immediately fell asleep. It had been 48 hours since he'd slept.

Moving about the camp, I noticed a group of men walking toward us from the south. Initially, a surge of adrenaline shot through me and I wanted to raise my rifle and fire at them. However, better judgment prevailed and I decided to wait and see who they were.

Two squads of Mike Force defenders moved to intercept them while the rest of us went to full alert. The distant figures approached the advancing Mike Force Platoons with their hands above their heads. As the assault force swarmed them, we recognized them as camp defenders who'd somehow managed to escape. Running past Daley's hooch, I screamed at him, "Wake up! We've got good guys walking in!" They were all wounded, hungry, and mentally and physically distressed. Approaching with caution, I realized that two of them were the Americans we'd been diligently searching for. One was standing erect, trying his best to communicate with the Mike Force Lieutenant.

He had wounds to his face and upper body and wore blood-soaked fatigues. The other American was in serious condition, so badly wounded that he couldn't even identify himself, basically a dead man walking. Lt. George intervened telling me his name was Sergeant Wilson. He'd been shot in the left forearm and the right side of his face with a small caliber weapon. A blood-soaked bandage covered his facial wound. His head was terribly swollen, black and blue from the trauma of the bullet striking with such force. His fatigues were riddled with small holes, all entry points of scrap metal.

Understandably concerned with the health of his bewildered friend, the Lieutenant was adamant that Sergeant Wilson be taken care of first. From out of nowhere, SFC Ed Fossit appeared, taking control of the Lieutenant. I would assist the badly wounded Sergeant. As I raised the young man's right arm to rest his weight on me, he turned his head looking into my eyes, staring at me through eyes blackened with terror and confusion. He was in shock, oblivious to his surroundings. As I tried to take his weight, I whispered, "Hey babe, I got you now, I'm taking care of you now." He was shell-shocked and most likely didn't hear a word I said. He simply turned his head back to the front and continued to put one foot in front of another, guided by an unknown person to an undisclosed location, he was just a soldier following orders. A few steps away, I sat him down, afraid to put him into a prone position. He stared off into no-man's land as I hoisted a splintered board into the ground to act as an IV bag holder.

Next, I cleaned his arm with an alcohol pad and tried to find a vein. After taping the bend of his arm, one responded and I inserted the needle deep in the vain to begin replacing the fluids he'd lost. Carefully cutting the blood-soaked field bandage from his head, I conducted a quick visual analysis. He had an entry wound from a small projectile in the left side of his face, just above the cheekbone. Feeling around gently, I was unable to locate an exit wound. Ed Fossit came over to assist and we determined that the bullet was lodged in his brain. Ed turned to me and said, "We've got to get him out of here now. Start another IV in his leg, open it up all of the way and keep pumping those fluids into him. I'll get a Dust Off launched and on the way here now."

As I reached for another IV bag, I felt a hand on my shoulder. Fossit was motioning for me to look over at Sergeant Wilson. His head was now bent forward; chin resting on his chest, eyes partially open, arms hanging limply at his sides. I moved to start CPR, but Ed grabbed my shoulder and said, "Let him go. He was dead before he even got here." That pissed me off. *"Another American dead, and for what?"*

While I realized that Ed was right, my emotions were at odds with my reasoning. I made another move toward the dying man and Ed repeated, "He's gone, Les let him go. He's a vegetable now anyway." Looking up at Ed, my eyes filled with hate as my jaw muscles tightened. All I could do was sit back and stare at the top of the dead sergeant's head. We'd been taught that there were reports of soldiers sustaining fatal head wounds and walking around for hours before suddenly dying standing up. What an eerie experience to have seen this mortally wounded young man walking around with a bullet in his head. What had made him move in the first place? He should have died as soon as the bullet entered his brain.

I looked at him sitting motionless, totally relaxed with his chin resting on his chest. I wondered if he knew he was dead. His eyelids covered half of his ocular sockets and his facial muscles no longer held his mouth closed. I laid him down on his back and closed his vacant eyes. Ed and I stood side-by-side as I blurted out, "Shit, is this place really worth it?" Ed didn't respond, he just quietly replied, "Let's just put him in a bag, Les." Leaning over the dead soldier, I found one dog tag around his neck and the other in his bootlace.

The Little People helped us place him in a bag and took him down to the landing zone to be shipped back to Da Nang. I made my way to the wounded Lieutenant to see if I might help him. Although he was suffering from shock and mental fatigue, he was trying to explain what had happened here at "A-101" the night before. We all listened attentively as he told of sappers infiltrating the wire and getting inside the camp. Before they knew what was happening, the medical and supply bunkers were blown to bits. Although he didn't have an actual count, he said sappers were everywhere 20 maybe 30 or more. After the initial blasts from the satchel charges placed on the TOC and medical bunkers, all hell broke loose. Sheer chaos and confusion reigned.

He relayed the story: "bad guys were running at us from every direction; they were all over us. Those of us that were left after the initial explosions and assaults attempted to run to our defensive positions and began fighting our asses off. But, it was already too late. We had more bad guys inside the camp with us than outside the wire." He went on to explain that the camp had VC sympathizers inside who had given the bad guys full access to the encampment. The Camp Commander, Captain Welsch ordered all Americans to retreat into the inner perimeter and defend from there.

Before leaving his 105mm Howitzer position, the Lieutenant had lowered the barrel onto the sand bags, put in a beehive round in the tube and pulled the lanyard. He said he had no idea if it hit anything because everywhere he looked; bad guys were overrunning the camp.

Dropping his head into his hands, the young officer began to cry. We stood by him, silently feeling his pain and anguish. With tear-filled eyes and a cracking voice, he continued, "When we started to retreat and run back to the command bunker, one second it was there, and the next it was gone. The charge was so heavy and intense that it threw me off my feet and it must have knocked me out. When I regained my senses, I could see and hear the NVA walking around me, screaming and hollering at their troops. I wanted to get up, but I couldn't. I had corrugated tin and shit all over me, pinning me to the ground. I was afraid, and I couldn't move my head because I was trapped under the debris. I lay there praying they wouldn't find me.

For about two hours, the NVA walked around looking for anyone still alive. I knew for sure they would find me. Man, I was so scared I pissed my pants. I could hear single shots being fired all around, but I couldn't see what they were shooting at or what they were shooting. I saw them drag some bodies across the compound, but I couldn't see who it was because it was dark. They placed them shoulder-to-shoulder. Then Captain Chu, the L.L.D.B. commander shot each one of them in the head. I wanted to kill the dirty little traitor, son-of-a-bitch, but couldn't move. The bastard let them walk right through the gates like they owned the place."

One of the Little People from the Mike Force handed the Lieutenant a cup of coffee he hesitated then took a couple of sips. We all stood silent, waiting for him to continue. With tears streaming down his face, he began again. "At about 0300 hours, I could hear someone shouting orders and then they were gone. I don't know why they didn't find me. I just don't know why they didn't. I lay still for 30 minutes, afraid to move. There was no longer any noise or shooting, so I began to try and free myself. I was pushing and shoving at the debris that covered me when I saw four Little People standing over me.

At first, I thought they were VC and I was prepared to meet my maker. But they turned out to be friendlies. They pulled the rest of the shit off of me and we searched for more survivors. We looked for 30 minutes and didn't find anyone. That's when I took all 11 who were left and went into our E&E net. Just as we were about to exit the camp, I saw Sergeant Wilson staggering around outside the perimeter. He had been on duty when the attack started. I ran up to him and tried to talk to him, but he wouldn't respond. I saw that he'd been hit pretty badly, so I put a bandage over his head then we passed through the area into our E & E net.

We moved until first light. Wilson just sat still, staring off into space while the Montagnards kept track of him for me. When we heard the choppers come in yesterday, we tried to make it back here. Around noon, we were about two clicks out when we saw a large unknown unit moving through the jungle. So, we held up. I was afraid it was more bad guys searching for us. We hid the rest of the day in the bush and started moving again early this morning."

The Lieutenant needed to be extracted and sent to the rear for evaluation. He would go into greater depth and detail during his debriefing once he'd rested and recovered a bit. As the doctor attended his wounds, Ed and I returned to our improvised hooch. Neither of us spoke because if we had, we would have blown a fuse. It was common knowledge that each camp had a certain number of VC and NVA sympathizers within their ranks. But to have the camp's L.L.D.B. commander turn out to be VC made me despise them even more.

The Dust Off arrived and extracted the dead Americans and the Lieutenant. The lone-surviving Lieutenant would have to carry this misery and pain with him the remainder of his life. For five more days, we buried the NVA dead and began the reconstruction process. Word came down that I was to return to the "C" team on the next available chopper and immediately report to my new assignment at CCN.

I returned to the "C" team on the evening of the seventh day after we'd futilely retaken Mai Loc. I arrived at my hooch and went directly to the showers. It felt great to be under the clean water. I was mentally exhausted and needed some sleep, but I had people to see. I finished showering, dressed in clean fatigues and went to the club to have a few beers and relax.

There were only four or five people, including the bartender inside. Recognizing no one, I went to the corner of the bar and asked for a beer. Gesturing in my direction, one of the guys said to the other, "Hey we got a fucking new guy." Looking directly at him, I replied, "Don't fuck with me. I just got back from Mai Loc." A sudden hush fell over the bar and the guy apologized and sent over a beer. Raising my glass to him, I nodded in gratitude, and proceeded to drink for hours alone until I passed out.

I woke up in my hooch with Sgt. Major Rodriguez yelling at me to get my lazy ass up and out to the jeep. Grabbing my gear, with my head feeling like it was about to blow up I headed to the awaiting vehicle. Sgt. Major Rod shook my hand saying he'd see me down the road. I didn't reply for fear of being sick. I put my black bag into the jeep and noticed that the driver wasn't wearing any rank on his sleeves or his collar. He was wearing a black bush hat and his uniform had a nametag with a US Army tag on it. He turned to me and said, "Let's go."

Moments later, we were heading South on Highway 1 toward CCN.

My head was throbbing. When we arrived at the CCN compound, I couldn't help but notice it was a fortress, definitely the most secure place I'd seen while in Vietnam. We stopped at the gate and a large black man named Troy came from inside the security building. He asked me for my identification card, looked at it then returned inside the security building. Upon his return he had issued me a temporary pass to be displayed on my fatigue shirt at all times while in the compound. The sincerity and urgency in his voice left no doubt in my mind that I was to do everything he asked, period. Troy told me to wear this badge on my uniform so that everyone could see it at all times.

Under no circumstances was I to remove it or be caught without it. He looked me dead in the eyes and said, "Sergeant, these people," pointing to the guards, "will shoot you and never get punished if you do not have your pass visible." With the comment still hanging in the air, he gestured his driver to take me on into the compound.

# CHAPTER 11 (HICKORY)

A highly classified joint Vietnamese Lead with American forces in support of an operation named Lam Son 719 was scheduled to begin in the very near future. The Republic of Vietnam's (RVNs) soldiers were to enter Laos and conduct search-and-destroy operations against enemy safe heavens and cache points, and try to detect enemy hospitals throughout the area.

The operation would kick off near Khe Sanh, Quang Tri Province with allied forces crossing the Laotian border and penetrating 20 miles westward, swinging south in an arching maneuver. The idea was to push the NVA toward an awaiting brigade of Vietnamese Rangers and Infantry who'd intercept and destroy them.

Before any military operation begins, ground commanders need accurate and timely intelligence on the area they plan to enter. Specifically, they need to know if it has friendly inhabitants and where they're located; where the water points are, and if they' sufficient to replenish men and equipment moving through; any known enemy locations and if they're currently being used, confirmation on suspected enemy equipment, morale of the enemy and if possible, the type of leadership they are under.

It's imperative that these small but important bits and pieces of intelligence be gathered and analyzed to provide the foundation from which mission plans, supply trains develop, replacements and schemes of maneuver are worked up by commanders. Military forces gather intelligence from a variety of sources including; aerial photos or photo interpretation, ground sensors, agents in the immediate area or captured enemy soldiers.

However, the best and most reliable source of intelligence is gathered with American Reconnaissance Patrols, teams of men commonly known as "deep penetration cross border recon teams." Even with our technologically advanced equipment, Special Forces recon teams were still heavily relied upon for this type of information.

In September of 1970, recon teams Python and Crusader were targeted to conduct a day insert into radio relay site Hickory and attempt a walk-off recon mission down into the Khe Sanh valley floor and surrounding areas and gather as much information as we could.

RT Python was to conduct an area reconnaissance mission of the north side of Hill 887 radio relay site Hickory, continuing down the north face of the hill to the valley floor and beyond. RT Python was to be extracted after seven days in the area of operation. RT Crusader was to conduct a similar recon mission, except they were to depart the radio relay site immediately after RT Python departed, then recon the west side of the Radio Relay site, proceed down the mountains sided down to the river at the bottom of the mountain, cross the river and recon the Kha Shan Valley floor.

Like Python, Crusader was to be extracted seven days after they departed the relay site. Our dual missions were designed to confirm or deny the presence of the enemy. We were instructed to photograph the area and collect soil and vegetation samples, which would be used to determine if tanks and heavy equipment could be deployed in this area in support of the upcoming mission. Every bit of the intelligence that could be gathered was vital to Lam Son 719 and the successful allied invasion of Laos.

Tension ran high as we prepared for our mission to walk off Hickory, especially since another American recon team had been inserted three days ago into a target area further into Laos and had failed to make their scheduled communications contact with Covey. A reaction force known as the Bright Light was inserting into the team's last known position to try and determine their status. When the Bright Light was called upon, it meant one of two things; either the team was getting the shit kicked out of them or they had all been killed or captured. We wouldn't know which case it was until the Bright Light returned and filed their report.

With deep concern over the missing team, we tediously prepared to insert into Hickory.

James E. Butler, the One-Zero (team leader) and I, the One-One (assistant team leader) were in the Tactical Operations Center studying every piece of intelligence that had been provided to us. We poured through visual area recon map data, analyzed terrain features to determine the most secure means of travel, memorized danger areas and prepared escape and evasion routes.

The TOC's (AST) pointed out bodies of water and verified the existence of trails and roads, including recent activity reports. While Jim and I studied the situation maps and prepared for the upcoming mission. The rest of the team packed their rucksacks with weapons, rations, ammunition, special radios, grenades, claymores, demolitions and physiological weapons. Once a team began preparing for recon mission, we stopped taking showers, shaving, using deodorant, after-shave or lotions of any kind so that we could better blend into the enemy's secluded jungle world.

Simply put, Americans had a different smell than Asians because of our diets and the fact that we tried to combat our body odors, whereas, the Vietnamese and Chinese didn't bother with perfumes or deodorants. Since we were going to be in Charlie's backyard, our lives depended upon us blending into the surroundings as best we could so we always started getting funky immediately upon being targeted for a mission. We needed to stink like the jungle. We went as far as stop smoking American Cigarettes and start smoking their brands instead, Ruby Queen's and/or Bastos.

After our equipment had been checked and rechecked, the team went into isolation. Again, this was a normal course-of-action for teams getting ready to be inserted into the areas of operation. This precautionary measure was done in order to get the deploying team away from the rest of the compound and out-of-reach of entities that might compromise the operation. Only authorized American personnel were allowed to enter and exit the isolation area. The isolation area also served as a gathering point for the team to assemble and prepare to brief the commander on our scheme of maneuver and follow-on mission.

An operational brief-back was always conducted prior to any team being moved to the launch site. Because we knew that enemy infiltrators or sympathizers were within our ranks, the destination and components of each mission was guarded with utmost secrecy. Americans have a bad habit of getting diarrhea of the mouth about what they are getting ready to do once they get among the boys and have a few drinks. Many times they would discuss their targets while sipping a few cold ones in the Recon Company Club. All the while, the female waitresses would be listening and passing information to the enemy before the guys had time to finish their drinks. Therefore, we implemented the isolation phase to protect the teams and the missions against enemy counterintelligence.

Both RT Python and RT Crusader had prepared long and diligently for their important recon missions. Each team moved into the fenced-in area of isolation, with the teams further isolated from each other into separate buildings.

RT Crusader was the first team to be called to the Tactical Operation Center Briefing Room to give an in-depth five- paragraph field order to a captive military audience. Teams normally spent around three hours or more briefing the Commander, the Operation Officers and other selected American VIPs on their targets and mission. Recon team Python followed Crusader. Our One Zero, James E. Butler presented a masterful debriefing to the commander, covering our mission in great detail. Satisfied with both brief backs the Commander released the teams back into isolation to prepare for immediate departure to the launch sites.

Jim Butler, was highly educated, came from a prominent family, attended the finest schools and held Masters Degree in Economics, in addition to a menagerie of countless educational credentials. He was high-spirited and had dedicated his life to gaining knowledge, trying to understand and research men and the odd reasons they made the choices they did. When Jim first arrived at CCN, no one could communicate with him because his analytical skills and educational background were so superior to the rest of the group. However, in time he regressed to the level of the rest of Recon Company and closed the communications gap between us.

Jim was a fine statue of a man, around six feet tall, weighing 175 pounds and had the body composition of a well-developed athlete. His physical appearance was deceiving because he gave off the impression of being studious and mentally unprepared for the perils of combat. However, Jim proved to be a legend within Special Forces circles, capable of performing incredibly cunning tactics, in addition to well-honed mental and physical prowess. In fact, he successfully accomplished some of the most daring recon missions ever undertaken.

At 1300 hours, our transportation trucks rolled outside the isolation compound and dropped their tailgates so that we could load our individual and special equipment from the isolation area into the trucks, concealing everything from outside view with canvas covers. As we left the compound hidden under the thick canvas covers, we joked and laughed, all anxious to get on with our missions. Our route to the airstrip, would take us past various American military compounds, Filco Ford, past "gonorrhea gulch" (the local red-light district,) through the outskirts of Da Nang, ultimately to our awaiting C-7 Caribou aircraft at the far edge of the Da Nang air base.

As we rode in the sweltering back of the truck, the Little People kept peeking out from under the tarpaulin that covered the 2 1/2 ton truck bed, becoming more talkative as we moved to the airstrip. I asked Jung, the interpreter why they were so excited? Grinning at me, he replied, "Soon we pass, gonorrhea gulch. Baby son, (our 15-year old) come here before, get clap. So when we go by all time, we throw gas grenade in whorehouse make everybody run. We do all time to whore house, girls very dirty, lie. We think they be VC."

Sure enough, as we drove past the whorehouse, three cans of tear gas were thrown from the rear of the truck into the makeshift corrugated tin roof houses and surrounding area. All of the locals shouted obscenities in Vietnamese as we continued on our way. The team thought this was one of the funniest things they had ever done. They laughed and laughed all the way to the airstrip.

The ever-efficient Air Force pilots who would take us to our launch site had their engines running, tailgate down and were waiting for our arrival. We jumped from the truck, grabbed our equipment, ran into the rear of the C-7 Caribou and watched as the aft doors slowly rose. As quickly as we loaded the C-7, the tailgate came up and we rolled toward the departure line. Finally, airborne Recon Teams Python and Crusader were heading for the launch site. After what seemed like minutes of climbing and leveling off, the C-7 Caribou began its descent into the Quang Tri air base. As we were landing, the pilot contacted the tower and requested permission to taxi to the secluded side of the airstrip to drop off its cargo of classified material. Permission was granted from the traffic controller, and as we taxied in the direction of our awaiting ground transportation. The loadmaster of the C-7 opened the rear of the aircraft while enroute to our debarkation area. No sooner had the crew chief cracked the seal on the tailgate of the Caribou, than the hot humid Asian air rushed in almost taking your breath away.

The relentless almost suffocating heat engulfed us and beads of sweat immediately covered our bodies, soaking our fatigues. We couldn't wait to get out and possibly feel a breeze. As soon as the aircraft stopped, we secured our rucksacks. Weighing in at 70-90 pounds each, these rucks contained all the equipment we'd need to sustain our lives for the next seven days, or beyond. A black enclosed-cargo van backed up to the rear of the aircraft and the doors swung open. Without hesitation, RT Python and RT Crusader enter the van. Once inside the doors quickly closed, then the van sped off towards the launch site, located another five minutes away from the airstrip. In the darkness of the van you could hear men and equipment hitting the sides of the van as we ran over unlevel road, potholes and speed bumps.

Everything in the rear of the cargo van was hot from the temperature outside in turn the inside was still and dark, like the insides of a coffin. All I could think about was getting out into the fresh air and seeing light. Tiny trickles of sweat inched down my forehead and down the sides of my face as I repeatedly wiped the sweat away that was running down into my eyes with the palm of my hand.

In an unexpected, unsuccessful attempt to maintain our balance, everyone was thrown to the front of the vehicle as it came to a screeching halt. The rear door locking system abruptly turned and the doors slammed opened to an almost unbearable level of brightness.

The brilliant sunlight rushing into the darkness was in such a reversible contrast to the darkness of the van's interior, we were all temporarily blinded as we tried to cover our eyes from the brightness. As our eyes slowly became accustomed to the light, we exited the van and were directed to our temporary houches awaiting insertion into our area of operation.

Each team member settles into our new isolation area, awaiting orders from our respective One-Zero. Jim follows the team into the hooch and instructs Jung to tell the little people to stay inside while he and I brief the site commander. Jung interpreted Jim's orders and the team attends to business like a well-oiled machine. While we walk to the launch site's Tactical Operations Center, Jim and I agree that the sooner we get inserted, the better. Arriving at the TOC, in the center of the compound was in full swing. A menagerie of safes, filing cabinets and wall lockers each filled with classified information, target folders and intelligence lined the walls. A huge situational map of the Top Secret area of operation was displayed on the left wall marked with boundaries of the Quang Tri launch site and its sister launch sites' areas of operations and what teams were currently working the area.

Target areas are distinctively marked by red boundaries, outlining areas of operations for specific recon teams. This huge map is continuously referred to and updated with projected recon operations and active targets being run at the present time. Each target with personnel on the ground was outlined in red grease pencil and labeled with a letter followed by a number i.e., M-5, A-2, A-5 etc. The typical recon area for a recon mission would only cover six grid squares by six grid squares on a map referred by us as a "6 by 6." A recon team map was a 6x6 squared, or a total of 36-grid square area of operation. Situation maps tell stories like a book, except they use pictures and symbols instead of words. Red dots plastered this map, indicating known enemy positions, enemy units or suspected sightings. Enemy unit designators were marked in red grease pencil, as were US Air Force seeded areas and US Air Force sensors.

My eyes moved to the massive radio communications unit directly to our front. Manned 24 hours a day, these radios were the team's lifeline. As Jim and I silently watch the operation, we hear that Covey is orbiting the Bright Light team who was inserted earlier looking for a lost team. RT Kansas, which inserted three days earlier, never came up for team confirmation on the second day. Failure to confirm a team okay was an automatic red flag for the Bright Light teams to go in search of the missing team.

It was common practice and good sense to make a daily contact with Covey when he flew over. Even though the contact was short, it let everyone know that you were still alive. The Covey's initial report was sketchy at best, only reporting "the Bright Light team is still on the ground moving in the general direction where RT Kansas was last reported to be. The Bright Light team is still moving with negative contact with any friendlies at this time. No new information is available, but we'll keep you advised as new info is received."

My attention was drawn from the radio to the far right wall, where a massive statistical board where the launch site Commander and Team Sergeant were feverishly transcribing information onto the board, as it was received from Covey. The launch site commander begins to give Jim and me a quick run down on the possible lost recon team and how the Bright Light had failed to make contact. He explains that an earlier transmission reported that the Bright Light might have picked up a trail, and now even that news they received earlier seemed to be inconclusive.

Everyone was anxiously waiting for word as to what was actually happening. The Launch Site Commander was Major Telliot, a West Point gradate who had served two previous tours in Vietnam with conventional military forces. Since he'd never pulled a Special Forces tour of duty, he had limited knowledge of what a recon team did on the ground, but was extremely capable of supporting this mission. Conversely, the Team Sergeant was a man by the name of Master Sergeant Kimberly O. "Pappy" Budrow, a seasoned Special Forces veteran, who'd pulled five tours in Vietnam in every special operations unit imaginable. Pappy was highly regarded throughout special operations circles and many Americans owed their lives to this man.

In the not-so-distant future, I too would be indebted to him for my life. Pappy looked to be about 40-years old and hailed from Pennsylvania. He was a large man in every sense of the word: size, heart and wisdom. Lines crisscrossed his forehead and crow's feet protruded from the corners of his eyes, bearing witness of experience, cunning and intelligence gathered the hard way. Underneath his well-worn facial exterior Pappy was a killing machine that had managed to master his fury, keeping it under control during most instances.

Pappy's eyes were dark brown, almost black. When he looked at you, it felt as though he was looking right straight though you, into our soul. Pappy had seen more death in his lifetime than I'd ever witnessed. His manner of speech, always speaking slowly and listening with genuine concern made everyone really pay attention to what he had to say.

Major Telliot and Pappy directed us to be in the briefing room in one hour to deliver our pre-launch briefing. Pappy added that headquarters had instructed RT Python to backup the Bright Light team currently searching for RT Kansas. Should the rescue team need help, our previously scheduled mission would be scrubbed and we were to launch immediately to reinforce the Bright Light. Without hesitation, Jim responded affirmatively, agreeing that we would comply completely. However, we were instructed to continue planning our original mission because the current circumstances and the situation were subject to change in a moment's notice.

Jim and I left the busy TOC and went to the Launch Site club for a quick beer. The staffs that weren't on duty were sitting around the table, talking to one another. As we entered all eyes looked our way and we were greeted with smiles, handshakes and laughter. There were only three people in the club. Everyone else was busy supporting the ground operation. We passed on a few stories of what was going on back in Da Nang and they brought us up on what had been happening here. We finished our beers and headed back to check on our Little People.

Our guys were relaxing, lying on their bunks or sitting on the floor playing Chinese poker. Jim and I went over to our bunks to relax for a few moments prior to our next briefing. For the past three days, we hadn't gotten much rest because of the constant planning we had performed for this mission. As I lay still on my bunk, with my right forearm shaded my eyes from the light, I began to mentally rehearse our upcoming mission. Next thing I know, Pappy is standing over Jim and me, telling us to come quickly to the TOC. News from the Bright Light has come in about RT Kansas. I sprang to my feet, following Pappy and Jim through the door at a dead run. As we quickly made our way to the TOC, I began thinking that our mission had been scrubbed and we were going in to get the Bright Light out because they were in deep shit.

To my surprise, as we rushed into the businesslike atmosphere of the TOC, everything was quiet and somber. Major Telliot turned to Jim and me and said: "the Bright Light has found RT Kansas. T he bad new is that the Bright Light reports no survivors. Preliminary speculation is that the recon team walked into an ambush. There were obviously two survivors, an American and a Montagnard. They were bound and moved approximately 25 meters from the ambush site before they were interrogated and then executed.

The Bright Light has met no opposition at the present time. They are putting the dead into body bags and loading them up to move to the extraction LZ. Jim, your team is still on emergency standby as Bright Light back up until the original Bright Light returns back here to the launch site. Any questions gentlemen?" We just shook our heads in a negative response.

Returning to our hooch, we waited patiently for the next three hours for any news of our fallen comrades. While we waited, I unconsciously began to sharpen by K-bar knife. My mind began to stress over my lost buddies. I had just been told that McAllory and Kitter were dead. I swore that I wouldn't believe it until I saw their bodies. Hell, only a week ago, we were all in the recon club trying to drink each other under the table. No, I would have to see the dead bodies myself before I would believe it. After waiting for two more hours, the hooch door swung open and one of the commo men screamed, "Bright Light choppers inbound."

Both RT Crusader and RT Python rushed out of our buildings to the chopper pad. We all stood silently looking to the West, where the choppers carrying the dead would appear. Time slowed as our hearts pounded out our silent fears. I took a Rudy Queen from my pocket and tried to light it. I must have been nervous because I couldn't get the lighter to meet the end of my cigarette. My hands were shaking. Suddenly, a hand grasped mine steadied the lighter to the end of the cigarette. Pappy was looking into my eyes as he said, "Boy, keep your cool. This ain't a place to lose it now." No one spoke as the helicopters came into view. As slick #1 came in at a low hover, I could see six body bags stacked on top of one another. Slick two three and four were suspended in mid air waiting to land.

Once the lead slick landed, the others followed suit, landing one behind the other in staggered formation. The troops on the ground walked quickly to slick #1 to assist in off-loading the body bags. With reverence and respect, we laid them down gently. With the blades of the choppers still turning, we gathered around the deceased soldiers, staring at each one in disbelief. Then, as if on cue, Pappy commanded in a loud voice, "Bright Light to the debriefing room. RT Python and RT Crusader back to your hooch. Launch site personnel, secure the dead and transport them to the airstrip for air lift back to Da Nang."

For a moment, we hesitated, but just for a moment; then our training took over and we followed Pappy's orders to the letter. As I slowly made my way back to the hooch, I wondered why men knowingly risked their lives, volunteering to go where they know death awaits, always pushing the law of averages, and for what? And, I especially wasn't immune to the insanity. Hell, here I was about to do the very same thing. I didn't know why I was doing this anymore. I only knew that I liked it and wanted to be part of it. *"I felt like I was on some type of tight wire with death,"* I thought, *"Or was I?"* Maybe I had some sort of twisted death wish. Because my heart genuinely ached for my fellow soldiers whose lives had been savagely taken from them, I would avenge their deaths. Someone would pay for every ache and pain afflicted on those I called my own. I wondered where my tears had gone. Not long ago, tears would have filled my eyes for the tritest of circumstance. Now, I could look at dead men, through eyes as dry as the Sahara. *Why wasn't I crying anymore? What was happening to me?*

Jim and I didn't converse while returning to our hooch. We simply walked in silence staring at the ground. Pappy came in a few minutes later and told us that neither Python nor Crusader would be inserted today. Instead, we would launch into Hickory at first light tomorrow. Jim relayed the change in plans to the interpreter, who told the Little People to eat and get some rest for an early insertion tomorrow. They immediately began to comply. Everyone knew what had happened and maintained his silence out of respect for the dead.

The afternoon sun was descending when a runner came into our hooch requested us to meet in the TOC. When everyone was present, Pappy began to speak, "It appears that RT Kansas walked into an area ambush and everyone was killed except an American and one of the Montagnards. The NVA bound the two of them and moved them south where they began interrogating them. Sometime during the interrogation, and brutal torturing of the two recon men the NVA got tired of screwing with them and finished the interrogation with a single bullet to the back of their heads." I felt my temperature rise as blood rushed anger with rage throughout my body. My chest hyper extending with every breath I took. Somehow, I was learning to contain my anger internally, waiting to unleash it as a deadly force when I needed to. I began to think of ways to physical and physiological revenge these inhumane acts against our soldiers. Its one thing to kill an enemy outright, but quite another to torture and execute him. I wanted to kill these unmerciful bastards; I wanted blood, and blood I would have.

After the briefing, Pappy dismissed everyone except Jim and me. We were instructed to provide him and the launch site commander with a brief back on our upcoming mission. This additional communications between recon team and our support vain ensured that all parties understood the concepts of the mission and how objectives were to be accomplished. It also ensured adequate support from the Launch Site. After hearing our full mission brief back Pappy seemed satisfied and dismissed us with, "Let's get it done." As we entered our hooch at about 2100 hours, all of the Little People were preparing to hit the rack. I did likewise, and in what seemed like no time at all pappy awakened us at 0600 hours in preparation for a 0900 insert into Hickory. As Pappy made his exit he cautioned, "weather's moving in, so be prepared."

Weather played a tremendous role in the way we conducted operations. If it was against us, we were crippled, unable to insert or have the ability to extract teams. Covey couldn't make daily contacts and most importantly, if a recon team got into any trouble during the monsoon rains, air support was grounded and you were basically on your own. The team would have to fight their way out or die trying. Anytime we received caution of approaching weather, we took it very seriously.

During the Monsoon season, you could set your watch by the time the rains would begin. In the morning hours, the sky was clear, sporting only a few puffy white clouds. However, as the day lingered on, those puffy white clouds would begin to consolidate over the mountains to the west, and then begin moving quickly west.

By 1500 hours, the rains were falling, with the downpour continuing anywhere from five to seven hours before beginning to dissipate. The rains would start up over and over again throughout the night. I speak casually about the way it rained in Vietnam because it's difficult to understand unless you've experienced it. The rains fell so hard and with such intensity, they appeared to be one constant sheet of water falling from the sky. I remember looking out from my hooch in Da Nang and feeling like I was standing beneath an overhang at the bottom of a waterfall.

No one spoke as we methodically secured our poncho liners and sleeping gear back into our rucksacks. I thought about yesterday and the loss of the recon team. I wondered what lay ahead for me. Were we destined to suffer the same fate as our brothers had? You just damned didn't know. No one knew! Then I wondered if anyone back in the world really cared what happened yesterday? Would anyone remember all of the Americans who gave their lives? Would anyone miss me if I met the same demise? I quickly chastised myself for thinking about such rot. I realized right then and there that the only people, who would remember us, would be us.

We left the hooch carrying our heavy rucksacks headed for the launch pad where the choppers were that would take us to Hickory. As if rehearsed, every member of the team placed his rucksack on the ground next to the helicopters and sat on it like a chair. We relaxed as the helicopter crews conducted preflight checks. I noticed Jung, our interpreter checking the magazine in his CAR-15. Jung was an extremely intelligent man, 26 years of age. He'd spent two years as a student at Ohio State University, spoke better English than most Americans, and hated the North Vietnamese with a passion. Our baby son, Chow (BS), sat immediately behind Jung. Chow was 15-years old, stood about 5'4" and appeared physically fragile. Yet, he was a typical teenager: full of vitality, always looking for adventure and afraid of nothing. Chow was mischievous. Largely due to immaturity, he would lie to us at the drop of a hat, earning him the nickname, BS.

As with any youngster who'd been slammed into war, he'd had no real childhood. He had only tried to survive, escape the continual terror and reality of war and preserve some kind of life for himself. The stories he told us were so far fetched that even he had trouble believing them. I think he told such bizarre tales for entertainment purposes.

And then there was Lou, different from the others in physical appearance. The majority of Asians stand about 5' to 5'6" tall. Lou, however, was close to 6' tall and skinny as a rail. His size earned him the nickname, Stick Man. Lou was 24 years old and his family had migrated from North Vietnam to the South when he was an infant. He told us through the interpreter that, "North Vietnamese think South Vietnamese be same, same as monkey. Treat South Vietnamese people very bad, some times kill them for nothing." Lou's specialty was booby traps, detecting them, disarming them and/or setting them up. Most of the time we put him on point, because we believed Lou had the ability to literally smell the NVA before the team could see them.

Our tail gunner Duo was the silent one, the old man on the team. He seldom spoke. But, when he did, the entire team listened attentively. He was the eldest member of our team, believing himself to be around 35-years old, but not really knowing for sure. While in the jungle, Duo had the eyes of an eagle, the cunning of a lion and could turn into a stone-cold killer in a heartbeat. The North Vietnamese had executed Duo's mother and father in front of him during the great migration from North Vietnam to South Vietnam. Of normal Asian size, Duo's face told the story of many battles, wisdom and pain deeply etched on his cheeks and forehead. His eyes were constantly searching, for what, only he and his God knew. While in the jungle, the entire team was at ease when he was around them. Duo had been wounded 15 times, escaped from the enemy twice and was known to have personally killed 50 plus NVA. When he killed an enemy soldier, it provided him with sheer satisfaction and a sense of personal revenge. Once when he and I were alone in my hooch, he revealed his reasoning, "When I kill VC, I think maybe I kill same VC that killed my family. Someday, I kill all VC and be sure."

Suddenly we hear the pilot yell back to the crew chief "coming hot" then the crew chief responds "Clear." Slowly, the turbine engines of the helicopters come to life and the crew chief motioned for our recon team to load up. In a matter of moments, we'd be on our way to Radio Relay Site Hickory. RT Python was assigned to aircraft one and two. RT Crusader boarded aircraft three and four. Both teams were sitting in the door of the helicopters, feet hanging out as we gave thumbs-up, confirming we were ready for take off.

As the birds climbed higher, I noticed the much faster Cobra gunships closing ground behind us to escort and support our insert into Hickory. Leaving the populated areas behind, we passed high over the lush green jungles of South Vietnam. After a 30-minute ride, we heard the all-too-familiar communications from Covey. Radio chatter between the Cobras and the UH-1s coordinates the insert into Hickory:

> Slick #1 and Guns #1, this is Covey 247, over;
>
> Covey 247, this is Slick lead, this is Gun #1, over;
>
> Roger, Slick lead and Gun #1, we'll be making an east to west approach into Hickory. The ground commander has relayed there is no enemy activity in the area at the present time, so we will do a standard insert. Slick lead, you'll lead the way in with your trail ships doing likewise. Slick lead, you'll come in hot, drop off your PAC's, come up and break left, then move off into the valley to assemble all of the birds out there, how copy? Over.
>
> Covey 247, this is Slick lead good copy, over;
>
> Gun #1, this is Covey 247, you and your finger man will escort each Slick in and out of the insert location. One of you is to escort on his three o'clock and the other escort at his nine o'clock. How copy? Over?
>
> Covey 247, good copy, over;
>
> Slick lead, this is Covey 247, direct your trailing chicks to keep about a four-minute separation so we don't get cluttered up around the landing zone, how copy? Over?
>
> Covey 247, this Spad #1, good copy, over;

Ok, Slicks and Guns, let's get these troops' feet on the ground; follow me in.

In the distance, I could see Covey breaking out of his orbit, heading toward Hickory, and a mountain top that spikes sharply skyward above all other peaks within a 2-mile radius. As we fly closer to our drop-off point, the lead slick and guns begin to move away from the trailing slicks.

Total compliance to Covey's directives was vital to everyone's survival. Leaning forward and looking out into our direction of flight, I saw green smoke coming from our landing zone. Not only does this smoke tell us where they want us to insert, it helps the pilots get a visual on the wind direction on top of the mountain peak during their final approach. Slick lead reaches his objective first and portion of the teams rapidly exit the silhouetted helicopter. As quickly as Slick lead was in, he's up and breaking away from the mountaintop, like a dragonfly escaping into the sky.

Our chopper is on short final as I struggle to see what kind of terrain we're dropping into. We're moving too fast for me to distinguish anything, except to see that the slopes off of Hickory are sheer drop-offs in every direction except one. As Slick two makes its pre-touch down, I take one last mental picture from my elevated position of the area we are about to negotiate. The terrain surrounding Hickory falls rapidly away from the crest of the hill a small ridgeline to the south overlooks the relay site. The jungle surrounding the Radio Relay Site has been cut or burned away from the bunker lines about 50 meters, giving the occupants on top of the hill complete visual dominance of the immediate area.

Hundreds of empty ammo cases, C-ration cans, mortar round containers, expended ammo casings and trash had been thrown down the hill resting along the jungle's edge. Defensive trench lines honeycomb the encampment. Radio antennas extend high into the air like flag poles on top of the communications bunker. Exposed mortar tubes and machine gun positions riddle the ground. A facade of total security is visible as you look down on the site from the air.

Feeling the skids of the helicopter touch down, we exit with rucksack in hand, CAR-15 draped around our necks and load-bearing equipment hanging loosely from our shoulders. As our feet touch the ground, we hear the torque of the helicopter raise in intensity. With rotor blades at peak rotation, the pilot snatches the chopper upward, propelling it up into the air, diving off and away from the hilltop. After the helicopter had cleared the landing zone, RT Python links up together and waited for our sister team, RT Crusader who was close behind us. One helicopter after another delivered its human cargo and returned to the sky.

# CHAPTER 12 (HICKORY 1)

As the Covey and the helicopters disappeared off to the east, serenity returned to the small relay site. A tall thin young man, wearing no rank on his fatigue jacket came toward us with his right hand extended, enthusiastically greeting each of us and welcoming us to his remote isolated "high mountain prison." He introduced himself as First Lieutenant Wolf, the camp commander and senior officer. In fact, 1LT Wolf was the only American officer who had been assigned to the top of this hill in years.

This assignment was normally reserved for senior enlisted men who really didn't want to run the bush anymore. As we would find out, Americans were sent up here either for a rest or because the Project Commander wanted to get the person out of his sight. Seventy five percent of the time, it was to get the individual away from the rest of the troops. In prior years, a tour-of-duty here at the radio site was a genuine support function, not punishment. However, this had changed over the past two years. Three Americans were now assigned to the radio-relay site: Lieutenant Wolf, Sergeant Henderson and Sergeant Warren. All were from CCN Security Company and had been residing here for the past three weeks.

As we were the first Americans they'd seen since they were sent to this duty assignment, they were elated to see us. Lieutenant Wolf was a 24-year old kid with a baby face, who stood about 6 feet tall. The reason he was here became apparent fairly quickly; his lack of self-confidence was evident in his apologetic manner of speech. You could tell he wanted to be "one of the boys" rather than take the leadership responsibility and authority required of an officer. He was sorely lacking in initiative and unwilling to sacrifice to reach lofty goals. Like so many other young Americans, he talked a good story, but had no solid idea of the sacrifices required to achieve success.

Sergeant Henderson, the communications operator, was a legend unto himself. He alone assumed the responsibility of running the relay site, and it was apparent that the other Americans were subservient to him. Sergeant Henderson saw himself as a direct descendant of God, destined to be a leader of men in the crusade against the evils of communism. In reality he was a loudmouth, opinionated mental midget of a man. Sergeant Henderson stood 5' 8" tall and grossly overweight. His jungle fatigues looked as though he'd been wearing them for weeks, with evidence of all manner of food having been spilled down the front of them. In general, he was an overweight slob, belly hanging over his belt, t-shirt too small and fat arms bulging through cutout sleeves. He resembled a big fat hog, with jowls dropping down from his face and a pug turned up nose. The fat around his face had accumulated in a manner that caused his eyes to squint in order for him to see properly.

The third American onsite was Sergeant Warren, the weapons man, and quite an odd character. Although he appeared to be intelligent and physically fit, his shy introverted manner was puzzling. Story was, he'd once been in recon company and had only gone on one mission. Apparently, his team had been hit hard and everyone was killed except him. Mysteriously, he came out of the battle without a scratch. When the Bright Light Team was inserted to extract the bodies of the decimated team, they found him wandering around alone in the jungle. He was returned to the base camp in Da Nang and flat out told the recon company commander he refused to run another recon mission. He'd experience periods of depression and exhibited violent mood swings, causing concern from our commander. In order to remove him from the compound, he was assigned to this post. Although he looked every inch an athlete, when you peered into his eyes, you could tell that the lights were on but no one was home.

As we made our way to the command bunker, Lieutenant Wolf proudly pointed out the defenses of the radio relay site. RT Python and RT Crusader followed him, scanning the surroundings as we passed through the camp. The outer portion of the command bunker contained a massive radio network tied into top-secret radio surveillance equipment. On the other side of the sand bag wall was the command bunker itself, which doubled as sleeping quarters for the Americans, and a very small briefing room should the need arise.

The Lieutenant led us out of the command bunker to the south side of the perimeter, where he stopped and announced that this would be where we'd stay for the night. We were shocked to say the least; he'd placed us in a portion of the trench line that encircled the camp with no overhead cover and no place to lie down and/or sleep. Dumbfounded, we stared at each other in disbelief. Captain Butler, who was familiar with Lieutenant Wolf didn't say anything except, "Okay guys, lets' make the best of it." As the Little People prepared sleeping positions, the two One-Zeros Captain Butler and Captain Dugan wandered off into another portion of the relay site to talk to the Lieutenant Wolf about their respective missions.

Lieutenant Danny Entricon and I approached the 81mm mortars to register them in our line of march for our defense in case it was needed when descending down the hill into our respective areas of operation. We registered each tube and developed overlays, registration points at every anticipated danger area. After completing our duties with the 81mm mortar, we toured the radio-relay site in it's' entirely. We walked the bunker line, peering down into the sandbag hooch's unimpressed with anything that we saw.

The U.S. Marine Corps had occupied these bunkers a few years prior, during the siege of Khe Sanh. Every once in a while, you could see where some young Marine had carved his name and the year he was here on the overhead support beams inside the bunkers. All of the bunkers were constructed with sand bag fronts with firing ports, wooden overhead beams covered with corrugated tin and two layers of sandbags on top of the tin. Grenade sumps had been dug into the corners of the trenches, in case they had to kick grenades into them to take up the detonation and shrapnel form the grenade when it detonated.

The current inhabitants had made life a little easier for themselves by stringing their sleeping hammocks from the overhead beams. They had also strung all of their individual equipment and weapons from one end of the bunker to the other. It was a shame that the current landlords condoned this unruly display from undisciplined troops. Disgusted with our observations, Lieutenant Entricon and I returned to our teams and spent the remainder of the day relaxing, checking our equipment and horsing around with our Little People.

Without any overhead protection above us, the afternoon sun was sweltering. Shortly, off to the west we began to notice water-filled monsoon clouds forming far off in the distance. Realizing that rain was on the way, we grabbed our ponchos and tired to construct some kind of overhead shelter for ourselves. We'd barely finished when rain began to pour down in great buckets. Harder and harder the monsoon sheets of rain fell to the earth, as we tried desperately to stay somewhat dry, to no avail to protect ourselves and our equipment from the deluge.

As evening approached, the rains subsided slightly, leaving us sitting or standing in pools of water up to the top of our jungle boots. Propped up in the bottom of the trench line with rain dripping off my bush hat, fatigues soaked to the core, I couldn't help but think this probably wasn't the best place to have a radio-relay site, with high ground to the rear. My tactical evaluation of the area, from the enemy's point-of-view, led me to believe this site could easily be overrun. All Charlie had to do was place some automatic weapons on the ridgeline to the south and he'd have total domination over the area. Eventually that exact scenario would play out; but that's another story.

Night finally brought a deep blinding darkness over the countryside. Neither sound, nor movement could be detected, only constant rain pelting down on the sandbags and our ponchos. Standing water had filled the bottom of the trench line.

It continued to rain all night without letting up. By 0200 hours, every member of RT Python and RT Crusader was awake and standing in six to eight inches of water. We couldn't get away from the torrential down pour of rain. We had even placed empty ammo crates from the mortar pits in the trenches to get us out of the water, but water still surrounded us. We were miserable the entire night. And, in a few short hours, we would walk off of this hill, tired, wet and severely short of the peak performance levels we needed to have. Hey, what's new? This kind of crap was commonplace in Nam. After another hour, the rain finally stopped. Soaked to the bone, everyone exited the bunker line, trying to escape out of the water-filled trenches for just a little while. We lay on top of the sandbags, exposed to the elements, looking up into a clear sky now filled with millions of stars.

I slowly began to relax as I gazed up at the stars then somewhere between awareness and sleep I felt something crawl onto my chest. Slowly raising my head and opening one eye to see what was on me, I was staring into the elongated nose and face of a huge rat. The rat was about the size of a normal house cat, only fatter. I didn't dare move for fear he'd bite me in the face; rats were notorious for carrying rabies and other diseases. I lay still, trying to think of a quick and safe way to remove him from my chest without getting bit and screwing up our mission.

Suddenly, I hear the muffled sound of a thud from a silenced weapon fire. The rodent sprung straight off my chest into the air, falling dead at my side. Turning my head toward Jung, who'd been sleeping beside me, I thanked him, and he responded back to me "no sweat trung si." Turns out, he'd seen the rat crawl up on me and pulled his silenced Hi-Standard 22 caliber pistol, shooting the rodent off my chest. After that incident with the rat in my face, we decided to stand guard over each other for the remainder of the night to make sure no other team members were in position to be rat bitten.

0500 hours in the darkness and quiet of the relay site bunker line, RT Python and RT Crusader made preparations to move to the staging areas and begin our walk-off of the radio-relay site down into our respective areas of operation.

The early morning sun slowly began to illuminate the eastern sky while both recon teams wished each other well as we began moving to the debarkation point off of the relay site. Lieutenant Wolf was there to be our guide. RT Crusader would be escorted to their jump off point by Sergeants Henderson and Warren leading off in another direction. We would travel off the hill through the semi uncharted old Marine mine field and enter our respective operational areas.

When RT Python arrived at our jump off point, everyone peered off into the jungle edges about forty meters on the other side of the Marine Corps minefield. The team was well aware that we had to leave the security of the camp trenches and enter a desolate open area. Hopefully, Lieutenant Wolf and his crew had done a good job of clearing the mines and marking a safe lane for us to travel through. Silently each of us wondered if Charlie was waiting and watching us from the tree line on the other side of the minefield? Terrorizing thoughts entered each of our minds. *Were they waiting until we got into the middle of the open field to ambush us?* The more I visualized the various disaster scenarios, the more my skin crawled.

The team became restless as Jim looked over at Lieutenant Wolf and asked, "What the fuck are we waiting on let's get to it?" Having worn all of his combat gear, as if he were going to accompany us on the mission, the Lieutenant got to his feet and started moving out of the defensive barbed wire out into the uncharted minefield. One by one RT Python passed through the barbed wire entanglement into the uncharted mine field, with Lieutenant Wolf leading the way. Inch by murderous inch, we moved deeper into the minefield, all of the while expecting an explosion. Everyone on the team stepped into exactly the same foot impression left by the man in front of him. Nervous sweat fell from our faces; as with each step we took we were totally exposed. My biggest fear was how the team would react if we took fire from our front or flanks. If we broke and ran, we would enter the heart of the minefield, almost guaranteeing certain death and injury.

However, on the other hand if we stood our ground out in the open and returned fire, death was just as certain because we had neither cover nor concealment. Any way you looked at this scenario and how it could play out, we were screwed. The entire team was aware of this; and yet, we continued our forward movement. When we finally reached the edge of the jungle, Lt. Wolf stepped to one side and allowed each man to pass him, moving in unison down and into the dense vegetation.

Next came the breath taking stench and dampness of the jungle floor and the continual mental sensation of an enemy lying in wait. Ahead, Jim gave the arm signal for a security halt. Lowering to one knee, our weapons and eyes working together, straining to see or hear anything out of the ordinary. We waited a full 10 minutes before Jim gave the signal to resume our forward movement. The terrain was steep, slippery and wet, thanks to the previous day's rains. The stench of rotting plants and trees, mixed with our own body order was intense. For hours we moved 50 meters at a time, then go into a security halt, and move another 50 meters time after time after time. Midday came and went while we steadily descended deeper into our target area.

By looking at the map, we had traveled approximately 600 meters when the sun began to set. Jim began to look for our temporary night position. Having located and passed through a tentative secure location we backtracked on our line of movement in a fishhook maneuver, finally coming to our temporary over night (RON) position. Slowly and methodically the team circled, moving back-to-back into our night defensive position. Back to back, rucksack to rucksack, the entire six-man recon team sat down simultaneously. We listened and watched with tension and apprehension, knowing that any recon team's most vulnerable time was either going into or coming out of its RON position.

As our surroundings and the jungle slowly darkened, I remembered that twilight was an unsettling time for any rookie combat soldier because the vegetation could very easily take on the false appearance of ghostly human figures. At last light, when we could barely see five feet in front of us, we rose up and fish-hooked back into our pre-designated RON site. If the NVA were in fact tracking us, their intentions would be to fire us up at last light, hoping we would run in different directions and have a split team tuning amuck in the jungles.

Slowly and cautiously, we moved through the jungle into our final RON site, where we listened intensely. Jim reached over and tapped us one-by-one to go out front and deploy our individual claymore mine as a means of night defense. As soon as one soldier returned, another left to set his mine. Finally, all of the claymores were deployed and the clackers were resting in each of our laps. Our simple circular defense was the best we could manage here. Again, for security purposes, one person ate at a time. And, as standard procedure, initiated by the Americans, we ate last. T his was done as a small gesture to show our Little People that we valued their welfare.

Eventually, we'd all had a meal, and everyone took his dextroamphetamine to help keep us awake. The all too familiar sounds of raindrops began to be heard falling on the vegetation and tree tops that surrounded us. The rains were late for some reason today. From a slow light pitter-patter of raindrops gently fall onto the leaves and ferns to a sudden down poor, the monsoon rains began beating down on us. It was like sitting directly underneath a water faucet and having someone turning the water on full blast.

We were quickly and thoroughly soaked to the bone and would stay that way for hours. As quickly as the rains abated, the mosquitoes arrived in full force, buzzing around your head and ears, trying their best to enter our nostrils, ears, eyes and attack any exposed skin they could find. Truly magnificent creatures created by God put here on this earth to be a sheer nuisance to man.

At 0500 hours, Jim reached over and tapped my leg, signaling me to begin the process of retrieving our claymores. One by one, we brought in the mines, ever watchful for enemy movement. Soon we were up and moving, I noticed that Jung had two leeches on his neck, so getting his attention I made the gesture for 'leech' with my finger and pointed to his neck. He in turn let me know that I had a leech on my right cheek and one at the corner of my mouth. After being sprayed with good old fashioned military issue insect repellant, the bloodsucking parasites released their grips from our skin falling back into the depths of the jungle floor, leaving tiny draining puncture wounds as souvenirs.

We did our best to travel erratically the remainder of the day, in order to confuse any trackers. Night once again approached and we repeated our perimeter defense. After we were set up in our final RON position, we could see through the sparsely cleared jungle down into the valley below. We also had a semi-partial view of the adjacent hillside. As night fell, we saw what appeared to be dim lights moving below us and on the opposite mountainside. At first, I thought it was my imagination because they appeared to be stationary. However, as the moonlight beamed down providing a limited amount of illumination, I aligned my CAR-15 barrel with the lights, and quickly determined they were moving and they were either flashlights or candles.

These sudden appearing phantom lights would move for about two hours and then disappear. Next, another set of lights would appear in the same vicinity and travel from there; the strange movement continued throughout the night until 0300 hours. Although we failed to detect them due to our secluded location, coupled with the down pour of monsoon rains we were unaware of lights moving above us on our ridgeline as well.

At 0400 hours, we began to hear distant voices and movement above us about 100 meters away. From down below, we heard faint sounds of something banging together like someone building something. Tension began to rise; each of us fully awake and coiled like a spring. The nerve-racking part was the possibility of the bad guys arbitrarily stumbling into our RON position. If they walked in on us without knowing we were there, we could blow claymores and cause mass confusion within their ranks for a few seconds. This would allow us some time to maneuver around them in the dark.

Finally, daylight crept over the mountains and we began retrieving claymores, fully prepared for an unsuspecting enemy soldier to appear. The tension and suspense was almost overwhelming. When all of our claymores were in, we began a slow and deliberate escape from the surrounding enemy, moving about 15 meters and pausing. We continued this meticulous motion for hours, all the while smelling the enemies cooking fires and hearing an occasional cough from the sleeping enemy.

After six grueling tense hours of constant movement, the sounds of our enemy became fainter until they had completely vanished in the depths of the jungle. Once we felt reasonably confident that we were a safe distance away from our adversaries we stopped, plotted on our maps where we had heard voices and their locations the night prior then wrote in our notebooks, recording everything we'd seen, smelled and heard during our escape.

Night was once again rapidly approaching. Because we'd only covered about 400 meters, Jim pushed us for another two hours straight down the mountain. He was trying to put as much distance between us, and our enemies as he could. The farther we moved down the mountain, the less dense the jungle became. By last light, we were in 6-feet tall elephant grass. I hate everything about elephant grass: it cuts you, slows you down and makes tracking you easy for our enemy because of the amount of noise you make negotiating your way through it.

With the current situation of enemy soldiers above us and across the valley from us, I couldn't help but think, "*This is just where we need to be. We've got half of the NVA Army in the valley with us and we're in elephant grass.*" Six of us against hundreds of them. To ensure we hadn't picked up trackers, we fish-hooked back through the elephant grass, we only put out three claymores because if we were hit, we would use the other three for deliberate ambush operations against our trackers.

After two hours of complete darkness, the flashlights suddenly appeared, just like the previous evening. However, this time they were much brighter than the night before because they were closer to us. In fact, they were now above us, below us, across from us and to our flanks. The team sat motionless, mentally and physically worn out. We hadn't eaten all day in an effort to keep from being discovered. Now, we began to eat or suck on dried rice and mutton. The raw rice was hard, but it filled the hole in our stomachs. And then, like clockwork, the rains came. Only tonight, we didn't have the luxury of the treetops to slow down their intensity. As huge raindrops pounded down on our heads, we knew it was going to be a long night.

With no way of preparing for our enemy, we felt like bait, just waiting for them to find us. Reaching into my jacket, I found two more dextroamphatimines to keep me awake. It had been two days since we'd slept. The best we'd had was small catnaps during this mission. I could feel my alertness and agility declining. I knew that I had to be careful not to allow my mind to begin hallucinating under the influence of the dextroamphetamine (green hornets).

The rains fell relentlessly for hours, until they were finally pushed away by a northerly breeze. As I shivered and tried to listen for approaching enemy troops, Jim elbowed me in the side, motioning for me to look into the direction he was pointing. I snapped my weapon to the front and wondered what it was he wanted me to see. I couldn't see anything. Turning my head back toward Jim, I could see by the moonlight that he was looking at something, but I couldn't see what it was. To make sure he had actually nudged me and that I wasn't experiencing a hallucination, I moved closer and looked at his shadow against the light colored elephant grass. He took my hand and used my finger to point with at the object he wanted me to see.

Finally, I saw a bright light fairly close to us. As I listened intently, I heard the familiar metallic sound of a pin being pulled on a grenade. Turning his way, I saw Jim preparing to let a hand grenade fly. I leaned close to him and whispered, "Wait. Let me stand up and see what it is before you frag it." He tapped my hand in approval. Ever so cautiously, I rose, maintaining a vigilant lookout on the light shining through the elephant grass. As I stood completely erect, I was able to see the light perfectly. I could barely contain my laughter, yanking my hat off my head and covering my mouth to stifle the laughter coming up from my throat.

The suspected bright shining enemy light was not our enemy but it was in fact the moon. Slowly, I knelt back down and whispered into Jim's ear, "You dumb ass, it's the moon!" With my hat still covering my mouth, I continued to laugh. Here we were, miserable, wet, cold and surrounded by the NVA and I'm howling into my hat with laughter. And poor Jim, having pulled the pin on a grenade in an attempt to frag the moon, now couldn't see well enough to put the pin back in the grenade.

I knew full well the gravity of our sad situation, but every time I thought about Jim trying to frag the moon, I laughed all over again. The remainder of the night, Jim sat with both hands tightly wrapped around the grenade, holding it all night with a death grip. As soon as there was enough early morning sunlight, Jim put the pin back into the grenade and breathed a sigh of relief.

Quietly, the team members retrieved our claymores and we prepared to move out once again. Within two hours of heavy crawling and humping, we'd re-entered the lush green vegetation of the jungle once more. The next thing we knew, we could detect sounds like those made during a building construction job coming from deeper down in the jungle. Chopping, hammering and sawing sounds filled the air. There was no doubt about it someone or the bad guys were building something, but what?

While Jim and the point man scouted the sounds and situation, we remaining four team members secured our en-prom-too defensive position waiting their return. For the next few hours, three Little People and I waited and listened to the continual nerve-racking hammering and muffled chopping sounds off in the distance. Noticing movement coming towards us and anticipating a firefight, my mind began to race. I was sure the enemy had gotten between us and Jim and was moving in for the kill. All of our weapons were trained on the distant movement, ready to engage, when Jim's smiling face appeared and he handed me his notebook.

I opened his note book and began to read, under heavy guard, the NVA was forcing Asian prisoners to build cages. The building was going on down in an escarpment. Cage's for what? Then it hit me we had found a POW staging area. We'd pinpointed its exact location. Jim's note read:

> Four NVA guards w/AK-47s, Khaki uniforms (Photo 1-5)
>
> Eight indigenous slaves (workers) (Photo 6-9)
>
> Cages (Photo 10-22)
>
> Triple canopy of area/thick ground vegetation
>
> Camp will hold 10-20 POWs with cages
>
> High Speed trail (N to S) (Photo 23-27)
>
> High Speed trail (E to W) (Photo 28-32)
>
> .51 Cal machine gun two positions (Photo 33-36)
>
> Time 1100 hours
>
> Location: LC45712546

After reading Jim's notes and realizing the importance of his intelligence, I signaled for us to move out of the area and request immediate extraction. This information and Jim's photos were invaluable as we had discovered a staging area to move American POWs too and from. What a fantastic accidental discovery. We began moving down the hill to the west, traveling about three hours before stopping to eat. The food tasted great. With all of the excitement of last night's moon-fragging attempt and the discovery of the POW staging area, my appetite was ferocious. My feet were burning because I hadn't been able to change my socks. For the past four days, I'd been wearing the same water-soaked socks and had the early stages of foot immersion, fondly known as trench foot.

Our hasty recon perimeter surveilled the area while Jim raised his hand to get us moving again. As fast as our movement began, it stopped. Noises were coming from our left flank, rapidly growing in intensity. Not more than 10 meters from our position, a squad or about a dozen NVA soldiers were making their way up the hill to the radio relay site. As they passed, I carefully took pictures of them with my 35mm Pentax camera. Minutes passed as we lay still. Squad after squad of NVA soldiers passed by us, all heading up towards the radio relay site. What was above us? What had we not seen? Movement continued for the next hour. We counted over 130 NVA regulars making their way up the ridge. Where were they going? With this many troops on the move, something big was going on.

After the last of the squads had passed, we waited 15 minutes before heading in the opposite direction, moving another couple of hours to locate a thickly vegetated area for our RON site. The thicker the better at this point. Just as before, heavy rains fell and bothersome mosquitoes danced around our heads. Everyone took dextroamphetamine (green hornets) and waited for morning. We began to notice an unusual quietness; something was wrong! As morning light broke through the darkness, we saw movement above and below us. Jim signaled the team to move. We slowly traversed the ridgeline as Jim and the tail gunner lagged behind. We were moving in unison when a thundering blast broke the silence of the jungle. Claymore mine detonated to our rear. Instinctively, we went into a security-halt position, weapons pointed in every direction. Jim and Doo came charging through the jungle like the devil was chasing them.

# CHAPTER 13 (HICKORY 2)

Directly below our security position, a state of confusion among the enemy was in full swing. As I stared wide-eyed off into the direction of the recent explosions, Jim and Doo came sprinting through the thick vegetation, their weapons at the port, nostrils flared and eyes wide open filled with fear. Within seconds, both managed to get inside our security perimeter when Jim got the team up and moving away from our known enemy location. We crouched as low to the ground camouflaging our selves as best we could while attempting to maintain a low silhouette and become less visible of a target for the enemy to shoot at.

Although we had rustling noises above us and below us from enemy troops that surrounded us, no firing had been exchanged due to their initial confusion and their inability to pinpoint our exact location. Our team performed a hooked maneuver in order to ambush any trackers who might have picked up our trail as we ran up hill. Halting momentarily, we heard the dreaded hissing of a B-40 rocket in flight, followed by a nearby impact accompanied with a deafening explosion. I felt a sudden stinging pain on the left side of my head and in my right thigh like a wasp had just stung me. I dismissed it, thinking I had scraped it on a tree limb while rushing through the brush.

Higher and higher we pressed into the smelly jungle, only to have fate empty us into a field of tall elephant grass. There was no time to find another avenue of escape. Jim ordered us to enter into the elephant grass. I hate elephant grass. Once again, Jim and Doo stayed behind as I painstakingly drove the team deep into the razor-sharp elephant grass at a high rate of speed. We were moving rapidly, when another explosion rocked us from behind. It wasn't a claymore this time; it was a grenade, but who threw it?

Unsure of Jim and Doo's location, I temporarily halted the team, and heard commands being given by the NVA directly in front of our line of movement. No sooner had we stopped and gone into a defensive security halt, when an NVA soldier came crashing through the elephant grass, unaware of our presence. His AK-47 was at the port, chest-high being used to ward off the sharp-edged blades of the elephant grass as he speed through. As he accidentally came into our perimeter, his eyes met mine. We both knew that he was not long for this world.

Engulfed in the elephant grass at an odd position, he tried to bring his weapon up, but he was too tangled to complete the movement. With my CAR-15 pointed directly at him, I pulled the trigger, driving a burst of 5.56 bullets into his body. He crashed backwards on to the jungle floor as if being yanked backward by the scruff of his neck. Simultaneously enemy AK-47 bullets immediately rained in on us from all sides. I screamed commanding the team to throw grenades, so we wouldn't have to give away our exact position until absolutely necessary.

My heart was pounding. I don't recall breathing; all I remember is everyone shooting and our team throwing grenades back at them. Jim and Doo crashed through the smoke covered elephant grass toward us at full speed, their faces streaked with blood trickling down their faces from the sharp-edged grass. As I momentarily watched them closing in, I saw Jim turn his upper body to fire in the direction he'd just come from. As he fired his weapon, I saw him do a complete slow-motion flip in mid air head over heals, landing on his back with his head facing me.

He'd been hit in the back of the head, but I couldn't initially tell how badly he was wounded. I reached him in three strides and two NVA soldiers slammed through the grass facing us. Since the butt of my CAR-15 was securely tucked under my right armpit, I used a lateral sweeping motion while squeezing the trigger. Short intentional bursts of semi-automatic fire impacted both enemy troops right on the money. One took three rounds to the chest and the other two rounds to the face. They immediately fell to the ground, without having time to realize what had hit them.

Jung was by my side, providing security while I cared for Jim. I reluctantly pulled Jim over, expecting to see a large gaping hole where the projectile had exited. The back of his head was covered in dark red blood, and already beginning to become matted in his hair because of rapid coagulation. As I cautiously turned him over, blood ran freely from the back of his head onto the ground. I tried feverishly to wipe the blood from his face and was amazed that there was no exit wound visible. Where was it?

As I held Jim's head in my hand, I searched for an exit wound. Jim opens his eyes and yelled in a slurred voice, "Fuck me, am I dead?" I didn't answer, just continued to rotate my hands toward the back of his head, finally feeling a crease in his skull, but no puncture or entry point. The superficial wound Jim received had only knocked part of his scalp away. Had he not turned his head and body in order to shoot at the enemy when he did, the bullet from the AK-47 would have entered the back of his head and exited out his face. I grabbed him by the shoulder straps and pulled him to his feet. Although he was wobbly, he began running towards the center of our defensive position. He fell to the ground twice because the wound had affected his equilibrium. He moved like a man who'd had too much to drink. Finally, we entered the perimeter, rallied the team and headed up the hill.

We made it another 50 meters up the hill when intense automatic weapons fire and grenades began exploded impacting and exploding all around us. Jim couldn't run any further; it was time to stand and fight. I ordered the team to set out claymores. This time, the mines had to be placed far enough out, yet dangerously close in order to protect us from enemy assaults and advances. Jim and I quickly hooked up the PRC-25 radio to the encrypted KY-38 system. Within seconds, we were ready to transmit. Jim began trying to radio Hickory. In between a whisper and a normal voice, he spoke into the handset:

Charlie Delta, this is Mike Foxtrot, over?

Again and again, Jim tied to raise Hickory. Seconds passed before a most welcomes voice:

Mike Foxtrot, Mike Foxtrot, this is Charlie Delta, we have extraction aircraft on the way to your location at this time, over;

Charlie Delta, this is Mike Foxtrot, we have two wounded, including myself, with bad guys everywhere. Need help or we're going to be guests of Charlie soon, over.

Mike Foxtrot this is Charlie Delta, Covey is five minutes out with a set of gunships on station, you should make commo with him any minute. From my position I see him now; I'll clear the air so he can help. Keep the faith brother, Charlie Delta out.

As Jim waited for Covey to come on station, I crawled around our small perimeter to see if I could spot the enemy. Nothing, I could see nothing through the elephant grass only voices could be heard and large masses of enemy troops maneuvering around us about 50 meters out, preparing to attack. I was trying to recall every counter tactic I'd ever been taught. I whispered to each of the team members to throw grenades only, no CAR-15 fire. They didn't know where we were yet, but they would try and pinpoint our location. If we were to engage them with shoulder-fire weapons, we'd be doing their work for them. Jung relayed every word, making sure everyone understood.

Baby Son looked at me with his large round brown eyes and said, "Trung Si, I have big surprise for VC." I didn't pay much attention to his comment, just turned and crawled over to give Jim more medical attention. Feeling a pinpricking pain in my leg accompanied by severe pain from the side of my head, I recalled running through the trees earlier just as a claymore went off. A limb must have been jammed into it as I was running. Heck, right now, I didn't have time to worry about it.

Jim was sitting upright, with his head hanging limply between his knees, with his arms lying limply down along his torso. I slapped him on the arm and asked, "You Okay?" Slowly raising his head and looking through glassy eyes, he responded, "I keep going in and out, my head really hurts." He was covered with blood; the blood from his wound ran down the sides of his head into his mouth, eyes, ears and nostrils. I whispered to him, "Keep your head back and give me the hand set."

Although he protested a little, pain and disorientation finally got the best of him and he gave me the handset. We could hear the engines of the

OV-10 Bronco orbiting overhead and a familiar voice talking, attempting to make contact with us:

Mike Foxtrot, this is Covey 237, over.

Covey 237, this is Mike Foxtrot, go green (Secure Voice Communications), over.

Mike Foxtrot, this is Covey 237, how do you copy this station? Over.

Covey 237, this is Mike Foxtrot, read you loud and clear, over.

Mike Foxtrot, the slicks are 15 minutes out, I have a set of Gunships on station are you taking any fire at this time? Over.

Covey 237, that's a negative, we're not taking fire at this time, but have enemy movement all around us about 25 to 50 meters out, 360 degrees around us, how copy? Over?

Mike Foxtrot, that's a good copy, I'll hold the gunships high and dry until you request them. I need you to pop smoke, so I can get a good tally on your position, over.

Covey 237, that's a negative. I repeat that's a negative at this time, Charlie doesn't know exactly where we are, and if I pop smoke, you'll be talking to Charlie instead of me, how copy? Over?

Mike Foxtrot, good copy, I'll stay on station ready to work when you need me, over.

Covey 237, this is Mike Foxtrot, thanks babe. Out.

With Covey circling above us, waiting to assist, the ground and surrounding jungle suddenly became deadly silent. Although we couldn't see them or hear them any longer we felt their presence.

*What were they doing? What were they planning?*

This was the nervy part of combat, trying to second-guess your enemy's actions. Crawling from man to man, I tried to reassure them that our extraction helicopters were on the way. As I told each one we were going to make it out, I could see fear and the mental anguish of death looming in their faces. The team was postured and ready to fight to the last man.

Jung reassured me as I crawled over to him, "We not die this day, Buddha not ready to receive recon soldiers, but many VC die today." The sincerity in his voice exuded confidence and something else, something I didn't understand then, but do now. When a man has a conviction to survive, there isn't much that will keep him from his fate. However, when the chips are down and he accepts that he will die, he looks at death through a different set of eyes. This is when you are mentally prepared and saying to yourself, "Today may be my day to die, but I'm going to take a hell of lot of them with me when I go," kind of attitude.

I checked our wounded Little People to make sure they knew our defensive plan. Creeping back, I saw Jim lying on his side, eyes shut, still bleeding and grasping the radio handset. As I got closer, I could hear Covey trying to contact us. My heart began pounding and I knew if I didn't speak calmly, no one would get out. Taking a deep breath, I called:

> Covey 237, this is Mike Foxtrot, over;

> Mike Foxtrot, this is Covey 237. Over;

> Covey 237, this is Mike Foxtrot, my One Zero has been hit in the head, and two soap bubbles have minor wounds, how much longer until the slicks are on station? Over.

> Mike Foxtrot, they are setting up now, I need you to pop smoke at this time, the gunships will give supporting fire during the extraction, how copy, over.

> Coveys 237, good copy, stand by for smoke, over.

Trying to hurry, I tugged at the yellow smoke taped to my equipment. My hands were shaking and my fingers weren't responding to my mental commands, so I started removing the black tape that held the canisters to my harness. Finally, I had the smoke grenade in my hand, pulled the pin and threw it just outside our defensive perimeter. When the spoon came off the smoke grenade, it made the usual popping sound signifying its activation. Then, all hell broke loose.

Enemy AK-47s were firing at us from every direction. The tiny recon team hugged the ground, trying to hide from the deadly projectiles. Doo was lying on his back and began to throw mini-grenades. The rest of the team followed his lead, hurling grenades in every direction, trying to suppress some of Charlie's fire. Seeing the hail of bullets being fired at us and the exploding grenades, Covey called in from above;

> Mike Foxtrot, this is Covey 237, over.
>
> Covey 237, this is Mike Foxtrot, over.
>
> Mike Foxtrot, I see you are in a world of hurt down there. I have a good tally on your position, I see yellow smoke, and I am sending the gunships in now, where do you want it? Over.
>
> Covey 237, I need some rockets along the tree line to my west and east, 50 meters from my position, how copy? Over.
>
> Mike Foxtrot, gun #1 is rolling in hot, with Gun #2 in trail. Get your heads down, over.
>
> Covey 237, we can't get much closer to the ground than we already are, Guns 1 and 2 you're cleared in hot, over.

I removed the radio handset from my ear and screamed "Gunships coming in hot! Everybody down!" Our yellow smoke had engulfed everything, including the elephant grass. I couldn't see where gunships #1 or 2 were because of the vegetation and smoke settling close to the ground blindly surrounding us. I prayed they had a good tally on our position and that their rockets landed between our location and the NVA, not on the other side of them and us. If that happened, it would push the enemy soldiers right into the perimeter with us.

Over the zinging of AK-47 bullets and cracking of grenade explosions, I heard the gunships making their approach, engines roaring, as they rapidly passed by. The detonation of the 17-pound high explosive rockets came down swiftly through the trees exploding delivering their deadly bite from their initial sweep from my west and east. The bad guys were surprised by the air to ground attack and frantically tried to escape death. Those who were less fortunate and couldn't run lay screaming in agony, a result of precisely placed ordnance from the gunships. The ranks of the enemy erupted in chaos and panic as men began crashing through the elephant grass in all direction, trying to escape the rain of rockets. Three NVA soldiers came running toward us, trying to outrun their own deaths.

Doo and BS rolled to their sides, weapons pointed at the sounds of men thrashing through the elephant grass towards us. Within a second, the evading enemy soldiers were running through our defensive perimeter when Jung's CAR-15s spit out the death it was designed to deliver. The NVA soldier on the left took three or four staggering steps after he had been hit in the face with a number of rifle rounds. His head exploded, snapping back from the velocity of the bullets as they impacted. He continued to stagger a morbid, lifeless dance, falling motionless on the opposite side of our fighting position.

The other two NVA soldiers were sprayed with 5.56 rounds in the chest, face and groin area. They too fell dead, landing on top of two of our Little People who lay prone in our defensive posture. Two of our little people, crawling on their hands and knees, pushing the dead bodies off their comrades, propping those same dead bodies up in front of their firing positions as shields against incoming AK-47 bullets. When you're under attack and out in the open, a dead body is very useful for cover. It might sound inhumane, but the dead are dead and the living must survive. So, you improvise. You use every resource available and live off of your enemy, whether he's dead or alive.

As the gunships completed their 17-pound rocket run, Covey directed them to bore holes into the sky and wait for further instructions on the target. Covey reestablished radio communications with me and asked for my next target:

> Mike Foxtrot, this is Covey 237, over.
>
> Covey 237, this is Mike Foxtrot, over.
>
> Mike Foxtrot, where is your next target? Over.

Covey 237, that was good shooting, you got them running all over, we're still taking fire from the North of my position about 50 meters out, how copy? Over.

Mike Foxtrot, good copy, I repeat, you're taking fire 50 meters from your North, guns 1 and 2 are monitoring and are setting up now, the slicks are five minutes out, how copy? Over.

Covey 237, good copy, I need to get my One Zero and our wounded Little People out quick, over;

Mike Foxtrot, that's affirmative, Chase will be #1 into you, put your wounded on the first slick, will have guns 1 and 2 fire flanking support, how copy? Over.

Covey 237, good copy, I'm standing by, out.

The intensity of the NVA's weapons fire had all but diminished because the Cobra gunships had put the 17-pound rockets directly on top of the bad guys. But now, once again I could hear an NVA soldier screaming out commands to his men. Jung crawled over to me and said, pointing north, above us, "VC attack soon from there," pointing in the direction of where I had just asked the Cobras to put in more 17-pound rockets. Again I worried that if the gunships fired their rockets behind the NVA, it would panic them and they too would run right into the perimeter with us. We didn't have much of a choice at this time, so I maneuvered two of our wounded Little People and myself over to the northern sector of our perimeter to wait.

Just as the gunships lined up to begin their dive, all hell broke loose. Screaming and shouting for their lives, the NVA charged down towards our defenses. I yelled over to Lue and Chow not to fire until I did. As if screaming and shouting wasn't enough from the attacking NVA, they had built up a heavy volume of AK-47 fire, coupled with B-40's and grenade explosions to add to our anxiety.

This was their ground commander's last-ditch effort to capture and/or kill us. With enemy bullets and grenade fragments flying in every direction through the elephant grass, our small element of men lay motionless waiting for our attackers. Very soon, within a matter of seconds we'd be putting it all on the line. The NVA was determined to extract this small menacing group of invaders and we were very shortly going to close the gap of destiny with them.

I suddenly experienced a calmness that came over me physically and mentally. At first, it was frightening. As I lay on my stomach with the tall grass semi-obstructing my vision, I realized my breathing had returned to normal, my mind was perfectly clear, my hands were not sweating and my body was no longer trembling. It was as though I had mentally become invincible to the thought of death.

The gunships shot by us and down into the valley, their lethal rockets of death impacted the jungle exactly where we wanted, causing crackling and exploding music to our ears. They also did a little something different this time; they separated their runs and spread them out.

Cobra #1 came in fired his ordnance about 25 meters from our position in front of the unsuspecting NVA attackers. Then Cobra #2 went about 25-40 meters higher up the hill and fired his rockets above and onto the attacking NVA unit. They caught the enemy soldiers in between their gun runs, trapping them in the middle of a steady stream of exploding orbs of death. The NVA thrashed wildly through the undergrowth. I blindly fired into the curtain of grass. Lou and Chow joined in the firefight, using a sweeping motion and spewing lead into the general vicinity of the retreating NVA attackers.

After firing massive amounts of 5.56 ammo, silence quickly fell over the jungle. I had expended my last round from my fourth magazine when I heard the helicopter blades cutting their way through the hot Vietnam air as it drew nearer. Crawling back to the radio, I listened for Covey 237 while giving appropriate call signs to him. I removed a second smoke grenade from Jim's load-bearing equipment, because I'd used mine earlier to initially mark our position for Covey.

With the handset pressed tight against my ear, I heard Covey 237 proclaiming that the slicks were on short final, ready to get us out:

> Mike Foxtrot, this is Covey 237, the choppers are on
> short final into your position, with Dust Off in the lead,
> pop smoke, over.

Covey 237, smoke's out identify, over.

Mike Foxtrot, I identify green smoke, over.

Covey 237, that's a roger over.

Mike Foxtrot, slick one can see your smoke, but you are going to have to talk him into our exact location, he's throwing the ladder out now, how copy? Over.

Covey 237, good copy, over.

Mike Foxtrot, this is Dust Off, over.

Dust Off, this is Mike Foxtrot, hey buddy you are about 200 meters down the hill from my location, we are at your 12 o'clock, come on up the hill, over.

Mike Foxtrot, talk me in, we're coming up, over.

Dust Off, keep coming, keep coming, Dust Off, I'm off to your two o'clock, about 30 meters, looking good, keep coming, I'm directly below you now, over.

The Dust Off pilot was frantically looking for us farther up the hill. I could see from my position that he hadn't believed that we were directly below him. Again he called over the radio:

Mike Foxtrot this is Dust Off, where the hell are you good buddy? Over.

Dust Off; look down between your legs, over.

Through the chin bubble of the helicopter, I saw the surprised pilot look down between his legs and smile. I raised my hand, wiggling my fingers in a greeting:

Dust Off, can you see me now? Over.

Mike Foxtrot, that's an affirmative, you crazy bastard, over.

The pilot laughed, told the crew chief where we were and the ladder came rolling out the right side of the chopper, slamming to the ground.

Woody, one of our Chase Medics was climbing down the ladder to help the wounded. We began to take sniper fire from a creek bed to the east. I called for Covey to support Dust Off with the gunships on station:

> Covey 237, this is Mike Foxtrot, Dust Off is taking sniper fire from the tree line to the east, about 50-75 meters away, down along the creek bed, over.

> Mike Foxtrot, guns 1 and 2 are rolling in hot at this time, over.

The sniper fire from the tree line was building in intensity, even though the door gunner inside Dust Off was shooting his M-60 machine gun in that general direction the sniping continued.

From high in the sky, out on our right flank came the gunships, belching 20mm rounds from beneath their fuselage. Their accuracy was deadly as they made their gun run down the creek bed, heading north. As they crested the hilltops and lowered their noses, they were lined up perfectly and immediately started firing the 20mm cannons. No sooner had gun #1 completed his gun run than gun #2 was putting hot lead in the same area. It was exhilarating to know that the Cobra gunships were on station with us protecting the aircraft while at the same time supporting us.

Meanwhile, Woody was now on the ground performed a quick inspection of Jim's wounds and had him up and headed toward the ladder. Lou and Chow, the two Little People that were wounded made their way to the ladder as well. As soon as the wounded were up the ladder and aboard, the pilot pulled pitch and broke hard right, gaining speed and altitude as he traveled back down the hill.

Slick 2 was coming in on short final at a high rate of speed. As he approached my position, I could see the pilot making adjustments with his feet on the pedals of the chopper. As he drew closer to our position with a rearing motion of his helicopter, he came to rest in a hovering position directly over us. The remainder of Recon Team Python got up and ran to the ladder that had been dropped for us to climb. Just as we reached it, enemy AK-47 fire began to cut down the elephant grass that surrounded us. I yelled over to Doo and Jung, "Just hook into the ladder with your snap links. Don't try and climb the ladder."

By hooking into the ladder and not climbing all the way up into the helicopter, we wouldn't be exposed to ground fire. We also didn't need to climb because it exposed the helicopter to more ground fire the longer he hovered. Even if we were hit coming out, we would still be secured to the chopper and wouldn't fall off. Jung and Doo took their snap link, still attached to their load-bearing equipment and hooked themselves into the metal ladder rungs.

As I hooked Jim's rucksack and myself up to the ladder, I notified Covey by radio:

> Covey 237, this is Mike Foxtrot, over.
>
> Mike Foxtrot, this is Covey 237, over.
>
> Covey 237, we are taking fire from three directions. Distance and direction of enemy fire unknown at this time. Need you to have the gunships fire up the area when we get airborne? Incoming fire too heavy to climb ladder, we are going to ride it out, how copy? Over;
>
> Mike Foxtrot, good copy, be advised that I have a set of fast movers on station and will bring them in hot on the bad guys after your extraction. We got you covered good buddy; see you back at the ranch, out.

The UH-1 helicopter pilot quickly ran up the r.p.m.s of the engine to begin our ascent. I could see and feel the chopper rising. Looking down at the ground as we gained altitude, the ladder now dangled below us. Looking over my shoulder at the extraction zone, an F-4 Phantom had just rolled in hot on the extraction area to decimate the area. It was eerie watching the canisters falling backward as they neared their target. Then came an air-sucking roar, as they collided with the ground, their ignition heard over the chopper blades. The fiery napalm spread quickly, covering an area of 50 to 75 meters. The second F-4 was right behind and released his canisters about 25 meters to the left of the initial F-4 napalm strike.

As we continued to gain altitude, I could feel the cool air of the heavens surrounding me refresh my body. I looked at Doo and Jung, who had crawled between the ladder rungs, using them to sit on. As we increased speed, the suspended ladder below us began to droop behind the helicopter. I looked up at the chopper and saw the crew chief lying on the floor of the chopper, his head out the door watching us and directing the pilot as we flew along. His vigilance on the ladder and us kept the pilot informed of where the ladder was in relation to the bird itself.

My body started coming down from the adrenaline rush. I was still on a high due to combat, but I could definitely feel the tension and stress begin to ease. As we flew along suspended from the ladder beneath the helicopter, the F-4's and Cobras that had gotten us out of hot water pulled along side us in flight. I waved at them appreciatively, giving them a gesture of thumbs up. They both tipped their wings in acknowledgment and flew away.

I looked over to my left and there was Covey flying along side of us with David Chaney once again in the back seat with Cat Fish the pilot in front, both gave me thumbs up through the canopy of the OV-10. Huge grins of approval were on their faces before they too banked hard away from us and headed off in another direction. I felt life running through every inch of my body. It felt good to be alive and heading back to the compound to tell of my exploits of war. Checking my leg for damage, I saw that blood was everywhere.

Feeling my face, I found it was bleeding as well. I reached down and felt a hole in my fatigue pants and discovered a piece of metal from a grenade sticking out of my leg. Since there wasn't much pain, I decided to leave it in place. The helicopter flew us directly to the 95th evac hospital, where medics and doctors were waiting to receive the wounded. As quickly as the chopper in front of us touched his skids on the pad, medical personnel had the wounded onto gurneys, and were carrying them into the hospital. Our helicopter slowed his forward movement and hovered, allowing us to slowly touch the ground.

Once our feet were well under us, the pilot gave us time to unhook our equipment and ourselves from the ladder. When we were completely out of the way, the helicopter landed and the crew chief began rolling up and securing the ladder back inside the helicopter. He then climbed in and headed back to the launch site, ready for another mission.

As I turned in the direction of the hospital, I saw Pappy and Passionate

Perry Parks coming towards me. I began to tell them about the mission when Pappy slammed a cold beer in my hand. As was our tradition when a recon team returned from a mission, each of the men took a piece of my equipment from me. Opening my beer with my demo knife, I took a long drink. The cold, wet fluid flowed down my throat and out the corners of my mouth onto my face. I turned to Doo, and Jung and passed it back to them. They too drank deep from the can containing the refreshingly welcome fluid. Walking together, I began to tell the guys about the intelligence we had gathered. They told me to be quiet and wait to be debriefed. Abruptly another beer appeared and I drank heartily and began to unwind.

When I entered the hospital emergency room, Jim was lying face down on a treatment table with two doctors and three nurses working on him. I went over to his bed and crawled underneath, so Jim could see me. Although the medical staff looked at me as if I had lost my marbles, I didn't care. I felt alive and full of vitality. Jim opened his eyes, looked at me and asked, "How'd we do?" I replied, "We kicked their ass, Di We." Jim then wanted to know where his beer was. My answer was, "Hey I didn't think you were going to make it, so Pappy let me drink your beer." We both laughed and the nurse said to me, "Sir, you are bleeding." She insisted that I allow her to examine my head and leg, so I crawled out and sat on one of the vacant surgical gurneys. A doctor came over, cut the pants leg open so he could examine the wound and instructed the nurse to take some x-rays before he tried to remove it. The x-ray showed that it was only a sliver of metal about 3/4" long and 1/4" wide. My head wound showed a metal fragment about 1 1/2" long buried under the skin.

Grabbing a pair of 5" Kelly's, the doctor pulled the metal out of my head and blood shot everywhere. The nurse scrubbed the wounds for about five minutes, and then flushed them with another syringe until she felt confident that she had cleaned both thoroughly. The next thing I knew, the nurse gave me an injection of Tetanus that hurt worse that my wound did. Chow and Lou had sustained similar wounds. After we were all patched up, we loaded into the jeep and headed back to the launch site for debriefing.

Upon entering the security gate, Pappy drove us to the TOC. Everyone was cutting up and laughing as we entered. Major Telliot stood waiting for our arrival and welcomed us back from the field. He wanted the film we were carrying so it could be developed for photo analysis. We also handed over our notebooks, containing our four-day mission information notes to the Intelligence Sergeant before we began the in-depth mission debriefing. Before we were finished, the photographs were presented to us so that we could explain each in sequence.

After the lengthy debriefing under the escort of the launch site Intelligence Sergeant, we made our way back to the hooch. As expected, the first thing we saw was a case of iced down beer. Everyone on the team went over to the barrel and got a cold brew. I sat on the side of my bunk and noticed that the hooch was quiet, each man thinking his own thoughts, reviewing the events of the past four days, smoking a most rewarding cigarette and nursing the beer in our blood covered, grimy hands.

I lay back on the exposed mattress, resting my head on the soft mildewed pillow and momentarily closed my eyes. Next thing I knew, someone was tapping my boot bottom and Pappy was standing at the foot of my bunk.

He announced in a loud voice, "OP 35 wants you and Jim there now. The Black Bird is 15 minutes out, and they want to debrief you personally. So get up, and get out to the jeep. It's waiting to take you directly to the airstrip." I asked, "what about our gear?" Pappy assured us not to worry about it because he was going back to Da Nang today and would take it with him. Jumping to my feet, I said, "Okay, color us gone." When we reached the awaiting jeep, I mentioned that I thought I'd be more tired than I was. Jim laughed as he replied; "We've been asleep since yesterday." I said in unbelief, "You've got to be shitting me." Jim just shook his head from side to side and got into the front seat of the jeep.

As we pulled onto the restricted aircraft loading area, a MACV-SOG Special Operations C-130 Black Bird with the MAC SOG Deputy Commander, Colonel Saddler stood on its tail ramp, waited for us to board. We quickly noticed there were other people inside the plane, who they were we didn't know they to were watching our approach. We shook the Colonel's hand and the aircraft quickly prepared for immediate takeoff. The intelligence that we'd gotten from the mission and passed on to higher headquarters was never disseminated back to us. We just simply collected the pictures and intelligence for them to decipher.

## DEPARTMENT OF THE ARMY, HEADQUARTERS, UNITED STATES ARMY VIETNAM APO SAN FRANCISCO 96375

GENERAL ORDERS                                         27 April 1971

NUMBER 1415

AWARED OF THE SILVER STAR

CHAPMAN, LESLIE A. STAFF SERGEANT United States Army, Command and Control North Detachment, 5th Special Forces Group (Airborne), 1st Special Forces, APO 96240

Awarded:            Silver Star

Dates of action:    16 January 1971

Theater:            Republic of Vietnam

Authority:          By direction of the President, under the provisions of the Act of Congress, approved 9 July 1918

Reason:             For gallantry in action while engaged in military operations involving conflict with an armed hostile force in the Republic of Vietnam: Staff Sergeant Chapman distinguished himself while serving as assistant team leader to a ten-man patrol during reconnaissance operations deep within enemy controlled territory. For three days the allied patrol observed enemy activity but all contact was avoided. Early in the morning of 16 January, the enemy element advanced toward their position. Amid the enemy onslaught anti-personnel mines were detonated, inflicting numerous casualties and temporary confusion in the enemy ranks. Immediately the patrol began moving to higher terrain, seeking a better defensive position. During this movement SSG Chapman discovered the team leader and another patrol member were missing. SSG Chapman returned and located the wounded team leader. Amid a fusillade of fire SSG Chapman assisted the team leader to the new defensive position while sustaining two wounds himself. Despite his painful wounds, SSG Chapman contacted helicopter gunships and directed their suppressive fire, allowing evacuation aircraft to successfully extract the besieged patrol. Staff Sergeant Chapman's gallantry in action was in keeping with the highest traditions of the military service and reflects great credit upon himself, his unit, and the United States Army.

FOR THE COMMANDER:

**CHARLES M. GETTYS**

**Major General, USA**

**Chief of Staff**

# CHAPTER 14 (A SHAU)

In the latter part of January of 1971, three Special Forces Recon Teams reported to the Command and Control North (CCN) Tactical Operations Center (TOC) to receive individual team target briefing on separate operations in the northern end of the A Shau Valley.

Two of the teams were to be inserted by helicopter into two abandoned firebases to establish static hill watch positions in the mountains overlooking the A Shau valley floor. The third team was to conduct an area recon, then establish a patrol base, run short recon mission from it all the while confirm or deny the presents of the enemy. Once the enemy was detected we were to call in air strikes on enemy positions and personnel traveling through the target area, as they were believed to be reinforcements headed to the Lam Son 719 operational area. As a follow-on mission, we were to confirm or deny the presence of NVA regiments moving up and down the A Shau Valley from the south to the north up the Ho Chi Minh trail.

Recon teams Python, Anaconda and Intruder were the selected recon teams to undertake these missions. Quickly after the initial briefing was conducted each team received their individual target folders. This type of mission was highly unorthodox for Special Operations Recon Teams. By definition, Special Forces Recon Teams conduct clandestine deep penetration, cross border operations, wire taps, POW snatches, raids and pilot recovery: our overall mission was to get in, get the intelligence and get out without anyone knowing we had been there. However, this particular mission into the A Shau Valley specifically announced and summoned the enemy to know of our presence. What's more, it was hoped through Senior Command Headquarters that the NVA regiments hidden throughout South Vietnam would divert from the Lam Son 719 allied push and attack us, instead.

Never in the history of Special Operations in Vietnam, had we intentionally placed ourselves in a semi-permanent position and waiting for the enemy to come and get us. Further complicating the matter, three Special Operations teams were not normally inserted in close proximity of one another, performing like missions on the like targets. Each and every American on recon teams Python, Anaconda and Intruder was confused; right up until the situation would unfold before us. We were about to become pawns for our government, to be purposely inserted into the Valley of death to intentionally lure the NVA into attacking us, thereby exposing their location, strength, capabilities, activity, units and equipment and ultimately diverting them from the Lam Son target area. We were to be the sacrificial lambs for the Military Assistance Command Vietnam Commanders.

The ultimate intent of our missions was for the higher command to learn the exact location of the Lam Son 719 reinforcements. If the NVA altered their reinforcement routes and hit the three recon teams (10-12 man units), it would take the pressure off the pre-invasion forces staging in the Khe Sanh, in the northwestern Quang Tri Province, who were preparing to cross the border into Laos. As the entire overview of our mission was revealed to us and commands scheme of maneuver, we listened in silence not believing what was being said for us to do.

On February 8, 1971, the South Vietnamese government would announce Lam Son 719, a limited-objective offensive campaign to be conducted in Laos. Armed forces of the Republic of Vietnam (South Vietnam) would invade Laos while the United States and our allied assets would provide logistical, aerial and artillery support. The objective of the campaign was to disrupt the NVA's key logistical artery within Laos, known as the Ho Chi Minh Trail. Since 1966, over 630,000 men, 100,000 tons of foodstuff, 400,000 weapons and 50,000 tons of ammunition had been moved through the maze of gravel and dirt roads, paths and river systems.

The U.S. portion of the operation, named Operation Dewey Canyon II, involved an armed attack by the US from Vandergrift Base Camp towards Khe Sanh, while the Army of the Republic of South Vietnam Army (ARVN) moved into jump off positions for the attack across the Laotian border. Phase II of the operation would began with an ARVN helicopter assault and armed brigade thrust along Route 9 into Laos. American helicopters would transport the ARVN ground troops, while the US Air Force, Navy and Marines provided air support.

American offensive operations would be limited to South Vietnam only due to the Cooper-Church Amendment, which prohibited US ground forces from entering into Laos. American artillery units would provide support to the ARVN effort because artillery pieces could shoot over 30 miles away. The allied mission would be a coordinated border crossing from Vietnam into Laos, near Kha Shan. Lam Son 719's allied forces' follow-on mission was to destroy strongholds, cache points, interdiction mission and destroy infiltration routes and disrupt enemy resupply efforts.

For the past several months, CCN recon teams had been launching into these denied areas continually compiling intelligence throughout the general area to aid the allied forces during their preparation for the border crossing. Our top-secret missions we had run into those denied areas coupled with the intelligence we had reported after our missions would be accompanied by high-altitude aerial photos and communication interceptions from sympathetic centers of influence. Every piece of intelligence accumulated confirmed that the NVA were conducting massive buildup of men, equipment and supplies in the countries west of South Vietnam (Cambodia and Laos).

Military Assistance Command Vietnam had determined that a joint allied military operation, specifically targeted at NVA supply routes, cache points and infiltration routes would weaken the Communist aggressors, forcing them to negotiate a peace settlement.

The NVA had for years used Laos and Cambodia as safe havens and launch sites to rest, train and organize large combat units. They would build up their forces, cross the Vietnamese border, hit a predetermined target and flee back across the border to safety. They knew what America could do and couldn't do and they used that knowledge to their advantage knowing all the while that conventional American units and allied forces couldn't chase them into these countries. Once back in the safe haven, they would rest their troops, re-fit and prepare for the next mission of death and destruction.

After much negotiation, bargaining, the allied forces convinced the adjoining countries to allow them to cross their borders and take the battle to the NVA. Months of joint top-secret planning and high-level classified briefings had undergone close scrutiny. Hundreds of high-level command hours of brainstorming and negotiation had been conducted prior to the allied forces reaching a final consensus for such a large operation.

It was exhilarating to know that the allied forces were finally going to take the fight to the Peoples Republic of North Vietnam and deal them a deadly blow. Soldiers and support elements were secretly briefed, realigned, resupplied and reinforced for the upcoming Lam Son 719 mission. It was imperative that all allied forces be in place simultaneously in order for the push to be effective. H-hour (the attack) was close at hand.

The A Shau Valley had never been hotter. Prior recon missions had captured documents indicating that the NVA had moved 11 counter-recon companies into the A Shau Valley to reinforce landing zone watchers, trackers, hunter killer teams and dogs' patrols with rear security units and enemy infantry regiments. Additionally, the NVA had two antiaircraft artillery (AAA) battalions defending the valley with one located at each end. The A Shau diversion was initially assigned to the 2000-man plus strong 1st Brigade, of the 101st Airborne Division. However, Senior Commanders analyzed and anticipated US forces loss estimates would be too high.

Instead, Military Assistance Command Vietnam would sacrifice Special Forces units that they assumed would be a smaller loss to the United States Government; so they assigned the mission to MACV-SOG. So, here we sat, stunned listening to the death mission brief, shocked at what we were hearing. All three teams, RT Intruder, RT Anaconda and RT

Python silently took notes while thousands of random thoughts danced around in our brains. We all knew what this mission would cost.

Every type of collected, known and suspected intelligence overview lay on the desks in front of us at our fingertips. Each recon team was to perform a well-coordinated, specific function in support of the overall mission. It was ironic; here we are three small recon teams (34-36 men to perform the mission) and had been ordered to take on half of the North Vietnamese Regular Army. Our over all mission was to try and keep the NVA from reinforcing their sister units in Laos, who would be fighting the allied forces as they crossed the Laotian border. This operation began to have the smell and feel of hunting a rogue elephant with a fly swatter.

RT Intruder would insert heavy with a 10-man Montagnard team. Commanded by One-Zero Captain Ronald L. "Doc" Watson. Captain Watson would be accompanied by his One-One Sergeant Allen R. "Baby Jesus" Lloyd and One-Two Sergeant Raymond L. "Robby" Robinson. Strap hanging with RT Intruder would be Sergeant First Class Charles F. (Wes) Wesley and Sergeant First Class Sammy Hernandez.

Captain Watson was a highly educated man, holding a Ph.D. in Social Sciences. At times, his vocabulary and articulation skills were so far superior to ours that when he spoke we just stare at him, unsure of how to respond. Truthfully, there were times when we had no idea what he had said. As time passed, he began to understand us and we him. Unfortunately, his mastery of the English language was brought down to our level. Doc was about 32-years young. He was a small man with a receding hairline, who wore black-rimmed military glasses and always had a pen and paper nearby for notes. We found out over time that he had previously been a well-paid college professor at a major university. Why in the world would he quit a safe, secure job to come here and run recon?

Doc had initially joined Special Forces, and then volunteered to come to Vietnam. Once he arrived in Nha Trang, Vietnam (Headquarters, 5th Special Forces Group), he requested Command and Control North the most dreaded combat unit within Special Forces and all of Vietnam. Doc told us he was here because he was going to be writing a book. His common statement to us was "You'll know who you are by what you have done." Unfortunately, as fate and destiny would have it, his notes would never be put into print. This brilliant man only had a few days left on this earth; this mission would take his life.

RT Intruder's One-One, Sergeant Lloyd was a tall lanky kid, about 20-years old, baby-faced, fun loving and a friend to everyone he met. Although he hadn't yet achieved anything spectacular, he longed to leave his mark on Special Forces. Just like the rest of us, Lloyd was secretly trying to be something he wasn't.

The One-Two, Sergeant Robinson was a medium-built guy, with long black hair. He fit in with the rest of us, crazy, wild and aware that his days were numbered just like the rest of us.

One of the straphangers was Sergeant First Class Sammy Hernandez. Sammy was of Latin descent with numerous years of conventional and unconventional combat experience under his belt. He was always serious and spoke very little. Sammy was average height and weight and about 28-30 years young.

The second straphanger was Sergeant First Class Charles F. Wesley who would also join the team, just going along for the ride and utilizing and applying his vast experience. Wes was known throughout recon company as the "professor or inventor." He'd spent many years in Vietnam in conventional units, Platoon Sergeant with the 1st Brigade, 101st Airborne Division, one tour as an "A-Team member and was now fulfilling his third tour with Special Operations.

Wes was a semi-introverted guy from Florida who was about 28-years old. I'm sure at one time he had a young man's complexion, but the many years in combat and vast amount of stress he'd endured in Vietnam had etched premature age lines deep into his skin. When Wes was sober, you wouldn't even know that he was around. But, when he started drinking, he came to life. Never loud or falling-down drunk, he just seemed to let go of his quietness and talk your ear off. As the past 30-plus years have passed by in my lifetime, Wes had become more to me than my best friend he would become my brother to the death and beyond.

Wes achieved his prestigious and notable title as "professor or inventor" while continuously conjuring up and attempting to develop a weapons system that would enable recon teams to break contact with the enemy. One of his greatest contact-breakers consisted of 20 mini-fragmentation grenades, a number 10 coffee can, plaster of paris and a six-foot length of 5/8-inch rappelling rope.

Our compound, Command and Control North sat at the base of Marble Mountain, Da Nang City, in I Corps. At one time Marble Mountain had been a Buddhist holy place, housing numerous shrines inside the caves that honeycombed the entire mountain. We in recon company used the base of Marble Mountain as our rehearsal range for diversionary team movement, breaking contact with the enemy and other assorted means of individual and team rehearsal, including fire and maneuver.

One day, while we were sitting in the recon company club drinking cold beer, Wes came in with a brilliant idea about constructing a contact-breaking device. He called it foolproof. After receiving our blessing on his contact breaker, he swiftly went to his hooch, laid out all the materials he would require for his invention and began constructing his weapon of destruction.

He mixed plaster of paris with water until it was becoming hardened ready to use. Next, he took six feet of rappel rope, tied a knot at the end of it and placed it in the bottom of the number 10 coffee can. As the plaster began to harden, Wes painstakingly added row upon row of mini-grenades inside the mixture. As the plaster of paris hardened, Wes carefully pulled the pins on each of the grenades, filled the container with more plaster, then with more grenades until he had filled up the coffee can with plaster, mini-grenades and the rappel rope.

To activate his invention, he placed the last mini-grenade into the plaster with the pin and spoon up, allowing this single grenade to detonate, projecting the other grenades in all directions simultaneously once it detonated. This enemy contact-breaking device was to be deployed similar to an athletic hammer throw competition during the Olympics. One man would pull the pin on the single exposed mini-grenade and another would swing the device in a circular motion in the direction of the enemy then let it fly. Theoretically, the device would land in the vicinity of the enemy then detonate, launching grenades in every direction. A true contact-breaker.

Early the next morning, having named the device, "the big chunk," Wes recruited his faithful companion, Sergeant Lemuel D. McGlothren to assist him in demonstrating his contact-breaking system. Together, they commandeered a jeep from the motor pool and headed to the range. Curious as to how the device would work, everyone in recon company gathered up on top of the bunker line overlooking the Marble Mountain range as Wes and Mac arrived. We were all properly equipped: beer in hand and two in our fatigue pockets. No one wanted to miss this historic event.

A US Marine 106mm artillery battery was stationed on top of Marble Mountain conducting fire mission drills at the same time the test was to be conducted. Before we knew it, some of the Marines took a break from their duties and were standing near the edge of the firebase looking down on the range waiting for something to begin. With great anticipation, we watched as Wes and Mac pulled out the coffee can with the rappelling rope attached. Quickly, they moved down range and laid it out.

Wes was to be the hammer thrower, while Mac pulled the pin on the grenade. Wes raised his hand high above his head, giving us the spectators the thumbs up signal. Turning back to Mac, Wes signaled the okay. Mac pulled the pin and ran away from the device back behind the jeep. Wes began his unorthodox Olympic hammer throw technique, spinning in a circle; all the while the device was extended out to the maximum distance of the repelling rope due to centrifugal force as it gained speed. One turn, two turns. As Wes made his final turn, he released the device and away it went, headed down range at a considerable rate of speed, gaining altitude and distance as it flew. There was one thing Wes and Mac neglected to calculate: mini-grenades only have a four- to five-second time delay fuse before they detonate.

While still traveling in flight, about 30 feet down range from "the inventor" Wes and his trusty sidekick, the primary grenade detonated, hurling mini-grenades in every direction. Next came a loud blast and a huge white cloud as the plaster of paris disintegrated. And, an unknown number of mini-grenades flew high into the air, landing inside the perimeter of the Marine 106mm battery on top of Marble Mountain. The Marine's thought they were under attack, they immediately went to battle stations. Meanwhile in the opposite direction, a number of the grenades made their way back into our compound. Basically, the device was working as designed grenades were being thrown and detonating in every direction. The Marines were frantically firing their 106mm recoilless rifles at unknown targets, beating back an imaginary enemy attack.

Those of us who happened to be on the bunker line were rolling around, howling with laughter until mini-grenades began falling all around us to. We dove for anything that resembled cover, seeking protection from this self-induced hell fire. Within seconds, the CCN compound was under full alert and the bunker line was active and protective friendly fire was being fired off in all directions, including down range, where Wes and Mac lay hidden. The haphazard uncoordinated firefight only lasted but a few seconds, but during those few mad moments, every weapon within a half mile of our location was performing at peek performance.

The CCN bunker line defenses and the Marine Corps 106mm battery were blazing away and every siren in the compound was screeching. After a few seconds, it all stopped. Why no one was injured or killed remains a mystery to this day. Slowly, we the spectators cautious emerged from our hiding places and watched Mac and Wes racing the jeep back down the dusty road headed back into the compound. We all left the bunker line and headed to the club, laughing hysterically at what we'd just witnessed. As soon as we crashed through the door into the recon company bar, we spotted Wes and Mac huddled together in a dark corner of the club, quiet as mice. We made eye contact with the two rocket scientists and immediately reverted to fits of laughter.

After settling down as much as we could, Wes explained what had happened while he and Mac were hiding behind the jeep after the first grenade went off. Wes said Mac grabbed him by the throat and began strangling him, yelling, "Son of a bitch, I told you it wouldn't work, I'll never do anything with you again. You keep me out of your fucking inventions. You're just trying to kill me, and the worst part is you really don't give a shit." Moments like these provided a unique bonding experience and brought a much-needed reprieve of humor to us all.

The A Shau Valley included 35 miles of fertile land, running along the extreme western frontier of Thua Thien Province. It was very similar to valleys found in Oregon, Washington or Montana, except its floor was covered in 15-20 feet tall elephant grass and bomb craters as large as backyard swimming pools. Running the length of the valley floor was Route 548. This NVA-constructed road was known to carry hundreds of enemy personnel and tons of supplies in support of operations against Hue and Da Nang. In spite of its natural beauty, the A Shau Valley exuded a foreboding aura of darkness and evil. So much so, that drawing a target into A Shau Valley was known as the "kiss of death" because nine times out of ten times, you weren't coming back.

Two days after receiving his initial briefing in the TOC, Captain Watson flew a visual recon (VR) of his target area. During his VR his observations and perspectives made it clear that RT Intruder would be unable to land directly on their desired primary landing zone, the firebase on the Laotian/Vietnamese border. Instead, he was forced to shift his primary Landing Zone (LZ) two clicks west and his team would be required to walk in. Once they arrived at the firebase, they were to secure it and call in resupply helicopters to deliver their prepackaged mission-essential weapons, ammo and equipment to the designated target area.

RT Python One-Zero Captain Jim Butler conducted his VR and announced that we would insert directly onto their primary landing zone (Abandoned Fire Base), set up a stronghold and try like hell to defend it and ourselves in the middle of the A Shau Valley. Captain Butler had chosen our designated defensive position, an abandoned firebase overlooking the legendary Hamburger Hill. In 1968, Hamburger Hill was the scene of a horrific battle between dug in NVA troops and where the 101st Airborne Division was dealt a crushing blow, almost annihilating an entire company of American soldiers. Captain James E. Butler headed up RT Python as the One-Zero, and I, Staff Sergeant Les Chapman would perform duties as his One-One. The two straphangers with RT Python were Staff Sergeant Larry Brazer and Sergeant Profitt.

Sergeant Brazer, a redneck hog farmer from North Carolina, had average physical features. Nothing in particular distinguished him from the rest of us, with the exception of a slow Southern tendency in everything he said or did. Nothing seemed to upset him, yet he was always extremely serious. I remember him talking about how he was going to be the largest pig farmer in North Carolina after he retired.

Sergeant Profitt was a newly reassigned youngster from CCN's Security Company, trying his luck at recon. Sadly, he was just another baby-faced kid who would run only one mission. The upcoming operation would provide more up-close and personal destruction in three days than a normal man would witness in two lifetimes. Profitt was about to be taken from the breast of fantasy and glory into the depths of hell and despair. He would witness firsthand the reality of war. It would be forever tattooed into his mind.

Diligently we prepared for battle, completing in-depth target analysis, and developing our plan-of-action and defenses. For days, we requested and received every piece of intelligence we could get our hands on in an attempt not to overlook anything. All of the One-Zeros for the upcoming missions gathered to inform one another of their separate missions, actions and concept of operations, in turn explaining how each team would provide mutual support while in the area of operation. This prior coordination would prove invaluable.

Before the start of any mission, nights in the club were quiet and uneasy. You could feel the tension in the room, among those who are about to deploy and those who knew what you were getting into. We all knew that most, (if not all) of us were not coming back, so we mentally prepared ourselves to die. You do the math: 30 to 36 men had been ordered to undertake a mission that normally called for three brigades (5,000 plus combat soldiers) of conventional forces against hundreds of hardcore NVA regiments.

However, we Recon Men with our ultra egos refused to reveal internal fears. As we headed down a long unforgiving road, we drank in silence making peace with our maker. Letters were written to love ones, assuring them that we were fine. None of us was capable of expressing our true feelings. Instead, we fed on hostility toward our enemy, mankind and ourselves in general. Our training and past combat experiences would pay off; we became calloused killers. Most of us were no longer in Vietnam for the sake of our country, or saving American lives through our high cost in men lost while gathering intelligence. We were in it for the thrill of the kill, traveling the last mile with your brothers and the smell the sweet aroma of revenge.

As was customary the night before a team went into isolation, we held an all-night drunk and each American placed $100 inside an envelope with written instructions for it to be opened in the event of our death by the Recon Company Commander, Captain Larry T. Manis. The funds were to be deposited into the bar for your own "kill party." This final gesture of paying your own way for one last hoorah was a big hit with the troops. Beer, wine and liquor flowed freely. Every soldier who would deploy in the morning was completely intoxicated. We joked about not coming back and who would crack open the safe to drink free on those who didn't return. We drank until the sun came up in the east.

As we prepared for destiny, Captain Ramsey the newly appointed One-Zero of RT Anaconda and SSG Houser, his One-One joined in the celebration. Captain Ramsey had been on two missions as a One-One, and neither of these operations had experienced enemy contact. He was a black officer, constantly complained to the Recon Company Commander about being a lowly One-One under a lowly Sergeants command. He felt he should have obtained the status of One-Zero immediately after becoming an officer and finishing his training.

Tired of listening to his bellyaching and boasting, Captain Manis granted his wish. However little did Captain Ramsey know or have any idea that in a very few painful days, his future was to change drastically.

Staff Sergeant Houser was of African American descent as well, he claimed to be related to the Blackfoot Indian tribe. None of us cared who he was related to; we only knew he was one of us. Houser's diverse background included conventional recon while serving with the 101st Airborne Division and Special Operations. He was of average height and crazy as a June bug. We had to watch our backs when he was around because he had a habit of sneaking up on you when you least expected it. Then he'd jump you from behind or straight on and force his tongue into your ear. After you reacted, turning to face him, he'd violently attack you, running his tongue down your throat.

Unlike other black soldiers I'd been around in Vietnam, Houser wasn't a racist, he didn't take 15 minutes to shake your hand, nor did he refer to every black soldier as his brother. He was a great, courageous soldier who called the guys in recon his brothers, and we were proud to claim him as our brother as well.

Two months prior to Lam Son 719, Houser was strap-hanging (accompanying another recon team to see how they operated in the field) while our then project commander Lieutenant Colonel (LTC) David P. Cole was visiting the MLT-2 Quang Tri launch site. LTC Cole was despised and hated by most of recon company. The recon team Houser was strap hanging with had moved out of their houches at the launch site and were sitting inside the helicopters ready to launch into their target area. The choppers were up and running, ready to take off, yet no one could locate Houser.

Understand the situation: the team is loaded, helicopter blades are turning the launch-site commander and project commander are standing by, waiting for the helicopters to depart. Abruptly, the launch-site communications door crashed open and a black guy is sprinting toward the awaiting helicopters. But, this running man wasn't just your everyday black combat troop it was Houser. Every eye focused in his direction, watching in disbelief as he ran toward the choppers. The commanders stood in shock as the Americans waiting with the bowels of the awaiting helicopters howled with laughter.

For there, running full speed towards the helicopters was Houser, rucksack on his back, load-bearing equipment over his shoulder, weapon strung across his chest wearing only a loin cloth, privates swaying in the wind with distinctive white lines of shoe polish below his eyes and across his forehead. Here he was a modern-day Zulu warrior! For his spear he even carried a broomstick handle with a bayonet duck taped to one end, representing the all-important Zulu spear. The only thing he lacked was a shield.

The entire command element stood speechless, totally stunned. As Houser ran past LTC Cole, he saluted and quickly leaped into the awaiting bird. Seeing the rage in LTC Cole's eyes, the pilot quickly torqued up the helicopter engine and, in a single swift motion, lifted the chopper off the pad before the old man could speak. Later, we learned that those left standing on the launch pad began questioning themselves, *"Did I really see that, or was I hallucinating?"* Within seconds after the departure of the helicopters, the radios began to smoke. The project commander was hot and wanted Houser's ass.

The pilot motioned for the team's One-Zero to put on the headset because the commander wanted to talk to him. The conversation was very one-sided, with LTC Cole stating, "If Houser has the misfortune of living through this mission he's to report to my office immediately upon his return. I reiterate, immediately to my office upon his return." Again, at times, we needed humor to break the monotony of combat.

At 0530 hours, the pace of our all night drunk took a rapid and sobering decline. In six short days, eight of our number would be dead; everyone else would be mentally and physically wounded for the remainder of their lives. Thankfully oblivious to what destiny and our future held, men staggered around in the early morning twilight, gathering personnel gear and equipment for the walk out to the transport vehicles which would carry them to the isolation area.

Now, there was no talking or joking around, only silence as we tried to unscramble our clouded brains. One-by-one, the teams loaded the vehicles stashing our gear and equipment in the rear of the trucks. Diesel fumes filled the confines of the tarpaulin-covered truck and intense heat and our earlier massive liquor consumption caused uncontrollable sweat to roll down our faces.

Thankfully, the ride to isolation would be short; a couple of left-hand turns and we were there. Most of us were on autopilot as we began offloading or just falling out the back of the truck. We were sluggish, yet somehow managed to drag our equipment and ourselves into the isolation cage. Once inside, each team was further divided and separated within the isolation area. From this time forward, no one team was allowed to have communications with anyone outside of their individual teams. Americans weren't concerned about us talking among ourselves; we were concerned with the Little People talking to each other for security purposes.

We knew that we had NVA sympathizers in our ranks; we just didn't know who they were. Therefore, any discussion concerning a team's mission was done under extremely controlled circumstances and only in designated areas and only among Americans.

Everyone stumbled around their respective building, looking for a place to lie down. I found an empty bunk and simply flopped down on my back, gazing up at the ceiling. My head was spinning, my stomach was turning and I thought I might vomit. Instead, I was fortunate enough to have passed out for six hours in the un-air conditioned inadequately ventilated building. I awoke to massive beads of sweat running down my face. My mouth was dry and my head felt like someone was inside trying to kick his way out. My entire body was completely drenched with sweat seeping from every pore in my body. I looked like I'd just got out of the shower and just put my cloths back on without even drying off.

As soon as my senses came to life, I smelled the pungent disgusting order of Nuc-mom. The team was busy eating rice and meat that had been brought to them from the mess hall. Normally we ate what the Little People ate so that our bodies would give off the same aroma, but at this point food and the smell of the fish sauce turned my stomach.

Propping myself up on my elbow, I looked for the Americans. Captain Butler was sitting in the corner of the small room studying the map of our target area. Brazier was passed out under my bunk, lying on the cool cement floor. Oddly enough, he was still wearing all of his gear, rucksack, load-bearing equipment and his weapon was draped across his chest. How he was sleeping was beyond me.

I slowly and painstakingly rose into a sitting position on the side of the bed. As I carefully stood erect, the Little People greeted me, saying, "Trung-Si, you boo coo drunk." I replied slowly, as the words hammered through my brain, "yes, Trung-Si be boo coo drunk." They laughed and started chattering among themselves. I'm sure I was the topic of discussion.

Jim Butler momentarily looked away from his map and smiled as I gingerly made my way over to him. Passing the map to me, Jim told me to look at the circled areas of concern. Jim had circled three distinct valleys that rose up from the jungle at the bottom of the A Shau valley, leading straight up to our future firebase. A quick glance through blood shot eyes revealed that there were three high-speed access points leading directly into our planned defense perimeter. If we didn't come up with some pretty innovative defensive measures, Charlie would be on top of the hill with us before we could even dig in.

As I sat meticulously studying every contour line and ravine on the map through glassy eyes, Jim handed me his canteen, knowing I was dehydrated from last evening's festivities. Jung approached us with two bowls of rice and some kind of meat and spicy Nuc-mon to share. With sincere appreciation, we accepted the food even though I wouldn't be able to eat for a while. I sat on the cool cement floor for a couple of hours, slowing regaining my senses as the scorching Asian sun passed overhead. I could see life slowly returning to Brazer and Profitt, both still sprawled under beds. Finally, they awoke in desperate need of water. Each man drank deeply from his canteen and went about the slow, painful process of sobering up. It was not a pretty sight to behold or experience.

For the remainder of that day and part of the next, we recovered, checked our equipment, cleaned weapons and waited for the TOC to call us in for our mission brief-back. After three days in isolation at 0700 hours. The AST came into each of the team isolation rooms and announced to the One-Zeros that all the brief- back would be conducted sometime today. However, RT Intruder was to be in the briefing room at 0900 hours. RT Anaconda was on stage at 1100 hours and RT Python was scheduled for 1300 hours. The AST further instructed us that each team was to bring all special equipment, physiological systems, maps, communications gear and weapon systems for the commander's review. Without waiting for any questions from us, the AST headed out the door and back to the TOC.

RT Intruder quickly gathered up their equipment and exited the isolation area with gear in hand, leaving their Little People where they were. After the commanders brief back they would return to get them and be transported to the chopper pad for movement to MLT-1 (Mobile Launch Team-1) Phu Bi launch site.

I glared at Jim, Brazer and Profitt; something was different, something was wrong; the brief-backs were going too fast. Something was happening that we weren't privy to yet. As if to confirm our suspicions, the AST returned and abruptly ordered in a loud voice, "RT's Anaconda and

Python, time change on your brief-backs: Anaconda, be ready in 30 minutes; Python, you be ready in one hour." We looked at each other in surprise, like deer caught in headlights.

RT Anaconda was up and moving toward the TOC. RT Python quickly readied our equipment. In no time at all, the AST was back, hustling us off to the TOC. Upon our entering the briefing room, we noted that it was filled with unfamiliar faces. We recognized a few, but the majority was strangers. Once we'd displayed our gear in the back of the room, introductions began. We had MACV command elements, Special Operations command elements, and two guys in civilian clothes whose names were never mentioned. We figured them to be CIA. After some brief handshaking, the CCN Commander directed, "Let's get started."

Once we were prepared to commence our briefing, the commander informed us that, upon termination of our brief-back, we were to move directly to the awaiting choppers and be transported to the launch site for immediate insertion. The Commander also told us that H-hour for Lam Son 719 had been moved up 48 hours for security reasons. Now all the hustle and bustle of the short briefings made sense. The NVA high command must have become aware of the allied push and mobilized everything to reinforce strategic enemy positions throughout Laos and Cambodia. MACV-SOG Command had mistakenly assumed that NVA reinforcements would come from the north. In actuality, they were coming from the south. Eight suspected regiments of hardcore NVA soldiers assumed to be on the move, heading straight up the A Shau valley.

Within 30 minutes, we'd conducted our brief-back and were dismissed without any mission clarification questions or comments from the Command element. Jim and I returned to the isolation area to get our gear, while Brazer and Profitt had been directed by the AST to get the team ready to walk to the chopper pad for transport to the launch site. Jim said in an angry tone "they sure want us out of here." We didn't get so much as a good luck or Fuck you very much." We all knew that we had all punched a one-way ticket into the A Shau Valley.

Our team was waiting at the isolation area, ready to move. Right on schedule, we exited, and began the hot short labored march up to the launch pad. Our rucksacks were heavier than normal because of the additional ammunition we were all carrying. Noises from approaching helicopters soon reached our ears. As we closed the distance on the chopper pad, we saw the other two recon teams sitting on the tarmac waiting for their air transportation as well. The noise we were hearing was from numerous helicopters coming in for all three teams at once, something we'd never experienced before. Instead of the usual compliment of four slicks and two Cobra gunships, we saw 15 slicks and six sets of Cobras.

Within moments, the big birds were on the ground, blades spinning, dust blowing and bits of sand stinging the fire out of any exposed skin as they hit. All of the teams loaded up for the trip to Phu Bai launch site.

RT Python was going into our target area extremely heavy. Each man carried three anti-personnel claymore mines, six M-14 anti personnel mines (toe-poppers), four ground flares each, two white prosperous grenades, 1,000 additional rounds of M-16 ammo, chow enough for seven days, 20 mini-grenades and an additional 300 rounds of M-60 machine gun ammo. Additionally, as part of our team equipment, we carried with us a 292 FM radio antenna, transponder, PRC-77 radio, extra radio batteries, KY-38 encrypted radio system, M-60 light infantry mortar with 50 rounds of high explosive (HE), 10,000 round of 7.62 machine gun ammo, three M-60 machine guns and our individual CAR-15 rifles.

RT Python had five UH1 helicopters assigned to insert our heavy team, with one set of Cobra gunships acting as escort and providing cover fire during our insert. Each American from within RT Python had been assigned to the first four helicopters, ensuring that if a chopper were shot down, all of the Americans wouldn't be killed at once. With rotor blades turning at maximum rotation and turbine engines torqued to the appropriate pressure, our mighty war chariots gracefully lifted into the air. As soon as we'd cleared the compound, the lead slick made a hard right pedal turn and headed for the coastline, using it as a guide until we reached certain terrain reference points. From there, the pilots would press inland to the launch site.

As usual, everyone grabbed a set of headset and listed to *Armed Forces Radio*. Rod Stewart was singing "Maggie Mae," while the Special Forces

Recon Teams Intruder, Anaconda and Python flew into the gates of hell. Half an hour had passed before the pilot made a hard left turn headed into Phu Bai launch site. We flew at low-altitude into Phu Bai, jamming to Credence Clearwater Revival's "Bad Moon Rising."

After landing on the helicopter pad at the launch-site, we unloaded and made our way to the TOC. Under American escort, the Little People went directly to their designated houches, while all of the American RT personnel reported to the TOC. We were met as we entered the TOC by the launch site commander Major Elliott and the assistant launch-site commander, Master Sergeant (MSG) Gover.

A politician in every sense of the word, Major Elliott was a power-hungry "yes man," who'd never been on the ground, yet always had the right answers for how it "should have been fought or done." Recon teams dreaded having to launch from this site because you could never tell if they were going to support you or not.

MSG Gover was six feet tall, overweight and sported a big alcoholic blue-and-purple nose. Although he'd run many recon missions in his younger days, he'd forgotten what it was like to be on the ground with your enemy everywhere, people shouting, people dying and facing certain death in every direction. We in recon company described Gover as a backstabbing, mealy-mouthed, son-of-a-bitch, who was a waste of skin and theft of someone else oxygen. I overheard one of the guys speak about MSG Gover in this way, "I wouldn't piss on him if he was on fire."

Gover and Elliott had a reputation for listening over the radio to teams in combat, making sly remarks and second-guessing the One-Zero's decisions. These two mental giants laughed and made jokes while soldiers, locked in mortal combat screamed and died.

As we entered the TOC, we moved directly to the briefing room to provide overviews of our missions. The entire time we explained our operations, Major Elliott doodled on a pad of paper while MSG Gover looked through a *Playboy* magazine. Clearly, they could not have cared less about our future, our mission or us; they were just going through the motions. After we'd finished our quick overviews of our missions, Major Elliott and MSG Gover stood and recited some kind of "let's do it for the kipper" pep talk, immediately followed by their assurance that their staff lived and breathed to support us, and would monitor our every move. I could not help myself from exclaiming aloud, "Bull Shit!"

MSG Gover responded violently towards me with "watch your mouth boy, he's an officer and you will damn-well respect his rank." I kept my eyes on the major. All the while MSG Gover screamed at me, Major Elliott stared in disbelief that I had the balls to have made such a comment. I matched his stares, glare for glare, hoping that he would do something stupid so I could kill him. As we walked out the door, having been dismissed, MSG Gover followed me and grabbed me by the shoulder, spinning me round. Instinctively and without hesitation, my weapon swung in the direction of my upper body as I turned. The barrel of my CAR-15 made contact with MSG Gover's left cheek. I calmly looked into his eyes and said, "Get your fucking hands off me or I'll blow your worthless fucking fat head off." Without moving a muscle, he stared into my eyes, feeling the cool steel barrel of my weapon pressed hard against his face. My finger was on the trigger and the safety was off. I'm quite certain he believed me. I would kill him as sure as salt.

Slowly MSG Gover removed his hand from my shoulder. As I looked him up and down in disgust, I whispered in his ear, "How many Americans have you and shit-for-brains let die because of your good-for-nothing images and egos?" He didn't answer, just tried to jerk away. As I lowered my weapon barrel, I told him emphatically, "The next time, I will kill you."

# CHAPTER 15 (A SHAU)

All three recon teams raced across the sky towards the A Shau Valley. Slick #1 was in the lead with RT Python's One-Zero and three Little People on board. The remaining four slicks followed suit, with me in slick #2, Brazer in slick #3 and Profitt in slick #4. Our trail helicopter carried Sergeant Woodham the chase medic, half of a set of twin brothers who were quite possibly the best chase medics in all of South Vietnam. The other Woodham twin was flying chase medic out of the Quang Tri launch site MLT-2.

I sat in the floor of the helicopter and thought about the altercation I'd just had with MSG Gover. I shouldn't have allowed him to rile me up, but the memory of four close friends being killed while he and Major Elliott frolicked in the local whorehouse pissed me off and, thoroughly disgusted me. Firsthand witnesses had reported to all of us in recon company that even after the two bozos returned from their fun-and-games and discovered they had teams in trouble, they were still too slow and conservative in the use of the airborne assets at their disposal to help the men on the ground.

Ultimately, their incompetence and lack of urgency lead to the two recon teams being totally annihilated. No one was spared; they died alone in the jungles screaming for help. To my way of thinking and all of the other guys in recon company, when a team is on the ground, the people in the support role back at the launch site should, (1) refrain from visiting the local whorehouses at least until the mission is complete and; (2) break out every resource and asset available in order to save of the team. Don't try and second-guess the team on what is happening on the ground because you are not there. And, don't try and conserve on the number of assets you call into action for the team's support. In my simple, single-dimensional viewpoint, they were playing guardian of the taxpayer's money in time of war, an action that caused the deaths of many soldiers.

I reflected on Gover and Elliott's lack of respect for us while we were at the launch site and couldn't help but wonder if they really cared if we lived or died. This wasn't the time to be thinking or concerned about them just prior to deploying on a mission. Conscious to the fact that I had to get my mind off of this negative train of thought, I reached up to the UH-1 ceiling console grabbed a set of ear phones and began listening to the chopper pilots communicate.

The RT Intruder pilots were broadcasting that they had trouble on the insertion. Apparently, they were flying low-level, just about to insert the team onto the firebase, when they spotted enemy personnel running all over the top of it. Therefore, the One-Zero aborted his primary LZ and opted to insert into the alternate landing zone. The slick was in and out before the dust settled, and the team informed Covey that they were safe and walking the two clicks up to their objective.

The pilot went on to say that the team was moving as planned, with negative enemy contact during the team's insertion into their alternate LZ. I thought to myself still listening to Covey talk to the pilots, "That's great to hear, no contact on insertion. That's a good omen." Little did any of us realize or know that everything from here on would turn to hell-in-a-hand basket over the next three days.

The bloodiest, most bitter loss of men and equipment ever recorded at CCN was about to commence. Our pilot announced, "Hey fellows, we're about 10 minutes out. Get ready to get it on. We're deep in Indian country!"

RT Python had chosen not to use air-to-ground or high explosive rockets or nail prep on our LZ during our insert. Jim's concept was for Slick #1 to insert first, set up a hasty perimeter, then secure the top of the hill and then call in the remaining team members, equipment and assets.

Covey directed one set of the Cobra gun ships (#3 and #4) and Slicks #2 - #5 to go into right-hand orbit 10 clicks to the east, while he inserted Slick

#1. Upon Slick #1's successful insertion, he'd call in the remaining assets. Covey followed up by directing Cobras #1 and #2 to provide cover and escort fire for Slick #1 while he was dropping off the team on the hilltops landing zone. Instinctively, the experienced pilots knew exactly how to unload Special Operations teams into denied areas, the helicopter pilots performed magnificently as directed. Slick #1, carrying Jim and three Little People, broke out of the flight formation and were immediately flanked by Cobras #1 and #2. The remaining accompaniment of UH-1s and Cobras went into a right-hand orbit east of the LZ, awaiting further instructions.

I began moving from one side of my helicopter (Slick #2) to the other, watching the insertion. I hoped we wouldn't have enemy troops on site, forcing us to change landing zones, as Intruder had to do. Changing positions as needed, I didn't take my eyes off Slick #1's aggressive descent into the target area.

Cobra #1 and #2 were lined up on each side of the lead chopper, prepared to return enemy fire if slick #1 started taking ground fire. Closer and closer Slick #1 maneuvered his aircraft towards the LZ descending rapidly. My mind began playing the maybe game: maybe Jim and the initial portion of the team would be blown out of the sky; maybe the slick would have a transmission failure and fall to the ground; maybe, maybe, maybe. All kinds of situations played themselves out in my mind within seconds. Staring intensely, I saw Jim's chopper continuing to draw nearer to the LZ.

Covey, circling high above the target location, suddenly executed a diving barrel roll with his OV-10 Bronco and fired a 17 pound white smoke rocket marking the LZ for the inbound choppers. Flying fast and straight, the smoke rocket impacted the western edge of the hilltop, accurately marking where he wanted the helicopter to put the team in.

This process was normal for Covey during insertion of recon teams, unless the One-Zero decided against it. Marking of landing zones assisted the slick pilots and the gunships in accurately recognizing the LZ. On short final, Covey turned the remaining portion of the insertion over to Slick #1. Slick #1 immediately began talking with Cobra #1 and #2, as they pressed closer to the LZ:

Covey 247, Slick #1 identifies white smoke on the LZ.

Slick #1, this is Covey 247, that's a good copy on white smoke. Over

Slick #1 is one mile out, over.

Slick #1 is 500 meters out, negative ground fire.

Slick #1's skids are down on the LZ. That's a Negative on enemy fire. The One-Zero's out conducting his hasty area recon of the landing zone. We'll maintain a sit-down awaiting clearance from the One-Zero to off-load and complete the insertion, over.

Slick #1, this is Covey 247, good copy, I'll stay high and dry, waiting to assist, over.

As soon as the helicopter landed, its rotor blades blasted up a dull colored red dust from the hilltop. As the dust and debris hung lifelessly in the air I could barely see the resting bird sitting idle, blades still turning on the LZ. From my vantage point, I had seen a man leap from the left side of the helicopter as it hit the ground. The man ran to the edge of the firebase and appeared to be searching the landing zone, trying to draw fire from the unsuspecting enemy.

Initially, I couldn't see the chopper or team as I watched Cobra #1 and #2 pull off into opposite directions, beginning their cloverleaf cover pattern. Slick #1 sat waiting for Jim to return, to give the UH-1 pilot an okay sign and off-load his cargo and men. Slick #1 hadn't removed his finger from the trigger mike on his cyclic, when he announced to the Cobras:

Snake #1 and #2, this is Slick #1, over.

Slick #1, this is Snake lead, over.

Roger Snake #1, we're taking fire from all directions. How about a little help down here, over?

Slick #1, we're in hot. I'll be coming in on your 3 o'clock and Snake #2 will be rolling in hot at your 9 o'clock, over.

Snake lead, that's a good copy, get these dinks off my ass, over.

The two Cobra gunships immediately went into a steep dive towards the resting insertion helicopter, as Cobra gunners cut loose with 7.62mm mini-guns, peppering the tree line on either side of the chopper. As we watched from afar, the Cobras performed their precision acrobatic flights in a constantly revolving wheel formation; coming in high, firing rockets and mini-guns, breaking off, then rolling back in hot again. The bright red tracers exploding from the Cobras' mini-gun looked like a single river of red. However, six other 7.62mm rounds, while firing at over 2000 mph were sandwiched between each tracer.

Over the radio, we hear Slick#1 passing orders to his follow-on slicks:

Slicks #2 – 4, this is Slick Lead, over.

Slick Lead, this is Slick #2, Slick #3, Slick #4, over.

Roger Slicks #2 – #4, deliver your packages, but be advised I am taking ineffective heavy enemy fire from all directions. Have your door gunners firing up the area as you come in hot. Be advised I am off loading my package and goods as we speak. Don't bring any fire on top of the hilltop; we have friendlies on top now. How copy, over?

Slick Lead, good copy, bad guys on the war path down there, Slick #2 is breaking orbit and lining up to deliver my package, over.

Slick #3, backing off, establishing separation between Slick #3 and Slick #2, over.

Slick #4, following suit, ditto, over.

While Slick Lead was giving direction to the rest of the insertion package, Snake Lead was communicating with the second set of Cobras, who were also orbiting with Slicks #2 - #4 as they set up for insertion. Snake Lead advised the second set of Cobras to escort the follow-on slicks in, firing air-to-ground rockets, 40mm and 7.62mm. They were directed to break off when they were 250 meters out and catch up with the next slick coming in to provide escort. Snake Lead and his wingman were going to continue providing cover fire until they were "Winchester" (out of ammunition) then Snake Lead would call them in to take over the attack.

> Snake #3 and #4, this is Snake Lead, over.

> Roger Snake Lead, this is Snake #3 and #4, over.

> Snake #3 and #4, we are taking fire from the tree line out to 50 meters in all directions. Concentrate you 17-pounders and mini-gun fire 25-to-50 meters off into the tree line, 360 degrees around the top of the hill, how copy? Over.

> Snake Lead, these is Snake #3 and #4, will be standing-by for your Winchester, and escort the slicks with their packages, into the LZ, over.

Again, from my vantage point, I noticed that after about 10 seconds in which the tiny figure ran clockwise around the hilltop, he then ran back to the helicopter and three other men from within the chopper jumped out. One went to the 12 o'clock position, one to the 3 o'clock and the other to the 9 o'clock. Boxes of ammo, supplies and rucksacks began flying out of the belly of the helicopter as the crew chief rapidly unloaded the team's equipment and cargo. At last, in another blinding cloud of red dust, Slick #1 drew pitch and flew off the hilltop.

As Slick #1 gained altitude quickly, I could hear him reporting to Covey and the gunships on his progress:

> Snake #1 and #2, this is Slick #1, I'm taking fire out the left side of my ship, am pulling pitch and making my break off to the south, over.

> Slick #1, this is Snake #1, good copy. We'll cover your flight, coming in hot, over.

> Covey 247, this is Slick #1, the One-Zero said for us to off-load and start bringing in the remainder of the team, do you have a good tally on me taking fire from the north? Over.

Slick #1, this is Covey 247, roger good copy.

Covey 247, this Slick #1, I'm clear, over.

The pilot of Slick #1 hadn't taken his finger off the stick mike when the Cobras started making their gun runs, firing in the southern and northern jungle tree line, where the unseen enemy fire was reportedly coming from. The Cobra gun fire and rocket fire was intense. After Slick #1 had successfully exfiltrated the LZ and started gaining altitude, he began providing orders to the remaining insertion package pilots:

> Slicks #2, 3, and 4, this is Slick Lead, start lining up for your insertion, separate for a one-minute interval between slicks, come in hot, hover, drop off your packages, cargo and equipment and make your break off the hilltop to the south. Link up over the valley then we'll make our break back to Phu Bai to the west. Over.

In ascending order, the follow-on slicks acknowledged slick #1's orders:

> Slick #1, this Slick #2, roger, over.

> Slick #1, this is Slick #3, roger, over.

> Slick #1, this is Slick #4, roger, over.

Then, we overheard Snake #1 giving orders to Snakes #3 and #4:

> Snake 3, this is Snake 1; take up a cover position at the 9 o'clock on Slick 2 – Slick 4, you follow Slick #2 in and Snake #1 and Snake #2 will dispatch to Slick #3 and escort them in. After you have provided cover for Slick #2, return to Slick #4 and cover their insert. How copy, over?

> Snake #1; this is Snake #3, good copy.

> Snake #1; this is Snake #4, good copy.

With that, the three remaining UH-1s and the two additional Cobras broke from their orbiting formation lining up for their attack. Slick #2 was in the lead, ready and driving hard to make his insertion. The remaining Slicks #3 and #4 were close behind, gradually allowing Slick

#2 to pull away from them, estimating the one-minute interval between package deliveries.

Returning to the right side of my aircraft, I sat down with my feet outside the door, resting on the skid. My CAR-15 was pointed at the ground as I watched the landing zone get closer with each passing second. About 500 meters out from the LZ, the world opened up with gunfire at the helicopters. Snake #3 and #4 were providing cover fire, shooting out each door of our chopper firing 40mm cannon fire as we closed on the hilltop. Enemy rounds began impacting the skin of Slick #2 as we broke into the 100-meter range from the hilltop.

Already on the ground, Jim had set up the PRC-77 radio and began giving instructions to the Cobras and to the remaining slicks coming in for the insert. Jim directed the gunships to fire 360 degrees around the top of the hill with 7.62 mini-gun fire and 40mm grenades. I could tell by the pitch in Jim's voice that he had landed in a hornet's nest. And, we'd be landing there as well sharing in the fight.

The pilots pressed on, despite the fact that enemy weapons fire was impacting the choppers. They were determined to deliver reinforcements, supplies and equipment, as was called for in their mission brief. They never faltered. They always held true to their code and continued driving forward into the hail of hot steel. A quarter of a mile from the LZ, Snakes #3 and #4 accompanied our slick as we closed the distance, firing out each side of the inbound chopper. Jim reported that the AK-47 (communist automatic infantry rifle) fire was now impacting the hilltop. He told Covey and the inbound slicks to keep pressing forward and deliver their packages. Every weapon in the helicopters, gunships and aircraft gun crews was delivering fire on the surrounding tree line as we closed on the LZ.

Within the blink-of-an-eye, Slick #2 bolted like a horse rearing up and came to a hover atop of our landing zone. We tossed out equipment and cargo from both doors and jumped to the ground, while Slick #2, nosed it over and zoomed off the hilltop heading south. While running to my pre-designated fighting position, I looked over my shoulder to see Slick #3 taking heavy automatic fire. He hovered on the top of the hill while men and equipment spilled from his belly. Like clockwork, Slick #3 pulled pitch, broke left and Slick #4 came in on short final. Like the three previous helicopters before him, Slick #4 held his chariot motionless, allowing a smooth exit for soldiers and equipment. We were inspired and reassured to know that our team and equipment had made it, and that the helicopter crews were safely on their way back to Phu Bai.

RT Python lay motionless, our M-60 machine-guns loaded ready to engage our invisible enemy. Suddenly, the enemy fire stopped and a chilling silence surrounded the area. We were in! As I watched my sector of the perimeter, I saw Jim running in a crouched position, checking on the team. After his quick check, he returned to the radio in the middle of our defensive perimeter and radioed Covey. After receiving confirmation on our team OK, Covey went about 10 miles away to our north and began boring holes in the sky there, waiting for something to go wrong on the ground. If by chance it did, he was close enough to us and could bring assets to support our position.

After some hard digging, all three M-60's were in place, cushioned by sandbags. Jim set up the 292 antenna while I readied the 60mm mortar for action. By placing the mortar in the center of the perimeter, it could provide accurate fire 360 degrees fire around us. I also began laying out the mortar rounds all the while cutting charges from the mortar rounds so that we'd have easy access to them in the darkness. We lay dormant watching and waiting for another hour and then started refortifying our individual fighting positions. One man acted as security while the other man dug. Within a short period of time, Jim had the radios running and had established communications with the Phu Bai launch site. I was responsible for making sure our fighting positions were dug in, and sectors of fire established prior to darkness.

Slowly, and under maximum security, we dispatched team members over the side of the hill top to put out claymores with white phosphorous grenades taped to the front of them for additional firepower and psychological effects. As I knelt over my fighting position with two claymore-blasting machines in my hands, an eerie feeling stopped me in my tracks. I felt like I was being watched. Hesitating momentarily to peek over the edge of the firebase rim, I was unable to see anything in the tree line. As a preventative measure, I moved to each position, ordering them to put their M-14 (toe-popper, antipersonnel mines) out to the front about 10 feet down the hillside. One by one, the little people exposed themselves to enemy fire in order to place the mines, all the while expecting to be fired upon. Still, there was no enemy fire. Something was wrong: I could feel it, but what?

Squinting my eyes towards the bright scorching sun, I knew with certainty that the next seven days were going to be hell. There was no overhead trees to shield us from the blistering sun or the unrelenting soon to arrive monsoon rains. Not to mention that we were surrounded on all sides by North Vietnamese soldiers, hell bent on killing us. We had landed in a place that we shouldn't have landed and the NVA wanted us out at all costs.

Our tail gunner Duo reported to Jim that while he was putting out his mines, he spotted three trails intersecting a larger high-speed trail about five feet wide, paralleling our entire southern and eastern position. Justifiably concerned, Jim decided to cover that area with M-60 machine gun fire and mortar fire. Jung, Duo and I climbed off the back of the hilltop, down into the ravine that led from the jungle tree line to the top of our fighting position. The ravine was deep enough to conceal men; giving them a good chance and opportunity of bring effective fire in on us after nightfall.

Nothing stirred while we were in the ravine, so we slowly yet cautiously maneuvered closer to the jungle's edge. We traveled about 30 meters then halted, weapons pointed into the jungle, eyes looking from tree to tree. About 15 meters from the tree line, we went into a security halt, to try and get a bead on the terrain. Directly to our front lay another camouflaged high-speed trail leading up to the firebase. Duo began booby-trapping the trail with tripwires and claymores. If and when the NVA came up this hill, they would be greeted by an unexpected thundering blast. While Duo rigged the mines, I saw two other high-speed trails interdicting with the main trail. Jung put out a couple of trip flares along this set of trails as an additional alerting device.

Within a matter of minutes, the deadly claymores were camouflaged, and ready to go. Careful not to disturb the quietness that surrounded us, we inched our way back up the ravine. About 25-feet from the top, we placed two more tripwire-activated claymore mines and buried 10 M-14 mines as an additional line-of-defense. Once we reached the top, each of us returned to our fighting positions, mentally preparing for battle.

Night would come in another four hours. Jung lay beside me and said, "Trung-si (Sergeant), I think there are boo coo VC here. 400, maybe 600 or more." He went on to say, "When the sun goes down, the VC will come. They are below us now, watching and making plans."

Because Jung's intuition and understanding of our enemy was so incredible, I immediately told Jim what he'd said. Jim got on the radio and informed the launch site of our situation and what we expected to happen when the sun went down. Returning to my position, I tried desperately to memorize the terrain below me because when it got dark, I'd have to rely on mental pictures of the surrounding features.

Our weather briefing during our brief back had informed us that there would be no lunar illumination during our entire mission. Surprisingly, a light breeze rolled across the top of the old firebase from the south, bringing a brief moment of relief from the blistering suns rays and heat. At one time, this mountaintop held five 105mm howitzers, which supported the 101st Airborne Division during their siege of Hamburger Hill. Accompanying the heavy artillery pieces was a full compliment of men, equipment and supplies. Now, it lay silent and disfigured by man's disregard for the jungle and surrounding area. As far as the eye could see, there were vast stretches of fern-covered rolling hills that blanketed the jungle floor. Long veins of endless valleys and ravines stretched in every direction. No movement, no villages, no friendly people roamed the valley only stillness.

All American forces throughout Vietnam referred to the A Shau Valley as the "Valley of Death." Running through the center of the valley laid the Ho-Chi-Minh Trail, or "Yellow Brick Road." From the air, it appeared as a massive yellow streak meandering its way north and south with tributaries roads breaking off in all directions.

There was a lifeless appearance to the Ho-Chi-Minh Trail because vehicles were seldom visible during daylight hours. This evil highway came alive at night with enemy personnel, equipment, vehicles and bicycles traveling in mass. The US Air Force repeatedly bombed the trail into oblivion. However, when the sun would rise the following morning, it appeared never to have been touched, only diverted from its original path. As soon as a section of the road was destroyed, the NVA had their slave labor force repairing it.

Off to the south, in the direction of where RT Anaconda was inserted, helicopter rotor blades and engines could be heard. Without warning, an earth-shattering explosion erupted on the south side of the perimeter. Our hearts jumped, racing to the surprise of the sudden break in silence. Brazier opened up with his M-60 in a long burst. His fire was concentrated in the tree line to his front.

After about 50 rounds of 7.62mm were fired, it was answered by another B-40 rocket that flew out from within the depths of the jungle. I ran over to Brazier's position to assess the damage. One of the Little People had taken some shrapnel in the face. Nothing serious, just a lot of peppering, puncture marks. Small trickles of blood ran down his swollen face. After I had given him first aid and a "no sweat" confirmation concerning his wounds, he re-entered his fighting position beside SSG Brazer. These Little People were tough, seldom complained and displayed a tremendous amount of loyalty to us and us to them.

Crawling over to Brazer who was still spellbound and peering down the barrel of his M-60, I asked what had happened. Without hesitation, he replied, "Man, one minute it was quiet, then I hear the fizzing of the B-40, then Bang! I almost shit myself. I just returned fire where I thought the rocket came from. I never did see an NVA soldier fire it I just fired at the dust it left. I just started firing at the dust."

He continued "I don't know if I got the guy or not, but he sure scared the hell out of me." I told him to relax, have a cigarette and keep his eyes peeled. If there was one B-40 man down there, you could be sure there were a lot more of them. Moving in a crouched position, I checked on Sgt Profitt. He was nervously jerking his head from left to right, frantically anticipating an enemy attack. His eyes were jerking inside their sockets, as his head constantly moved from side to side.

I asked him how he was doing. He responded, "Dude, I think I just wet my pants." Trying my best not to laugh and calm him down, I said, "Don't worry about it. I think I just did the same thing." Looking over at me, Proffitt gave me a reluctant grin. I answered with a tap on his shoulder saying, "You're going to be all right, just stay low and keep alert. The bad guys are just trying to see what we have as far as firepower. If we get any more B-40s, engage them with your CAR-15." As I tapped the receiver of the M-60, I continued, "Don't use this baby unless you see that we are under a full on ground attack. We'll keep it as a surprise and kick their ass when they come to visit."

I ran back to my position, crawled into my foxhole and began to dig it a little deeper. Taking the entrenching tool in both hands, I swung the shovel high over my head forcing the blade of the entrenching tool into the cement-like ground. The sharp blade never even penetrated. Instead, it bounced back at me again and again. At the most, I probably dug about an inch in a period of thirty minutes. It was apparent that our fighting positions were going to be very shallow, 10-12" at best. Jung took over the painful duties of digging and I gladly handed over the shovel. I was beat.

I collected my load-bearing gear, rifle in hand leaving our foxhole to check our perimeter again. The team's baby son, B.S, was up to his usual horseplay, like any other 15-year-old. He was doing everything except what he was supposed to do. I asked him what he was doing. His reply: "Trung-si, I do very good work, I work very hard." In reality, his teammate, Than had been doing all of the work while B.S. screwed off. I told Than to get out of the foxhole and pushed B.S. in. Next, I handed Than a tree limb switch I had found on the ground, and told him to swat B.S. every time he stopped working.

Than turned his head back to B.S., tapping the switch in the palm of his hand as he waited for B.S. to start digging. Little B.S. looked surprised and pointed his finger at me, saying, "You very mean man to B.S." Then turned to his foxhole and began working and then started to laugh. As I crawled away, I thought about what a great group of men I went into battle with. Every member of the team was well seasoned; everyone got along with each other, they were good men to be in combat with.

After completing the perimeter check, I located Jim again. Still hearing the choppers in the distance, I asked him what was going on. He didn't answer me immediately, maintaining the radio handset next to his ear. So, I asked again, "What is going on, Jim?" Gesturing for me to wait a minute, he continued to listen to the radio. Seconds passed before he explained, "RT Anaconda is getting the shit kicked out of them." According to Jim, Anaconda got their first chopper on the ground okay. When Slick #2 was on short final, Charlie opened up on them. Slick #2 took a lot of hits and had to break off and come back around, while the Snakes shot up the countryside.

On the second attempt to insert the team, Houser's chopper got in, and was followed by the rest of the team. They were all on the ground and in the midst of insertion, with Captain Ramsey and his troops providing cover fire. SSG Houser is now on the radio reporting that for some unknown reason, Captain Ramsey stood up and began "John Wayne" firing, taking two rounds in the chest. He went down like a ton of shit. Houser called in a Prairie Fire and the recon team was successfully extracted and is now on their way back to Phu Bai.

Houser reported that he has three dead Little People, and had to leave one of them on the LZ. Captain Ramsey is in pretty bad shape. Houser reported that the two rounds Captain Ramsey took, almost blew out his back. The pilot was shot in the left foot and the peter pilot took one in the face, dying instantly. The fast-movers are on their way to burn up the area. We'd find out later that when RT Anaconda was on short final, the choppers were taking Russian .51 caliber rounds from all directions. Houser later said that Captain Ramsey had told him he was going to get a Silver Star out of this operation or he wasn't coming back.

Captain Ramsey should have called off the insertion and reverted to his alternate LZ. However, he was apparently so set on getting a medal that he not only got himself shot up, but got three men killed in the process. He jeopardized everything for his own personal gain. Captain Ramsey lived, but his left lung, spleen, gal bladder and part of his intestines were removed. Pointing north in the direction of RT Intruder's landing zone; Jim informed me they had made contact and were trying to get extracted. We were their only link to the outside world now.

# CHAPTER 16 (A SHAU)

North of our definitive position, RT Intruder had aborted their primary landing zone, Hill 1528 because enemy soldiers were spotted running all over the immediate area. Captain Watson had reverted to his alternate LZ, which lay 800 meters inside of Laos. Although he had performed a visual recon of the area, this landing zone turned out to be a poor choice once the team touched down. The U.S. Air Force had defoliated the area a few months earlier, but the vegetation in Vietnam grew at a high rate of speed causing the jungle to look completely deep jungle.

RT Intruder's 14 men inserted onto the alternate landing zone without incident. They quickly assumed their team movement formation and headed towards the security of Hill 1528. They'd come in light, with 40-pound rucksacks, load-bearing equipment and personal weapons. This way, they would be able to move quickly without jeopardizing themselves. Once they reached the security of the hilltop, they'd request the resupply choppers to deliver the remainder of their prepackaged supplies and equipment.

Forward they pressed, determined to reach Hill 1528 before nightfall. They moved swiftly through the knee-high vegetation towards the heavenly arms of the jungle about 100 meters to their front. Once there, the recon team would be concealed inside the thick vegetation, possibly avoiding detection.

As RT Intruder reached the edge of the jungle, they went into a security halt while two men moved ahead to make sure no enemy lay in wait. The two-man recon unit returned, giving Captain Watson the thumbs-up. One by one the recon team slowly disappeared into the jungle, moving methodically toward their objective. Normally, they would have moved slowly; however, they were rushing because the sun was beginning its downward swing into evening. They had to reach the top of the firebase before dark.

Captain Watson brought the team to a security halt every 100 meters to listen for any enemy movement. RT Intruder had moved for more than three exhausting hours, covering a distance of only 300 meters. They encountered almost impassable obstacles and treacherous rock formations, cascading straight up. Watson set up a hasty team security formation and sent SFC Wesley forward with three Little People to recon the rocky cliff that lie in front of their movement, and find a way for the team to climb it.

Captain Watson gave SFC Wesley a 15-minute head start to blaze a trail up that cliff for the remainder of the team. Wesley and his team moved forward and slowly yet methodically negotiated the slippery stinking moss-covered rocks. Higher and higher they climbed, each step becoming steeper. After about what seemed like a 50-meter climb, the rock formation opened up into a gently rising jungle terrain again.

Having reached the crest of the cliff, Wesley dispersed the three Little People into a defensive security perimeter. Four exhausted men lay quietly in the undergrowth, their backs to the edge of the cliff, facing off into the direction of the inclining jungle floor leading to yet higher terrain. Silently and vigilantly they watched for enemy movement. Returning to the edge of the rock face cliff, Wes secured one end of a 100-foot rappelling rope to a tree, and then threw the running end down to the team that patiently waited at the base of the cliff.

As the four men provided security, the remaining recon team began their exhaustive climb negotiating the foul smell of the slippery molding rock formation. The sounds of men and equipment banging against rocks echoed through the jungle. Wes became uneasy and agitated because of all the noise the climbers were making as they climbed. He could hear boots sliding off the slippery moss-covered rocks and equipment slamming against the cliffs.

A half-hour passed between the time Wes and his small team had reached the top of the rock face cliff until the first team member emerged. Each soldier was drenched in sweat, their fatigues covered with the slimy black moss from the rocks. The stench from the mold-covered rocks was intense, but blended in perfectly with the jungle. As each member of the team reached the crest of the cliff, he crawled to his respective security position, awaited Captain Watson's next order. Each of the men lay quiet trying to recover from the exhaustive and strenuous climb.

With map in hand, Captain Watson moved slowly around the perimeter, attempting to locate their position in relation to their objective. He radioed up to Covey (Captain Tom Yarbrough) requesting he make a low-level pass over their objective. As it turned out, they were about 300 meters away from their objective. Watson also learned from the map, that the rock formation they'd just climbed was a sheer 25-meter drop-off on either side of them. God forbid if they were hit from the high ground, it would be all over except the crying; they had no where to go except to stand and fight or die.

Realizing the gravity of the situation, Captain Watson quickly reformed the team and began moving up the ever-inclining slope. Their objective (Hill 1528) was about 200 to 300 meters up ahead of them and they needed to reach it as quickly as possible. The team hadn't moved 100 meters when the point man abruptly halted, raising his hand above his shoulder, fist clinched tight, signaling the team to stop.

Watson strained to see through the jungle vegetation ahead of him but couldn't detect anything. Slowly and with purpose, he cautiously moved up alongside the point man. There, hanging about two feet off the ground were three strands of black communications wire. Further complicating matters, a high-speed trail ran five feet on the other side of the suspended wire.

This wasn't just a footpath; large numbers of enemy soldiers could and are walking side-by-side up and down on this trail. The high-speed trail paralleled the communications wire strung through the trees and vegetation. Captain Watson spotted five to ten more communication lines, draped higher up throughout the trees. Captain Watson's heart was in his mouth, as he slowly rose to his feet and motioned for the team to come to him. Once all of the Americans were kneeling around him, Watson, whispered, "We're going to have to abort the mission and request extraction. I suspect we've come up the back side of an NVA regimental headquarters and they're waiting for us up on the high ground." Captain Watson continued, his voice cracking as he spoke, "We have a well traveled high speed trail to our front, with five to ten strands of communications wire strung throughout the trees."

As the One-Zero presented his recommendations to the team, chills ran up their spines. There was no way in hell that the NVA hadn't heard them making their way up the rock face; they were sure to have an ambush in place just up ahead. Off in the direction of the halted team's right flank, a single gunshot cracked from about 100 meters to the north. The entire team automatically snapped their heads and weapons in the direction of the shot. Nervously maintaining their poise, they refrained from firing. Instead, they stayed perfectly still focused on the general direction from where the single shot had come from. Within seconds, the first single shot was answered with another single shot rang this time from the south or left of the team's position, again about 100 meters away. The NVA had the team bracketed in between them, and these shots were confirming such.

Suddenly, from above the halted teams location they could hear men running towards them down the high-speed trail off to the right front of the hiding Recon Team. As the startled Americans turned in the direction of the approaching soldiers, the point man and two Little People opened up with automatic fire on five NVA soldiers. Their aim was true bullets savagely penetrated the enemy troops bodies, spewing blood and tissue into every direction. The NVA soldiers were dead before their brains could inform their bodies.

The team was now compromised. Captain Watson ran into the middle of the trail, where the dead soldiers lay. The remainder of the team crashed out of the bush and set up security positions around the One-Zero. Most of the team's security posture was oriented toward the upper and lower directions of the high-speed trail, covering the tributary paths that intersected it. RT Intruder's search team quickly stripped the bodies of the dead NVA soldiers, securing their weapons and small packs. The enemy rucksacks contained medals, documents, a little money and photographs. All of this would be delivered to MLT-1 Phu-Bai for Intel to study. As quickly as possible, the team was up and moving at a high rate of speed down the trail in single file. Watson hoped that this unorthodox maneuver would throw the NVA off. About fifty meters down the trail it tapered down into a single one-man path.

Surveying the situation, Captain Watson gave the signal to set up a defensive perimeter and prepare for battle. Their tactical position could not have been worse; they were channeled. The left flank held the high ground, leading up the hill and on the right flank lay a sheer 25-foot drop-off. Wes and Sammy set up the M-60 machine gun aiming it up the high-speed trail. Two Little People ran back up the path with claymore mines, attempting to plant them far enough out to provide a standoff capability. Jamming the legs of the mines into the ground, they returned and connected the blasting machines to the outstretched electrical blasting wires.

Wes and Sammy directed two more of the little people to place out other claymores to defend the team's location. Time was running out, and everyone knew it. Covey was flying overhead, trying desperately to make contact with the team on the ground. Captain Watson reached for his handset of his PRC-77 and began whispering into the mouth piece:

Covey 174, this is Zulu Tango, over.

Zulu Tango, this is Covey 174, over.

Covey 174, we have run into a suspected NVA regimental size headquarters down here. They have communications wire strung in the trees and on the ground. We made contact with the enemy, killing five NVA. We are compromised and I'm declaring a Prairie Fire, over.

Zulu Tango, this is Covey 174, roger, understand you are declaring a Prairie Fire, will have assets launched immediately. They will be here in approximately 45 mikes. How copy, over?

Covey 174, that's a good copy, do you have any guns or fast-movers on station at this time, over?

Zulu Tango, that's a negative on guns or fast-movers on station, but will assist you with my guns if you need me to until additional assets arrive! My front seater is calling for assistance at this time, how copy, over?

Covey 174, good copy, no further contact with the NVA since we killed the five NVA back down the trail, but it is just a matter of time. We anticipate enemy contact any second, over.

Zulu Tango, I'll stay high and dry and wait for your call. Need to go up high now to make contact with Hillsboro for additional assets, will monitor your transmission, how copy, over?

Covey 174, this is Zulu Tango, standing by, over.

Zulu Tango, be advised that the weather is moving in on you, with any luck we'll have you out before it socks you in, over.

Covey 174, thanks for the good news, am still standing by, out.

The news Captain Watson had just received from Covey was akin to being stabbed in the back with a dull stick. If the weather came in before they were extracted, the assets might as well not come until tomorrow; the team would already be dead. There was nothing to do but lay motionless and wait for the inevitable attack because sure as shit, it was coming.

Sgt. Robinson signaled to Captain Watson that he could hear voices in the distance. In an instant, the others heard them too. It appeared the enemy soldiers were maneuvering into position for the attack, but were confused as to the exact location of the team. The NVA were intentionally making noise trying to get the hidden recon team to fire at them, thus pinpointing their position.

Dangerously close, the noises continued to grow louder. The trapped recon team stared through bloodshot eyes with fear and anticipation. Every one was keenly aware that the monsoon rain clouds were forming and if they moved in, it was all over but the shouting. There was nothing they could do except hope the extraction choppers came in time. Agonizing, stressful minutes passed, and still no sight of the enemy. For

40 mind-bending heart-pounding minutes, RT Intruder laid waiting on the threshold of total chaos, fear and anxiety.

Finally, off in the distance the extraction helicopters began to be heard. At first, some thought it was just their imagination, but as the sounds intensified, so did their spirits. Abruptly, Captain Watson's radio came to life:

Zulu Tango, this is Covey 174, over.

Covey 174, this is Zulu Tango, over.

Roger Zulu Tango, the slicks are 10 minutes out. I'll be requesting a smoke to get a good tally on your exact location. Also Zulu Tango, have you made contact with the bad guys yet, over?

Covey 174, this is Zulu Tango, that's a negative on making contact with the enemy at this time. I repeat that's a negative on contact with the enemy at this time. Covey, I don't think the bad guys really know where we are. I'll wait until the last second to pop smoke and give our position away, over.

Zulu Tango, this is Covey 174, roger bow understand will be standing by, over.

As the sounds from the helicopters gained in intensity, excitement within the ranks of the recon team increased. Captain Watson waited for five minutes before throwing a smoke grenade into the center of the formation assuming that Covey and the extraction package were in position and ready for the extraction. As the smoke made its way into the sky, the One-Zero was back on the radio with Covey:

Covey 174, this is Zulu Tango, smokes out, identify, over.

Moments passed with no response from Covey 174. Captain Watson held tightly to his handset, then:

Zulu Tango, this is Covey 174, I identify yellow smoke, how copy, over?

Covey 174, that's a good copy, over.

Zulu Tango, the clouds are about 200-300 meters from my location. You're too high. Air's to thin; we'll attempt to pull four people at a time. Will direct Slick #1 to drop ladders in on your position and pull you out, how copy, over?

Covey 174, this is Zulu Tango, good copy on weather and will be sending out two straw hats and two soap bubbles on the first lift, how copy, over.

Zulu Tango, This is Covey 174, Slick #1 is coming into your location at this time, keep me advised as to ground fire and also vector Slick #1 into your location, how copy, over?

Covey 174, this is Zulu Tango good copy, break, break.

Slick #1 was frantically trying to make his way up the mountain. It was going to be quite a trick getting the team out at this altitude. The dark gray monsoon clouds now crested over the top of the mountain tops charging down the mountainside as the helicopters scrambling up. It was a vicious race of man against the elements. Inch by inch, the choppers climbed up the steep mountain.

As soon as the aircraft was hovering directly over the team, an aluminum ladder came rolling down from out of the right side of the bird, quickly unfurling as it crashed to the ground. Robby, Wes and two Little People crawled over to the suspended ladder and snapped their rucksacks to the first rungs of the ladder then slowly started climbing. As soon as the four men were on the ladder Warrant Officer Steve Dieh, the pilot of the UH-1 was struggling to maintain his hover and was experiencing great difficulty because of altitude he was at and thin mountain air.

Pulling up hard on the helicopter's cyclic and with full pitch of the blades, he tried to raise them out of the jungle. Realizing he didn't have enough power to go any higher, Diehl attempted to nose the helicopter over and dive off the hill. Unfortunately, the chopper hadn't gained enough altitude, so as he dove away he began dragging its dangling passengers below through the trees. As the bird began a slow turn, the ladder became twisted in the treetops with the four men still attached.

The helicopter would have crashed if Robby, Wes and the two Bru hadn't jumped from the ladder just seconds before the crew chief cut the ladder away from the belly of the helicopter. Crashing down through the trees the four men fell, snapping tree limbs with their bodies, bouncing down through the timbers like balls in a sick pinball game. It was a horrifying sight for those still left on the ground watching as the four men fell helplessly through the trees down into the jungle. Ironically, the four men crashed through the trees impacting the ground directly on top of the five dead NVA soldiers they had encountered and killed earlier. Instinctively, the men who fell from Slick #1 quickly gathered their senses and started running back toward the rest of the team, all the while, hearing enemy voices ahead and on both sides of them as they ran.

Believing Wes, Robby and the Little People to be dead, Sammy and one of the Bru heard men running toward them. As Sammy's finger began to squeeze the trigger, he thought, *"Well, here we go."* As his finger began to squeeze back on the trigger he recognized his teammates running towards him and took his finger off the trigger, grateful they were still alive. As Wes and Robby passed through the lines of the perimeter, Sammy whispered to Wes, "Damn man, I thought I was going to get drunk on your money in the safe." Wes didn't respond he just ran directly to Captain Watson's position.

Wes was out of breath and bleeding from the numerous small lacerations he'd received during the fall down through the trees. All Wes wanted to know was who was being extracted next. Captain Watson told him that he and the same package were going out on the next chopper by means of Stabo. Wes, Robby and the two Bru quickly prepared themselves for the string ride out. The second helicopter was coming up the hill searching for the team when Captain Watson relayed he was directly overhead. Four stabo ropes came crashing down through the tree smashing to the ground with a thud. Again, Wes, Robby and the two Bru crawled to the stabo rigs; snap-linked themselves into the D-rings of the stabo ropes and gave the crew chief the thumbs up.

In seconds, they were catapulted up through the trees and screaming back down the hillside, headed to Phu Bai. For the next 30 minutes, the four men hung below the helicopter in the stabo rigs their legs slowly becoming useless due to the lack of blood circulation to their legs caused by their body weight being carried by the two leg straps that held them into the stabo rig. Their legs slowly lost all feeling. They were in excruciating pain from the leg straps cutting into their legs and the extra weight of their individual equipment they had around their bodies.

Little did they know the pain and agony of their extraction wasn't over yet? As Wes and the others began to slowly approach the 101st Airborne Division firebase, instead of the pilot lowering them to the ground directly onto the landing pad gently, the helicopter came in too fast and to low slamming the four suspended men against the hard ground outside the firebase perimeter, dragging them through the fire bases defensive perimeters concertina wire.

When they impacted the outside of the perimeter Robby hit a metal engineer stake that stood upright holding the razor sharp concertina wire in place thrusting the stake deep into his leg. When the pilot realized his error and miss calculation of the landing pad he immediately yanked the chopper skyward clearing the men out of the concertina wire. Then as gently as possible, the pilot placed them on the designated chopper pad. The pilot leaped from his helicopter while it was still running and ran over to the men he had just extracted apologized profusely. The guys lying limply on the ground due to lack of circulation in their legs who had just taken the long stabo ride and frolic through the barbed wire were just grateful to be out of the jungle.

The pilot Chief Warrant Office -2 Mr. Diehl informed Wes and Robby that two helicopters were waiting for them over on the other side of the pad and would take them back to the launch site and the hospital. After applying immediate first aid to Robby's leg temporally stopping the bleeding, the four men hobbled over to the waiting helicopters then loaded into the belly of it headed toward MLT-1 Phu Bai and to 95th Evac hospital. The pilot carrying the extracted men motioned for Wes to put on a headset then informed him that CW-2 Mr. Berg's chopper had crashed with Watson, Lloyd and Hernandez attached to strings.

Wes with his heart leaping out of his chest instructed the pilot to return to the extraction location and see if they could find the crash site. Wes's reasoning was that with the help of Covey, Wes and the two Little People accompanying him would rappel directly onto the crash site, secure it and check for survivors. The heavy monsoon rains and daylight was quickly becoming a premium. The pilot replied back to Wes that it was impossible to return to the crash site at this time due to limited visibility over the area of operation.

Captain Watson called in the next extraction helicopters to continuing getting the remainder of the team out. With the third chopper hovering above the team, four Little People hooked themselves into the Stabo D-rings with their snap links that hung from the apex of their load bearing equipment. Eager to be lifted out, they looked skyward and gave the signal that they were ready for extraction. Captain Watson knew the crew chief couldn't see the men below due to poor visibility.

Using his PRC-77 radio, Watson informed the pilot that the men were attached and he could begin lifting them up and over the trees. No sooner had Captain Watson radioed up to the pilot the slack in the stabo ropes was out of the once slip dangling ropes. Although Captain Watson could no longer see the men on the ropes, he knew the chopper had left the area because of the sounds from its rotor blades quickly faded into the distance. Time was of the essence in extracting the remainder of the team. Slick #4 was below the team's location, inching his way up the mountainside through the blinding monsoon grayish dark clouds and trashing rain hammering against his wind shield. The courageous pilot never broke his approach cautiously creeping his way up through the dense clouds and pounding rain, searching for the team. Again, these courageous helicopter pilots disregarded their own safety to slowly and blindly climb through the clouds and enemy gun fire.

Inch by inch the helicopter climbed, until it was directly overhead. The crew chief couldn't see the team on the ground and the team couldn't see the chopper above. Captain Watson was in total control of the helicopter's mobility and was responsible for the accuracy of the chopper's movement. He never moved the radio away from his ear as he continued to strain his neck and head looking skyward talking the pilot in. Nothing could be seen; from the ground up or from the helicopter down, only the sounds of the rotor blades popping above them breaking the air molecules as they titled the blades to maintain their hover.

Just then, enemy automatic weapon fire came from all around the surrounded team. A common tactic used among the NVA was to allow part of a team to be extracted and then pin down the remainder waiting for reinforcements to come causing more casualties and shooting down aircraft. They knew reaction forces would be close behind. Now, they had a split team, half the team was out and the other portion of the team was stranded on the ground.

The NVA were firing blindly in the general direction of the helicopter sounds, hoping to hit it while it hovered. Bullet after deadly bullet impacted the ground around the remaining stranded warriors who lay helpless. The enemy fire was so intense that the vegetation around the men on the ground started falling from it stocks as the enemy projectiles cut their way through.

Meanwhile, Slick #4 continued his deadly motionless hover, while round after round of enemy fire pelted his helicopter. The enemy ground fire began to build in intensity with each passing second. B-40 rockets and Chi-Com grenades began peppered the area in and around the team. Explosion after deafening explosion intermixed with rifle and automatic weapons fire rained down on the stranded team. They were in a nasty situation and their only hope for survival was hovering above.

The cloud cover had now turned into a dense ground fog. Captain Watson continued to communicate with the pilot hovering above, using only the sounds of the rotor blades as his reference point. The blind helicopter continued its totally exposed hover high above the destitute recon team waiting patiently for the team to give him the OK to pull them out.

All the while as the helicopter hovered, the mountainside on the ground came alive with people screaming, shooting and assaulting down on the destitute three-man team who lay waiting Sammy grabbed two of the claymore clackers and waited until he saw six enemy soldiers break through the vegetation about 20 meters above him. With a quick squeezing motion of his hand, Sammy sent the electrical current down the claymore wire, detonating the mine. Instantaneously, a blast erupted; hurling hundreds of bee-bee sized deadly projectiles toward the approaching enemy troops.

Sammy and Lloyd began blindly throwing hand grenades off into the jungle, not wanting to fire their individual weapons until they absolutely had to. They still hoped the enemy was merely trying to identify their position instead of launching a ground attack. But it was too late; the NVA soldiers knew exactly where the remaining three-team members were. Sammy grabbed another claymore clacker just as a B-40 rocket was launched echoed through the trees, detonating dangerously close to Captain Watson. The situation on the ground became more critical real quick with each passing second. Air support was impossible because the men were completely engulfed in the monsoon cloud. The remnants of RT Intruder were on their own. Sammy fired off another claymore, followed by the screams of wounded and dying men. Still, the income enemy fire continued to intensify.

Out of nowhere, three stabo rigs came crashing down through the trees slamming to the ground, initially startling Captain Watson and Lloyd. With bullets flying through the air, Captain Watson continued to bark orders up to the invisible helicopter pilot over his radio, hovering somewhere above his position. The only men left on the ground were Lloyd, Sammy and Watson. These three brave recon men were completely surrounded, stranded and fighting for their survival.

Captain Watson yelled above the friendly and enemy gun battle that was in process and told Sammy and Lloyd to blow the remaining claymores and hook up to the awaiting stabo rigs. Both remaining claymores detonated, momentarily wiping out all of the enemy weapons fire. While two men were engaging the enemy with their CAR-15's and M-60 machine gun fired, the other hooked up to the stabo rigs. Once connected, he tapped the other on the shoulder and took up the rotation until all three were strapped in. All three men now lay on their stomachs, facing outward in a small wheel formation; feet in the center of the wheel and their upper bodies poised outward providing defensive fire for one another. They lay in a three-pronged wheel style defensive fighting position as they waited to be brought up through the trees.

An explosion to their right threw hot shrapnel onto the defenders burning holes in them. Having thrown a grenade at three NVA soldiers sneaking into the perimeter, Lloyd noticed that when the smoke cleared, only their remains lay smoldering on the ground. The three Americans felt a violent tugging jerking sensation radiating down their stabo ropes as the rescue helicopter began to pull up attempting to rapidly gain altitude. Calm, experienced, and clear thinking flew above the team. Higher and higher the helicopter lifted the Americans towards the tree tops, each still firing his weapons at invisible targets as they rose up through the trees.

Enemy bullets blindly whizzing past their heads and bodies as they were suspended in midair no cover to hide behind or under, completely and totally exposed to enemy fire. As they rose higher and higher the dangling men below on the stabo ropes could hear the AK and automatic weapon rounds impacting the helicopter above them. Still they climbed 40, 50, 60 feet into the air then finally they had cleared the treetops when they felt a severe jerking motion radiating down the ropes as the chopper took hit after hit. The pilot made a desperate attempt to dive away from the enemy fire, in all the excitement and confusion banking left instead of right brought the last helicopter heading directly into the major volume of enemy fire.

Meanwhile, Jim Butler was trying desperately to relay the status of RT Intruder extraction when from out of nowhere a series of enemy B-40 rockets impacted our perimeter. We returned fire immediately, only to be answered with yet another volley of enemy rockets exploding on the rim of our perimeter. Pieces of hot metal and rocks spewed down among us. Diving head first into my fighting position for cover, I brought my weapon up and slowly peeked over the embankment of the hilltop. Right there, in the open were 10 to 15 hardcore NVA infantrymen charging up the hillside at us. Two of the enemy soldiers were armed with B-40 rocket launchers. The remainder of the small NVA assault squad was carrying AK-47s and 7.62 SKS rifles, with bayonets fixed. I quickly reached into my ammo pouch and grabbed two mini grenades. Making sure to stay well behind the natural berm of the firebase, I pulled the pin and threw the first grenade into their direction, while two of our Little People fired their individual weapons at them as they blindly continued their charge.

The detonation of the first grenade brought down two of the assaulting enemy soldiers. I pulled the pin on the second grenade, let the spoon fly and counted, "1001, 1002" threw it high into the air, trying to get an air burst over the advancing enemy soldiers. The grenade exploded about three feet off the ground. Once again peeking over the berm, I saw only jerking, flopping contorted bodies. They all appeared to be dead or close to it. Rather than take a chance, two indigenous personnel and I threw three additional grenades down into them to make sure they were dead and not just playing possum.

At this point in the firefight, Jim arrived at our position to lend a hand and analyze the situation. All three grenades exploded within the motionless formation of the enemy men, tossing bodies and body parts high into the air and down the hill.

We spent the next 15 minutes watching for any signs of life among the assumed dead soldiers. After making sure they were dead, we checked our perimeter and let the rest of the team know what had just happened. The enemy was definitely probing our position to see where our automatic weapons were so they could bring maximum fire power to bear against them. Shortly the NVA would hit us again from a different direction trying to gain more information on the exact location of our automatic weapons during the next probe.

After feeling assured that the enemy attackers below were in fact dead I returning to the center of our perimeter, squatted down I lit a cigarette while Jim listened to the radio maintaining vigilance on the situation with the other team. Jim sat silent only listening for the next five minutes, never moving a muscle before surprisingly sitting straight up and telling me that the last helicopter extracting RT Intruder had been shot down. A gut wrenching feeling of helplessness swept over me as I reluctantly turned my head and eyes off into the general direction of where RT Intruder's had inserted. Since we'd observed the extraction package carrying men on stabo rigs out prior to our skirmish's, we assumed the whole team was on the way back to Phu-Bai.

Looking towards the west, I could see that the monsoon clouds and rains were nearly upon us. Shortly, we wouldn't be able to see our hands in front of our faces. Covey and two sets of Cobras circled overhead close to the extraction site, trying to stay out in front of the ever-advancing cloud cover. I questioned Jim if he knew who was on the downed chopper. He didn't have names, just solemnly replied there were three Americans and the slick crew.

According to Jim, Covey had launched an Air Force Sea Air Rescue (SAR) mission to try and rescue the men and the downed helicopter crew. This was the largest and most powerful helicopter in the US arsenal, known as a Jolly Green. Two A1-E Sky Raiders, better known as Spads, Fire Flies, Nails or Hobos, would compliment the Jolly Green providing it security as it went in to extract pilots and recon teams.

Although the downed helicopter hadn't established any communications since the crash, the last transmission received from the pilot was that he was hit in the chest and that his peter-pilot's head was gone, and he was losing altitude.

As Covey flew over our position, still attempting to stay ahead of the clouds, Jim radioed him for a status check. The pilot was Cat Fish, (an Air Force Captain), with his back seater Sergeant First Class Jose Fernandez, as Covey Rider.

> Covey 237, this is Oscar Mike, over.
>
> Oscar Mike, this is Covey 237, over.
>
> Roger Covey 237, this is Oscar Mike everything down here is Ok for the moment. We made contact with the locals but terminated all of them. We are anticipating another attack at any time. They will probably hit us when we are under the clouds and rain, over.
>
> Oscar Mike, this is Covey 237, good copy on your situation. Am going to patch you to the back seater and he will provide you with an update on what's going on. I need to work with the inbound SAR, over.
>
> Roger, Covey 237good copy, over.
>
> Oscar Mike, this is the back seater. We don't know much at this time, only that we have a chopper down with four American helicopter crew- members and three straw hats (Americans). Over

Covey 237, this is Oscar Mike, can we be of any assistance, over?

Oscar Mike, this is Covey 237, that's a negative to assist at this time, got to go babe, the SAR mission is five minutes out, keep your powder dry, over.

Covey 237, this is Oscar Mike, roger standing by, out.

We heard the huge CH-53 Jolly Green and its A-1E Sky Raiders coming from the east long before we could see them. What an amazing spectacle they made as they passed overhead, speeding toward the downed team. The radio traffic suddenly intensified as Covey began to brief the Jolly Green that he'd lead him into the crash site and then break off, corkscrewing up and out of the clouds. As Covey, the Jolly Green and his accompaniment of Sky Raiders executed hard left turns heading off into the direction of the crash site, they were all but cloaked by the thick covered monsoon clouds making them completely invisible to us on the ground. We could only listen over the radio as the operation unfolded.

Finally making contact with the Jolly Green, Covey reported he was lost in the clouds, unable to see 10 feet in front of his cockpit. He ordered the CH-53 and A1-Es to abort the mission. Following Covey's orders to the letter, the three rescue birds flew out of the dense clouds then began orbiting off out in the middle of the A Shau sky awaiting further instructions from Covey.

Jim still keeping the handset next to his ear looked at me then stated, "Covey's lost in the clouds. He's trying to corkscrew his way out without crashing into the side of a mountain." I could only imagine the fear and anxiety they were experiencing inside that cockpit at this moment. We both sat aimlessly staring at the radio, as if it could relieve our minds or do something.

Thankfully, after two or three grueling minutes a familiar most welcomed voice filled the airwaves, "this here's the old Catfish checking in. We just cleared the tops of the clouds and will be back at your location in about three or four minutes." Jim and I grinned at each other with a collective sigh of relief. Realizing that I needed to refocus my attention back on our current situation instead of dwelling on what was happening at the crash site; I made my way back to my little cement-like foxhole. Just about that time, heavy rain began to fall from the sky. My watch read 1530 hours (3:30 pm).

Everyone would soon begin to bail rainwater out of the bottom of his foxholes with C-ration cans. We were all drenched, tired, hungry and miserable. I ordered a rotation for the evening meal one man could eat while the other pulled security. Jim sat with the radio constantly pressed tight against his right ear, listening so attentive to the emptiness of the radio waves. He as well as the rest of us were hoping to hear a distress radio signal from the downed helicopter crew and lost recon team.

I could barely see Jim's eyes in the twilight as he spoke to me, "Les, we are their only means of communication with the world. If they're down there hurt, still fighting and alive, we have got to gut-it-out up here, no matter what, until they are extracted." Knowing that all of the other Americans were equally as concerned with the fate of our brothers, I made my rounds and informed them of the current situation with RT Intruder. As I made my way from each fighting position to my position we all tried to reassure one another that the team and helicopter crew were all right, just running and hiding from the bad guys. But deep down, we refused to admit it outright but we all knew that once again death filled the air in the A Shau Valley.

It had been raining continuously for over four hours now and the darkness of the night was blindingly pitch black. Water logged and tired, we wanted something to interrupt the nothingness of the night. Finally, the rains changed from a deluge to a steady mist, immersing us in wet foggy clouds. The jungle floor was saturated from the terrestrial rains, a muddy sloppy mess. The rainy season made it almost impossible for Charlie to move heavy equipment down the Ho-Chi-Mien trail but foot soldiers and their equipment he was a master at. Likewise, the Allied Forces experienced extreme difficulties moving equipment and men in the wet surroundings.

Yet, the NVA could and constantly did move mass numbers of foot troops down the A Shau Valley without ever being detected because of the constant ground/air fog. That's why we were here in the first place to locate, intercept and call in visual air strikes as they mobilized reinforcements headed towards Khe Sanh. Another problem during the rainy season was hearing approaching enemy troops. Because of the ground saturation, the normal rustling of vegetation and snapping of twigs was muted to the point of complete audible obscurity. It didn't take a mental giant to realize that the NVA would soon be probing our perimeter once again, trying to find our weak spots.

Patiently, the defenders of this small parcel of land watched the darkness and listened to the rainfall camouflaging our enemy's movements as we silently waited for Charlie to physically make his appearance.

# CHAPTER 17 (A-SHAU)

Back at Phu Bai launch site, excluding Robby who lay in the hospital the survivors from RT Intruder were busy debriefing and preparing for a Bright Light (recovery) mission back into the A-Shau where their chopper and split team had gone down. RT Habu was called up from Da Nang to perform the duties as Bright Light. RT Habu was made up of experienced, battle-seasoned veterans including, Staff Sergeant Danzer (Hoot) Owls, as the One-Zero; Sergeant Lemuel D. McGlothren, his One-One; Staff Sergeant Cliff Newman and Sergeant First Class Jimmy Horton, straphangers with Sergeant James (Woody) Woodham, as the chase medic. There was to be a total of five Americans and six Little People on this Bright Light team.

Wes was still at the Phu Bai launch site, debriefing all levels of command concerning what had occurred on their target. The briefing was in-depth and very specific so that the commander and his staff could conduct detailed coordination and planning for the recovery attempt. Wes skillfully walked them through the sequence of events from the time RT Intruder inserted up through the heroic extraction attempted by Captain Watson and the flight crews of Company A, 101st Aviation Battalion. His report included the estimated size of the enemy, their activity, the assumed location of their base camp, the suspected location of the downed helicopter, including the time of the incident and the types of weapons used against them.

After Wes had completed his debriefing, everyone stood motionless in the dimly lit smoke filled debriefing room silent, each man was either staring at the large situation map that hung on the wall or at the CCN

Commander; all anxiously awaited their orders. Finally, the Commander stood erect and reluctantly turned his focus and attention towards Wes. The old man asked Wes directly "Wes would you volunteer to go back into the target area with The Bright Light to help them locate the downed helicopter and recover any survivors and/or the possible Killed in Actions (KIAs) at the crash site."

Wes staring in disbelief and surprised at the commander trying to register the old mans request, Wes was outwardly stunned at what he'd been asked to do. An internal tug-of-war raged within Wes's mind. Frantically searching his mind, body and sole for the correct and moral response back to the old man wrestling internally "*Should I go back in and face another round with death, or should I decline and stay alive one more day?*"

Glancing around the room through the smoky haze Wes saw recon officers and support staff respectfully waiting for his response. Deep within his heart, Wes new the aching answers to the request even before it was asked, an answer known only to those who've lived through combat and been where we've been and done what we've done.

Wes reasoned within himself, "*If it were me down there, I know they would be forcing their way on the mission to rescue me, or die trying.*" The answer to the Old Mans request was plain as day; of course he'd volunteer. Slowly turning his head from the situation map Wes looked into the Commander's eyes, and then slowly spoke, "What the hell, my wife can use the insurance money. Yes sir, I'll guide The Bright Light back in." The TOC immediately went into action as Special Operations men began the coordination efforts with multiple external support units for equipment, aircraft and fast-movers for the insert of The Bright Light into the A-Shau Valley at first light.

Physically exhausted and mentally drained, Wes silently thought about what he'd gotten himself into, but didn't have time to dwell on it long. He simply grabbed his load-bearing equipment, weapon then tilted his jungle hat down low over his forehead, exited the TOC door and headed for the club. After his first drink, he felt his composure slowly return as he silently made peace with himself and God. According to his watch, it was 1800 hours or 6:00 pm. just then; a young Special Forces soldier entered the club, loudly calling out, "Hey Wes, they want you're back over at the TOC. The Bright Lights here and is getting ready to receive their initial in brief from the old man."

As Wes quietly entered the TOC, he was almost knocked over by Doc Woodham rushing out the door headed for his dispensary to fill a medical supply list for The Bright Light mission. The Bright Light team leaders were all huddled over the situation map that lay on the big planning table, deep in discussion. Without being noticed, Wes glanced over SSG Danzer's shoulder, causing him to quickly turn around to see who was standing over his shoulder. Quick handshakes were exchanged and Danzer stated, "Glad to see you're still alive and going back in with us." Wes nodded his head and replied, "Guys, this is going to be an ass-kicker. Take only ammunition and water, cause we ain't staying long." Further explanations were unnecessary. They would have to fight their way in and they knew for sure that they were definitely going to fight their way out, if they were going to be able to get out at all.

Wes began to informally brief the Bright Light on what had taken place only hours before, covering the initial insert of RT Intruder, the route taken by the team, the discovery of the high-speed trail and communications wire, climbing the slippery rock face cliff, a quick description of the targets terrain, the enemy they encountered and the last known location of the remaining American, prior to his extraction.

Every member on the Bright Light gave Wes 110% of their attention as he methodically pointed out reference points on the map. Suddenly, the door slammed open and Sgt John Fettler announced, "RT Python just reported that they have picked up a beeper. They're alive!" Everyone rushed toward the radio room, hungry for information. Just after a squelching noise, Captain Jim Butler's voice rang out:

Sierra Zulu, this is Whisky Mike (RT Python), over.

Whisky Mike, this is Sierra Zulu (MLT-1, Phu Bai), over.

Sierra Zulu, we have been picking up a beeper on our survival radio. An American must be manning the survival radio because he is allowing five beeps from the URC-64 or 68 to be transmitted, and then there is silence. The emergency signal is being repeated again and again, how copy, over?

Whisky Mike, this is Sierra Zulu, have you been able to make contact or hear any American voices over the survival radio, over?

Sierra Zulu, have made numerous attempts to make contact, but no response. I think the mountain between them and us is blocking the transmission, over.

Whisky Mike, this is Sierra Zulu, continue to monitor and attempt to make contact with the beeper. Will have traffic for you in approximately six zero mikes, over.

Sierra Zulu, this is Whisky Mike, standing by, out.

This tiny bit of hope spread to everyone throughout the room, stimulating a more determined resolve to successfully launch the Bright Light, extract the survivors and hopefully kick Charlie's ass in the process. Everyone was aware that 12 brave recon men remained in position refusing to come out and save their own hides because they were the only means of communication between the survivors and the launch site. RT Python had already refused extraction twice. Unfortunately, the next few days would be filled with unquestionable misery, agony and emotional ups and downs that would be remembered for years to come by the men about to enter the A-Shau Valley.

Indeed, the events that were about to unfold would be permanently tattooed into these Special Operations soldiers' minds and sole. The men at Phu Bai launch site worked feverishly coordinating and reconfirming assets and supplies for the upcoming Bright Light mission until the wee hours of the following day. Constantly preparing, checking, coordinating and communicating so that everything would come together successfully all at the same time. Without warning, the silence of the room was broken by a radio transmission from RT Python:

Sierra Zulu, this is Whisky Mike, over.

Whisky Mike, this is Sierra Zulu, over.

Sierra Zulu, this is Whisky Mike we are under heavy ground attack on the southern section of our perimeter. No casualties yet, I suspect this is another ground probe. Keep this line open, will keep you advised, how copy, over?

Whisky Mike, this is Sierra Zulu, good copy. You suspect this is a ground probe by the gooks, no casualties. Do you require any assistance from us at this time? Over?

Sierra Zulu, this is Whisky Mike, that's a negative on assistance at this time, however would appreciate it if you could make it stop raining, we are all but swimming in the trenches, send LBRBs (Little Bitty Rubber Boats), over.

Laughter suddenly radiated through the room. Butler's request for LBRBs broke the stress momentarily that weighed so heavily throughout the TOC.

Whisky Mike, this is Sierra Zulu, that's a negative on stopping the rain on our end, babe, that's between you and the man upstairs. However, we do have some LBRBs we could send your way, how copy, over?

Sierra Zulu, this is Whisky Mike, disregard the LBRBs, we will continue to tread water. Be advised that the enemy fire has ceased, will continue to monitor, out.

Sighing with relief, everyone returned to their portion of the massive coordination effort. Major Elliott announced that the brief-back would begin in five minutes. Slowly, the REMFs (Rear Echelon Mother Fuckers), as we affectionately referred to them, picked up their paperwork and meandered into the briefing room.

The Bright Light team had been steadily working on their scheme of maneuver within the confines of the briefing room, away from the massive administrative coordination going on in the other rooms. After the briefing, the commander released the staff to get some rest prior to launch. The TOC quickly emptied out, except for Sgt. John Fettler the radio operator and Wes, who stayed behind to smoke a cigarette.

Although it had been 24-hours since Wes had any sleep, his mind wouldn't stop working. He relived his close encounter with a well-trained enemy and his quick but horrific peek at death. A chill went down his spine, causing him to tremble slightly as he mentally tried to prepare himself for the return to the valley of certain death.

The silence was broken when John Fettler spoke up, "Wes, I don't blame you for being scared about returning to the A-Shau. I've never been there, but I can only imagine how afraid you must be." Turning to meet John's gaze, Wes replied, "Man I'm not afraid, I'm scared shitless. I only got out of there by a thin margin the first time, and here I am getting ready to go back to the same hell hole. I must be crazy! But why should I worry about the inevitable? If The Man upstairs throws my Ace, I'm dead anyway."

With that, Wes stepped out of the TOC into the hot night air, making his way to the Bright Light hooch.

Although the Americans and Little People on the team were continued to prepare their equipment and supplies for the mission, Wes was too tired to help. Instead, he simply sat on the edge of an empty bunk and stared aimlessly at the wooden floor at his feet. A Montagnard soldier from the team handed him a bowl of hot spicy noodles, which he humbly accepted. Mentally and momentarily reentering the world of the living, Wes realized that he hadn't eaten since yesterday morning, prior to the insertion of RT Intruder.

Famish he devoured the tasty noodles followed by the noodle soup, turning up the container to drinking the last drops of warm liquid. Within a few minutes, exhaustion set in and Wes stretched out to rest his weary body and mind. As Wes laid on the bunk his right arm shading his eyes from the light that hung over head RT Habu continued to diligently prepare for the early morning insertion into the A-Shau Valley.

SSG Danzer, the One-Zero was about 26-years old and hailed somewhere from the Midwest. Since he'd only been in recon company for six months, his expertise as a One-Zero was limited. Although he'd just taken over the team, he had yet to be baptized under fire. Danzer stood about 5 feet 9 inches tall, with a slender build and an extremely pale complexion. He'd spent one previous tour with the Big Red One (First Infantry

Division) down south. He was big-hearted and generous, but his killer instincts had never been tested.

RT Habu's One-One was a young kid named Sgt. Lemuel (Mac) D. McGlothren. Because he was the youngest in all of recon company, Mac was always having pranks pulled on him. He had a good nature and let most of the ribbing and practical jokes slide. Mac was from somewhere in Florida or Alabama and even though he was short on years, he'd been on a number of missions with SFC Lloyd (Snake) Adams and SSG Jimmy Johnson and had proven himself more than once. Snake Adams and Jimmy Johnson were known in recon circles as "the redneck team." The two-strap hangers on the team were SSG Cliff Newman and SFC Jimmy Horton.

Cliff Newman was a quiet mountain of a man, standing about 6 feet 5 inches tall. He was well known for his competency and leadership abilities as a professional soldier. Newman and Sammy Hernandez were the best of friends. So, when Cliff learned that Sammy had gone down with the helicopter in the A-Shau, Newman volunteered immediately without hesitation or reservation. No one, but no one could have kept him from going in to retrieve his friend.

The second straphanger was SFC Jimmy Horton, a well-seasoned recon man with numerous missions under his belt. He'd been in all three SOG organizations: Command and Control south, central and now north. Horton was a wild man, always game for any target, anytime, anywhere. Standing about 5 feet 8 inches tall, slender built like the rest of us and had red hair to match his temper. Horton's face was a road map of experience, and his constant bloodshot eyes read like a book of horror stories that only he knew. He was highly regarded and respected in recon circles.

Recon team Habu was a Bru Montagnard team with lots of experience and countless missions to their credit. The interpreter was a Montagnard Prince, named Kuman. All the Montagnard on the team obeyed him to the death. They never questioned Kuman and their loyalty to him was beyond reproach.

While Wes slept, the Little People went through his equipment, reloading every magazine, restocking his mini-grenade pouch and filling his canteens with fresh cool water. Slowly The Bright Light Team began to wind down. Everyone soon found a bunk and tried to get some rest. 0500 hours (5 AM) arrived and John Fettler entered the hooch to roust the team for preparation and their soon departure. Having vigilantly remained next to the radio, Fettler was able to provide an accurate status report to the Bright Light. RT Python had been fighting off the NVA all night. He also relayed that the weather was holding and everything looked good for a first-light insertion. Choppers are in route and would be on the pad at approximately 0630 hours.

In less than 30 minutes, The Bright Light had gathered their gear and headed to the launch pad. The entire Da Nang and Phu Bai Command Staff was waiting for them on the tarmac. Heavily loaded down with ammunition and weapons, each man was also carrying a body bag. The Bright Light team moved into their respective loading positions. Thirteen warriors stood or rested a top their rucksacks waiting for their sky chariots to arrive then carry them to the aid of their fallen brothers.

Covey now flying an O-2A Sky Master, had taken off prior to the sun coming up to check on RT Python and get a visual recon of the crash site. Leading the Covey team as the pilot was 1st Lieutenant James Hull, an experienced pilot who'd graduated from the Air Force Academy and SFC Jose Fernandez as his Covey rider. The men of Recon Company held Covey pilots in the highest regard and considered them to be one of our own. All Covey pilots could rest assured that if they went down, we would be coming in to get them.

Inbound choppers suddenly illuminated the landing pad like the noonday sun as their skids slowly and methodically searched for the ground. Within moments, the six helicopters were loaded with men and equipment. Each American quickly grabbed a headset to begin briefing the pilots on the mission and what might be expected from the hostile natives in the A-Shau Valley.

Luckily, three of the six pilots inserting the Bright Light team had been on yesterday's insertion and partial extraction of RT Intruder, and were just as eager as the Bright Light to assist.

Anxious to get the show on the road, Slick #1 instructed the other choppers to follow his lead indicating that they would coordinate with them further while in flight. Previous Bright Light missions had proven that the NVA was astute to the American moral obligations to retrieve their dead from the battlefield and in turn search for any of the missing. During this short period between preparing for a Bright Light recovery the NVA would return to the area and would have plenty of time to prepare for their return. More than likely, they'd already moved additional NVA combat forces into the area to repel and/or destroy the responders.

As the flying UH-1 armada lifted off the tarmac in the shadows of the morning dusk heading down the runway gathering speed with each second that passed, Cobra gunships suddenly flew in formation on each side, rapidly pressing ahead to link up with Covey. Slick #1 announced to the trailing helicopters, "We're 30 minutes out, door gunners lock and load, test fire your weapons." Without a word, the door gunners pulled the charging handles of their M-60 machine guns to the rear, let them fly forward and pulled the trigger, releasing short bursts of automatic weapons fire from each gun. Slick #1 was leading the armada and instructed Slicks #2 - #5 to form in a right echelon flight formation to the target area. He further instructed Slick #6 to pull slack on the formation and wait high-and-dry until called to come in.

Covey came up on the frequency and began briefing the helicopter pilots on what they as a team were preparing to do. Silence rang out inside the guts of the helicopters as the destiny of each man visited his maker. For twenty minutes the Bright Light team flew without saying a word to one another only listening. Then came the announcement over the internal helicopter radio headsets. "We're ten minutes out, get your shit together for insert."

Covey, this is Slick #1, I'm two minutes out, over.

Slick #1, this is Covey 297, I'll fly to you, pick you up and lead you back into the target area, over.

Covey 297, this is Slick #1, I am looking for you at this time, over

Roger, Slick #1, this is Covey 297, I'll lead you in and mark the LZ with smoke, land on the smoke, drop your cargo, come up and break right, go into orbit ten clicks east and stand by. How copy, over?

Covey 297, this is Slick #1, good copy, will keep my eyes on you

Break, break. (Talking to another set of pilots)

Slicks #2 - #5, this is Slick Lead, do what I do and regroup five miles off to the east after insertion, Slick #6 - orbit five miles out and stand by high and dry. How copy, over?

Slick #2, good copy.

Slick #3, good copy.

Slick #4, good copy.

Slick #5, good copy.

Slick #6, good copy, staying high and dry.

Easing out onto the helicopter skids for a faster exit, the men had their faces disfigured by the gusting wind as they looked forward of the fast descending helicopters approaching the landing zone. Hanging outside of each door their bodies completely exposed to enemy ground fire. With an impressive rapid insertion, each chopper delivered its valuable cargo without incident. The Bright Light Team hit the ground, ran into the jungle and quickly reassembled 50 meters inside the vegetation to wait, watch and become adjusted to the jungle's sounds.

For five long minutes, the team waited for an enemy attack that never came. As unnerving as the strange absence of NVA fire had been during the insertion, it was even worse now that the team was alone in the jungle. They were outmanned, outgunned and fully aware that their viper-like enemy could strike at any moment. Cautiously, the Bright Light moved slowly toward the downed helicopter. Wes was near the front of the team so he could direct the One-Zero to the crash site. Normally, two Americans wouldn't be placed in close proximity to each other, but Wes knew the terrain firsthand and was needed alongside Danzer. The jungle was thinning out with each step the invaders made, and as the jungle vegetation began to spread out, so did the team.

For the second time in less than 36 hours, Wes was in the same unforgiving jungle, and he was starting to get a little jittery. The helicopter wreck lay off to the west about 600 meters from their insertions landing zone. The team cautiously made its way through the sparsely vegetated area and entered back into the dense heat smoldering jungle, stopping only momentarily for a security halt.

Danzer sent two Montagnards back to the edge of the jungle to determine if they had picked up any bad guys or trackers. Intense observation, listening and waiting followed until the signal from the Little People was rendered to SSG Danzer that they hadn't picked up any bad guys. Again, they were up and continued to close the distance toward the crash site before assuming the next unexpected security halt. As they knelt, each man slowly and deliberately scanned the jungle floor their head and eyes in unison with their weapon. The jungle was quiet and alarmingly silent. Evil lurked within the shadows.

Danzer passed through the security formation to the point mans location to investigate the cause of the halt. As Danzer left the formation, he signaled back to the waiting team members that he could see a path or trail to their front. The team signaled back confirming that they understood the signals and would wait for further instructions.

Danzer and the point man slowly disappeared into the jungle only to be gone for a minute or two. When he returned he motioned for the team to move forward until they were in sight of the trail. Slowly and carefully, the team moved into flanking positions to prepare to cross the danger area. On approach towards the trail, they found it to be well groomed and well traveled, with numerous footprints deeply embedded in its red clay surface.

From the edge of the jungle where Danzer halted the team, he could see about 25 to 30 meters up and down the trail. Crossing a trail or road for any size unit was extremely hazardous especially for a small combat unit. The NVA were notorious for placing lookouts on the trails, to watch for enemy crossings.

Normally, the NVA trail watchers would allow half of the team to get across to the other side and then open up on both sides at once, effectively splitting the team, having broken the team down into smaller groups easier to kill. Once these NVA scouts opened up on a team, a larger enemy force would quickly respond, join in, and the fight was on. Once Danzer felt relatively secure about their situation, he sent the first portion of the team across, moving in sets of twos.

The first set swiftly crossed the trail to the far side of the danger area, quickly searching the other side making sure there were no bad guys waiting in ambush. After they had performed their recon of the far side, one man stayed about 25 meters deep in the jungle to secure that area, while the second man returned to the edge of the trail to signal the One-Zero to send the rest of the team across.

Without hesitation once the one-zero had received the all-clear signal, Danzer sent the second, third, and fourth two-man teams across. Now, only Danzer and two far flanking security men remained. Giving a slow and deliberate hand and arm signals to the flanking security men to fall back and join him, Danzer and the two remaining men crossed simultaneously.

All of their previous repetitive rehearsals below Marble Mountain and team training for crossing these kinds of hazardous obstacles had paid off. Each team member knew exactly what he was supposed to do and performed his task flawlessly under real-world conditions. The team regrouped quickly on the other side of the trail and continued their forward movement. The Bright Light was on the same trail through the jungle that RT Intruder had taken the day before. RT Habu had been moving for about two hours now without incident.

Wes knew and felt that they could be ambushed at any moment. He recalls back in 1968 when his platoon from the 101st Airborne was ambushed on the other side of the A-Shau Valley while conducting a search and destroy mission. It was still fresh in his mind; they'd lost nine dead and 24 wounded within a matter of seconds. The NVA were masters at ambushing Americans.

When the team stopped again, Wes knew why the point man had halted them; he'd come upon the communications wire hanging in the trees. Danzer signaled for Wes to come forward and accompany him to the point man and together all three would move forward. Just as he'd thought communications wire was strung in every direction. Just beyond the tangled wire, lay another well-traveled, high-speed trail.

At that very moment, Covey surprisingly passed over the team's head, coming in from the direction of the rescue team's landing zone. Danzer questioned Wes, "Why is he flying so low over the LZ?" As Covey flew off into the distance Danzer could hear the right seater calling on the radio:

> Mike Hotel, this is Covey 247, over.
>
> Covey 247, this is Mike Hotel, over.
>
> Mike Hotel, This is Covey 247, I need you to count your people. I have an unidentified person in the middle of your insert LZ popping a panel.
>
> Covey 247, this is Mike Hotel, standby, over.

Danzer turned to the team and gave the hand and arm signal for the last man in the formation to pass up the count. All of his people were accounted for.

> Covey 247, this is Mike Hotel, over.
>
> Mike Hotel, this is Covey 247, over.
>
> Covey 247, this is Mike Hotel; I have all of my people with me, over.
>
> Mike Hotel, this is Covey 247, roger understand that you have all of your people accounted for. I am going to make another pass over the LZ and check it out. Will be right back, how copy, over?
>
> Mike Hotel, standing by, out.

Danzer, Wes and the Bright Light team heard the 0-2 pass low off to their west directly over their previous insert LZ.

> Mike Hotel, this is Covey 247, over.

Covey 247, this is Mike Hotel, over.

Mike Hotel, whoever it is popping the panel looks like one of us. I am sending in a slick with a set of guns as escort to check him out, over.

Covey 247, standing by, out.

Danzer decided to continue to move the team closer to their objective. If Covey did have a good guy on the ground, Danzer didn't want his team to be standing still to await the news. The enemy was most likely looking for them and they couldn't take that risk.

Covey called for any SOG helicopters that were up from either MLT-1 Phu Bai or MLT-2 Quang Tri. He received immediate response from three helicopters and two gunships out of MLT-2. He reported to them what he'd found on the landing zone and asked for their assistance. Replying in the affirmative, the pilots would be on-scene in less than 15 minutes.

Flying on the chase bird was the Recon Company Sergeant Major (SGM) Billy Waugh. Covey briefed the responding helicopter crews as they closed in on the area where the unknown person was still popping a panel. The chase bird was ordered to go in and identify the person. A set of guns would escort him, providing over cover fire if needed. Slowly the helicopter and two guns descended making their way down to the LZ where the figure was now vigorously popping the panel jumping up and down. Once the helicopter was directly over the figure, SGM Billy Waugh radioed to the pilot that he recognized him as SFC Sammy Hernandez.

Following orders to drop strings to Sammy by the pilot, the crew chief quickly dropped out one stabo rope. As the rope fell SGM Waugh lay on his stomach inside the helicopter looking at the ground. The rope hit the ground and Sammy looking up at the hovering helicopter made an immediate distinguishable gesture with his finger up to the hovering aircraft. Billy Waugh immediately understood started laughing and directed the pilot to land and pick up Sammy.

Later, Sammy stated that he would never again ride a stabo rig or string out of a target again. Upon his return to Phu Bai, Sammy told the TOC that he had recovered Wes' rucksack when he'd fallen down through the trees. Sammy still had his CAR-15, his rucksack and the M-60 machine gun when he and Doc Watson and Lloyd were being extracted. The extra weight he was carrying possibly saved Sammy's life by causing the rope to break, hurling him through the trees like a ping-pong-ball as the chopper with Doc Watson and Lloyd went down and disappeared off into the jungle.

Sammy continued by saying that he'd been knocked out and lay in the jungle for hours before regaining consciousness. He'd hid in the thick vegetation all night, evading the enemy who'd been searching for him with flashlights. At one point, the NVA search parties came within five feet of him. Sammy said he hid all night and tried to signal anyone with his survival radio. That was the beeper that RT Python reported hearing. He'd laid low until daylight then cautiously moved back to the original insert LZ.

Mike Hotel, this is Covey 247, over.

Covey 247, this is Mike Hotel, over.

Mike Hotel, this is Covey 247, roger babe, the person on the ground is a Mexican American, one of the straphangers. Over.

Covey 247, this is Mike Hotel, that's good news; I am continuing to move the team closer to my objective, will contact you later, out.

# CHAPTER 18 (A SHAU)

Danzer momentarily halted the team to up date the Americans that Sammy had been recovered. Wes grinned, inwardly thankful his friend was alive, and then returned his focus back to finding Doc Watson, Lloyd and the helicopter crew. Having moved the Bright Light team into the general vicinity of the crash site, Danzer set up security on the same trail RT Intruder ran up the previous day.

Stepping onto the well-worn path, Wes saw a pool of dried blood intermixed with red clay from the five NVA soldiers they had killed the day before. The bodies were gone, but the bloodstained earth remained. Danzer sent two Little People up the trail about 20 meters past the bloodstains and directed them to act as early warning for the team should any enemy soldiers come down the trail.

Two other Montagnards were sent 20 meters down the trail to perform the same duty as early warning. Once security was in place, Wes and Danzer walked around the area, spotting two rucksacks and a stabo rope beside the trail. Danger signs immediately bombarded the two men's brains as they stood staring at the rucksacks and limp stabo rope. This set-up scenario had all of the ear marking and appearances of an NVA booby trap. Moving forward vigilantly, Danzer asked Wes what he thought. After staring at the rucksack intensely for a few seconds, Wes blared out, "Hey, that's *my* rucksack. How did it get all the way down here?" Wes went on to explain that he'd lost it when they'd jumped from the stabo ropes on their first extraction attempt.

Wes decided to tie his rappelling rope to Danzer's and attach the other end to the rucksack's shoulder strap and pull it out. That way, if it was booby-trapped, and it did explode none of the team wouldn't be hurt by the explosion. Danzer directed that two members of the team methodically continued to visually search the immediate area for trip wires or other out-of-the-ordinary items. Wes carefully tied the running ends of the ropes together, tying one end to his rucksack and taking the slack end, back and away from the rucksack.

Looking over his shoulder, Wes signaled that he was going to pull the rope. In turn, Danzer signed to the team to prone out on the ground. After everyone was safely down, Wes yanked the rope and the rucksack jerked toward him. No explosion. After lying still for a few more seconds, Wes rose to his feet and gradually headed toward the rucksack, opening it slowly in case trip wires were attached inside. He carefully examined the contents, pulling each item out one at a time. His claymore mines, M-14 toe poppers, chow and water were missing.

While Wes continued to search through his rucksack Danzer began to reform the team preparing to continue their mission towards the crash site. When the team was once again ready for movement Danzer had them up and pressing forward. The thick vegetation became thicker and more laboring as the team slow climbed the mountain side.

The vegetation below the double canopy was staggeringly thick. The smells of the jungle itself were pungent and almost took you breath away. Below the tree tops the breathable air seemed to evade each man's lungs as he put one step in front of the other. Profuse sweat saturated their fatigues as the sweat continued to form all over their bodies and run down their faces as they slowly continue to press forward.

The undergrowth on the floor of the jungle was horrendous and the terrain constantly became steeper with each step they took. Wes couldn't help but think about his M-14 toe poppers and claymore mine the enemy had taken from his rucksack. *"What if they had planted them around the downed chopper?"* While this possibility was real enough the only thing worse would be if the enemy troops were waiting for them to arrive at the crash site. If that happened, the team wouldn't be able to fight their way out.

Five hours had passed since the Bright Light had been inserted. Covey 247 had returned to base for fuel and had been replaced by Covey 224.

Danzer requested Covey to locate his position and make corrections to their line-of-march so that the team wouldn't over shoot or miss the crash site. Covey replied that he'd provide directions as soon as he located them on the ground.

The previous night at RT Pythons tiny hilltop fortification, the rain that had chilled us for hours was slowly dissipating. Since it had been quiet for over four hours now, I was concerned with what Charlie was up to. When I heard someone approaching my position from behind, I slowly repositioned my rifle for a confrontation. Jim Butler was making his way to me. Just as he came within arm's reach, a B-40 rocket broke the silence of the night and came hissing up at us from within the jungle, followed immediately by an explosion.

Everyone on my portion of the perimeter was temporarily blinded by the flash of the round as it impacted the hilltops edge, our night vision was totally eliminated by the unexpected sudden flash. The initial explosion triggered a volley of additional enemy rockets taking flight. One after another deafening blast shook the night, sending adrenaline pumping through the team's veins as we tried to sink deeper into our rain-filled foxholes.

Crawling forward to the front of my foxhole, I spotted an NVA gunner standing upright holding the weapons system on his shoulder as his rocket flew at us spewing a rain of deadly fire from behind it as it flew. Jim rushed back to the center of the perimeter to relay the ground attack information back to Phu Bai. As he picked up the radio, three more B-40s flew across the sky, followed by loud detonations as they impacted about five meters short of Profit's machine gun position.

Luckily, Profitt didn't return fire. Charlie was conducting yet another ground-probing action to get the defenders to fire back at them isolating and identifying the location of our automatic weapons. With my body half-submerged in the rain-filled foxhole, I moved to the front edge of my fighting position once again for a better view of the downhill slope. Watching for enemy movement down through the jungle that lies below us, seeing no moment or aggressive actions against us. I exited the back of the foxhole, leaving Jung with security detail. I wanted to see if Profitt or his crew had been injured, and to check for enemy soldiers creeping up the hill under diversion of the rockets.

Upon reaching Profitt, I asked if he was injured. His reply: "Hell, I don't know how I'm doing. I'm still cleaning the crap out of my pants." Without taking a breath and excited he continued, "We couldn't see anything during the B-40 attack, but I can hear heavy movement and talking down below about 25-40 meters away. They are up to something." Profit had barely finished his statement when more rockets were fired directly into our area. One ricocheted off the steep terrain and the second went above our heads off into the jungle behind us.

Over the detonation and explosions of the B-40s, I yelled over to Profit, "Don't fire your machine-gun; throw grenades. They're trying to get you to commit your machine gun so they can lock in on the weapon. Do not fire unless you have definite enemy targets or an all-out ground attack. And for Pete's sake, keep your ass down." Profitt screamed back at me, "I can hear them moving down below." I told him to hang tight and wait. He grabbed two M-26 grenades, holding one in each hand. Reminding him once again, I relayed, don't throw them yet. They're all still in the tree line. Let's wait and catch them out in the open."

As we both watched over the edge of the berm, a trip flare was set off on the southern sector of our perimeter, followed immediately by machine-gun fire. I made a mad dash over to Brazier, who was still firing the machine-gun. As I moved alongside him, I told him I was coming in behind him so he would know that I was there and wouldn't become frightened turn and shoot me. Moving forward I tried to see how many bad guys were coming up on us. Twenty NVA soldiers were charging up the hill directly in front of Braziers position. With the help of his assistant gunner, Brazier worked quickly and efficiently. The tracers from Brazier's machine-gun were on target.

As the 7.62mm M-60 machine-gun rounds entered then quickly exited their bodies, blood, tissue and parts of their uniforms were torn away and thrown through the air violently in every direction. They screamed in agony as Brazier's bullets tore through them. Another ground flare suddenly illuminated in the darkness about 25 meters to the right from the last one as we were looking down at their lifeless bodies. Again

Brazier swiftly orientated his machinegun in the direction of the ground flare and red tracers from his M-60 began filling the air with streaking, glowing red dots of death. Brazier fired only short distinct bursts. We weren't receiving any return fire so Brazier ceased firing and began his visual observation down the hill off into the battle field directly to his front. Occasionally, one of the NVA bodies would jerk from their motor nerve response. Although the NVA soldiers were quite dead, their nerves and brains were still firing off electrical impulses. Brazier had done an excellent job of stopping the advancing troops with very little expenditure of ammunition.

He and I lay still for 15 minutes watching, vigilantly scanning the down hill area before determining that the enemy assault on this position was temporarily halted. As I was leaving to find Jim, Brazier asked, "Any word on when the Bright Light will be going in to get Doc Watson, Sammy and Lloyd?" Turning back around, I replied, "We haven't heard much of anything back from Phu Bai, other than the Bright Light has been identified and will launch at first light tomorrow. Wes and Robby made it out. Wes is going to be leading the Bright Light team back into the crash site, at first light."

Brazier didn't respond, he just turned his head back to the front and maintained his attention back over the receiver group of his M-60. Brazier knew as well as anyone that the chances of anyone surviving the helicopter crash especially when they were on strings were almost nil. Although we tried to be optimistic, we knew deep down in our hearts that their chances were not good. I hurried to find Captain Butler. When I didn't spot him, I assumed he was out checking on his troops.

Without making a sound, Jim placed his hand on my shoulder to let me know he was there. I jumped in surprised fright turning rapidly towards him, "Shit, you scared the hell out of me. Man, I could have done you in. Don't pull that shit on me again." As he grinned and chuckled a little, I told him what had happened on Brazier's section of the perimeter. Jim began telling me of his suspicions, "Les, get ready for a push real soon from the NVA. While you were over with Brazier and Profitt, I heard a lot of rustling around down in the brush on the northern side, down in the ravine. I think they are going to send a small unit up that ravine and try to come in from behind us. I also think they are going to try a diversionary tactic on the opposite site of the perimeter, while this unit comes in from behind us. This is either going to happen tonight or prior to first light. We'll find out soon enough." Since that was my sector of the perimeter, I assured Jim that I would take care of it.

With that, I moved back towards my foxhole, attentively listening and watching for anything suspicious off in the direction of the ravine area. After an hour had passed, I was in desperate need of sleep. Out of sheer necessity, I fumbled around for my pillbox and grabbed two dextroamphetamines. No question about it, I had to stay awake and alert, especially now that the enemy was preparing another ground assault. Suddenly, a nicotine craving came over me and I grabbed a Vietnamese Bastos cigarette from my pocket. The aroma from the cigarette would gag a maggot, but it tasted good to me. Another 15 minutes passed, bringing the rising sun closer to illuminating this side of the world. The pills were beginning to revitalize me as I felt my second wind.

Jung tapped me on the arm, whispering in my ear, "NVA come." Sure enough, 20 meters down the hillside; a full squad of NVA regulars was coming out of the shadows. Evidently, they'd found our trip flares and disarmed them. What they hadn't realized was that they were moving through one of the only areas that had been defoliated. Their shadows and movement stood out as clear as day against the lighter background of the dirt. They had miscalculated in believing they could sneak up on us while it was semi-dark. Most likely, they had planned to move up into the ravine, lay low until a diversionary tactic was initiated and then rush up behind us while we fought the diversion from the front on top of the hill they would attack gaining access to us from the ravine area providing a surprise rear assault.

Fully aware of their attempts to back door us, I whispered to Jung, "I need you to come with me to interpret what I'm about to do. After you finish explaining to these guys, go back to our position and maintain security on our side of the hilltop." Jung and I rushed to the furthermost fighting positions and explained what we were about to do to two of the Little People. My plan was to slide off the backside of the hill and intercept the squad of NVA soldiers as they came up the ravine. After Jung verified that they fully understood the plan, I turned to him and stressed, "You just remember that we're down there, don't fire my ass up. Don't mistake us for the bad guys. Understand?" Jung replied, "No sweat, Trung-si."

Because each passing second brought more light, the three of us ran to the far side of the perimeter and quickly crawled off the hilltop before being spotted. The ravine we were in formed a semicircle around the foot of the hill, gradually emptying on the top. To their credit, the NVA had a good plan, had they initiated it earlier. Thankfully, we spotted them during their movement. Two Little People and I moved quietly through the shadows of the ravine, anticipating contact with the enemy at any moment.

The Asia sky continued to brighten as we made good time. The ravine made a hard right turn, leading down the hill away from us. I gave an arm signal to spread out. They responded without question or hesitation onto the other side of the narrowing ravine. Above us and to the south on the other side of our defensive perimeter came an explosion, followed by what sounded like hundreds of AK-47s firing. The response from our defenses was somewhat delayed, because initially there were no targets. All the enemy fire was coming from within the shadows of the jungle.

Almost on cue, the CAR-15s and M60 machine-guns began barking hot lead back down into the jungle. Firepower from both sides picked up in velocity and intensity. This was the diversion meant to draw our attention away from the north side, where the NVA soldiers were aggressively pushing up the ravine toward my two Little People and me. The three of us lay motionless, trying to blend into the last of the twilight shadows while enemy soldiers scurried upwards through the ravine. As they drew closer, they sounded like a herd of stampeding wild buffalo. I suddenly saw one NVA soldier round the corner of the ravine. Four others real close behind him, with the remainder of the squad trailing, closely followed him. They were running as fast as they could while climbing the steep hillside maintaining their eyes and focus on the ground as they climbed. Steadily, they advanced to within 10 meters of our small ambush position.

Bracing my CAR-15 against my side, I pointed at six NVA soldiers who were completely exposed in the center of the ravine I squeezed the trigger. My weapon came to life, immediately followed by my Little People's rifles. Empty .223 cartridges flew from the right side of our weapons as the bullets found their target. Three of the first group of NVA soldiers was killed instantly from our initial volley. They were dead before they had a chance to even point their weapons at me.

The NVA soldiers were totally unprepared for this offensive maneuver, never considering that we would meet them with force before they crested the hilltop. They had allowed themselves to become channelized in the ravine and we had the advantage of the high ground. There were only two ways for them to go, either up or down. Jung and his silent M-60 were patiently waiting for them to come out of the ravine. He would kill those that we missed as they chaotically retreated. Either way, they were all going to die.

After the first group of NVA soldiers had been killed, the fourth and fifth men fell to their knees, raising their rifles attempting to shoot us. However, by this time we'd reloaded we were just a split second faster, they to fell under the full wrath of three CAR-15s. The impact from the rounds literally picked them up and threw them back down the ravine head over heels. It was clear they were dead as their blood and tissue was tossed in every direction from the impact of the projectiles from out weapons. Unsure of our position, the rest of the squad began firing wildly. One of the enemy soldiers was so rattled that he killed two of his fellow soldiers shooting them in the back in the confusion of our counter ambush.

The small group of remaining troops turned and retreated back down the ravine. I began chasing after them while reloading, my attention focused solely on their backs, as they were the only thing visible. We lit them up. They didn't even know what hit them. The last four soldiers running down the ravine that we hadn't killed were now out in the open. Probably believing to be shielded from view, they headed back into the direction from which they'd come. Jung gave them a second surprise. Deadly with the M-60, Jung fired about 50 rounds of 7.62 mm, killing every one of them.

Although the fighting on this section of the perimeter had ceased, the other side of the hilltop raged violently with weapons fire. Realizing that Jim needed us, we ran back up the ravine. Our breathing was labored, sweat rolled down our faces and our leg muscles were on fire as we aggressively made our way back up. Finally, the hill top embankment came into view and I moved to the front of the formation. I wanted to be the first person to be scene by the team as we crested the hill top and reentered back into our perimeter so that our Little People didn't get mistaken for bad guys and get fired up.

As we reached the top of the hill, Jim knelt there waiting, weapon at the ready, concern in his eyes. He yelled, "Man, get your ass up here. They are hitting us from two sides at once. We've got wounded. We need all of the firepower we can get to beat back the attack." Jim and I together sprinted to the south side of the perimeter where Brazier was traversing his M-60 from left to right. Just prior to reaching his position, Jim and I went down on our bellies, crawling alongside him. Seeing that he was frantically firing, we peeked over the embankment and saw 30-50 hardcore NVA soldiers charging up the hill and closing the distance on us very quickly.

I remembered that I'd set up the 60mm mortar and ran back to the center of the perimeter. Grasping the mortar tube in my left hand, I sat down on the base plate to orient it straight up-and-down. Next, I grabbed one of the 60mm high explosive mortar rounds, dropped it into the tube and fired it straight into the air. Quickly recognizing that I needed help as I fidgeted around for another round, one of the Little People left his fighting position to come to my aid. I didn't need distance with these explosive rounds, I needed close in firepower. As the Little Guy reached my position, he slid into the shallow mortar pit like he was sliding into second base. Quickly, he handed me another mortar round. With the tube still oriented straight up-and-down, I began dropping round after round down the tube.

Five rounds were in flight when the first one hit the ground detonating behind the advancing NVA assaulters. The first was too long. However, the second, third and fourth rounds began walking their way into the advancing forces. Jim screamed over the explosions for me to bring it in closer. Then, again he screamed "Damn it, I said bring it in closer." Canting the tube more, I shoved three rounds in and waited for Jim's corrections on where they were landing. Obviously, the winds above were pushing the rounds towards our attackers. My assistant gunner had six more rounds ready for me to drop down the tube. The second set of mortar rounds began hitting directly on the southern slope with great accuracy, impacting right in front and on top of the still enemy solders. Again Jim yelled, "Keep it up! Drop some more rounds! You're hitting dead on target."

The first round exploded in the middle of the NVA troops, while the second and third threw red-hot shrapnel throughout their ranks; bodies, masses of blood and flesh exploded in every direction, altering their advance. In a desperate attempt to escape the hell of hot metal falling down some of them, broke-off the attack and ran back down the hillside as Brazier fired his machine-gun at their backs for another few seconds.

As I prepared to drop another three rounds down the mortar tube, all gunfire stopped. Silence mysteriously returned to the battlefield. I sat motionless listening to the ear piercing silence then slowly raised to my feed and left the mortar position with reservation, I headed toward Jim and Brazier.

Brazier didn't acknowledge my presence he maintained his focus and total attention over the barrel of his smoking machine gun. Jim ran back from Braziers fighting position to call in a situation report with the Phu Bai launch site, pulling his handset away from his ear long enough to yell over to Profitt, "Watch your sector. They are going to hit us from that side at any second." Jim then yelled over to me, "Get me a situation report on our dead and wounded, quick!"

As Jim reported our situation to Phu Bai, I began appraising the enemy killed, weapons they carried and the overall determination of our current friendly situation. I reported to Jim who kept the handset to his ear as he echoed my report into the radio as I spoke:

Delta Zulu (Phu Bai), this is Whisky Mike, over.

Roger Whisky Mike, this is Delta Zulu. We are prepared to copy, over.

Delta Zulu, approximately 50 to 70 NVA killed, unknown number of NVA wounded. We were attacked by an estimated reinforced platoon-sized element, standard weapons: AK-47s, RPDs, SKSs and B-40s. We have sustained six wounded and no KIAs at this point. We beat back their initial assault and are preparing for them to launch a second attack, how copy, over?

Whisky Mike, that's a good copy. 50 – 70 NVA KIA, attacked by an estimated reinforced platoon-sized element, enemy weapons AKs, RPDs, SKSs and B-40s. Understand that you have sustained six wounded. Are you declaring an extraction at this time, over?

Jim suddenly screamed angrily into the handset:

Delta Zulu, this is Whisky Mike, that's a negative on extraction. I repeat that's a negative on extraction. We will stay in this position while the Bright Light is on the ground. If we come out, the Bright Light will have no commo back to you. We will let you know our decision on extraction when the Bright Light is extracted from the AO (area of operation) and all personnel are accounted for and not until then! Do you understand? How copy, over?

Whisky Mike, this is Delta Zulu, good copy on negative extraction, will be standing-by, over.

Jim continued to listen to the person on the other end of the radio; then like a rocket lit at both ends Jim went off:

Delta Zulu, this is Whisky Mike, listen to me, asshole. We are staying. We will be able to take care of ourselves until you get the Bright Light is out, we are not going anywhere, negative further, out.

Jim threw the radio handset at his rucksack, becoming more irate, "those sorry fuckers, I can't believe how stupid and ignorant Elliott is. How he ever became an officer is beyond me. He said we are on our own if we don't come out now. If he were here, I would personally toss his ass off this mountain and let the NVA deal with him." Knowing better than to say anything, because it would be like throwing gasoline on an open fire, I just let him rant and rave. As he slowly began to calm down, he took a deep breath then inquired, "How's our ammunition holding up?"

I told him I hadn't checked that yet, but would get right on it. Calling to me as I left, he said, "Hey, make sure our people are all okay." I didn't respond I just went about my duties as One-one. We had sustained six minor wounded and had no friendly KIAs. I patched up the wounded, removed any visible shrapnel from their bodies and put them back in their positions.

Our ammunition supplies were in good shape, the team's spirits were high and we were ready to take on whatever the bad brought our way. I returned to the commo position and before I could render him a report Jim updated me on the Bright Light team that had been inserted about 30 minutes previously. As he was explaining the current situation with Bright Light, Covey low leveled directly overhead about 30 feet off the hilltop causing us to duck for cover.

Surprised, at the sudden roar of Covey's engines directly overhead, we all dove to the ground. I didn't know until then that Jim had been wounded in the back while we were conducting our ambush. I immediately went to work on his wound. He'd caught some small fragments in his back from a grenade or B-40. As I lifted his jacket, I saw three small fragmentation wounds with small droplets of blood trickling out of each puncture hole. There wasn't anything I could extract, just pinhead-sized fragments just below the skin. As I put some dressings on him I joked, "Man, you'll be picking this shit out of you for a long time. Every time it bugs you, think of me."

I could tell from Jim's expression that he was worried about our friends Doc Watson, Lloyd and the remainder of RT Intruder. Turning to face me, he asked, "Les do you think Doc and the others made it?" I responded honestly, "Jim, I sure hope so. But you know as well as I do, if they went down with the helicopter, it's all over. If they were alive, they would have used their beepers. On the other hand, they may have had bad guys around them all night and couldn't transmit. I sure hope we hear some positive response from RT Habu because they'll relay the information back to Phu Bai thru you." Pulling Jim's fatigue jacket back down over his back, neither of us said anything more.

When I returned to my foxhole, I addressed my assistant, "Jung, you did real well today taking down those NVA out in the open. We need to make sure the M-60 is oiled and ready to continue to operate. It rained quite a bit last night and I don't want our weapons rusting up on us. I'm pretty sure that when the sun goes down again, we are going to be doing a lot of shooting." Nodding his head in agreement, Jung pulled out his weapon cleaning kit and went to work oiling the M-60.

Next, I checked on Profitt, who was still cautiously peeking over the lip of the embankment. He turned to me and began a dialogue, "man, when all those B-40s came firing down on us, I almost crapped my pants. By the way, what happened on your side of the hill? I saw you and a couple of the Little People slide off and then it sounded like you were having your own private little war of your own down there. And while that was going on, Brazier's M-60 went nuts. Man, I tell you, this type of shit is not what's happening I think I'll just stay a REMF."

I replied, "Hey bubba, you ain't seen nothing yet. Wait until the sun goes down and it gets dark again." Continuing with the story, I explained, "As for what happened in the ravine, a bunch of gooks tried to sneak up on us. I saw them and we laid out an ambush of our own. You should have seen their faces when we opened up on them." Profitt shook his head and said, "Man you've really lost it, going over the side like that. What if you had been hit down there, there would be no way we could have gotten to you. Man, you're nuts! Please do not do that kind of shit anymore. Please!"

Leaving Profitt still shaking his head, I moved to Brazier's position. Brazier had already oiled his machine-gun and was back on security watch, staring down emotionlessly at dead NVA bodies his eyes roaming back and for the along and down the edge of the slopes leading down from his fighting position. I lit a cigarette took a hefty drag then passed it over to him he took it in turn took a long drag off of it them pass to over to his assistant gunner.

Without speaking, I lay down beside Brazer and his assistant gunner. None of us had gotten any sleep over the past 36 hours and we were beginning to drone (staring off into space, in a daydream like trance). I broke the silence by saying, "Babe, you really know how to work that machine-gun. If it hadn't been for you, I think that they might have gotten on top of the hill with us." Brazier didn't respond, he just looked over at me and slowly turned his head back to the front. He was on his second trip here in the Nam and it still bothered him to have to kill men. Brazier had performed his job perfectly, and the proof of his efficiency lay dead in front of his position.

Leaving him alone with his thoughts, I crawled from post to post making sure everyone was awake and alert. After visual confirmation that the team was okay, I made my way back to Jim's radio position. Since he had the headset to his ear almost all night and today, I asked if we had heard any more new or info on the status of The Bright Light. Without speaking or moving the handset from his ear, he motioned negatively with his head. I told him that everyone was tired and that our adrenaline rush was definitely on the downward slide. I asked if there was any specific task he needed me to take care of. Again, he shook his head negatively.

I was in dire need of rest but like the others I couldn't let down my guard, I returned to my foxhole to sit with Jung. The noonday sun glared down on us with a vengeance from overhead, as we lay completely exposed to its full intensity. Many of the Little People propped their ponchos up over their fighting positions to get some relief and shade from the blistering sun and heat. After lying down for more than three hours, I made another tour of the perimeter. The enemy hadn't made any moves against us since their early morning thrust. However, at this stage of the game, it was highly likely that they would and could attack any moment. As I passed each position, I directed everyone to take two dextroamphetimines and stay alert.

Jim was still at his radio listening position, handset glued to his ear. No one was transmitting over the air. Jim just sat listening just in case they came on line. As I was returning to my defensive position, I noticed a couple of the Little People staring oddly at an adjacent hill about 75 meters away. When I asked them what they were looking at, they pointed in the direction of a lone tree surrounded by tall elephant grass then returned to jabbering among them selves. I immediately called Jung over to find out what was going on. He explained calmly, "they see a VC on the hill, looking at us. He is moving with the elephant grass from behind the tree when the wind blows it from side to side. Every time the elephant grass moves, he moves with it."

Curious, I sat down and began focusing my total attention on the tree and elephant grass that surrounded it. For more than half an hour, I watched, and began to think they might have been hallucinating from the lack of sleep and the consumption of the dextroamphetamines (green hornets). I decided to watch a couple of more minutes, when suddenly I picked him up as he moved with the blowing grass. He was checking out our positions to report back to his superiors in preparation for the upcoming night attack.

I decided to take care of him once and for all myself. As he moved behind the small tree, waiting for his next opportunity for an outward movement, I assumed a prone firing position with my CAR-15 extended, tightly pressed into my right shoulder taking aim at where I had last observed him.

I didn't have to wait long for him to reappear. Ever so slowly, he began to make his appearance with the movement of the elephant grass. Once his head and upper body were completely exposed, I squeezed off a single round, striking him above his throat. His head and body jerked back violently, skull exploding from the impact then disappearing. Jim came running to see what was going on. I explained what had transpired. We all lay motionless, staring at the last known position in case an undetected spotter was set to continue the task. Finally, we felt confident that we'd remedied the spying situation and returned to our positions. For the remainder of the day atop the abandoned American firebase, RT Python's exhausted defenders simply waited, and then waited some more for an attack.

Not a single moment went by without Jim or me holding the radio next to our ear, listening for any word from the Bright Light. The sun slowly began to make its way off into the west, and the monsoon rain clouds began forming. Suddenly, a horrible thought washed over me, "if they don't get the Bright Light out prior to the rains starting, then they won't have any overhead aircraft cover to support them if they get into a world of hurt. If they get into trouble, they'll be on their own to fight it out."

# CHAPTER 19 (A SHAU)

Recon Team Habu was less than 300 yards from the crash site. Having traversed more than a mile through the jungle, they were drenched in sweat, tired, hungry and mentally drained. Despite sensing they all knew they were entering a trap, still they drove hard, negotiating almost impassable terrain in hopes of recovering RT Intruder and the downed pilots and crew. Partly due to physical exhaustion, the team was becoming somewhat careless and was nowhere near as observant as they were immediately after insertion. The hot Asian sun was now completely blotted out by thick concentrated monsoon cloud cover and the rains began to pour down on them with a vengeance.

The water assaulted down on RT Habu as if being blasting from a fire hose. Danzer quickly gathered the team in search of a rest-overnight position, having spotted a location during their travels on the way up the steep terrain. As the team knelt in a security halt, Danzer and two of the Little People went to recon the RON site. Thirty minutes passed while they scouted the area, finally deciding they were fairly safe with the site selection Danzer had chosen. The two scouts returned to the team and everyone moved into their respective RON position.

After an extensive waiting period in the RON site, the men went about positioning the claymore mines out and proceeded to eat their evening meal. Every other man on RT Habu quickly ate, while his teammate maintained watch providing him security. Within 30 minutes, the entire team had eaten and was back on full alert. Everyone tried to bolster their position by camouflaging the immediate area around them. Night was quickly approaching and who knew what the evil it would bring with it?

Somewhere high above the clouds, Covey raced his engines, alerting the One-zero that he had information to pass to him. Danzer keyed the handset and began transmitting to his invisible life-line high above:

Covey, this is Charlie Whiskey, over.

Charlie Whiskey, this is Covey 227, over.

Covey 227, we are in our RON position, about 200 meters south of the crash site. We'll continue to move to the crash site at first light to recover any survivors or bodies, how copy, over?

Charlie Whiskey, this is Covey 227, that's a good copy. Be advised that I just tried to fly over the crash site but couldn't get in due to the heavy cloud and rain cover. It's going to be another wet one. I will not be able to cover you tonight, but RT Python is monitoring our conversation as we speak. They'll stay on the horn all night listening on your frequency if you need them, over.

Covey 227, understand RT Python will be monitoring the radio all night. We are going to hunker down and wait for the sun to come up before we move to the crash site. Also, will you be on station when we get ready to move to the crash sight at first light? We may need some help, over.

Charlie Whiskey, this is Covey 227 that's affirmative, will be with you prior to first light and stay with you until I am low on fuel. Then, I'll be replaced by Covey 221 to cover you until I return good buddy, over.

Covey 227, thank you much. Hopefully, we'll see you when the sun comes up, out.

As Covey's engines slowly faded, Danzer reattached the radio handset back to his web gear for easy access during the darkness. The valley below was now completely obscured and the team was surrounded by fog, rain and darkness. They lay with their feet toward the center of the perimeter in a wagon-wheel formation, each man representing a spoke on the wheel. Hours passed with everyone being soaked to the bone and shivering uncontrollably as their body temperature dropped. Finally, it became so miserably wet and cold that Danzer crawled around the perimeter suggesting that every other man climb into a body bag to get some warmth and relief from the rain while the others held watch.

As instructed, the first group hesitantly climbed into the empty reinforced rubber bags. The idea of getting into bags designed to carry dead soldiers was mentally challenging and physiologically horrifying, to say the least. However, it was their only means of sheltering themselves from the down pour and cold. Eventually, everyone took his turn inside the bags.

Everyone that is, except Wes. Initially, he flatly refused to get into a body bag to escape the elements in this bizarre fashion. Only after his intense misery and discomfort constantly increasing beyond his level of tolerance, did he realize it was his only option. Almost as soon as he entered the bag, Wes began to think about the dead. He'd read that the brain continues to emit slight brain waves even after physical death. Then another horrifying thought crossed his mind, *"If your brain is working after you are dead, your hearing must be working too."* His emotions and imagination began to overtake him as he continued along this line of insane reasoning.

*"What if you were dead, locked inside one of these rubber coffins, and you could hear men on the outside telling the world that you were dead? How many men have I put into body bags while they heard me talking about them being dead?"* It was too much for Wes to handle; Wes couldn't breathe anymore. Desperately, he searched for the zipper as the bag began to slowly squeeze in on him, clinging to his skin and wet fatigues. He felt entombed; and he had to break free. Just before he was about to pull out his SOG knife to cut himself out, he found the zipper and jerked it all the way down. T he cool breeze rushed over him, bringing reality back with it. Wes returned to his defensive position, quite satisfied to lie in the rain and cold.

At 0300 hours, the rains finally stopped. Danzier directed the men in the body bags to pack them back into their rucksacks. As quickly as possible, they followed his directions, silently returning to their defensive positions. Because the morning twilight had yet to arrive, they had no visual defenses. Instead, they strained theirs ears to hear approaching enemy movement. Unknown to them, the NVA had purposely allowed them in, and had been monitoring their every move. They'd let them in, but they didn't intend to let them out.

Finally, the sun began to force itself upon the earth, revealing an oppressive three-foot high fog sheet swirling over everything for miles. Hidden beneath the fog, the team was visually obscured from sight. Instinctively, some of the team members wanted to stand and gaze above the ground fog to see what the NVA was up to. With great self-discipline and training, the brave men of The Bright Light remained hidden beneath the ground fog. Recognizing the need for movement out of the team's RON, Danzer ordered the retrieval of the claymores, and then moving the team off in the direction of the crash site.

Covey 224 was overhead and began racing his engines. Danzer reached for the handset awaiting Covey's transmission. The radio squelched:

> Oscar Bravo, this is Covey 224, over.

> Covey 224, this is Oscar Bravo, over.

> Oscar Bravo, this is the back seater, if you are moving at this time, squelch your radio handset twice, over.

Following the directions of the experienced covey-rider, whom Danzer recognized as Fernandez, he confirmed their movement.

> Oscar Bravo, this is Covey 224, roger babe, understand that you are moving to the crash site at this time. Just have a little information to pass on. Do not acknowledge just listen. RT Python got hit pretty hard last night and again this morning. Some wounded, but they are refusing to be extracted until you are extracted. I'll be circling around over RT Python's position, waiting for you to make contact when you reach the crash site. If you understand, squelch your radio twice, over.

Once again, Danzer acknowledged that he understood the transmission.

RT Python sat atop their tiny firebase as night fell. Everything had been quiet since their early morning attack, although the NVA still had us surrounded. Occasionally, we'd hear heavy troop movement off in different sectors of the jungle below us and we would lob an M-79 (40mm grenade launcher) rounds in the general vicinity of the noise. So far, they hadn't returned fire, but we knew they were maneuvering into position for a last light or middle-of-the-night ground attack.

Like clockwork, ugly gray clouds began to form off to the west. Meanwhile, the unforgiving hot sun continued to blister down on us. The breathable air a top the firebase was extremely heavy there wasn't any type of breeze even slightly moving only the stillness of the jungle and the surrounding areas. While most of the team tried to get some rest. I'd been unable to sleep because of the dextroamphetamines I'd taken earlier. All I could think of when I was trying to rest was, *"Damn it is hot up here."*

Jim out in the open sat with the radio plastered to his ear, regularly informing me of the Bright Light's status. According to the last report, The Bright Light had made it to the crash site and was in the process of removing the bodies, placing them on top of the burned helicopter, awaiting extraction. As I slowly conducted another perimeter check, Jim began frantically waving his arms at me trying to get my attention. I quickly moved to his location and he blurted out, "Danzer and the Bright Light just made contact with the enemy. Covey is over them now, providing them air support and trying to expedite the extraction choppers from Phu Bai to get them out."

In the middle of the explanation, he abruptly stopped, gesturing with his free finger for me to wait. Something else was coming in over the radio. For a few moments Jim sat motionless, listening closely to the transmission and conversation. As he slowly pulled the handset away from his ear, he cursed, "Holy Hell! Covey's been shot down, just south of the crash site. The Bright Light is in heavy contact with the enemy and was forced to retreat, leaving the bodies on top of the downed chopper. Damn, what else is going to happen?"

Not knowing what to say, fear and concern for my brothers in the field radiated wildly throughout my very sole, I stared wide eyed at Jim in disbelief. It was extremely uncommon for a Covey to get shot down.

Since my arrival at CCN, two Coveys had gone in; both ran into the side of a mountain during limited visibility. Never had I heard of one being shot down by ground fire. The Bright Light was in a hornet's nest just north of us. As I continued to stare at Jim, his facial expression reflected anger and deep concern. He wanted to do anything possible to help the Bright Light. But, all we could do was listen over the radio.

Seeing that Jim was busy coordinating for assets in a futile attempt to help, I rose to my feet. As I stood erect, subconscious mental pictures of each of the team member's faces flashed before my eyes. We were hopelessly standing by, unable to help them just simply listening to our brother's die. Knowing it was vital to stay focused on our situation, I continued making perimeter rounds, passing information on concerning the Bright Light's status and the downed Covey as I went. If the extraction package didn't make it quick, the Bright Light would spend the evening fighting off the NVA.

Back at MLT-2 Quang Tri, Pappy Budrow had diverted their Covey to the downed O-2 crash site and to provide assistance to the Bright Light should they need it. The back-seater, Sergeant First Class David Cheney had run lots of recon missions and was known as one of the best covey-riders in all of Southeast Asia. David was tall with a slender build. Although only 32-years old, he looked to be in his 40's with lines of close calls etched deeply into his face. Hearing Covey approaching, I moved to the center of our perimeter where Jim joined me. Standing side-by-side, we looked to the north as Covey circled and waited for the extraction package to arrive.

As I watched, I thought of Jim's tenacity and continuous vigil in monitoring the radio hour after hour any other conventional commander who have gotten off this hill top after the first major contact with the enemy. In a few minutes, I wandered back to my foxhole and sat down in the shade of the cover Jung had temporarily constructed.

Movement was slow, physically draining and psychologically challenging for the Bright Light team as they moved. As the RT Habu began closing in on the crash site, the once almost impassable thick vegetation began thinning out somewhat. Off to the left of their line of movement was a 20-25 foot sheer drop-off, a natural rock formation they were being forced to follow. The terrain began to become steeper and much slicker, with thick clumps of jungle vegetation scattered in every direction. Stopping the team, Danzer motioned for Wes to come to him. Whispering, he asked, "Wes, how much farther to the site?"

Wes had been watching the terrain features all the while the team was moving, but was unable to recognize much. Because the jungle changes daily, it's common to become disoriented. Looking back at Danzer, he replied, "This area doesn't look the same to me. I don't think we came in from this direction. I think we were more to the south. Let's go up about another 100 meters and let me have a look there." Danzer nodded in agreement and signaled the team to proceed higher up the mountainside, traversing more to the south along the ridgeline.

Beads of sweat rolled down their faces as they struggled forward. The team had gone another 100 meters when Danzer motioned for the group to stop. Wes once again came forward and knelt along side Danzer, searching with his head and eyes at his surroundings for any recognizable terrain features. Shaking his head, he replied, "Man, nothing looks the same. It's like we're in some other world. We're not in the right place, we have to be farther south."

Danzer had concluded that this stop-and-go movement was taking too much time. The easiest and quickest way for them to reach their objective was to have Covey come over and talk them in. Reaching for his radio, he spoke softly into the mouthpiece:

> Covey 224, this is Oscar Bravo, over.
>
> Oscar Bravo, this is Covey 224, over.
>
> Covey 224, we are having trouble finding the crash site, need for you to talk us into it. How copy, over?
>
> Oscar Bravo, this is Covey 224, that's a-roger I'm on my way to your location now. Talk me into your immediate location. The back-seater and I will be looking for you, over.

Knowing what was transpiring high in the air and on the ground, the team patiently maintained a security posture, keeping a close watch out of their perimeter on their surroundings. Covey's engines could be heard through the jungle as they approached the semi-lost team. Danzer had one of the Little People break out his signal panel and began popping it. As Covey drew nearer, Danzer began to talk Covey into the team's general location.

Covey 224, this is Oscar Bravo, over.

Oscar Bravo, this is Covey 224, over.

Covey 224 this is Oscar Bravo, from your current direction of flight, we are off to your three o'clock, over.

Oscar Bravo, this is Covey 224, roger, over.

Covey 224, keep coming, keep coming. Bingo, Bingo, Bingo, over.

Oscar Bravo, we have a good tally on your location. You are about 100 meters north of the crash site. You need to continue climbing up the mountainside, pressing hard northwest. If you follow the information I just provided, you'll run right into it. I'll fly directly over the site and gun my engines to orient your movement, how copy, over?

Covey 224, this is Oscar Bravo, thank you much, we're up and moving now, out.

While still on the radio, Danzer gave the signal to move out and the point man acknowledged his understanding of their direction of movement. The team tightened up the formation so there was less distance between troops, and made it to the crash site in less than an hour and a half.

Immediately upon entering into the crash site Danzer directed Cliff Newman to be in charge of establishing site security while another portion of the team was directed to begin searching for the bodies. Cliff ordered the Little People to place the claymores out he positioned their automatic weapons systems facing towards those danger areas that he had identified. Within minutes, the team's security element was in place and prepared to intercept the enemy if they attempted any type of ground movement against the team's location.

As Mac, Jimmy Horton and Wes stood beside staring at the once flying machine it looked distorted, and un-recognizable as once having been a helicopter. What was left of the helicopter lay bent and distorted scattered all over the wet jungle floor. It gave off the appearance of a metallic fly after it had been hit by a giant fly swatter. Having burned it self out, the chopper's magnesium frame and skin were just molten chunks of nothing all melted together. The only part recognizable of this molten pile of junk was a portion of the frame, skids, part of the chin bubble, a small portion of the tail section and of course the charred bodies inside.

Both pilots were still strapped into their seats, harnesses burned and melted into their chests. Hopefully they had been killed before they crashed or died upon impact, thus denying them the agony of being burned to death with the aircraft. Both bodies were nothing more than black; foul smelling charred hunks of meat, burned beyond any human recognition.

Moving directly to the lifeless bodies, Wes and McGlothren proceeded to slowly and respectfully cut them out and away from their seats. Rigor mortis had set in on the pilot and was preventing them from getting him into the body bag. They had to forcibly press down on his limbs to bend them back into their natural position in order to get him totally inside the bag.

Mac was on the verge of vomiting the entire time they were performing their gruesome duty. They then began removing the peter pilot. It was obvious that he had died an agonizing death in the flames. His arms were raised as if he were trying to frantically climb out of the flaming inferno, but had been overtaken by pain and the tremendous heat from the fire. As they removed him from his chair, he literally fell into pieces. Shocked and startled, Wes and Mac dropped him both men jumping back and away, recoiling away from the separated limbs of this thing that had once been a human being. Quickly regaining their composure, the two men began picking up the body parts, individually placing them into the black body bag.

With both pilots respectfully placed side-by-side on top of the burned helicopter, Wes, Mac and Horton began cautiously looking for the crew chief and assistant crew chief. Their bodies weren't inside or around the chopper, which meant they had either been captured, escaped or were thrown away from the aircraft upon impact. The search didn't take long for not more than about 25 meters from where the helicopter rested; they found the body of the crew chief in the fork of a tree. He was on his back inside the fork of the tree, staring blindly toward the heavens. His eyes were half closed and his facial muscles drawn tight, as if he had been in great pain. Before he could relax from the pain, he had died.

Wes pulled off his rucksack, removed the body bag he'd carried in spread the bag at the foot of the tree as he watched Mac climb to the fork and begin lowering the dead 20-year old crew chief down to their waiting arms. Wes and Horton reached as high as they could to receive the body.

Suddenly, a chill came over Wes as he recalled his terrorizing experience inside the body bag the previous night. He couldn't fight off the thoughts that ran through his mind when he was in the bag, *"I wonder if he can hear us and know what we are doing to him?"* When Wes and Horton placed the lifeless young man into the bag, they were startled. As soon as the body hit the ground, the air that had been trapped in the dead soldier's lungs escaped, passing by his vocal cords, resulting in a gasping noise. Wes dropped the dead young soldier's body to the ground with a thud and stood looking down at him. Wes then leaned over re-grabbed the young man by his shoulders and swung his swollen body inside the bag, then quickly yet firmly zipping it shut.

They returned his body to the helicopter and gently laid the crew chief beside the two pilots. A single leg had been found close to the crash, but there was no body attached to it. Where could this man be? The team spread out and began a clover-leafing maneuver in and out of the perimeter, searching for his remains. Most pilots and crew laced one of their personal dog tags into the bottom eyelets of their bootlaces for this very reason. It was just added insurance that if something like this were to happen, they could at least be identified and properly tagged.

Thus far, they had recovered Specialist Gary Johnson, Chief Warrant Officer George Berg, Warrant Officer Gerald Woods and the leg of Specialist Walter Demsey. But the body of Demsey couldn't be located.

The search continued for an hour until they had extended past their security perimeter. Then, they'd begin the search again but to no avail. They jointly began to review various scenarios of what might have happened to Demsey, the most plausible being that Demsey had been trapped under the burning helicopter when it crashed. They theorized that he had been thrown clear of the chopper as it came down through the trees, and fell beneath it as it impacted the ground, killing him instantly. Despite there agreed upon assumptions, they continued to search for his body.

As Jimmy Horton extended his search deeper into the jungle near the rock-face cliff, he came across three stabo ropes lying on the ground, trailing off and over the edge of the cliff. Holding the ropes in his hands, Jimmy came to the lip of the cliff that plummeted straight down. His visibility was obstructed by thick vegetation hanging over the naturally camouflaged ledge. Lying on his stomach, he placed as much of his body out over the edge as possible to try and see what hung from these ropes. After several moments, Jimmy was able to focus about 20 feet down the cliff.

There, hanging smashed against the rocks were the bodies of Doc Watson and Lloyd. There was no movement; they simply hung limp and lifeless in their stabo harnesses. Their arms dangled at their sides. Their weapons were still snap-linked to their stabo rigs and hung loosely against their chests, rucksacks still on their backs. Rising quickly, Jimmy left one of the Little People at the site while he moved rapidly through the jungle to report his discovery. As Jimmy moved, he heard thrashing noises in the vegetation coming toward him. With his CAR-15 raised, safety off, set on fully automatic, Jimmy knelt to camouflage himself in the thick vegetation. That was when he saw Danzer, Mac and Wes coming through the undergrowth towards him.

Jimmy stood up and announced "I found Watson and Lloyd over the side of the cliff, hanging from their stabo ropes, smashed into the rock-face cliff." The four men moved directly to the cliff. It was obvious that the NVA hadn't investigated the crash site yet or they would have cut these ropes, causing the bodies to plunge to the bottom.

Slowly and cautiously, the four men lay on their stomachs stretching as far as they could to peer over the edge. Just as Jimmy had said, there dangling from the ends of the stabo ropes were Doc Watson and Lloyd. Trickles of blood had run down the sides their mouths, ears and nose. Lacerations and abrasions were also highly visible. Before the search party could put together a plan for retrieving their fallen comrades, one of the Montagnards came running, reporting to Danzer, "VC come." The tail gunner had observed two NVA soldiers watching the team recover bodies. Danzer and the other three Americans sprinted back toward the defensive perimeter.

The security posture Newman had put in place was not meant to defend the crash site for a long period of time or as a final fighting place. Their primary mission was to recover survivors or bodies and get out. To stay at the crash site and attempt to defend it was ludicrous. The site contained helicopter debris, obstacles, jagged metal and other obstructions too dangerous to negotiate in the daylight much less at night. If darkness set in or the One-Zero had to move internally in the darkness, he was a sitting duck. Danzer knew he had to move post haste. He signaled the team to recover their claymores. Once this was completed he directed the team to execute an immediate action (IA) withdrawal drill, heading back down the hill while not firing, only quietly moving away from the crash site.

They were all reluctant to leave the bodies of the crew on top of the helicopter, not to mention Doc Watson and Lloyd left hanging from the side of the cliff. Nevertheless, they had to get away from this crash site. If enemy observers were watching them, the main body of the NVA wasn't far away. Danzer wanted to put as much distance between the Bright Light and the enemy as possible.

As they continued to execute their withdrawal drills, the cliff's sharp drop-off to their left flank looming like a death sign, the jungle suddenly came to life with enemy automatic weapon fire directed at them from three distinct directions. The NVA had purposely allowed the team to walk into the crash site. Now it was time to deny them the recovery of their fellow soldiers and kill them in the process. The Bright Light instinctively returned fire at invisible targets. Danzer grabbed the radio to contact Covey:

Covey 224, this is Oscar Bravo, over.

Oscar Bravo, this is Covey 224, over.

Covey 224, this is Oscar Bravo we have made contact with the NVA and are receiving automatic weapons fire from all directions. I'm declaring a Prairie Fire; I say again I'm declaring a Prairie Fire. I need some help now! Over.

Oscar Bravo, understand that you are declaring a Prairie Fire, will have the extraction assets launch immediately to your location.

Break, Break.

Oscar Bravo, this is the back seater, the pilot is calling back to the launch site for the extraction package to be launched. Need to know how many and where the bad guys are. Over.

Covey 224, this is Oscar Bravo, babe unable to determine how many bad guys at this time, only know that we are taking heavy enemy fire from three different directions, about 50-60 meters from my location. Am popping smoke at this time for you to pinpoint our location, over.

Oscar Bravo this is Covey 224, the extraction package is on its way. We are rolling in at this time to pick up your smoke. I will identify, how copy, over?

Covey 224, that's a good copy, over.

The team continued to lay down a heavy base of fire against the enemy's automatic weapons locations. Despite the Bright Light's massive return-fire, the enemy's consistent high volume of fire never faltered. From their positions, Wes and Horton observed four NVA soldiers charging them less than 10 yards away. The two Americans responded by firing their CAR-15s simultaneously and with deadly accuracy. Wes watched as the CAR-15 bullets impacted the advancing troops. Enemy uniforms and flesh exploded into a cloudy pink reddish mist. Not only did the impact penetrate vital organs, it tossed their bodies backwards and all over the ground.

Wes lay on his back, reloading his Car 15 when he observed Covey up through the double canopy trees as he flew over their location. The O-2 appeared to be in a steep left bank. All Wes could see was the top of the wings where the fuselage should be. Thinking to himself as he flew past that Covey couldn't see their smoke if he was flying upside down. Wes immediately realized something was terribly wrong with Covey. He could hear Covey's engines performing at maximum RPMs, followed by a whining sound. A few seconds passed. After one second seeing Covey upside down his engines roaring and so low a thunderous crashing sound echoed from off to the south, then dead silence from the Coveys engines.

Through the hail of enemy gunfire, everyone on the ground looked horrified at each other with disbelief with what they knew just occurred. What had they just witnessed? Had in fact Covey crashed? Cliff Newman through the hail of enemy bullets crawled forward to Danzer and said, "What the fuck was that noise? It sounded like Covey crashed." Danzer just nodded his head in conformation, adding, "I don't have commo with him anymore.

Immediately, Danzer was on the radio back to MLT-1 reporting his suspicions:

> Oscar Mike, Oscar Mike, this is Oscar Bravo, over.
>
> Oscar Bravo, this is Oscar Mike, over.
>
> Oscar Mike, I report that Covey 224 is down east of my position. I repeat Covey 224 is down east of my position. How copy, over?
>
> Oscar Bravo, this is Oscar Mike, good copy. Did you see any parachutes or are you receiving a beeper, over?
>
> Oscar Mike, this is Oscar Bravo, that's a negative. I repeat that's a negative. What are your orders? Continue mission or attempt to break contact and go down to the Covey crash site to search for survivors, over?

> Oscar Bravo, this is Oscar Mike, continue to monitor your survival radio and we are going to call in a SAR (US Air Force Sea, Air, Rescue) mission, over.

> Oscar Mike, this is Oscar Bravo, continuing mission, out.

MLT-1 had immediately called for the launch of a SAR mission out of NKP (Na Kom Pha Nom), Thailand. Unknown to the launch site, Lieutenant Hull had already alerted NKP to launch a SAR Mission in anticipation of the Bright Light team not getting out of the crash site. The SAR mission consisted of one Jolly Green (CH-53) helicopter and a set of A-1E Sky Raiders (known as Spads, Nails, Fire Flies or Hobos).

Having heard that Covey 224 was down, Covey 247 (Captain Yarbrough) did a hot refuel and was on his way back to the area of operation to assist the teams on the ground and the SAR mission. As he listened to his radio he heard confirmation that Covey 224 had indeed just crashed, Wes thought to himself, *"This is really getting fucked up."* About that time, Covey 247 made contact with Bright Light's One-zero:

> Oscar Bravo, this is Covey 247, over.

> Covey 247, this is Oscar Bravo, over.

> Oscar Bravo, the Jolly Green is on its way. The number one priority at this time is to get the pilot and rider out first. If there is still enough daylight remaining and the weathers works with us, the Jolly Green will return and extract your team and the bodies as well. Out.

The intermittent enemy explosions and gunfire continued for another 5 minutes. Suddenly, the Bright Light could hear the mighty Jolly Green and his escort of A-1Es approaching. Surprisingly, the SAR mission flew directly overhead down into the A Shau valley, making a beeline for the Covey crash site. Joining the rescue helicopter and the A-1E's were three UH-1 helicopters sent from MLT-1. The recon company commander had sent a second Bright Light team with the UH-1. They were to get on the ground and retrieve the bodies and/or survivors of the downed Covey.

Inside the UH-1 helicopter was Captain Fred (Lightning) Wonderlich, his One-one Staff Sergeant Klowecki and two Montagnards. They would lead the second Bright Light in on the downed Covey recovery mission.

Lightning having run some pretty hairy recon missions in his time, Lightning was well respected and admired. He was also one of the most experienced One-zeros in CCN's recon company. Lightning came by his nickname justifiably many months earlier when he'd been at one of our many radio relay sites "Sugar Loaf" in Laos and was conducting a walk off recon mission. Since many of our missions were being run in the middle of the monsoon season, it normally rained from beginning of the mission to end.

The story goes that Lightning was moving his team through the jungle for four days of wet, miserable humping and, seeing no sign of the enemy that he had been targeted to recon for. He'd become highly upset, indignant and socially unacceptable. In short, he was pissed. While he was moving, Lightning looked up into the sky during a downpour and said, "God damn you God, make this fucking rains stop."

Lightning's request was quickly answered, when without warning, a lightning bolt flew from the heavens and hit in the middle of the team. The power and strength of the lightning bolt literally picked the team members up off their feet and threw them like pieces of paper in every direction. The team had been strung through the underbrush and into treetops from the ferocity and unchained power of the lightning bolt. Each man had been knocked unconscious, burned and rendered completely helpless. Lightning said he didn't know how long the team was unconscious, but when he came to, he gathered up his scorched team and requested extraction.

After his recovery, Captain Wunderlich had a local seamstress make cloth lightning bolts and had them sewn onto the right sleeves of every set of fatigues he owned. He told us that he would never make such a request again because God would not be so gentle next time; the next time I bet He'd run that lightning bolt up his ass.

Once the CH-53 had located the downed Covey, he began orbiting the site, coordinating with the UH-1's while enroute with the experienced Bright Light team aboard. Quickly, the UH-1 was on station and the two forces linked up, coordinating their rescue plan. The Bright Light team was going to rappel directly onto the crash site, recover and extract the dead. Then, the team would be extracted. As soon as the coordination was complete and the plan set, Slick #1 rolled in and hovered over the downed Covey crash site. As it did so, a set of Cobra gunships began orbiting directly over the helicopter, ready to tear up the area if any enemy fired at the slick. The A-1Es would assist, and stayed high-and-dry circling with the Jolly Green.

As soon as the chopper began to hover, rappelling ropes were thrown out the doors of the helicopter and the four-man Bright Light team hooked up and climbed out and onto the skids. Two men were positioned on each side of the helicopter with ropes flailing and dangling wildly below them from the down thrust of the rotor blades. After Lightning saw that all four men were ready, Captain Lightning looked across the open doors and gave the command, "Go!" four men quickly descended down the 120 foot ropes coming to rest on the water soaked jungle floor

Once on the ground, the Bright Light recovery team moved directly to the O-2A. As they approached the downed bird, it became obvious that they weren't going to get 1LT Hull out; he was pinned by the back engine to the front engine. SFC Fernandez was still sitting up right in his seat; leaning forward, his head was bent down resting on his chest, his upper body being restrained by the seats harness.

Lightning recovered the body of SFC Fernandez, placed him in a body bag and had to leave 1LT Hull in the wreckage because it was impossible to remove him from the aircraft. The CH-53 arrived overhead, dropped the jungle penetrator and Lightning attached SFC Fernandez's body to it and watch it rise up into the air. Suddenly, one of the Little People opened up on a squad of NVA soldiers who were also looking for the downed Covey. Without hesitation, the Jolly Green's escorts responded, making bomb runs over suspected enemy positions. Once Fernandez was removed from the jungle penetrator, the crew chief sent the jungle penetrator back down again and again to retrieve the four-man Bright Light Rescue team.

# CHAPTER 20 (A SHAU)

Fifteen kilometers north from RT Python's position, the fighting escalated with each passing moment. Not only were enemy automatic weapons hammering the Bright Light, but also B-40s were coming in on them from every angle. The One-zero knew he had to move or they were going to die in place. On command, the team began evasive action to try and break contact with the enemy and put some distance between themselves and the enemy. The well-disciplined team retreated performing immediate action drill repeatedly over and over back down the hill. Even though they executed their retreat for more than five minutes, it became obvious that the enemy was strung out all along their path of their retreat.

Receiving fire from every direction, there was no relief from the intense onslaught of rounds. RT Habu's One-Zero knew that if he allowed the team to continue their repetitive withdrawal, eventually the NVA would figure out their maneuvers, lay a deadly blocking maneuver and annihilate the entire team. The team had already sustained two wounded and feared the worst was yet to come.

With Covey down, the sun descending, and monsoon rains quickly approaching, things didn't look good for the home team. Danzer decided to establish a defensive fighting position against the onslaught of the NVA. As the team halted, the enemy fire suddenly stopped. Danzer's reasoning was that if the team were in a halted defensive posture, they would have a better chance of survival if a ground attack were to ensue, rather than be in the middle of an Immediate Action Drill having to deal with a split team.

Anxiety permeated throughout the small recovery team; their breathing heavily labored, hearts pounded, sweat poured from physical exertion, coupled with the unforgiving humidity and temperature of the jungle elevated their nervous system screaming out danger signs over-and-over. Their final defensive position consisted of a 25-foot rock-face cliff to their backs, which provided total assurance that the enemy couldn't move in behind them. This would allow the team to concentrate all of their attention to their flanks, to the high-rising mountain slopes to their front and on the high-speed trail running north and south.

Although the replacement Covey had been trying to contact the Bright Light team as they were retreating, Danzer couldn't hear him until they were actually stopped and in their final defensive posture:

> Oscar Bravo, this is Covey 271, over.

> Covey 271, this is Oscar Bravo, over.

> Oscar Bravo, this is Covey 271, you had me a little worried; thought you might be having tea with old Charlie there for a moment. Covey from Quang Tri should be on-station in about one zero mikes. Also, Covey will be picking up the extraction package from Phu Bai and leading them to your location, how copy, over?

> Covey 271, this is Oscar Bravo, that's a good copy. We have moved into a defensive position down and away from the crash site. We are preparing for the bad guys to attack at any second. I have two wounded and had to leave the bodies of the Americans back at the crash site. All personnel are accounted for, over.

> Oscar Bravo, this is Covey 271, roger good copy. Understand everyone accounted for at the crash site. Am standing by to assist as needed? I am going up high and get some fast-movers on station, over.

> Covey 271, this is Oscar Bravo roger babe good copy, out.

The team listened to the jungle noises intensely, peeking through and below the underbrush for any enemy movement. Their fields of vision were very restricted and narrow because of the thick vegetation that they lay in for concealment. Sounds of men moving about from within the jungle indicated that the enemy was positioning troops to further surrounding them, in preparation for a massive ground attack. Jimmy, Wes, Mac and Cliff spread themselves out evenly throughout the defensive perimeter to provide constant supervision over the Little People. Time was running out. The rains would soon begin, preventing the defenders from hearing the enemy's approach, being extracted or living through the night. A slight breeze lightly rushed over the backs of the Bright Light as they waited.

Suddenly, the welcome sound of Covey's engines roared overhead as he closed the distance between the valley floor and their location.

The handset squelched and David Cheney's voice came over the radio:

Oscar Bravo, this is Covey 217, over.

Covey 217, this is Oscar Bravo, over.

Oscar Bravo, this is Covey 217 catch me up on what is going on down on the ground, over.

Covey 217, good to have you back with us babe, we accounted for all the crash victims. We recovered all the crew, but could not recover two straw hats, hanging off and over the side of a cliff, still in their stabo rigs. We were preparing to recover the two on the stabo rigs when we saw bad guys watching our position. We retreated south and away from the crash site and are surrounded by an unknown large sized enemy element. Covey went down somewhere east of the helicopter crash site. We have had negative contact with the downed Covey or received any survival beeper signals at this time. We are preparing for a suspected and anticipated NVA ground attack at any moment. We have set up a defensive perimeter on the west side of a 25-foot rock face cliff, about 100 meters south of the helicopter crash site. Have two soap bubbles wounded, how copy, over?

Oscar Bravo, this is Covey 217, roger good copy babe, the extraction package is about 10 minutes behind me. I will remain high-and-dry, waiting for the fast movers and the extraction package to arrive. Will be monitoring your frequency at all times, how copy, over?

Covey 217, that's a good copy, out.

The sounds of Covey once again slowly faded as he flew eastward to retrieve the extraction package coming from Phu Bai. Unlike the previous day when the clouds normally stayed relatively high, this day they actually dropped down onto the jungle floor itself, filtering down over the mountainside down into the valley.

Small droplets of cool rain began to fall on the jungle treetops. The thick heavy clouds quickly blotted out the sunlight over the entire area. It was like someone had pulled down the shades blocking out the sunlight. If the team was going to be extracted, it would have to be quick or they would have to try and hold out until sun up.

The UH-1 helicopters out of Phu Bai were now on station, orbiting over the A Shau Valley. The One-Zero of The Bright Light waited patiently for Covey 217 to make contact. The team on the ground knew coordination between aircraft took time, precious time, which was now in extremely short supply. The suspense of waiting was at last broken with the radio squelch:

Oscar Bravo, this is Covey 217, over.

Covey 217, this is Oscar Bravo, over.

Oscar Bravo, this is Covey 217, Slick #1 is two minutes out from your location, talk him into your position. Do not pop smoke. I repeat, do no pop smoke? Talk him in. Slick #2 will be following behind, with the rest of the package close behind. We're going to have to bring you out on strings, how copy, over?

Covey 217, this is Oscar Bravo we're ready for extraction, will send the wounded out first. Remind the chopper crews that it's hot down here with all kinds of bad guys and they are going to take fire from all directions, over.

Oscar Bravo, this is Covey 217, roger babe have already told them that they are going to be going into a hot extraction LZ. The slicks are coming at you now,

Break; break.

Slick Lead, this is Covey 217, take your orders from the One-Zero on the ground. How copy, over?

Covey 217, this is Slick Lead, good copy,

Break; break.

Oscar Bravo, this is Slick Lead, over.

Slick Lead, this is Oscar Bravo, be advised that there are enemy automatic weapon positions all around our defensive position, and up the hillside about 100 meters. We're off at your two o'clock, on the edge of a rock face cliff, keep coming, and keep coming. Bingo; Bingo. Over.

Oscar Bravo, this is Slick Lead, good copy. I have a good tally on your position. We'll drop strings, over.

Slick Lead this is Oscar Bravo standing by, over.

Oscar Bravo, strings are out, over.

As Slick Lead came into a hover above the Bright Lights position, the rotor blades began thrashing and whipping the treetops around violently. No sooner had the pilot announced that the strings were out, than three stabo ropes crashed down through the trees coming to rest on the ground, in the center of the team's position. The two wounded Little People crawled to the stabo harnesses and fastened themselves in. Slowly, Slick Lead rose higher, taking the slack out of the ropes as he climbed. The Montagnards looked skyward, in anticipation of being pulled out through the tops of the trees.

Slick lead continued his steady upward climb as the Little People below danced around on the ground from left to right, forward and back, trying to stay directly underneath the helicopter to avoid passing over the enemy's position. As they began to slowly rise up off the jungle floor, automatic weapon fire immediately filled the air followed by green tracer cracked through the trees upward at the helpless men dangling defenselessly below the chopper.

Danzer radioed to the pilot screaming, "You're taking fire. You're taking fire."

The pilot pulled up hard on the cyclic, and then yanked the two Little People straight up through the trees, vanishing off into the abyss of the monsoon clouds. After confirming that the stabo ropes were clear of the trees, he headed toward the 95th Evacuation hospital in Phu Bai.

Immediately, Slick #2 began maneuvering his aircraft into the Bright Light's defensive position, regardless of the enemy ground fire. With each passing microsecond that escaped the enemy fire picked up in savage intensity. Slick #2 slowly crept forward through the dense rain and blinding clouds when a B-40 hissed by, followed by two others. Three stair-step explosions rocked the sky and Slick #2 sent a distress call over the air,

> "I'm hit. I repeat I'm hit. I'm coming out. The LZ is too hot. Enemy B-40s, automatic weapon fire is coming in from everywhere."
>
> Covey 217, this is Oscar Bravo, over.
>
> Oscar Bravo, this is Covey 217, over.
>
> Covey 217, Slick #2 is taking heavy ground fire and B40 rounds from the ridge above. They're trying to take down another helicopter. We need some fire suppression down here quickly. Are the fast movers on station or do we have any gun ships, over?
>
> Oscar Bravo, this is Covey 217. Babe I can't help you with suppressive fire. We can't see you and don't know where you are in all of this soup. How copy, over?
>
> Covey 217, the enemy green tracers are coming from

above us now and firing blindly off into the valley at the sounds of the helicopters. Stay clear until this crap thins out down here, over.

Oscar Bravo, this is Covey 217 that's affirmative we'll stay clear. We can see the enemy fire coming up at us from out of the clouds, but we are well north of their fire at this time, over.

Danzer and the team knew full well that any rescue or attempt at extraction was futile at this point. They simply couldn't take the chance of another helicopter being shot down. The monsoon rains and clouds completely blanketed the western mountain range accompanied by the thick ground fog that inched its way down through the jungle into the A Shau Valley itself. The monsoon pressed hard from the west, the rain and clouds persistently pushing the extraction package farther away from the team on the ground with every second that passed. Visibility was now completely nonexistent in the air and on the ground.

As each of the Bright Light team members lay in the rain-soaked jungle, preparing for the inevitable all-out ground attack, they knew this mission had been jinxed from the get-go. Everything they'd tried to do or attempted to do continually turned to shit. They had resigned themselves to the fact that they wouldn't be pulled out of this Valley of Death today and maybe never. Danzer began to prepare for the worst, directing the Americans to take charge and place all claymores out as he got on the radio with Covey:

Covey 217, this is Oscar Bravo, over.

Oscar Bravo, this is Covey 217, over.

Covey 217, I can't see a thing down here and I know that you can't see anything down through the cloud cover either. Charlie's down here patiently waiting for the next helicopter to come in. If you send another chopper in, they will surely shoot it down. What do you advise? Over?

Oscar Bravo, this is Covey 217, I hate to agree with you, but I think we're all screwed. I'm being pushed out deeper and deeper into the valley with each turn of my plane. I can't get support aircraft in to assist you without endangering them and all of you. The only thing I can recommend is to put up as much of a defense as you can, try and hold out overnight and I'll be up on station prior to first light with an SAR extraction package. How copy, over?

Covey 217, this is Oscar Bravo, roger babe I've come to the same conclusion. Lord will and the creek don't rise and if we make it through the night, I'll see you at first light, over.

Oscar Bravo, good luck to you old buddy, I'm going to try and get a Stinger (a C-119 gunship with 60mm cannons, 40mm cannons and 7.62mm mini-guns). And/ or a Specter (a C-130 gunship with a 105mm Howitzer, 60mm cannons, 40mm cannons and mini-guns) gunship on standby to look over you during the hours of darkness. How copy, over?

Covey 217, this is Oscar Bravo, thank you much bubba, and thanks for your help good buddy. With any luck, I'll buy you a beer back at the ranch, out.

Specter and Stinger were used by the U.S. Air Force to fly the trail (Ho Chi Min Trail) at night and take out any targets of opportunity they came across. They had technically advanced infra red capabilities, heat sensors and other assorted goodies that could pick up enemy locations and personnel, regardless of the weather. Recon teams often used them for just this purpose. Every team member carried a mini-transponder that the gunships could pick up with its computer, enabling them to locate friendly troops even under the worst weather conditions.

Once Danzer had given the command to deploy claymores, everyone knew they were staying put. Initially, they were reluctant because they were sure they would be extracted. However, as reality set in, so did their courage and training. They went about their duties like a well-oiled machine. Within minutes, 10 claymores had been placed 20 feet out and away from the defenders. Since the mines weren't far from their perimeter, Danzer ordered everyone to remove his rucksack and place it to his front of his position to act as a shield once the claymores were detonated.

When claymores detonate, they threw vegetation, rocks, and anything else it towards the enemy and like wise back at the defenders as well. Many a soldiers have been wounded or killed from the back-blast of a claymore mine. Although the enemy weapons and B40 fire had stopped, The Bright Light could still hear enemy soldiers running around through the vegetation above and on their flanks in preparation for the attack. Slowly removing the handset from his ear, Danzer's face was troubled as he signaled the Americans to meet him in the center of the perimeter. Slowly each man responded and crawled to meet with him. In the center of the perimeter they all lay on their stomachs, heads close together waiting for Danzer to provide them with his scheme of maneuver.

Lighting a Ruby Queen cigarette, Danzer looked into each of their eyes and said, hesitating momentarily he spoke softly "well guys, we're not getting out of here today. Covey says we are completely covered by the monsoon clouds, fog and rains. They can't even give us any air support because they don't know exactly where we are in all this crap. Covey is going to try and get a Specter and Stinger on station above us all night. We need to get the transponders out and ready so when they arrive they can lock in on us during the night. I hope everyone put their money in the company safe because the ways things are looking, some of the guys are going to be drinking on us." Everyone knew they were getting ready for the fight of their lives and that some, if not all of them were not going to see the light of day.

Danzer took another drag off the Ruby Queen cigarette and passed it around. Carefully reviewing the details, Danzer quizzed, "Are all of the claymores out?" The Americans nodded their heads in the affirmative. Then Danzer queried them "I'm open for suggestions if anyone has anything to add." Wes spoke right up, "if we get hit during the night, which way are we going to escape and evade? I recommend we climb down or jump off this rock-face cliff into the jungle below. It'll take Charlie hours to come after us or find us with that much distance for him to cover."

Everyone was stunned at his recommendation and wore expressions of complete surprise on their faces. Finally, Horton chimed in, "Damn, Wes, we'll kill ourselves jumping off this rock cliff during the night. Bubba you must be eating dog food again or drinking battery acid." The men laughed nervously at Jimmy's statement.

Wes was quick to answer, "Well babe, its either jump and take our chances jumping off the cliff, or stand here, fight and die. Me, I'm for jumping off the cliff if we have to!" In reality, jumping off a high cliff in the middle of the night wasn't the wisest plan for escaping and evading the enemy. However, in their particular rapidly deteriorating situation, it seemed to be the best course-of-action and the only course that was available to them.

Danzer directed each American to take two dextroamphetimines now in preparation for the long night of darkness ahead of them. As they each took their pills, Mac suddenly decided to voice his opinion. Looking at each man, he turned his baby face and whispered with his southern drawl, "Next time you assholes decide to go somewhere, leave my raggedy ass name out of it. I'll stay back at camp and keep the beer cold. You're all crazy, and I'm just as crazy for being here. You're trying to get my ass killed."

No one replied at first. Then, they suddenly on cue they all broke into a subdued laugh, pressing their bush hats hard against their mouths attempting to stifle their giggling and laughter. That little bit of reprise from the pressure and gravity of their situation helped them return to their defensive positions with a better attitude. The team had prepared well; they'd brought a lot of ammunition, grenades and claymores. Feeling somewhat confident, the brave men of The Bright Light lay back and wait for the inevitable attack that was yet to come.

# CHAPTER 21 (A-SHAU)

Darkness was only an hour away. RT Python hadn't seen the enemy since the early morning attack, although we were still completely surrounded by the NVA, we lay in wait. Occasionally, we heard heavy troop movement coming from down within the jungle and fired M-79 rounds in towards the sounds. The movement made me skeptical of the adversary's plans for the evening; I was sure we had a full night of fun and games ahead of us.

Ever vigilant, Jim never took the PRC-77 handset away form his ear. He monitored every conversation, just in case we could provide some sort of aid to our fellow soldiers. Covey was trying to extract the team, but an intense cloud cover was moving in too quickly restricting their extraction. I painfully raised myself over the side of my foxhole and caught a quick glimpse of men's shadows running through the jungle. Instead of running laterally, they were heading back down the hillside into the depths of the jungles vegetation.

What were they preparing to do? I thought for sure they were getting ready to pound us with B-40s, but nothing happened. They were only moving from place to place. One second they were there, the next, they were gone. I began to wonder if the NVA movement was only a figment of my imagination, a chemical reaction from the drugs I'd been taking to stay awake.

Jim was up and pacing again. He had the radio handset pressed hard to his ear and his left hand on his hip, as he kicked at the dirt and began moving in a tight circle. He was obviously pissed, so I decided to give him some space and stay where I was. After he appeared to have calmed down a bit

I would find out what had upset him so much. My attention was drawn to the helicopters as they flew north of our position headed towards RT Habu's position. I knew they were headed to extract the Bright Light team. The extraction package was closing in on the extraction site, yet they seemed to be waiting. I could see Covey darting in and out of the clouds prior to he himself out of the clouds orbiting to the east of the Bright Light's extraction location. I thought maybe they were just doing some final coordination and fine-tuning prior to the extraction.

What was going on? What were they waiting for? Suddenly Slick #1 broke formation and headed behind the mountain range and out of sight. Minutes passed before two figures were scene hanging below the chopper, flying east toward the launch site. Slick #2 then made his move into the clouds. Within seconds, he reappeared with green tracers chasing him close behind. The entire extraction package was being pushed further and further off to the east because of the monsoon clouds and rain towards the center of the A Shau Valley.

Quickly the once distant monsoon clouds were now directly over us and rapidly descending down lower and lower we lost sight of Covey and the choppers in the clouds that now covered our position. At the center of our perimeter, I watched as Jim began pitching a fit; kicking equipment, throwing his web gear and generally went on a rampage. Something bad had just happened during the extraction that I had to find out about. Glaring at me through water covered black-rimmed, military-issue glasses; Jim spit it out, "Slick #2 just got shot out of the extraction LZ. The Bright Light team is taking heavy enemy fire and the monsoon rains have completely obscured any vision in or out." Every time we try to accomplish anything, we are always stymied by either the NVA, the weather or by Murphy's Law.

I added my two cents aloud, "well, the intelligence about this shit hole sure was right. They wanted us to confirm or deny the presence of the enemy. We sure enough have. They've got us all surrounded, just like they want us." Slapping his leg in disgust, Jim shouted, "They had to abort the fucking extraction because the God damn clouds are like soup around the team, and Covey doesn't want to risk having another chopper shot down. David, Covey's directed the Bright Light to dig in and make the best of it. Covey will be back over them prior to first light, with the Jolly

Green and Spads to get them out tomorrow at first light. Covey is trying to get them some overhead coverage from Specter or Stinger tonight." "And the hits just keep coming."

I shook my head in disbelief and left Jim, still shouting to anyone who would listen, that this entire mission was going to hell in a hand basket and there was nothing we could do about it. Shortly, the mountain range where The Bright Light team was courageously dug in became totally obscured from our view by the gray clouds. Our position would also be covered shortly. Covey flew off to the east of us and began relaying information to Jim. Finally, Jim dropped the handset from his ear and walked away from the radio. We were all dumbfounded at the sequence of events that had plagued us over the past 48 hours. Knowing that Jim needed a break from radio duty, I sat down and listened to an empty handset for a couple of hours.

We had to constantly monitor the frequencies in case The Bright Light needed help or wanted to pass information. Within a matter of minutes we would be submerged under another night of miserable down pouring of rain. As normal, it began lightly then built to a flood, gradually filling our foxholes and gushing down the hillside like a waterfall.

As much as I hated to, I ordered everyone to take down their makeshift overhead shelters. We had to suffer through the rain and be ready for combat tonight. We couldn't afford to become relaxed or comfortable, and in turn we had to maintain strict noise and light discipline through the hours of darkness. Knowing that tonight the NVA would test us in every way, I made sure the 60mm mortar position was ready and all the mortar rounds were stripped of their charges, and ready to be put into action.

While conducting one final trip around the perimeter, I reiterated at each mans position that everyone had to stay alert and watch to their front. Darkness drew down on us quickly, as though someone had suddenly flipped a light switch to the off position. The only sounds around our perimeter were hard-hitting raindrops. We relied solely on our M-14 toe-popper mines to alert us to any enemy advances.

Around 2330 hours, the rains began to subside and I became convinced that we were about to be hit? So, I made my rounds again, stressing to each man that our survival hinged upon 100% alertness all the way until first light. When I reached Profit's position, he was leaning out over his weapon, looking down the hill for something. Cautiously I crawled over to him through the mud and asked what he was looking for? He didn't respond right away, just kept staring over the edge of the hillside. I repeated myself, "What the fuck are you looking at." Turning his head to me, he asked, "Les, do you hear a bear growling down there?" Confused by what I thought I'd heard, I replied, "What did you say?" Again, he repeated, "Man, I'm sure there is a bear down there growling."

Crawling forward to look over the lip of the hilltop, I too began to hear something that sounded like a bear growling. Then it hit me; I questioned Profit if he'd been taking dextroamphetamines all day? When he replied yes, I laughed and explained, "Asshole, you're hallucinating, and I must be too. There is no bear down there, now get your shit together, quit worrying about Smoky the Bear and start thinking about killing those little gook bastards." Crawling away, I laughed to myself.

From somewhere in the deep jungle, a voice called out over a loudspeaker. The language was Vietnamese, so I rushed over to Jung and asked him what they were saying. Listening for a while, he turned to me and said, "Trung Si, they say, if we give you up to them, they will let us go." The invisible voice kept repeating the same phrase again and again. Nervously, I bolted over to Jim and reported what they were saying to our troops. Jim whispered to me, "Man, they're getting ready to hit us. I sure hope our Little People hang with us, but go around the perimeter and tell the Americans to be prepared for anything."

I quickly made the rounds to the other Americans informing them of what is being said then returned to my mud hole. Jung whispered, "Trung Si, VC lie. We know they kill all of us too. It has happened many times before." Sighing under my breath, I told Jung to go around to the Little People and tell them to stay in their holes because the fighting would soon begin. Jung scurried off into the darkness, doing just as I had instructed. As he slithered back in our foxhole, he reassured me, "Trung Si, all team stay with you and fight VC. We no surrender to VC." Although still cautious, I also felt proud to be fighting alongside men of this caliber.

The tormenting high pitched twanging voice continued blaring out the same phrase for another hour. Our nerves were frayed from listening to the same words again and again. Then, as quickly as it had started, the amplified messages ceased. Momentarily startled at the silence, everyone grabbed their rifles and moved to the forward edges of their fighting positions in preparation for the inevitable enemy attack. Minutes passed as we listened and maintained 100% vigilance on our sectors of fire.

Finally, the wait was over. Eight B-40s began hissing as they took flight from within the jungle, followed immediately by blinding flashes of light and deafening explosions as they impacted the edges of the hilltop. Dirt, mud, debris and body-piercing hot metal and the pungent scent of burnt phosphorous filled the air. Volley after volley of B-40s continued to fired impacting all around us.

Suddenly, a trip flare ignited and Brazier's machine gun once again came to life. Knowing better than to abandon my fighting position to investigate, I remained in place. During the flashes and explosions from the B40s, I looked over the edge of the berm and saw camouflaged enemy soldiers crawling up the hill, not more than 15 meters away. Instinctively, I screamed to Jung, "Roll grenades down the hill. Don't throw them, just pull the pin and roll them down the hill. The NVA are crawling up the hillside towards us to get inside our perimeter."

I reached for the M-26 fragmentation grenades I had pre-positioned previously, pulled the pin out of the first grenade and let it simply roll out of my hand. Just as I released my grenade, Jung did the same. Time seemed to drag as we anticipated the explosions. We pulled two more grenade pins and sent them on their way rolling down the hillside as well. No sooner had I pulled my hand back from laying out the third grenade, than the first two grenades detonated seconds apart. Men screamed in agony. I glanced quickly over the edge and saw NVA soldiers being thrown through the air. Body parts were being blown off and scattered over the hillside. More importantly, the advancing NVA were no longer crawling; they were on there feet, charging up the hillside towards us.

With bayonets fixed to the end of their weapons, they fired as they closed in on our position. I grabbed one of the claymore blasting machines and squeezed. An immediate flash, followed by a deafening blast rang out, as this wasn't an ordinary claymore. I had taped a white phosphorus grenade to the front of it, adding physical and physiological impact.

For a single second, there was a decrease in the number of B-40s and heavy weapons firing coming in on us. Next came the thud of Chi-com hand grenades impacting the ground on top of the hill. One exploded so close to my position, that it bounced me back against the wall of the foxhole, causing an immediate ringing in my ears. Everywhere I looked, I saw brilliant flashes of light, followed by explosions and heavy automatic weapon fire. The NVA had launched a two-sided ground attack, trying to divert our attention from one side of the perimeter to the other.

Our machine guns were chattering, spitting out fiery red balls (tracers) of death. Off to my rear, a parachute flare suddenly took to the air. Initially I thought it was an enemy B-40 rocket being fired from behind me, but it was launched by Jim to provide us with some type of illumination. As the flare made its way up into the heavens, we continued to fire in every direction.

A hazy artificial light suddenly appeared followed by a light distant popping sound throwing light down on the hilltop and surrounding jungle as the flare burst overhead deep within the clouds. Normally, it would have given off a million candlepower of brilliant light. But this one was subdued because of low cloud cover; it gave off just enough light for us to distinguish advancing NVA soldiers allowing us to identify our targets and fire directly into them. There they were about 50-60 NVA soldiers charging up the hill, stepping over their own fallen comrades bodies as they relentlessly continued to close the gap between them and us. I reached for two more grenades, throwing them both into the advancing soldiers.

Enemy and friendly explosions and gunfire were no longer distinguishable. It seemed like the whole world was shooting. I felt a stinging, burning sensation on the backside of my left shoulder and realized I'd been hit with either a bullet or shrapnel. As I continued to fire my CAR-15, I felt blood running down my back down into my fatigue pants. I knew I couldn't stop and see how bad I was hit because I had to fight or die. We were fighting for our lives and everyone had to pull his own weight to survive. I had to suck it up and stay in the fight. Blocking out the pain, I moved forward in my foxhole as bullets bounced in front of me, throwing dirt and debris into my face.

In between my ducking and bobbing, I caught a glimpse of a large number of NVA about five meters off to the right oblique of my position. Jung was busy firing to his left flank when I screamed for him to detonate his claymore. Without hesitation, Jung masterfully maintained his right finger on the trigger mechanism of the M-60 while he reached over with his left hand for the blasting mechanism, giving it a hefty squeeze. The brilliant flash from the claymore temporarily blinded both of us. Our vision returned as the light from the flare Jim had fired earlier suddenly came out from beneath some low-lying clouds and lit up the surrounding area.

My heart jumped into my throat. A large concentrations of 50 to 100 enemy soldiers were everywhere below us. Jung began to bear down on the M-60 just before we were both thrown to the rear of our foxhole from the concussion of a B-40 impacting directly to our front. The explosion was earth- shattering. Yet, none of the metal fragments from its warhead hit us they flew over our heads and off into the darkness. Despite the pounding in our skulls, Jung and sprung back forward in our foxhole and resumed firing at the advancing troops.

To my rear, I heard screaming and yelling as four NVA soldiers crested the edge of the hilltop. Leaping from the foxhole, I ran at them, determined to kill each one. Without bringing my weapon up to shoulder level or using my sights, I fired at them while on the run in the fully automatic mode. Jim had also seen them as they came up out of the darkness and he too was firing and advancing toward them at the same time I was. He was shooting at them from their right flank, while I attacked from their front, catching them surprised and totally off guard.

As they foolishly ran into our hail of bullets, all four men suddenly bent in the middle of their torsos like folding a piece of paper. They'd been hit so many times by Jim and I that the impact of our bullets literally picked them up and threw them back off the hilltop.

Grabbing me by the shoulder and shouting above the explosions, Jim made it clear, "we can't let them get up here with us, or we've had it!" Looking up to see the parachute flare burning out, Jim frantically dug into his fatigue pant pocket and retrieved a second parachute flare, reversed the ends quickly he squatted down them slamming it against the earth. The primer detonated and the flare swished like a rocket into the semi clear sky. With a popping sound, the flare ignited, this time providing us total illumination.

Abruptly, five more NVA soldiers appeared from the same side as the first four and began running to the center of our perimeter as they blindly fired their weapons at any target of opportunity. Jim and I together charged at them, firing side-by-side as we walked into the hail of enemy bullets. Three of the four NVA soldiers dropped like sacks of potatoes. The other two fell to their knees, dropping their weapons to the ground and grabbing at their wounds. One of the dying NVA reached for his face as he had taken a round directly in his upper lip. He didn't know it, but the back of his head was gone. His body jerked and his arms then flailed up and down because his nerves were allowing normal muscle response due to the pain. The last NVA soldier grabbed at his chest then fell face first to the ground. Just to make sure we'd killed all five, Jim and I reloaded and quickly shot each one in the head.

Behind us on the opposite side of the perimeter, Brazer had just killed an NVA soldier in close quarter combat. He had another on the ground, running his SOG knife down into his chest all the way to the hand guard. Every side of the perimeter had NVA soldiers popping over the rim of the hilltop. With no place to hide and no cover, we were now fully engaged in close quarter combat with the NVA. The enemy was on the hill with us and we had to kick their ass off of it if we wanted to survive.

We shot at anything that moved. The fight was fast and furious. When it was over, 28 NVA soldiers lay dead at our feet and we were no longer receiving incoming enemy fire. We had momentarily achieved the upper hand. We'd some how had beaten back another full-scale hardcore NVA infantry ground attack. Jim and I stood motionless by each other breathing hard; sweat running down our faces and adrenaline pumping feverishly through our veins. We stared at each other, saying nothing. We both knew we hadn't seen the last of the NVA; this was only the prelude to what was to come.

The NVA were determined to take back this hill and kill us in the process; there would be no prisoners taken. This was going to be a fight to the finish. Winner takes all. Jim slowly staggered back to the center of the perimeter, shouting orders over his shoulder as he moved, "Americans, check your Little People, redistribute ammo, tend to your wounded, and get ready for another attack."

"Jung" Jim screamed. Jung responded immediately, "Yes Die We (Captain)." Jim continued, "Get some men and start throwing these dead NVA bodies over the side. Let's clear this place off before they hit us again." Jung called out the names of two of the Little People, Chow and Nhe and relayed the task at hand. One by one, they threw the dead NVA soldiers over the side of the hill. The enemy's weapons and ammunition was divided among the defenders of the hilltop. In turn, the Americans began redistributing our own ammunition to equal it out, in preparation for the next attack.

Jim tried contacting MLT-1 Phu Bai over the radio, with no response. Over and over he called, becoming angrier by the second. For 10 minutes straight, he tried to reach the launch site with no response. Then, a familiar voice sounded out, not from Phu Bai, but from MLT-2 Quang Tri launch site. It was Pappy Budrow. One of the originators of recon missions, Pappy was a Master Sergeant E-8 and had been to Vietnam in every capacity imaginable. He'd run hundreds of missions and was always there when a team needed him. He'd pull out any and all of the stop to get a team back safely.

Pappy was about 32-years old, balding and meaner than a snake. He had the attitude of a mad hornet, yet Pappy had more experience in his little finger than all of us combined. He was always serious and hardly ever smiled or made small talk. Pappy was dedicated to the mission and the recon men on the ground. No matter what it required, he took care of his men.

Jim immediately began feeding information to Pappy:

> Mike Oscar, this is Quang Tri base. Hey babe heard you calling Phu Bai with negative response. Maybe they are having radio problems. Can we be of any assistance, over?

Quang Tri base, this is Mike Oscar. We just had a major NVA ground attack launched against us. Don't know what our personnel status is yet, but will know momentarily. We were hit by an estimated reinforced company-sized hardcore NVA element. They broke through our perimeter and tried to overrun us, but they were unsuccessful, over.

Mike Oscar, this is Quang Tri base, good copy. From the sounds of it, you need help and need it right now, over.

Quang Tri base this is Mike Oscar, Pappy we need some overhead cover, I think we're fighting that NVA regiment we were sent in here to find and call in air strike on, over.

Mike Oscar, roger babe. Will see what I can round up, you stay close to that mouthpiece; will call you back soon, out.

While Jim waited for Pappy to radio back, I inspected what was left of our defensive perimeter. Although we had no dead, everyone was wounded, either from frags, bullets or knives. We had plenty of ammo, and a few claymores and antipersonnel mines were still in place. We were all experiencing survivors' adrenaline high, ready for round two.

I returned to Jim's post to report our status and found him digging through his rucksack like a badger. Walking closer to him, I asked, "What are you looking for at a time like this?" He explained that Pappy was trying to get us some overhead cover tonight and Jim was trying to locate our transponder so they could pick us up via transponder frequency. Excitement immediately over took me, I exclaimed, "Sweet Jesus, we're going to kick their ass now if we get a Stinger on station above us." Jim finally found the mini-transponder and raised it above his head like a prized trophy. Thankfully, he'd replaced the batteries just prior to our departure from CCN. When the time came, Jim could turn this piece of equipment on and the Stinger would automatically lock in on our position. Once locked in, Stinger could bring death and destruction against the NVA 360 degrees around us up to within 10 feet, without hitting us in the process.

As our adrenaline levels began returning to normal, we turned into a tired bunch of soldiers. I once again reached into my pocket and was preparing to take another coupled of dextroamphetamine to amp me back up. I secured two green hornets, grabbed my canteen and washed them down.

I leaned over to Jim and recommended he take a couple of pills himself. He obliged me without question. It was now 0200 hours in the morning and two long hours had passed since the last ground attack. Being amped up from the drugs, I was rejuvenated, even though I was beginning to feel my wounds. No one could look at how bad I was hit until daylight, so I just had to gut it out. I knew that if I sat down and relaxed for more than five minutes, I would pass out from fatigue. We'd been up for more than 42 hours without any solid rest. I continued to move about the perimeter in order to stay awake and alert.

As I neared Brazier's machine gun position, I asked him how things were going. He quickly replied, "Les, I think I have some type of malfunction with this M-60. It doesn't want to cock and place a round in the tray." Moving to the other side of his weapon, I took it out of action and began to disassemble it. We had to make sure this firearm was in good working order, especially tonight. So, together we began to break it down. After finding and correcting the problem, we scrambled to reassemble it in the dark. Before we had completed the task, a ground flare went off over the eastern side of the perimeter. Profitt opened up with his M-60 and was answered instantaneously with a volley of enemy B-40 rockets.

The NVA was renewing their ground attack against another part of the perimeter. I fumbled feverishly trying to rapidly get the M-60 machine gun back into operation. Meanwhile, once again the tree line below us came to life with enemy soldiers charging up the hillside toward us. My attention was diverted from the assembly of the firearm, because I was partially focused on what was going on in the other portion of the perimeter. Brazier quickly abandoned the effort, grabbed his CAR-15 and joined his assistant gunner in engaging the NVA soldiers advancing up the hill.

While the southern and eastern sides of the perimeter were fighting it out with the NVA, I was blindly searching the ground for the missing part I'd dropped as the B-40s impacted. After what seemed like an eternity, I found the part, inserted it into the firearm and it was ready for use. As soon as Brazer heard the charging handle and slide slam forward, he pushed me out of the way and grabbed the weapon. He loaded a 100-round belt of 7.62 machine gun ammo, cocked it again and began firing.

I raced over to Profit's position, where he was firing continuous bursts at the enemy soldiers. No sooner had I arrived than Jim came in behind us. He took one look at our situation and returned to the command post to get on the radio. Looking over the hillside as Profit continued to fire, I knew something wasn't right. There were only 20-25 soldiers advancing toward us. The enemy was attempting another diversion, sacrificing their men on the eastern side of the perimeter.

Sure enough, a claymore detonated on the west side of the perimeter in the Little People's sector. They were firing volley after volley of CAR-15 fire into the small ravine we'd fought in early yesterday morning. Jim fired a parachute flare into the sky then ran over towards the western perimeter to support and direct the Little People. He quickly determined that 30-40 NVA had channeled themselves inside the steep ravine, with no place to go except toward us or back into the jungle. Jim took out mini-grenade after mini-grenade, pulled the pins and simply held his hand over the side of the hilltop, and allowing them to just roll out of his hand down into the advancing enemy.

Horrifying screams radiated from within the ravine as hot metal entered men's flesh followed as the mini grenade exploded. Jim rolled two more M-26 fragmentation grenades down the hill, increasing the distance with subsequent grenades. Within a short period of time, Jim was throwing grenades like an NFL quarterback, as deep into the ravine as he could. One of the Little People joined him in the grenade toss, while the third man continued to fire blindly down into the dark ravine. Horrifying yet memorable screams of men dying echoed up and down the ravine.

High above our position a parachute flare lit the countryside. The immediate flash of light enabled Jim to see what he was up against. He had to determine if the NVA were alive, dead, wounded, or just scampering about in the small confines of the ravine trying to avoid the hail of hot metal pounding down on them in the death funnel they were in. Enemy bodies covered the ground, while other NVA who had only received minor wounds tried to continue to climb up the ravine toward Jim. Some of the wounded soldiers made a futile effort to crawl up the sheer faced walls of the ravine to delay their ultimate meeting with death.

On the eastern perimeter, Profitt fired until all 20 plus NVA soldiers lay motionless on the ground in front of him. As quick as the NVA had initiated the attack, the enemy and friendly fire became spotty and sporadic. Then, all at once, it stopped. Total silence rang out. Except for the distant moaning and groaning of the severely wounded NVA soldiers that lay dying at the base of the fire base itself.

When the parachute flare died out, it was as if someone had closed a closet door down in a basement, blocking out the light. Each member of RT Python lay motionless, our hearts beating loudly, our breathing almost nonexistent due to fear and our anxiety. For hours, we lay listened for enemy movement. Slowly, I reached over and touched Profit on the shoulder. He jerked, startled by my touch and partially out of fear. I grabbed him tightly and asked, "How you doing there Bubba?" Profit turned and blurted out "Man, if I ever ask to straphang again with you, tell me to stay the fuck home and guard the compound. Damn-it and, I volunteered to come with you, holy shit I must have had my head up my ass." I laughed, slapping him on the back as I headed back to the command post.

Jim was standing with his back to me. After he realized I was behind him, he said solemnly, "Les, I don't know how many more of these ground attacks we can withstand and still hold this piece of dirt." Without waiting for a response, he raised his head to the sky and asked, "Where is that Stinger Pappy is sending us?"

While the rest of the team refitted equipment and ammo, Jim and I sat by the radio to rest and strategize. Jim asked how much ammo I thought we'd expended. I replied, "off the top of my head, I'd say we shot about 3500 rounds of 7.62 machine gun ammo, used up over half of our grenades and I have Brazer and Profit checking with the Little People to see how many loaded CAR-15 magazines each man has left. We are down to our last line of defense with the claymores, not counting the thirty or so 60mm mortar rounds remaining."

Jim shushed me into silence, "do you hear that?" Straining to listen to the empty sky, I faintly heard the humming of an airplane, off in the distance. We sprang to our feet as the radio squelched, breaking the silence and startling us. My heart raced with anticipation, hoping it was Stinger or Specter.

> Station calling, station calling this is Mike Oscar, over.
>
> Mike Oscar, this is Stinger 121, over.
>
> Stinger 121, this is Mike Oscar. Boy, are we glad to see you. I'll give you an update on our current situation and what we've had to deal with over the past 12 hours. Stinger 121, keep coming, I am off to your 10 o'clock, over.
>
> Mike Oscar, this is Stinger 121, heard you boys are having a little tussle down there. We just thought that we'd mosey on over here and see if we could join in the party and give you a hand with taking care of these bad guys, over.
>
> Stinger 121, this is Mike Oscar, if we get out of this alive, the beer's on me. Over

As Jim began to render the situation report to the Stinger pilot, I scurried around the perimeter, informing everyone that we had a Stinger above us and stressing the importance of staying low to the ground. I reminded them not to expose too much of themselves once the shooting started. Making my way back to Jim, I heard the conversation as Stinger was telling Jim what kind of weapons systems he had onboard.

Mike Oscar, I have two 7.62 mini guns, a 40mm cannon and a 60mm cannon, all on the port side. We are loaded to capacity and prepared to give you fire support as soon as we locate you on the ground. Understand that you have a mini-ponder ready to transmit your beacon to us, over.

Jim quickly knelt by his rucksack, placed the mini-ponder in his hand

and turned the system on. He then keyed the handset and called to Stinger 121.

Stinger 121, this is Mike Oscar, over.

Roger Mike Oscar, this is Stinger 121, over.

Stinger 121, this is Mike Oscar the system is turned on and you should be receiving our signal at this time, over.

Mike Oscar, this is Stinger 121, say babe I am not receiving any signal at all. Turn the system off and on a couple of times and we'll try it again, over.

Jim did as he was instructed. Three separate times he turned the miniponder on and off. On the third and final attempt to get the system to signal, Jim left it on and attempted to make contact with Stinger 121 once again.

Stinger 121, this is Mike Oscar, over.

Ah roger, Mike Oscar, this is Stinger 121, over.

Stinger 121, this is Mike Oscar. We have followed your direction and turned the system on and off three times. Are you receiving our signal at this time? Over.

Mike Oscar, this is Stinger 121 that's a negative good buddy. I'm still not picking up anything. Your system must be hosed or malfunctioning. Over.

Stinger 121, this is Mike Oscar our system must be out. Can you see us with your infrared capabilities? Over.

Mike Oscar, this is Stinger 121, that's a negative babe there are so many bodies down there, I can't make out who is who. I can't support you with accurate fire until I have positive conformation of the friendlies on the ground. Over.

Realizing the urgency of our situation, I grabbed two parachute flares and headed for the center of our perimeter. Upon reaching the center, I yelled to Jim to have Stinger watch on his monitors for something. That will be the center of our perimeter.

Stinger 121, this is Mike Oscar, over.

Ah roger Mike Oscar, this is Stinger 121, over.

Stinger 121, watch your screens, you are about to see something. Try and lock in on what you see, that will be the center of our perimeter, over.

Ah roger Mike Oscar, this is Stinger 121 standing by, over.

Jim yelled over to me "Ok Les, let it fly." Kneeling on both knees, I took the cap off the flare, reversed it so the primer bottom and the striker were touching. Then with a hefty downward thrust, I struck the parachute flare tube hard against the ground. It immediately shot into the dark sky. At the same time the parachute flare shot out of the tube, enemy B-40s ignited and came crashing in on us from the southern, eastern and northern sectors of the perimeter. Instantly, they began exploding. It sounded like there were 10 or more B-40s fired at us simultaneously. Over and in between B-40 rocket explosions I screamed to Jim, "Did they get a fix on us yet?" Jim quickly replied, "that's' a negative. Fire off another one."

Just then a B-40 or something detonated directly behind me, picking me up of the ground and throwing me violently back onto the ground like I was a piece of paper. My head was spinning as I gasped for the air that had been knocked out of me. I was semi-confused and shell-shocked. One minute I was on my knees, and the next I was flying through the air, slamming into the ground. Regaining a small portion of my senses, I returned to the center of the perimeter and uncased a second flare. Again I called to Jim, "Have Stinger watch his screen. Something is coming up at him."

As Jim began speaking to Stinger, I shot the second flare into the sky. I hadn't received a response from Jim when I heard the thudding sound of an M-79 grenade launcher (40mm weapon have a very distinctive sound) followed by another explosion on top of the hill close to me. I screamed, "The NVA have M-79s." I hadn't gotten the words out of my mouth when four more rounds impacted, exploding all around the top of the tiny hilltop. My face felt like I'd been swarmed and stung by a hundred angry bees at once. I'd been hit in the face and left leg.

For a moment, I lay stunned, and then sat up to feel for the damage. Jim yelled to me as I sat upright and I tried to grasp the meaning of his words, "Stinger has a positive lock on our position. He'll deliver fire on the bad guys as soon as he is in position. I'll have him ready to fire a 360-degree circle around our position, 10 meters out, then work his way down the hill into the jungle 50 meters, okay?"

Jim was unaware that I'd been peppered with shrapnel. I yelled back to him, "Cut him loose on those little bastards."

As Jim continued his communications with Stinger 121, I did a quick inspection of my wounds. I had three pencils lead sized puncture wounds to my face and about the same number to my left leg. Blood poured down my face onto my fatigue jacket. The blood gushing from my leg felt like I had peed on myself. Carefully, I stood up and felt ghastly pain radiating through my face and leg. I began to hobble over to the southern sector to assist Brazier, who was shooting down the slope into the jungle. He shot another burst and looked over the edge, stunned to see nothing but dead bodies. Maintaining his attention forward, he said, "I don't see anyone. I think they are back off in the jungle, lobbing M-79 rounds in on us." I agreed with his analysis as we tried to pinpoint where the grenade launchers were firing from then we could accurately engage them.

Over on the eastern sector of the perimeter, Profit was still shooting short bursts from his M-60 into the tree line below his position. I yelled over to him, "Profit, if you don't have a target, stop shooting." He didn't hear me, so I went over to him to repeat the command. Instead of one M-79 shooting at us, there were more like four or five firing from various locations in the depths of the jungle.

Painfully, I ran over to Jim, reporting, "off in the eastern and southern sectors down in the tree line about 75 – 100 meters in we have about three, maybe five M-79s lobbing rounds up at us. Tell Stinger to spray that area and kill those gooks." Returning to Brazier's position, together we continued to try and locate the M-9s. We couldn't see any specific enemy gunners. We could only hear the weapons being loaded and fired up at us. The thudding distinct sound of another volley of M-79s was being fired off.

Over my shoulder, I screamed, "Incoming!" They were becoming more accurate with each round they fired. Two, maybe three rounds had detonated on or near the command post where Jim and the radio equipment were. A smoky dull haze filled the air as I jumped to my feet. As I made my way through the dust-filled air, I saw Jim still giving directions and distances to Stinger. He'd been hit with M-79 fragmentations to his right arm and side. Even though we were both wounded and knew virtually nothing about our troop status, we did know that if we stopped, we were going to die; we had to press on at all costs.

As Jim continued to direct Stinger, the firefight gained in intensity. We had to get Stinger to bring hell down on the NVA before they really started tearing us up. Jim raised his head and screamed, "Stinger is coming in hot. Tell the boys to get their heads down." I hustled around the perimeter as best I could, passing the word about Stinger preparation to fire. I had just scurried back into my foxhole when a bright red river of fire suddenly came down from out of the darkness from above.

Red tracers of death rushed down from the sky, followed by the long deep burping sounds of the mini-gun as it fired. After Stinger gave them a taste of his mini-gun he began placing a ring of 40mm cannon fire 25 meters down the hill away from us. Next, he fired his 60mm cannons into the surrounding jungle where the M-79 grenade rounds were being fired from? I heard a dragging sound of equipment coming from behind me and saw Jim pulling his rucksack with all of the radio equipment, still talking on the radio.

Jim asked me, "how was that?" Although he couldn't see me, I was grinning from ear-to-ear when I replied, "wonderful, just fucking wonderful. Tell Stinger to take his fire about 25-50 meters deeper into the jungle to our east and south on his next run."

Stinger 121 this is Mike Oscar, over.

Ah roger Mike Oscar, this is the old Stinger 121, over.

Stinger 121, this is Mike Oscar, my One-One is jumping up and down, and just loving what you are doing. He asked me to have you take your fire another 25 to 50 meters deeper into the jungle, if you would be so kind sir. Over.

Mike Oscar, this is Stinger 121, tell your One-One to sit back, relax and watch this. Here's hoping this brings love into his heart and a smile on his face, over.

I walked to the edge of the hillside for a more advantageous observation. From high above came the roar of the invisible 40mm and 60mm cannons. One second the jungle was black and silent, the next it was filled with explosions impacted about 10-20 meters inside the tree line.

Brilliant flashes of light brightened the once dark and mysterious jungle depths. Stinger's fire was accurate and deadly, taking only about ten seconds. When he had terminated the run, we heard the enemy's screams. Stinger had delivered an initially devastating blow that the NVA was unprepared for. Furthermore, Stinger's continuous circling sounds reminded them there was more where that came from. Jim was dragging his rucksack back to the center of the perimeter and I knew something was wrong.

Joining him, I realized that his total attention was drawn away from our situation to our sister unit the Bright Light team screaming for help:

Charlie Delta, this is Mike Oscar, over.

Mike Oscar, this is Charlie Delta, over.

Charlie Delta, understand that you have four wounded and are evading the enemy at this time, over.

Mike Oscar, this is Charlie Delta. Ah roger, we have four wounded and the bad guys are all over us. Do you have any overhead cover that we could use? Over.

Charlie Delta, this is Mike Oscar, that's ah roger babe on the overhead cover, I have Stinger 121 overhead. Do you have a mini-ponder with you? If so, I will divert my assets over to you to give you some relief from the bad guys, how copy, over?

Mike Oscar, this is Charlie Delta, that's affirmative on the mini-ponder, appreciate the loan of your Stinger if you could send him over to my location I sure could use some relief. These guys are kicking my ass, over.

Charlie Delta, this is Mike Oscar, roger babe, standby while I talk to the asset above. Over

Break. Break.

Stinger 121, this is Mike Oscar, over.

Ah roger Mike Oscar, this is Singer 121 I was monitoring your conversation with the other team on the ground. How can I be of assistance, over?

Stinger 121, this is Mike Oscar. The Bright Light team is approximately 6 to 8 clicks directly to our north. I would appreciate it if you could leave us for a while and head on over that way. Give the bad guys up there a taste of your firepower, over.

Mike Oscar, this is Stinger 121, that's ah roger. Are you going to be all right if I leave your area for a little bit? Don't want the Indians to be talking to me on the radio when I get back, over.

Stinger 121, this is Mike Oscar we're going to be okay for a while. I think you just swimming around in the area will make the NVA think twice before they try another action against us at this time. I would appreciate you heading on over and taking care of our partners, over.

Mike Oscar, this is Stinger 121, roger that. I'll mosey on over there and see what I can do, but, I'll be listening in case you need me back here real quick, out.

Break. Break.

Charlie Delta, this is Mike Oscar, over.

Mike Oscar, this is Charlie Delta, over.

Charlie Delta, this is Mike Oscar I have a friend coming over to stay with you for a bit and join in on the festivities. Have your mini-ponder ready to transmit he should be making contact with you at any time. How copy, over?

Mike Oscar, this is Charlie Delta, good copy. Thanks for the help good buddy. We'll get back with you later, out.

I hated to hear Stinger leave, but RT Habu needed help right now, not 10 minutes from now. We would have to make due until he returned. With any luck, the locals were all laying low licking their wounds. Since Stinger didn't go very far away, we could still hear his aerial firepower. Time after time, he made his gun runs in support of the evading Bright Light team. We felt confident that Stinger was beating back the enemy attack, but this was normal for running recon missions, even though they had fire support above them, only those fighting on the ground knew if the situation was improving or if they had a chance at all.

While Stinger supported the Bright Light, we prepared for another NVA attack. I checked our 60mm mortar to see how many rounds we had left. I also made sure I'd stripped all of the charge bags off each of the remaining rounds that we had left. There wasn't any need for us to fire more than 100 meters away. If necessary, I would straddle the tube again, point it straight up and down, and fire until we had completely expended all of our 60MM mortar ammunition.

As we once again redistributed ammo along the perimeter, enemy movement could once again be heard. They were going to launch another assault against us even though they knew we had overhead cover. We readied ourselves as massive quantities of adrenaline pumped through our veins. Deep down inside, I had a selfish thought, "Damn, I sure hope Stinger gets back here pretty quick." Glancing in the direction of the Bright Light, I saw Stinger delivering a red stream of fire from above and knew it would be some time before he was over us again. To my way of thinking, the NVA commander was most likely going to marshal his troops around the hilltop and hit us with everything he's got. A well-coordinated enemy attack from every direction at once would almost guarantee him success.

It was blindingly dark, the deepest dark I have ever seen or experienced in my life. The distant jungle tree line that lay just below us looked like a veiled black curtain. Eerie blood curdling sounds of evil softly began radiating from deep within the jungle, distant and quietly at first then continuously building in intensity. The tapping sound came from the left, like two sticks being beaten together in a continuous rhythm, tap, tap, tap, tap and tap. Then a second set of rhythmic beating sounds rang out to our front, followed closely by the third and fourth sets behind us and off to either flanks of our position. The initially beating of the sticks in all directions was in disarray then it became one beating sound in total unison with the others that surrounded us as it grew louder and louder.

The sound continued to intensify with each second that passed, tap, tap, tap, tap and tap. Its purpose hit me like a slap in the face as I quickly peered over the edge of our mountain high fortress to get a look down the slope. Initially I stared blindly seeing nothing then slowly I began seeing movement of men slowly clearing the jungle's edge. First one line of NVA troops appeared completely encircling my front, left and right sectors. Then a second and third row of NVA followed behind the first group of NVA.

I screamed over my shoulder "Here they come." The tapping was a way of keeping all of the troops in line as they marched upward. They were walking up the hillside shoulder-to-shoulder, closing ground towards us with every tap of the sticks. Jim sent a parachute flare into the sky. As it burst and illuminated the area, my heart jumped into my throat.

Four continuous circles or lines of NVA ground troops were literally marching up the hill, the first rank was now within 25 meters of reaching the top. The second, third and forth ranks were five to ten meters behind each other. They hadn't started firing their weapons yet they were waiting for us to initiate contact so they could concentrate their fire on our exact fighting position.

Brazer, Profit, and Jung simultaneously brought their M-60 machine guns to life, firing down into their ranks. The enemy soldiers immediately retaliated with a heavy volume of return fire on each M-60 machine gun position. Realizing that we needed heavy firepower, I scrambled back over to the 60mm mortar. With the mortar tube between my legs once again pointing it straight up and down, I dropped the first round down the tube. A thudding sound escaped the tube as the round quickly fired skyward. Without hesitation, I dropped round after round as fast as I could load. I'd dropped five 60mm mortar rounds before the first fired mortar round impacted our northern perimeter. Sitting on my butt with the tube between my knees, I began to tilt it slightly in various directions as I fired.

Although the mortar rounds hammered down on the advancing enemy troops the NVA continued to press forward. NVA Bodies were being thrown high into the air, blood flying freely in all directions as our mortar rounds and bullets tore sections of their bodies away. Heads exploded, leaving torsos with floundering arms and legs, performing a morbid last dance of life before it fell lifeless to the ground. Yet, they kept coming.

After I'd expended every mortar round we had, I ran to my foxhole to assist Jung, who was still franticly firing our machine gun. We knew, without a shadow of a doubt, that their numbers were too great for a small force like us to defend against any longer. It would only be a matter of time before we'd be wiped out entirely. Steadily they continued to advance, and we continued to fire, hoping and praying that we could mow as many of them down as humanly possible before we ran out of ammo or they were on top of the hill with us.

My desperate thoughts were on Stinger; where was he? How much longer before he would be over us again? Or would he be too late? Every time we killed one or a group of NVA soldier, others immediately took his place. They were now within 10 meters of reaching the top of the hill. As our final line of claymores detonated, one explosion followed another and flashes of blinding light encircled us. At this point, you couldn't tell the difference between friendly and enemy explosions, it was a free-for-all. In order to conserve ammunition, I turned my CAR-15 from automatic to single shot and began taking determined aim at any advancing NVA adversaries. One of the NVA soldiers was so close to me that I could see he carried his weapon at the port, head and eyes looking up. I slammed my rifle into his face, feeling it give against his skin and pulled the trigger. His head exploded with such force, it threw gray matter in every direction, including into my face. He never knew what happened.

Jung had been hit by shrapnel from a B-40 and lay bleeding at the bottom of our foxhole. I didn't have time to help him, I had to fight off this assault or we were both going to die. I had to overcome my natural instinct or desire to look behind me to see how the rest of the perimeter was faring. Instead, I kept my focus and attention concentrated on my sector and continued firing at enemy soldiers at every opportunity and direction that I could.

Now they were within arms distance of my position. As I fired into the advancing troops, I caught movement out of the corner of my eye and swung my rifle around. Four NVA soldiers had crested the top of the hill and momentarily stood searching for targets to engage. Reflexively, with a flip of my finger I switched my CAR-15 from single shot to automatic and fired at them in the full-auto mode. The hail of bullets impacted their faces and chests, collapsing them immediately.

Each passing second brought an increase in the fighting. As I turned back to my front, I saw a B-40 rocket ignite and dove to the bottom of my foxhole lying on top of Jung. The round missed our position and flew off down into the A Shau valley to detonate off into the shadows.

Rolling to one side, I fired in the direction the rocket had been fired from, dropping the gunner with the launcher still mounted atop his shoulder looking through the sight. Jim had the forethought and opportunity to fire another flare, providing us with the much-needed illumination during the heat of the battle. I somehow got back on my feet only to see another NVA soldier running directly at me, screaming at the top of his lungs. His bayonet was affixed to the end of his SKS rifle and he intended to run me through. Why he didn't fire his weapon at me as he charged, I'll never know. Since I hadn't had a chance to reload, I swung the butt of my rifle like a baseball bat into the side of his head, crushing his skull. Blood spewed all over me.

Losing my balance due to the force at which I swung my CAR-15 at the enemy soldier I fell on top of him then rolled to my side and grabbed for another magazine. I quickly loaded another magazine, tapped the bottom of it with the palm of my right hand and staggered to my feet. I saw Jim firing his weapon at NVA soldiers as they crested the hilltop on the southern sector of our perimeter. At my last glimpse at him I could see five or six dead NVA bodies lying around him and more coming.

At this point, everyone was shooting; using anything they had as a club or bat. Everything that could be construed as a weapon, rocks, sticks, knives, guns, and dirt, whatever it took to kill the enemy was being deployed. We were fighting to survive and it wasn't a pretty picture. Suddenly an inner calm came over me. I guess that mentally I knew I was about to die, I wasn't afraid anymore. I knew there was nothing I could do about what was to come, so I stood erect as the enemy came at me. Each time I pulled the trigger, an NVA soldiers fell.

I remember reloading four separate times because I was mentally awe struck with how peaceful it felt. I wasn't rushed or scared I just calmly kept loading one magazine after another into my weapon and continued to fire.

Surprisingly, the savage fighting only continued a few more seconds. As it came to a halt, we all stood erect around our perimeter, our hearts pounding, breathing heavily, and covered from head to toe in the blood of our enemies and of our own. We held our weapons at the ready and searched the perimeter in a blind stupor, completely numb. Some of the enemy had retreated, while the rest had been killed during the assault. The stench of blood filled my nostrils, and the taste of death filled my veins.

The hilltop was scattered with bodies and body parts, yet the tiny hilltop was still ours. I knew then how the Roman gladiators must have felt after they'd battled it out with swords and spears still being alive. Even though death and mayhem surrounded me, I felt no personal remorse for what I'd done. I was a soldier and I'd done my job. Stumbling over to me, Jim scanned the area and mumbled gasping for air, "Les, we did it. We beat them back again."

Continuing, still breathing hard he asked, "Why do they keep coming? We've held them off four times in one night. How many more times are they going to come at us?" I didn't respond, I just reached into my pocket and pulled out a Ruby Queen cigarette. After taking two deep drags off the foul smelling cigarette allowing the smoke to go down my throat and fill my lungs, I handed it over to Jim. I felt neither sorrow nor shame, instead, I felt victorious and alive.

Jim suddenly grabbed me by my arm, interrupting my moment of self-glory and commanded, "We've got to check the boys and see how many of them are still alive."

Stepping over bodies, I moved from position to position taking the casualty report. Everyone had been wounded; no one was spared. However, miraculously, no one was dead. We were down to 60% of our original fighting effectiveness. I walked back and gave Jim the report of our casualties and the amount of ammunition we had remaining. As we were conversing, the radio at our feet began to squelch, indicating incoming radio traffic. Jim picked it up to hear:

Mike Oscar, this is Stinger 121, over.

Stinger 121, this is Mike Oscar, over.

Mike Oscar, we are back on station at this time. Saw from a distance that you boys were having a little trouble with Charlie. Sorry it took so long to return but your buddy's to the north of you we're in a world of hurt, over.

Stinger 121, this is Mike Oscar, we had more than a little trouble, and we nearly got over run. We have about 50 to 60 dead NVA on top of the hill with us at this time I don't know how many dead NVA are below that we killed on their way up. We are getting low on ammo and don't think we can hold them off if they hit us again like they just did. The entire team is wounded. I don't know how much longer we can hold out, over.

Mike Oscar, this is Stinger 121, Jesus Christ, man. What kind of people do you guys have down there? You guys are killing machines, over.

Stinger 121, this is Mike Oscar, we need some help and some relief from these little gook shit heads. You got any ordnance left, over?

Mike Oscar, this is Stinger 121, that's a negative good buddy. However, we have radioed ahead for another Stinger to be on station in approximately 10 mikes that will replace us and stay with you because we're Winchester. We'll stay circling overhead to keep the bad guys off of you until my replacement arrives on station. How copy, over?

Stinger 121, this is Mike Oscar, good copy, thank you much, I'll buy the beer if, and that's a big if when we get back to the ranch, appreciate all of your help. Pass on our thanks to your crew. Over.

Mike Oscar, this is Stinger 121. That other team you sent us to help is more than likely going to need more assistance tonight also. They got Indians all over them. I'm trying to get another Stinger to come and support them, while I try and rustle up another Stinger for you. If I'm lucky we might get a Specter (C-130 Hercules gunship) to supports you. Those boys are in as much shit as you guys...They have two-dead; six wounded and are evading the enemy. Over.

Stinger 121, this is Mike Oscar. Thanks again for update and your help. We'll be standing by for the Stinger and/ or Specter you have on call, out.

I made my way back to my foxhole and began patching up Jung as best I could in the dark. My own wounds were giving me a great deal of pain and I was beginning to stiffen up from them. Hopefully, when the sun came up, we'd hear that RT Habu had been extracted and we too could get off this hilltop. Stinger was now informing Jim over the radio that he had company up there with him. However, this time it wasn't a Stinger it was a Specter gunship that had arrived on station.

Mike Oscar, Mike Oscar this is Specter 09, over.

Specter 09, this is Mike Oscar, over.

Mike Oscar, this is Specter 09, hear you boys have been having quite a party down there tonight. From the sensors I have on board, you have a large body of bad guys moving around about 100 meters to your north, on

the opposite ridge line adjacent to you. If you don't mind,
I'd like to take care of that situation for you, over?

Specter 09, this is Mike Oscar be my guest, you're cleared
in hot, over.

No soon had Jim finished the clearance for Stinger 09 to fire, than a
huge cracking sound followed from high up in the sky, followed by a
tremendous explosion on the ground about 100 meters north of our
position rang out. The explosion was followed immediately with a steady
stream of red tracers lighting up the dark night sky, then suddenly again
the cracking sound from up high followed by a second detonation.

Jim quickly jumped on the radio and called up to Specter 09.

Specter 09, this is Mike Oscar, over.

Mike Oscar, this is Specter 09, over.

Specter 09, this is Mike Oscar, what was that explosion
up in the sky? Were you hit, over?

Mike Oscar, this is Specter 09, (laughter from the pilot
lasted for about three seconds). We're fine up here that
was a 105mm howitzer specifically fitted for this baby.
By the way, you won't be having any action from that side
of the hill the targets have been neutralized, over.

Specter 09, this is Mike Oscar, could you continue to
scan around our immediate area, out to about 200 meters
for any bad guys nearing our position and terminates
them, over?

Mike Oscar, this is Specter 09, ah that's ah roger babe it
will be my pleasure. It looks pretty calm down there at
the present. I'm going to head on over and check on your
buddies up north of you. I'll be right back, over.

Specter 09, this is Mike Oscar, roger, good copy, out.

For the next three hours, Spector-09 flew back and forth between the
two teams; firing at multiple targets until he himself was Winchester
(out of ammunition).

# CHAPTER 22 (A-SHAU)

RT Habu lay face down on the jungle floor. The Bright Light tried their best to blend in with the vegetation, anything to hide from the enemy that surrounded them. Their backs were literally pinned against a 25-foot rock-face cliff. While providing rear security for the team, the cliff had a huge drawback. In order to escape if they had to they'd have to jump over the side of it. The North Vietnamese soldiers lay motionless in front of them and just off both flanks, waiting patiently for the right time to annihilate the small group of defenders.

Every man on The Bright Light searched the darkness with his eyes. Back and forth they scanned the blackness of the jungle, hoping to get a glimpse of the enemy, before he saw them. The monsoon rains poured down on them like faucets, drenching earth, man and equipment. Deep beneath the jungle, the aquifer became so saturated, it made it impossible for the ground to absorb any more water. An inch-high stream of muddy stinking water ran through the perimeter of the Bright Light off and down the rock face cliff that lay behind them.

Any other time, the tranquil sounds of water cascading off the cliff would have been soothing. Tonight, however, they brought uneasiness, constantly reminding the team of their awkward position and what might be required of them in order to escape. Hours passed without a sound or movement as darkness fell deeper over the A-Shau Valley.

Wes lay facing the southeastern end of the defensive perimeter, having placed the blasting machine for his claymore directly under his chin for quick access. Still, there was no movement or visual of the enemy. Being a seasoned veteran, Wes knew the silence wouldn't last much longer. From somewhere deep within the jungle suddenly came the sound of a weapon hitting against a piece of equipment. Even though the noise was faint, it was definitely a metallic sound that only a weapon produces. Some one out there made a mistake.

Anxiously, The Bright Light prepared them selves for the coming attack. Again, the metallic sound reverberated, this time from a different direction. Wes thought he saw a shadowy figure moving about 20 meters away kneel down. Wes had to call on every ounce of self-restraint and discipline he had not to fire at the faint shadowy object. The object would remain still, completely motionless like a rock statue, Wes constantly watching the image or figure kneeling down, patiently waiting.

The silence was broken when something came at the team flying through the tree limbs, followed by a squishing thud on the water-soaked jungle leaves. One after another, unseen objects began sailing through the air in the team's direction; the enemy was throwing grenades trying to draw fire. The first grenade exploded only 10 meters to the front of the team, followed by an earthshaking then another, then another. The concussion from the grenades radiated through each member of the Bright Light as a wave of pressure violently pulsed through the air. Having anticipated the NVA would use grenades to pinpoint the team's exact location, the team maintained silence, still searching the darkness for movement, resisting the urge to return fire. The enemy knew the American recon team was close, but they weren't sure how close.

Six more grenades were thrown, all detonating out in front of the team. Once again, rustling vegetation could be heard in every direction as the NVA closed the distance. With each passing second, the opposing sides drew closer together, destined to fight it out face-to-face.

If the NVA continued to close the gap in on The Recon Team as they blindly search for them the next time they through their grenades, they would be landing directly inside the perimeter. Either way, the fight was about to begin. Fingers went from being relaxed alongside receivers, to curling around triggers. Claymore firing mechanisms were taken off safe and made ready to detonate as the Bright Light prepared for the next group of grenades to be thrown. Stealth and deception by the team was no longer going to be an option.

Hearing the flight of the first grenades rustling through the vegetation, Danzer squeezed his claymore clacker, blowing the first of many personnel mines off in the direction of the concealed, ever-cautious advancing NVA. The unsuspected detonation filled the air with hot metal, tearing its way into flesh at a high rate of speed. Unknowingly, Danzer had blown his claymore while three NVA soldiers were standing directly on top of it. Hot pieces of metal fanned out in a 120- degree arch, hurling dirt and debris back onto the team.

Wisely, the Bright Light had placed their rucksacks in front of their heads to ward off the majority of the flying back blast debris the claymores generated, although they had no protection from the concussions that followed. Once Danzer had detonated his claymore, other team members followed suit, firing off two more of the mines.

Within seconds the NVA's small arms attack picked up in intensity. Bullets whizzed overhead, not affecting the team, as they were all prone at ground level. In an effort to keep their exact location under wraps for a few more minutes, the Bright Light did not return rifle fire. The detonation of the personnel mines and the enemy throwing hand grenades had momentarily ceased. The only sounds echoing through the darkness were from wounded soldiers.

Off in the distance, just south of them, Wes heard faint sounds of explosions and gunfire. He couldn't help but think to himself, "Well, I'm glad someone else is fighting their ass off. I'd hate to think we're in this alone and having all of the fun." Explosion after explosion rang and echoed throughout the A-Shau Valley, accompanied by a distant faint barrage of automatic weapons fire.

Cliff Newman listened to the battle sounds and thought, "RT Python must really be in the middle of it. I hope they are dishing it out instead of being on the receiving end of an ass-kicking." The Bright Light team members were very much aware that RT Python was to the south, providing them communications support and actively involved in a firefight. They prayed the NVA wouldn't overrun the team, cutting off their only source of communications with Phu Bai.

An hour passed as an evil silence fell over the A Shau valley. Everything was still; quiet, both up close and off in the distant. The only constant sound was the light tap tap, taping sounds of raindrops falling from the treetops down onto the wet jungle floor like that of a dripping water facet.

Finally, enemy movement sounds began to be heard as men ran through the jungle bush and an occasional commander shouting out orders. Danzer and Wes knew that when they were hit this time, it would be the real thing, an all-out NVA infantry ground attack. There would be no more reprieves. The team was enduring a hellish period of mental anguish and anticipation, knowing the enemy was moving in on them, and ultimately knowing they had no place to escape to except off the cliff down into the dark abyss that lay at their backs.

Wes realized that the figure he'd seen earlier wasn't the result of his mind playing tricks or his imagination, it was an enemy soldier sent to try and detect the Bright Light's movement. The shadow was apparently well trained, patient and disciplined, moving slowly then stopping for long periods of time, biding his time as he drew steadily closer. If successful, he'd eventually be within arms reach of the hidden recon team. When the attack started, the hidden NVA soldier would have the advantage of surprise over the unsuspecting team members. Wes continued to watch the phantom figure, as it was now within 5 meters of his defensive position directly in front of his weapon.

Unknown to the Bright Light, the NVA had deployed troops four to five men deep in preparation of the assault. The NVA unit was a reinforced company-sized element of 120 to 150 hardcore NVA infantry troops. They had deployed platoon-sized elements consisting of 30 to 45 men in three specific locations for this initiative.

Suddenly, all the distant noises ceased.

Wes's battle experience took this as a signal that the enemy was in position, simply waiting orders for the attack. As Wes continued to watch the sly ever persistent NVA soldier creeping up on them, he knew he couldn't allow him to get any closer or he'd be shooting them in the back as they focused on the enemy to the front and flanks. Wes slowly reached under his chin for the claymore clacker grasping it in his left hand he gave a healthy squeeze, resulting in a sudden flash of light, an ear-piercing explosion and a premature launch of the NVA's ground attack against the destitute but prepared Bright Light

As soon as the enemy troops heard and saw the explosion, they assumed it was their signal to attack. Standing erect and rushing wildly toward the team, the NVA soldiers apparently failed to realize that their muzzle flashes marked their exact locations like beacons in the night. The Bright Light members instinctively used the remainder of their claymores against the attackers. Almost simultaneously, the hidden mines detonated, saturating the area with pieces of hot metal, delivering devastating death and destruction to the NVA. Instead of the NVA surprising the Americans, the tables had been turned and their attack was temporarily thwarted.

Those who were dead from the initial blasts were spared the wrath of the American team's grenades and gunfire. As soon as the third claymore exploded, the Bright Light opened up with everything that they had, delivering a savage, violent onslaught of M-60 machine fun and CAR-15 fire. The battle was quick and decisive, lasting no more than 30 seconds. Only the tell-tell screams and crying of men dying and wounded provided the evidenced of the deadly clash. Without being told, members of the Bright Light team reloaded their weapons prepared for a follow-on attack. All but three claymores had been fired during the last assault. The NVA had been hurt, but they wouldn't make the same mistakes the next time.

Both advisories were blinded as to exactly what lay in front of them. The NVA had the upper hand when it came to the ability to freely maneuver about the jungle. This was their backyard and they knew approximately where the team was located. They also knew the Bright Light team had nowhere to go, because their backs were against a 25- to 30-foot cliff. The NVA assumed that no one in there right mind would take the chance of jumping off a cliff in the middle of the day, much less during the hours of darkness. Therefore, the NVA felt confident they would kill or capture the team.

Moving quietly among his men, Danzer stopped at each position, gathering an estimate of his losses. His situation was grave; they had one Montagnard dead and three wounded. So far, all of the Americans had escaped injury but were mentally charged up from the last attack. It would be impossible to take the dead Montagnard out with them at this point, especially if they had to fight their way out.

That was one of the many hazards of being a recon man; if there were any possible way, your team would bring your body out when they were extracted. But, sometimes they couldn't or the situation didn't permit the body to be removed from the field of battle. Likewise, it was often possible to get a recovery team back in to retrieve the dead, but not always.

Almost on cue, Danzer returned to his command position when a hail of enemy grenades started flying through the low-lying vegetation. Their effectiveness with the grenades was much improved; this time they were falling directly inside the Bright Light's perimeter.

One of the enemy grenades landed directly by Jimmy Horton's right leg, almost taking off his foot just above the ankle. Quickly rolling to his right side screaming in pain, Jimmy reached and found his syrrets of morphine and jammed the sharp point instrument deep into his right thigh muscle, injecting himself with the painkilling drug morphine. In turn he ripped off his A-7-A strap he used as a belt and tourniquet off his stump.

Jimmy knew that he didn't have the luxury of succumbing to his pain; a ground attack was in progress. Granted, he was severely wounded, but his chances of survival were much better if he kept fighting. In spite of a great amount of blood loss and almost unbearable pain, Jimmy picked up his weapon and continued to fight alongside his teammates. The Bright Light returned fire in a futile effort to prevent the NVA from throwing more grenades into the area. It was useless; enemy grenades were continuously landing within the perimeter. Without question, Danzer and his team were compromised and would surely be annihilated very quickly if they didn't break contact and evacuate their position immediately.

Taking a deep breath in desperation, Danzer screamed, "Blow the claymores and break contact. Jump off the cliff." The words were barely out of his mouth when all three of the remaining defensive claymores detonated in unison, launching their deadly pellets in the direction of the enemy. Ignoring the hail of bullets, B-40 rockets and Chi-Com hand grenades, Cliff Newman crouching at the waist, grabbed a hold of

Horton by his stabo rig and began dragging him toward the cliff. Upon reaching the edge of the cliff, the two men momentarily stopped and skeptically peered off into the deep darkness and prayed they would survive the fall. Although they had no idea what lay below or how far it was to the bottom, they had to jump.

Cliff leaped blindly into the abyss of darkness dragging Jimmy with him; their midair flight would only last a few seconds before impacting the rocks below. They impacted the flat rock-covered ground with a horrifying thud, shooting spears of pain up their feet and legs. Horton let out a bloodcurdling scream as he landed on his almost-amputated foot. Since their adrenaline levels were high, the initial pain was bad but not bad enough for them to just lay there. Once they'd regained their composure, it would be even more excruciating and almost intolerable to move.

Cliff and Jimmy had no time to waste, as they knew other team members would soon be making the jump, possibly falling on top of them. They had to move and move quickly. Cliff sluggishly got to his feet, grabbed Jimmy by his stabo rig and drug him away from their landing site. Although they didn't know it, three other team members were already on their way down at that very moment. Cliff and Jimmy had moved off just in time to avoid the barrage of falling bodies crashing down onto the rocky surface, grunting loudly from the pain of the impact.

Cliff had drug Jimmy off to a safe distance from the rock face landing zone and began to try and desperately determine the severity of Jimmy's injury to render him first aid as best he could in the darkness. Meanwhile, at the top of the cliff, enemy grenades continued to fly into the perimeter, causing the remaining defenders to crawl toward the cliff's edge. Wes was prepared to simply just slide off the edge of the cliff instead of jumping performing a commando role or drop. However, the intensity of the detonations of the weapons systems behind him encouraged him to vigorously leap out and away from a top the rock-face.

As he fell, he mentally willed himself to relax and bend at the knees to absorb the fall. Without warning, he hit the bottom with a smashing thud, knocking the air out of his body. As quickly as possible, Wes began to stagger away gasping for air just as he heard something crashing down through the trees above him smashing the ground. Realizing it was Danzer; Wes reached over and tried to help him to his feet, guiding him out of the landing area. Both men limped away, painfully making their way to the team's rallying point.

Danzer reached for his radio handset trying to reach RT Python, just a few kilometers away to render them a status report:

Mike Oscar, Mike Oscar, this is Sierra Mike, over.

After seconds passed with no response, Danzer tried again:

Mike Oscar, Mike Oscar, this is Sierra Mike, over.

Still no response from RT Python as Danzer pressed the radio handset against his ear. Reaching over Danzer's shoulder in the darkness, Wes followed the radio handset cable down to the radio contact connection. Upon reaching the end of the cable, Wes found that there was no radio and began a fit of nervous laughter.

Whispering in Danzer's ear, "You dumb shit. All you got in your hand is the radio handset. You jumped off the cliff and left the radio up on top with the bad guys." In disbelief, Danzer grabbed the cable, following it along to a frayed end. In a hurry, excited and in fear for his life he jumped off the cliff, never realizing that he'd forgotten to grab his rucksack that held the radio. Wes was still laughing out loud when they reached the rallying point where the first part of the team laid exhausted and in pain.

Danzer dropped the handset on the wet jungle floor and reached for his URC-68 survival radio, began transmitting over it instead.

Keying his survival radio an URC-10 immediately sent out an emergency distress beeper over the Guard channel. Captain Jim Butler the One-zero of RT Python quickly responded to the emergency call from the URC-10. Recognizing Butler's voice, Danzer gave a quick situation report. As he spoke, an explosion on the other end of the radio temporarily halted their conversation. Minutes passed as Danzer tried to reestablish communications. All manner of terrible thoughts went through Danzer's mind as he repeated the call sign for RT Python over and over again. Finally, the call was answered:

Sierra Mike, this is Mike Oscar, over.

Mike Oscar, this is Sierra Mike, we are in some serious shit down here. Have you got any overhead cover at your location yet, over?

Sierra Mike, this is Mike Oscar, that's a negative at this time. I have been informed that a Stinger will be arriving at my location in approximately 10 mikes. Once I beat back this NVA attack if we can, and they don't overrun us I'll send him over to you, how copy, over?

Mike Oscar, this is Sierra Mike, hang in there buddy. I know you're getting your asses handed to you, but I'm not having a beer-drinking contest over here either. So keep the faith, I'll be standing by to receive Stinger when and if he arrives in time, out.

As the remainder of the Bright Light team limped painfully off into the rallying point, they instinctively took up security positions, forming a hasty defensive perimeter. They lay motionless, hoping the NVA wouldn't realize they'd jumped off the cliff. Up top, a massive round of enemy firepower announced the NVA's final assault into the abandoned Bright Light position. It became apparent that at least three of the enemy soldiers on the assault team were unfamiliar with the terrain, as they charged head long off the cliff. Their bodies could be heard smashing against the rocks, bones breaking, skulls bursting as they impacted the rock face cliffs bottom.

A deafening silence closed over the area just before enemy conversations could be overheard on the higher ground above the team. Habu's interpreter listened intently and whispered to Danzer, "They know we jump, they throw more grenades down on us, very soon." He'd barely finished the sentence when one landed close to the team. Hearing the grenade land with a bouncing thud, Mac threw himself over Jimmy to protect him from close proximity of the enemy grenade. While shielding his fallen comrade, Mac absorbed a grenade fragment that would have killed Jimmy had it hit him. A large piece of shrapnel about two inches in length had lodged in Mac's back as blood gushed from the wound.

Hearing that Mac had been hit, Doc Woodham crawled over and felt his back, as his hand moved across Mac wet back he came across a large piece of metal protruding from the wound site. Taking Mac's field dressing from his load-bearing equipment, Doc dressed the wound as best he could in the darkness. More enemy grenades were on their way down through the trees bouncing off the rocks as they hit. In a last-ditch effort to get the team away from the explosions, Danzer ordered them to crawl away from the cliff to the east. Cliff and Wes grabbed Jimmy and began dragging him through the jungle on his back.

For 10 pain-filled minutes, the wounded Bright Light team crawled through the darkness. Each stretch of their weary arms and strenuous push of their legs took them farther away from the Chi-Com grenades that were hurling hot metal through the air. Everyone kept his chest and face hugging the wet appalling smell of the jungle floor as they crawled out of range of the deadly grenades putting distance between them selves and the NVA.

While RT Habu blindly crawled through the darkness their bodies against leech-infested jungle floor, Danzer directed a hasty perimeter be established while Doc Woodham prepared to work on Jimmy's severed leg. Quietly reaching for another morphine syreet, Jimmy once again injected himself with the powerful morphine painkiller. Becoming semi-sedated from the morphine flowing through his body, Jimmy lay so quiet and still that Doc Mac and Wes thought he might have died. Wes was almost directly on top of Jimmy when Jimmy uttered aloud, "Whoever that is, get off my fucking hand, you heavy son-of-a-bitch." Relief washed over Wes as he laughed and whispered into Jimmy's ear, "Hey Hound Dog, it's Wes and Mac Doc Woody is working on your foot."

Slowly and deliberately, Doc Woodham began to feel down Jimmy's injured left leg starting at the groin and ending up where once Jimmy's jungle boot should have been. Jimmy's foot was partially blown off, with only jagged bloody bone fragments and tissue remaining from the instep forward. Taking one of his own morphine syrret, Doc Woodham jammed it into Jimmy's right leg as the wounded man cursed, "Damn Doc you jammed that one all the way down to my ass hole. Doc didn't reply, he just continued to work on Jimmy in the pitch-black darkness.

Removing Jimmy's second first-aid field dressing and extending it to its maximum length, Doc gently began to tie off the severed foot by process of touch-and-feel. Jimmy moaned softly as Doc applied the field dressing to the exposed bloody stump. Concerned with the amount of blood still coming from the foot Doc called Mac over to apply direct pressure to slow down the bleeding.

It became apparent that the bleeding wasn't decreasing; Doc took about a foot of duct tape from his web gear, tore it in half and stuck it to his chest for easy access. He then took out his own field dressing, put it on top of the bandages he'd just applied to Jimmy and began running the tape under the almost-detached jungle boot.

He brought the ends of the tape under the boot and up the calf, securing them off there. Once the tape and second field dressing was in place, no further wetness could be felt. The bleeding had stopped and in a couple of minutes, the second and third syreets of morphine would kick in. Doc leaned over to Jimmy and whispered, "Hang in there babe. We're going to get you out of here, the morphine will take affect soon and you won't feel any more pain. Just hang in there."

As strange as it sounds, Jimmy had a tremendous advantage of having been wounded four previous times on different operations. Although he'd never lost a body part, physiologically he was acquainted with the pain and how best to deal with it.

Doc Woodham moved over to inform Danzer of the seriousness of Jimmy's wound. The team had now sustained three dead and everyone had been wounded; Jimmy and Mac were the worst. If they didn't get out soon, Jimmy would bleed to death. Danzer was very aware that their current position and situation was very grave at best. They needed to move farther away from the rock-face cliff but would be hampered and slowed down by the wounded team.

Crawling over to Doc Woodham, Danzer asked if Jimmy could be moved. Surprisingly, Jimmy himself answered, "Yeah, hell yeah, I can move. Just get me someone to lean against. I'll have to sit this dance out, but I can move."

Mac volunteered to be Jimmy's crutch and Danzer ordered just loud enough for the team to hear. "Point man out, and move 100 meters to the east as fast as we can." The Montagnard point man replied, "No sweat Trung Si." In the darkness, the team members slowly followed the point man, each holding onto the man in front of him, maneuvering eastward down the hillside. The travel was painful, and slow.

One of the cardinal rules of running recon missions is you're taught never to move through the jungle at night, unless it's a life-or-death situation, and this incidence qualified. Since Mac was acting as Jimmy's crutch, he was unable to hold onto the man in front of him. Therefore, he had one of the Little People act as his guide through the thick vegetation. The bewildered Bright Light made slow and painful progress as they struggled to maintain some type of security and movement through this pit of darkness.

Now that their ears were ringing less, they could hear the humming sound of an approaching aircraft. Danzer's URC-10 came to life:

Sierra Mike, this is Stinger 121, over.

Stinger 121, this is Sierra Mike, over.

Sierra Mike, this is Stinger 121, your buddies to the south of you sent me over, saying you may need a little help down there, over.

Stinger 121, this is Sierra Mike, you bet we do. We have three dead and everyone is wounded, with two Americans seriously wounded. Say old buddy could you put some fire down 100 meters to our west, over?

Sierra Mike, this is Stinger 121, that's ah roger I'll be more than happy to assist. But, first I need to pinpoint your location, so I don't fire you up, over.

Keeping the URC-68 close to his ear, Danzer asked, "Wes, do you still have the mini-ponder?" Wes replied, "Yeah, in my rucksack." In a soft voice, Danzer ordered the team to halt and directed Wes to set up and activate the mini-ponder for transmission. During all the excitement and explosions of the past 30 minutes, The Bright Light hadn't been able to hear Stinger providing fire to RT Python.

It only took Wes a few moments to extract the mini-ponder from his rucksack and start its transmission:

Sierra Mike, this is Stinger 121, over.

Stinger 121, this is Sierra Mike, over.

Sierra Mike, this is Stinger 121, old buddy your partners across the way said that you could use a little company over here. Could you bring up your mini-pounder so I can get a good lock on you locations, over?

Stinger 121, this is Sierra Mike the mini-pounder is transmitting have you got a good tally on my position at this time, over?

Sierra Mike, this is Stinger 121, that's a roger babe, I have a good tally on your location. Now, lets get down to business where did you say your bad guys are, and we'll see if we can get them off your back over?

Stinger 121, this is Sierra Mike, I have a large re-enforced company size element moving against me could you give me a 360-degree wall around my position about 25 meters out. Then move your fire out 100 meters to my west, and put fire down all in that area, how copy, over?

Sierra Mike, this is Stinger 121, be advised that my fire will be danger close. I'll need your initial for the record before I can fire, over.

Stinger 121, this is Sierra Mike, initials follow: Romeo Lima Delta, over.

Sierra Mike, this is Stinger 121, I'm coming in hot at this time. Get your heads down here it comes. I'm going to light their fire and rock their world, over.

While Stinger 121 was communicating with Danzer, he'd locked in on The Bright Light's location and began maneuvered his aircraft into firing position. No sooner had Stinger directed the team to get their heads down, than high in the darkened sky, a bright river of red tracers began screaming down around the team.

Although the aircraft itself was obscured from their vision, its familiar belching sound from their mini-guns rang out clear. Stinger placed a red ring of tracers around the team as they lay in their defensive perimeter. Instead of impacting the ground and bouncing as they did on normal hard surfaces, the tracers sunk into the wet jungle floor being absorbed into the saturated jungle.

Sierra Mike, this is Stinger, 121, over.

Stinger 121, this is Sierra Mike, over.

Sierra Mike, how was that? With your permission, I am going to move my fire up the hill side a little, about 100 meters and introduce my self to them and my 40mm cannon, how copy, over?

Stinger 121, this is Sierra Mike, good shooting. I sure feel better now that you're above us. Adjust your fire 100 meters due west and you're cleared in hot, over.

Sierra Mike, this is Stinger 121, ah roger, cleared in hot, over.

A few mere seconds passed before the sound of Stinger's 40mm cannon began thumping and firing, detonating into the jungle above, 100 meters west of the Bright Light team. Screams from the NVA filled the air down into the center of the A-Shau Valley as Stinger tore them to pieces. Then, a different sound erupted from above as Stinger employed his 60mm cannon against the enemy. Explosion after explosion echoed through the jungle for a full five minutes. As soon as Stinger had completed his attack, Danzer called to him:

Stinger 121, this is Sierra Mike, over.

Sierra Mike, this is Stinger 121, over.

Stinger 121, this is Sierra Mike. Hey babe, we can hear the bad guys above us screaming and yelling every time you fired. Request that you go high-and-dry and standby for additional targets as they present themselves, over.

Sierra Mike, this is Stinger 121, that's ah roger, going high-and-dry, just call me if you need me. I'll be boring holes up here in the sky, out.

Distant moans and groans filled the jungle from the wounded and dying that lay above the team sounded like something out of a horror movie. Death and gunpowder hung heavy in the air. Stinger had performed his task magnificently; he'd hurt the enemy severely, and they were now licking their wounds, aware that circling high above was a fortress of firepower and death. The only question now was how long would this temporary delay in enemy action last against the determined NVA? Stinger told Danzer of his plans for flying back and forth between the two recon teams, supporting each until he ran out of ammo. He also informed Danzer that he had made arrangements for another gunship to replace him when he was Winchester.

True to his word, Stinger alternated his support between the two beat-up recon teams, ultimately circling over RT Python as his replacement came on station.

As Jim and I sat around the radio, we heard another aircraft closing in on our position. Jim turned to me and said, "That must be 121's replacement. It sure feels good to have these guys flying above us." As before, Jim kept the PRC-25 handset next to his ear, even when he and I conversed.

Mike Oscar, this is Stinger 121, over.

Stinger 121, this is Mike Oscar, over.

Ah Roger Mike Oscar, this is Stinger 121 my replacement is on station and will be contacting you momentarily. I have been briefing him, and he is aware of your situation and that of the other team to the north of you. Good luck and keep the faith; this is Stinger 121, out.

Stinger 121, this is Mike Oscar; say if and when we get back, the beers are on me. Thanks for getting our butts out of a crack. You saved our ass, out.

Mike Oscar, this is Stinger 127, over.

Stinger 127, this is Mike Oscar, over.

Mike Oscar, this is Stinger 127, hear you boys are up to your eyeballs in Indians down there. Could you provide me with a signal so I can lock in on your position? Understand that your mini-ponder is out, over.

Stinger 127, this is Mike Oscar, glad to have you with us. We're just having a gay ole time down here. We got bad guys all around us, I'm sure you were briefed by Stinger 121. He gave us great support. I'll be giving you a signal in about one mike, how copy, over?

Mike Oscar, this is Stinger 127, that's a good copy, am standing by for your signal, over.

Jim told me to go back out to the center of the perimeter and fire a parachute flare so Stinger 127 could lock in on our position. As I skeptically secured another hand flare and hobbled to the center of the perimeter, I thought, "The last time I did this, all hell broke loose and I got hit. Wonder what's going to happen this time?"

Cautiously I bent down to the ground, my CAR-15 hanging around my neck then I removed the cap from the flare. Reversing the cap to the other end, I raised it over my head and slammed it hard against the ground. As designed, the flare shot straight up, heading high into the air, marking our current location. This time , there was no response from the NVA, only the swishing sounds of the flare rocketing skyward. Once it had reached its maximum altitude, the world was lighted up.

Mike Oscar, this is Stinger 127, over.

Stinger 127, this is Mike Oscar, over.

Ah roger Mike Oscar, I have a good lock on you, but that flare sure made me a little nervous. I thought for a minute there that I was taking fire, and then I realized what it was. Mike Oscar do you have any targets for me at this time, over?

Jim started to respond, when green tracers could be seen headed skyward from off to the south of our position.

Mike Oscar, this is Stinger 127, over.

Stinger 127, this is Mike Oscar, over.

Mike Oscar, this is Stinger 127, did you see what that little bastard just did? He shot at me. Hold on a second and I'll be right back, I going to tear his ass off for him, the little asshole, out.

As Stinger 127 slowly drifted to the south, a stream of red tracers came down from the heavens, followed by the delayed burping sound of the mini-guns, as they fired in the distance. A second and third wave of mini-gun fire followed, down into the same location.

Mike Oscar, this is Stinger 127, over.

Stinger 127, this is Mike Oscar, over.

Mike Oscar, this is Stinger 127, I took care of that little bastard who just shot at me. Can you believe he shot at me? Mike Oscar, let's get back to you situation, do you have any targets for me at this time, over?

Stinger 127, this is Mike Oscar, yea babe when you make it back over here, I need for you to fire down into the jungle tree line to my north and east about 25 meters, then work your way out to about 100 meters, how copy, over?

Mike Oscar, this is Stinger 127, that's ah roger. Mike Oscar, I'm going to make my run and intermix my fire with 7.62 Mike Mike mini-gun, 40 Mike Mike cannon and follow it up with 60 Mike Mike. How copy, over?

Stinger 127, this is Mike Oscar, good copy; you're cleared in hot, over.

Stinger 127's massive display of fire power followed by explosions and its magnificent light display was amazing, as it reassured us that he was here to deliver lifesaving support for our survival. For the next hour, screams and cries from the explosions could be heard as men died alone in the darkness. Stinger had delivered yet another blow to our enemy, hiding like the evil that he was within the shadows of the A-Shau Valley. Both NVA personnel and supplies were being destroyed as Stinger dished out his aerial death. Repeatedly flying short-tees back and forth between RT Python and The Bright Light, Stinger 127 provided lifesaving support and a boost to our morale as well.

Mike Oscar, this is Stinger 127, over.

Stinger 127, this is Mike Oscar, over.

Roger Mike Oscar, I'm Winchester and have to RTB (return to base) but have contact with Specter 124 who is coming in on station at any moment. I've already briefed him on your situation, and he is prepared to make contact with you as soon as he gets in the area. But, I'll stay with you until he gets here, I'll bore some holes in the sky above you and stay around for a while, how copy, over?

Stinger 127, this is Mike Oscar, that's a good copy. Appreciate your assistance, and like I told Stinger 121, the beers are on me if and when we get back. Tell your crew up there that we appreciate them also, out.

For the next 20 minutes Stinger 127 flew a wide circle above RT Python and the Bright Light, letting the bad guys know he was still in town warning them to stay away. It was now one o'clock in the morning and call signs for each team had changed at midnight. This was standard operating procedure for recon teams when we deployed into the field. Call signs were changed every 24 hours for security purposes. Our call signs were pre-designated by our communications section back at MACV headquarters. RT Python had now taken on the call sign of Whisky Zulu, and the Bright Light was now Bravo Delta.

Whisky Zulu, this is Specter 124, over.

Specter 124, this is Whisky Zulu, over.

Whisky Zulu, this is Specter 124. Roger babe, I'm loaded to the gills and ready to assist. I got your general location from Stinger 127 while in flight and will be coming over to get a positive on you. My sensors will pick you up when I fly over, how copy, over?

Specter 124, this is Whisky Zulu, a roger good buddy, no targets at this time, but once you have us locked in, sure would appreciate if you would scan the area and take on any targets of opportunity that you pick up, how copy, over?

Whisky Zulu, this is Specter 124, I have a good tally on your location at this time and will continue to scan your area for Indians. Understand that you have another unit on the ground, approximately 10 clicks to your north that also needs support, over.

Specter 124, this is Whisky Zulu, that's ah roger on our sister unit to the north. Would appreciate you going over and checking on them once you have scanned our location, over.

Whisky Zulu, this is Specter 124, that's a good copy, out.

Specter 124 flew over our position for about 10 minutes before he departed to make contact with the Bright Light.

Break. Break.

Bravo Delta, Bravo Delta, this is Specter 124, over.

Specter 124, this is Bravo Delta, over.

Bravo Delta, this is Specter 124, how you doing down there guys? Your friends across the way sent me over to check on you and see if I could be of any assistance, over.

Specter 124, this is Bravo Delta, roger babe, sure glad to see ya. Do you have a good tally on my location? I have my mini-ponder on at this time, over.

Bravo Delta, this is Specter 124, that's ah roger on your

mini-ponder, I have a good tally on your location. Do you have any targets for me at this time, over?

Specter 124, this is Bravo Delta, we can hear bad guys moving around us up to my west, approximately 50 to 100 meters. They are trying to make their way down a rock cliff face to get to us. Would appreciate it if you could let them know that you are above, how copy, over?

Bravo Delta, this is Specter 124, that's a good copy. I can see them on my monitors. You are pretty accurate on your assumptions it looks like about sixty to eighty bad guys. I'll be back after I greet them with my calling card, out.

Danzer passed the word that Specter 124 was on station and getting ready to make a gun run off to the west. Specter 124 maneuvered his C-130 Hercules into position and began his orbit over the Bright Light's position. Without warning, he announced his presence to the NVA who were frantically trying to hide behind anything they could attempt to conceal themselves from him. Their efforts were stymied within seconds as Specter 124 opened up. All hell broke loose as the big gunship began firing to the west of the Bright Light team.

Specter was right on target; his sensors brought the guns directly onto the enemy with deadly accuracy. The run was short and sweet. Danzer's radio came to life as contact was made:

Bravo Delta, this is Specter 124, over.

Specter 124, this is Bravo Delta, over.

Bravo Delta, this is Specter 124, we took care of that little band of Indians that you had lurking above you. Do you have any other targets for us at this time, over?

Specter 124, this is Bravo Delta, hey babe we can hear the bad guys screaming and hollering down here. You must have bloodied their noses. Sure appreciate your help. I have negative targets for you at this time, over.

Bravo Delta, this is Specter 124, okay good buddy, I

think I'll just mosey on back over to your partners to the south and see what's for breakfast. If you need me, I'll be listening, out.

Specters 124 called RT Python while enroot.

Whisky Zulu, this is Specter 124, over.

Specter 124, this is Whisky Zulu, over.

Whisky Zulu, this is Specter 124, say babe from my screens you have a large enemy-sized unit, about two to three platoons or more moving toward you on the backside of a ridge adjacent to your position that you can't see. Specter 124 requests permission to engage those targets at this time, over.

Specter 124, this is Whisky Zulu roger you're cleared in hot Specter 124. Give them a taste of what you're serving, over.

Between RT Python and the Bright Light, Specter 124 fired upon the unsuspecting enemy and halted their movement for the time being. Neither team could accurately report back to Specter 124 on his air strike and render an assessment, only that he was bringing heavy concentrations of fire down on the enemy.

# CHAPTER 23 (A-SHAU)

Having fired his entire load of ordnance in support of the two recon teams on the ground, the Specter gunship 124 was replaced by Specter 128

This state-of-the-art C-130 Hercules was armed to the teeth with two 7.62 mini-guns, one 60mm cannon and a 105 Howitzer.

These special aircraft were primarily used during the hours of darkness along the Ho-Chi-Min Trail they were capable of taking out any of the NVA's modes of transportation and eliminating antiaircraft gun positions. Specter 128 had infrared capabilities, possessing the ability to detect people, warm metals and a host of other objects used for search-and-destroy missions. Like the C-130 before him, Specter 128 would provide air cover for both teams the remainder of the night.

The first Specter had proven to be the saving grace for RT Python and the Bright Light, as they lay surrounded by large NVA elements. Time after time, the aircraft expended its ammunition in support of the teams against strategic targets designated by the men on the ground. Over the course of the evening, the two Special Forces recon teams would completely expend two Stingers and two Specters of all of their ammunition. First light was due in less than an hour.

The wounds I'd received over the past few days were beginning to take a mental and physical toll. They weren't disabling or even life threatening there were just a lot of them. My entire body had been repeatedly peppered by tiny pieces of metal slivers. Each time I made the slightest movement, they cut into my skin, inching their way into my nerves and sending waves of pain up to my brain.

My fatigues were becoming stiff from the dried blood, which covered me from head to toe. Some of it was mine, but most of the blood had come from my enemies. I smelled horrible, a wicked mixture of dried blood, gunpowder, horrendous body odor and sweat. I'd sweated so profusely that my joint areas of my fatigues were marked with visible white salt stains.

As the daylight slowly overtook the darkness, we could see dead and dismembered NVA bodies sprawled out from the jungle's edge up to the crest of the hilltop we sat upon. The decimated bodies were just heaps of flesh, broken, mangled and bloody. This grotesque aftermath of war was branded into our minds. Despite the tremendous number of dead, we heard even more enemy movement deep in the jungle.

Undoubtedly, the NVA were preparing for another strike against us. If they hit us again, it would result in another bloodbath. We felt and assumed that we'd destroyed the majority of their forces. Between the three Specters and two Stingers who supported the two teams, we'd killed at least 500 to 600 of them in a fairly short time.

I turned my attention to our battle-weary team and noticed that no one smiled, laughed or even spoke. We were zombies, slowly and deliberately checking our equipment, redistributing ammunition, all in a daze. It had been three days since we'd had any real rest, sleep or food. We were physical wrecks. How any of us kept going is a mystery to me, even to this day.

Brazier sat on the back portion of his foxhole hunched over, his elbows resting on his knees a lit cigarette dangling loosely from his mouth. Brazier's eyes steadily fixed on the bottom of his foxhole, staring off into a void where only he was allowed to venture. Hundreds of expended 7.62 machine gun cartridges and machine gun ammo links lay in large heaps surrounding his M-60 machine gun position. Occasionally Brazier would raise his blood-covered head scanning the area with his blood shot eyes. Slowly Brazier moved his head and eyes from left to right.

He like the rest of us was completely physically and mentally exhausted and weary over the past three deadly days of death and agony. I thought to myself, *do I look as bad as Brazier?*

My now zombie like gaze left Larry and lazily moved over to where Duo our tell-gunner and Baby-son (BS) were. Duo had suffered numerous shrapnel wounds to his right and left sides to include all of his upper body. BS still full of vim and vigor wasn't wounded at all. I would have bet my paycheck that Duo watched over him like a hawk and protected him during the fighting. However, Duo was tired, weary and weak while having to put up with BS and his untiring joking around and playing. I couldn't hear what was being said but I guess Duo had, had enough of BS then threw an empty CAR-15 magazine at him as BS laughed and quickly danced away from him.

Prophet sat motionless the butt of his M-60 machine gun pressed hard against his right shoulder his cheek resting on the stock of the weapon. Prophets assistant gunner was busy grabbing hand full after hand full of expended 7.62 brass and machine gun links then throwing them out of their foxhole off the side of the hilltop. Prophet never moved he simply maintained the weapon against his shoulder staring mindlessly off into the dense hot jungle that lay silent below his position.

Jim as usual was busy talking on the radio while two other little people moved back and forth through the command position from one location to another. As Jim looked over at me not realizing that I was checking him out his eyes were circled with black bags under his eyes. His face was swollen from the wounds he had received and one of his lenses to his black-rimmed glasses had been cracked during the fighting.

Yet it didn't deter his completion of his mission. Jim's fatigues were a mixture of red clay, blood and sweat. It was a dingy reddish brown color with circles of body salt sweat rings.

In every direction that my eyes moved they fell on the remains of deformed dead men, body parts, enemy equipment, the blood stained ground coupled with the burnt spots where ordinance had detonated on the hilltop. All the signs and true signatures of men engaged in war. Death surrounded us, and in many cases we were the tools that brought about that death.

The smell of burnt iron ore or some type of metal filled my nostrils with the once living cells that had died in man that begins to fill the air with that pungent lingering slaughterhouse smell of flesh and blood. The harsh rustic order of burnt blood and tissue that was once human flesh filled the air. In turn that rawhide smoldering smell circled us from every direction even with the slight breeze from the east the odor saturated every air molecule that the very oxygen released from my lungs was replaced with its consistency and death.

Even with all of the death, misery, suffering, hunger, fatigue, adversity and danger we had faced over these past few days we still stayed the course. We kept the faith with one another and maintained our silent but solemn pledge to our fellow recon men to die if necessary to preserve a friend's life.

The sounds of an OV-10 engine broke the silence of the early morning. The extraction package for the Bright Light was on its way. Soon the outnumbered, outgunned recovery team would be on their way back to the launch site. Somewhere to the north, Covey flew high above the Bright Light's position, circling as he waited for the arrival of the SAR mission. Danzer and the Bright Light team lay quietly hiding beneath the cool jungle growth, waiting for the Jolly Green and its escort of A1-E Sky Raiders.

According to the sounds coming from the rock-face cliff, the NVA had successfully negotiated the drop-off and was moving in on the team, despite the devastating fire brought against them from above the previous night. If the enemy could move against the wounded Bright Light team and destroy them, it would be a tremendous physiological victory for them, and would discourage other recon teams.

Wes lay on his stomach with his eyes moving from left to right in anticipation of an NVA soldier emerging through the jungle. In order to get close to the hidden team, Charlie would have to maintain slow and deliberate movement. Wes slowly looked over his shoulder at the group of men waiting for the arrival of the CH-53. Each tried to blend in with his surroundings long enough to be extracted. Hearing the aircraft raised their anxiety. As they envisioned freedom from above, while death stared them in the face here on the ground.

Danzer had kept his radio on all night to direct fire. As a result, his batteries were drained so he'd turned the communications and extraction over to Cliff Newman. Cliff attentively listened for the voice of Covey. He didn't have to wait long:

> Bravo Delta, Bravo Delta, this is Covey 224 (David Cheney the back seater and Captain Yarbrough the pilot of the OV-10), over.

> Covey 224, this is Bravo Delta, over.

> Bravo Delta, this is Covey 224, how are you guys doing down there? Big bird is approximately 15 minutes out. We have monitored all of your radio traffic through RT Python situation reports. You guys had a pretty rough night, but I'm here to take you home for some chow and beer. Are you and the team prepared for extraction, over?

> Covey 224, this is Bravo Delta we've been ready since yesterday. Everyone is beat, hungry and tired. Our seriously wounded need extraction immediately. We have bad guys all around us and anticipate a ground attack any moment. Did you bring any fast-movers with you? Over

> Bravo Delta, this is Covey 224, that's a negative on fast-movers but have two sets of Hobos escorting the Jolly Green approximately five mikes out. Once they get on station, I'll turn you over to them to use, as you need. I'll be monitoring your frequency while my front-seater continues to brief the Jolly Green on your situation and plan for extraction of the team. How copy, over?

> Covey 224, this is Bravo Delta, good copy. What's the status on RT Python, over?

> Bravo Delta, this is Covey 224, the team south of you has had it pretty bad all night, heavy fighting and casualties. They've refused extraction until you are taken out first. I have a complete UH-1 extraction package on the way

from Quang Tri and Phu Bai to get RT Python at the same time the SAR mission is extracting your team. I'll be flying back and forth between both of you to coordinate extraction. How copy, over?

Covey 224, this is Bravo Delta, good copy. We'll be standing by waiting for the SAR and Hobos to make contact with us, out.

While Cliff talked with Covey, Danzer moved about the perimeter, checking on the team and preparing the wounded to be extracted. They would be going out first, followed by the rest of the team. All eyes were on Cliff as he removed the radio from his ear. He smiled and gave the thumbs-up sign, indicating to the team they would be extracted today; the package was on its way.

An immediate sense of relief washed over everyone although they knew the extraction wouldn't be easy they would be going out under fire. The NVA had fresh troops, ample light and heavy weapons and a complete knowledge of the area and how the extraction would progress. The Bright Light team had been in tight situations before, but none quite like this. Should they actually make it out alive, this was going be one hell of a war story.

Covey moved farther east to intercept the SAR mission. They didn't want to provide advance warning, with the extraction package so close. As Cheney sat patiently in the back seat of the OV-10, he listened to Captain Yarbrough and the Jolly Green pilot discussing the situation and planning their extraction.

SAR-2, SAR-2, this is Covey 224, over.

Covey 224, this is SAR-2, over.

SAR-2, this is Covey 224 glad you guys could join the party. Are you the same SAR that tried to extract the team yesterday before we had to divert? Over

Covey 224, this is SAR-2 that a roger, roger I was with your yesterday, Over

SAR-2 this is Covey 224 let me bring you up to speed on

what's been going on with the team since our diversion from yesterday. Three Stingers and two Specters have supported the Bright Light team all night. The team on the ground has been in constant contact with the NVA since yesterday. The One-zero, the man on the ground has advised me that you have numerous Russian .51 Caliber or Chi-Com weapons to the north, east and west of the extraction site. An unknown large number of NVA are in the area at this time. The team has sustained numerous wounded and dead. The area they are hiding in is single canopy. Recommend that you extract the team with strings or jungle penetrators, over.

Covey 224, this is SAR-2, that's a good copy on the situation on the ground and that's affirmative. I have two sets of A1-Es armed with maximum load of 250 pounders; CBU (cluster bomb units), napalm and 20mm cannons. Also Moonbeam has dispatched two sets of fast-movers orbiting at 20 thousand feet at this time, over.

SAR-2, this is Covey 224, that's a good copy. This is going to be a hot LZ. Recommend you have your A1-E escorts make contact with Bravo Delta on the ground prior to your approach. Bravo Delta needs some help. The Indians are moving in for the kill. How copy, over?

Covey 224, this is SAR-2, Roger good copy. Will have escorts make contact with your team on the ground prior to my approach, over.

The peter pilot of the Jolly Green had been listening to the conversation between Covey 224 and the SAR pilot. He then relayed the information on to the Hobos.

The SAR-2 peter pilot directed one set of the A1s to make contact with the team on the ground, providing them pre-extraction support, while the second set of A1s stayed with the Jolly Green.

SAR-2, this is Covey 224; I'll have the team identify

their location with smoke, then turn the extraction over to you. I'll go high-and-dry and be ready to support as you direct, how copy, over?

Covey 224, this is SAR-2, that's a good copy, over.

SAR-2, this is Covey 224 I'll take the A1s in and make contact with the team at this time. We are approximately five mikes out, over.

Two radio squelch breaks acknowledged that the SAR-2 commander understood what was about to transpire. Cheney had been busy taking notes and recording the support coordination on the OV-10 protective glass canopy. He simultaneously was listening for the Bright Light team to contact him if they got into trouble

This was standard procedure for the back-seater to take notes and know what type of support he had at his disposal once the extraction started. It was important to know who was where, what you had to call on and what they were carrying as far as ordinance. It took great coordination and professional combat experience to make all of this work effectively.

Cliff gave the signal for the Bright Light team members to put on their stabo rigs. Every other man suited up while the others provided security and vigilance, knowing the enemy was close. Within minutes, the entire team was rigged and ready to go. Anxious for extraction and prepared for the inevitable ground attack, the men knew it was only a matter of time. The once sparse noises of the enemy movement rapidly increased. The Bright Light team was out of claymores; their only line of defense would be their individual CAR-15s, M-79 grenade launchers and hand grenades. It wasn't looking too promising for the home team. If Charlie hit them prior to or during the extraction, it could go either way real quick. It all depended on who was more determined. How much longer would it be before someone called checkmate and initiated the attack?

As the OV-10 continued to orbit, the faint image of the Jolly Green and its two sets of A1-Es flashed through the treetops of the single canopy jungle silhouetting it self against the blue sky as they grew closer.

Suddenly over the radio waves came a distress call from RT Python.

Covey 224, Covey 224, this is Whisky Zulu, over.

Whisky Zulu, this is Covey 224, over.

Covey 224, this is Whisky Zulu, I'm under heavy ground assault at this time. I estimate regimental size infantry NVA unit. I'm declaring a Prairie Fire. I repeat, I'm declaring a Prairie Fire, over.

Whisky Zulu, this is Covey 224, can you hold out until I get the Bright Light team extracted, over?

Covey 224, this is Whisky Zulu I'm being hit hard from all sides at once. I have an estimated regimental-sized infantry element assaulting up the hill toward my position. My ammo situation is critical, and I don't know how much longer we can hold out, if at all, but we'll try until you just get the Bright Light. Hope we're here the next time you try and make contact, out.

Covey was now between a rock and a hard place; they had an extraction mission in the making for one surrounded friendly element with heavy enemy contact. And now, they had a second team, not more than 10 clicks to the south declaring a Prairie Fire.

RT Python stood a good chance or being overrun and killed very quickly. The dilemma was that the SAR mission hadn't even begun. Nor had the One-zero of the Bright Light team linked up with the A1-Es for support. What else could go wrong?

There weren't enough immediate assets to go around, and there wasn't enough time for another Covey to be brought on station. Cheney would have to do both extractions at once, jumping back and forth coordinating the two missions.

Once the Jolly Green, A1-Es and the Bright Light linked up, Cheney would temporarily abandon the RT Habu to coordinate then conduct the extraction and support for RT Python. The SAR commander and crew were more than capable of extracting the Bright Light team.

Back at the Phu Bai launch site, Sergeant John Fettler the communications sergeant had left the communications bunker and TOC long enough to get Major Elliott and Master Sergeant Dover from their houches to respond to the Prairie Fire RT Python that had just declared.

Quickly David Cheney discussed their devastating dilemma with the front-seater and together they decided to split forces. The SAR mission would take care of the Bright Light extraction while Captain Yarbrough and Cheney provided support for RT Python. Captain Yarbrough contacted the SAR-2 commander and requested permission to use one of his sets of A1-E Sky Raiders to support RT Python. Permission was granted and the SAR commander released the aircraft over to Covey. Cheney hurriedly made contact with the Bright Light One-Zero, explaining the situation:

> Bravo Delta, this is Covey 224, over.
>
> Covey 224, this is Bravo Delta, over.
>
> Bravo Delta, this is Covey 224, am between a rock and a hard place up here old buddy. RT Python is in a world of hurt. They're getting hit as we speak by an estimated regimental-sized element. They need air support and I'm the only one on station at this time. Am turning you over to the SAR mission commander while I support RT Python, how copy, over?
>
> Covey 224, this is Bravo Delta, roger good copy. You best hurry and give the boys some help. Between me and the SAR commander and crew, we can handle it from here. Get out of here, and go help RT Python, over.
>
> Bravo Delta, this is Covey 224, the front-seater is now briefing the SAR-2 commander on the overall situation. I will ensure that you have commo with the SAR mission before I leave you, over.
>
> Covey 224, this is Bravo Delta, no sweat, am standing by for SAR-2 commander to make contact with me. I have already been talking to Hobo One-One and One-Two. Over
>
> Bravo Delta, this is Covey 224, good copy, will see you back at the ranch. Out

Break. Break.

Phu Bai base, Phu Bai base this is Covey 224, over.

Covey 224, this is Phu Bai base, over.

Phu Bai base, this is Covey 224 RT Python has just declared a Prairie Fire. Need for you to launch the extraction package immediately. I'll extract the team as soon as they get on station. RT Python is under attack by an estimated regimental-sized force and doesn't think they can hold our any longer, over.

Covey 224, this is Phu Bai base we launched the extraction package and another Covey 10 minutes ago. You should have them on station within the next 20 mikes, over.

Phu Bai base this is Covey 224 am heading over to RT Python's location with a set of Hobos at this time, will contact you later, out.

Cheney could still hear the front-seater coordinating with the SAR mission. While Yarbrough talked with the SAR, Cheney made contact with RT Python, informing them he was on the way to their location.

Whisky Zulu, this is Covey 224, over.

Covey 224, this is Whisky Zulu, over.

Whisky Zulu, this is Covey 224, have turned the SAR mission over to the One-Zero on the ground. I'll be at your location in less than a minute, over.

Covey 224, this is Whisky Zulu you better make it quick because we are getting the living shit kicked out of us. Don't know how much longer we'll be on station. We're fighting them off within five meters of the top of the hill, and they just keep coming, over.

Whisky Zulu, this is Covey 224, roger babe understand. I have a set of A-1Es with me. We'll take some heat off you when we get there, over.

> Covey 224, this is Whisky Zulu, appreciate your help,
> its getting so bad up here that their going to be on top
> with us within the next few seconds. Will be standing
> by, I hope, out.

Cheney had flown with all of the other Covey pilots for months now. Because they had worked together through so many emergency situations, they all had a pretty good feel for what the other would do. A Covey pilot and back-seater who worked well together was the greatest commodity that a recon team could have when you're on the ground crying for help.

Coordination's between Covey, the SAR-2 commander, Phu Bai base, The Bright Light and RT Python had been efficiently made in less than three minutes. Once again, the professional combat experience of the Covey Pilot, Covey Rider and their assets were a lifeline for all recon teams.

As Cliff Newman listened to the radio traffic being passed between Covey and the teams, he realized that their attempt to extract both Special Force units at the same time would be hairy, to say the least. The Bright Light patiently waited for the extraction to commence, all the while they fully expecting an attack against them from the NVA. Needless to say, the anticipation had a nerve-wrecking effect on the team members. The enemy was playing a physiological game now, making lots of noise to keep the hidden team nervous, upset and on an adrenaline high. This wears down a soldier real quick.

A sudden deafening quiet pervaded the area as the NVA poised for attack. Wes thought to himself, *"Damn, how much longer before we get out of this shit hole?"* As if in answer to his silent question, Cliff began to coordinate with SAR-2, the Jolly Green commander:

> Bravo Delta, this is SAR-2, over.
>
> SAR-2, this is Bravo Delta, over.
>
> Bravo Delta, this is SAR-2, can you provide me with
> the current situation on the ground, and the number of
> friendlies with you at this time, over?

SAR-2, this is Bravo Delta I have five Americans and five Little People with me at this time. To my west, back up the hill proximately 100 meters from my location, along the ridgeline; there is an unknown number of Russian .51 caliber or Chi-com automatic weapons. We have enemy movement 360-degrees around our position, and anticipate an all-out ground attack at any moment. We are surrounded by at least a company or larger, maybe two companies of hardcore NVA. How copy, over?

Bravo Delta, this is SAR-2, good copy. I'm going to send in the Hobos first to link up with you. You direct their fire for your support. How copy, over?

SAR-2, this is Bravo Delta, am standing by, over.

Bravo Delta, this is Hobo 01 and Hobo 02, over.

Hobos 01 and 02, this is Bravo Delta. We have a large number of bad guys all around us, waiting for the order to attack. Also, be advised you have an unknown number of .51 caliber automatic weapons off to the west of my position. I'm ready to pop smoke on your command. Also be advised; that as soon as I pop this smoke, all hell's going to break loose down here, over.

Bravo Delta, this is Hobo 01 and 02, good copy, I'll be rolling in 100 meters to your north and dropping some snake on top of those suspected gun positions. Hobo 02, will be rolling in about 25 meters to your south, down the ridgeline with snake also. How copy, over?

Hobos 01 and 02, this is Bravo Delta. That's a good copy. You're cleared in hot as soon as you have a good tally on my position, over.

Bravo Delta, this is Hobos 01 and 02 rolling in at this time. Pop smoke, over.

Hobos 01 and 02, this is Bravo Delta, smoke's out identify, over.

Cliff pulled the pin on the smoke canister and tossed it on to the wet jungle floor in the middle of the perimeter where it began smoldering releasing the compacted smoldering elements that began emitting yellow smoke out the top and bottom of the canister. Initially, the smoke hung low in the jungle, obscuring the team's vision from within their own perimeter. There was a long hesitation from the Hobos who flew high above, waited patiently to see the smoke so they could provide fire support. It was obvious that initially the smoke couldn't be scene from the air because of the denseness of the jungle tree tops. Slowly the smoke inched its way up through the trees. Seconds ticked by and still no recognition. Finally, the welcomed voice of Hobo 01 was heard clearly:

> Bravo Delta, this is Hobos 01 and 02, I see yellow smoke. I repeat, I see yellow smoke. How copy, over?

> Hobos 01 and 02, this is Bravo Delta, That's ah roger on yellow smoke, you're cleared in hot at this time. My initials are Charlie November, over.

> Bravo Delta, this is Hobos 01 and 02, get your heads down guys because we're coming in hot, over.

No sooner had the Hobo pilot relayed his intentions, than the air filled with hissing sounds of B-40 rockets in flight. Before the first rocket impacted, The Bright Light returned fire. As the B-40s exploded, they sent hot steel fragments through the undergrowth surrounding the defenders. Rolling in from the south to the west, Hobo 01 began dropping CBU bombs approximately 100 meters up the hill above the Bright Light.

As Hobo 01 completed his initial pass, the distinct deep bellowing of a .51 caliber Russian or Chi-Com heavy barrel machine gun rang out. Unknown to Hobo 01, as he pulled up, he was taking fire with green communist tracers hot on his trail. Cliff called to him:

> Hobo 01, this is Bravo Delta, you're taking fire from up on the ridgeline. I repeat, you're taking fire from up on the ridgeline, over

Hobo 02 had been maneuvering into his first gun run when he too saw the green tracers chasing his cohort. Abandoning his previous flight pattern, Hobo 02 diverted his attention and weapons to the enemy machine gun emplacements. He came in high, lining up and firing his 20mm cannon and releasing four 250-pound bombs directly at the antiaircraft position.

Just as he pulled up and away, the 250-pound bombs hit home and the machine gun emplacement was a thing of the past. How many more .51 caliber machine guns were still down there? In order to protect the Jolly Green during extraction, the Hobos had to find out. Using height as his safety, Hobo 01 watched as Hobo 02 came up after his gun run.

Sure enough, he spotted a second .51 caliber machine gun firing at his wingman from approximately 200 meters farther south. Hobo 01 rolled in hot, firing his cannon and dropping his bombs on the new target. He was dead-on and the second antiaircraft position was destroyed as well. Without missing a beat, Hobos 01 and 02 went back to their original coordination with the One-Zero on the ground and began making their gun runs, preparing the area for Jolly Green to maneuver into the extraction site.

Enemy ground fire against the Bright Light became more intensive. In between reloading his CAR-15, Wes saw enemy ground troops assaulting their position with their weapons stocks tucked under their armpits, firing blindly in on RT Habu's position. Wes screamed, "Ground attack," as the NVA charged forward. Every team member began frantically returning fire against the assault troops. If the NVA swept through the perimeter, it would be all over but the crying. Because of the enemy's close proximity, it was impossible for Cliff to call in air support without killing his own troops in the process.

Unanimously, each member of the Bright Light decided to fight for all they had or die in place. No rules of engagement would apply; it was kill or be killed. Cliff kept the radio pressed hard against his ear while firing his CAR-15, still advising the SAR commander of the ground attack as it transpired. Friendly bullets ripped through flesh as the enemy rockets continued to detonate. The entire jungle area was filled with gray smoke. Although seriously wounded and under the anesthetic effects of the morphine, Jimmy Horton lay on his stomach and emptied an entire magazine into two advancing NVA troops. His fire was deadly, the rounds tearing through their bodies, taking out large chunks of tissue as the unknowingly dead NVA continued to move toward Jimmy, the dead bodies collapsing only a few feet away.

As the ground fighting escalated, the Jolly Green crept forward toward the Bright Light's position, his escorting A1-Es scattering CBU bombs onto the attacking forces. All of a sudden, Wes felt and recognized the ear-crushing roar and prop blast from the Jolly Green's mighty rotor blades, along with the tremendous down-thrust of air that overpowered the explosions and flying bullets. The treetops and jungle vegetation whipped about and thrashed violently back and forth as the huge chopper hovered over the battlefield.

Observing exactly what was going on below, the Jolly Green's crew chief harnessed the power of his mini-gun, encircling the faltering Bright Light with 7.62 mini-gun fire. Spitting out death from its belly, the Jolly Green abruptly put a halt to the enemy's fierce firing and assault. Those NVA who were spared from the devastating effects of the mini-gun faced the fire and wrath from the Bright Light, still actively engaged in the firefight.

One after another, enemy soldiers fell to the ground; their dead bodies so numerous lay at the feet of the Bright Light team that they could have almost formed a protective wall around the team. As the close-quarter fighting continued, the slow moving A1-Es amped up their support, bringing fire so close that occasionally pieces of shrapnel wounded some of the team members. But, that was the price you paid for close-in support against a hardcore adversary like the NVA.

The explosions and detonations from the CBU units sounded like an alligator in a chicken yard, snap-boom, snap-boom, and snap-boom as they filtered down through the treetops down upon the NVA.

Hobos 01 and 02, this is SAR-2 command, over.

SAR-2 command, this is Hobos 01 and 02, over.

Hobos this is SAR-2, begin your defensive cloverleaf tactical cover for me while I get these fine young men out of here, if you please, over.

> SAR-2 command, this is Hobos 01 and 02, ah that's
> ah roger, going into defensive flight patterns starting at
> your 3-o'clock and 6-o'clock, then at your 12-o'clock and
> 6-o'clock at this time, over.

The Bright Light was fighting off the remaining enemy assaulters, using hand-to-hand combat where necessary. Within a matter of seconds, the experienced Americans and Montagnards had killed each and every one of the initial assaulters, leaving their bodies to rot where they lay.

If they hadn't been previously wounded, every one of the Bright Light team was now, some two and three times. Blood ran down their bodies, yet no one attempted to stop fighting and render themselves or their fellow combatant first aid; they couldn't afford to let their guard down until they were inside the Jolly Green. The majority of the wounds the Bright Light had sustained appeared to be minor and could wait. However, there were a few with serious wounds, like Jimmy Horton, Mac and two of the Little People.

Supporting himself on his elbows, Wes turned and looked up to get a look at the Jolly Green, hovering above them. The dark green and black helicopter was monstrous in size, looking more like a spaceship from underneath, blades turning, thrashing the treetops. As the jungle penetrator slowly made its way down to the ground, the A1-Es provided suppressive fire 360-degrees around Jolly Green. As the penetrator reached the ground, Cliff standing upright like a giant oak tree in the middle of an open area pointed at Horton and Mac, ordering them to mount the jungle penetrator and be extracted together.

Without hesitation, Mac grabbed Horton by his upper web gear, and placed him onto the penetrator then he climbed aboard. Once the crew chief saw that the two men were aboard he started wrenching the two wounded soldiers up through the trees nearing the safety of the rescue helicopter with each second that passed. Once the two wounded were removed from the jungle penetrator and safely inside the Jolly Green, Mac and Horton were immediately greeted by an Air Force PJ and the other Woodham brother. Again, the jungle penetrator came winching back down from the CH-53. Two Little People were up next, followed immediately by two more.

Enemy weapons fire continued to sporadically rain down on the remaining Bright Light team members. Those remaining on the ground were anxiously waiting to get aboard the giant helicopter and get the hell out of this place. Unprepared for the enemy's next tactic, the three remaining Americans, Cliff Newman, Charles F. Wesley and Ronald Danzer were hit by another fierce volley of automatic weapons fire. Wes, Cliff and Danzer were now kneeling back-to-back, facing the onslaught of the enemy attack. Their weapons chattering sending hot lead in retaliation against the enemy ground attack.

Ejected shell casing flew out of their weapons as they fired. Even though the jungle penetrator lay dormant on the ground not more than five feet away, they couldn't move or stop firing.

Suddenly the sounds of screaming and yelling gave the remaining recon members advanced warning that the NVA assaulters were up and running toward them. Magazine after magazine the three brave Americans fired. With each pull of the trigger, NVA soldiers began falling in heaps one body falling top of another onto the damp jungle floor. They never hesitated or relented in their assigned task to kill or capture the team even as they were being killed or wounded by the intensity of the Americans weapons fire their resolve was solid. Still, they continued to advance, jumping and stumbling over their fallen comrades, determined to kill the men on the ground.

From above came the most beautiful sound ever heard, the roar of the Jolly Green's mini-gun. This time, the friendly mini-gun fire was so close to the stranded recon men that they could feel the heat from the tracers as they impacted the jungle that surrounded them. It only took two short blasts from the mini-gun for the enemy assault to cease. NVA dead bodies were piled up like cordwood at the feet of the three recon men still on the ground. The NVA bodies lay dead so close to the American recon men that some were actually lying at the tips of their boots.

Cliff made a life-or-death decision, and he made it quickly. As it was impossible to allow one man to remain on the ground, Cliff and the two other Americans would ride the penetrator up at the same time. Undoubtedly, this would definitely put additional stress on the extraction system far beyond its tolerance and capabilities, but there was no other choice. With a temporary lull in enemy fire, the last three men boarded the penetrator.

Two of the remaining recon men climbed on either side of the penetrator and sat down on the blades and the third straddled the pole. From within the Jolly Green, the crew chief waited for the thumbs-up signal from the men below. He didn't have to wait long as they all raised their arms to signal they were ready to be pulled up. The retrievable wench system of the penetrator began creaking and squeaking with the additional stress being placed on it, as it performed far beyond its maximum hoisting capabilities.

The crew chief didn't let up, lifting the men higher and higher. As they rose towards the Jolly Green, bullets whizzed past them. So, instinctively they did what any soldier would do in the situation, they returned fire. Sensing the possibility of being shot out of the sky, the door gunner let go a long burst of mini-gun fire, indiscriminately saturating the area.

Still firing continuous bursts from his CAR-15, Wes thought to himself, *"Man, I can't die this way, being extracted, being shot up in the air."* While the men drew closer to the Jolly Green, the A1-E's were meticulously firing in support, firing surgically with their 20mm cannons, dropping CBU canisters and bombs into the surrounding jungle.

Finally, the door to the Jolly Green was within arms reach and the three men noted the concerned facial expression of the crew chief. Clinging tightly to the metal penetrator with one hand and firing with the other, the Americans fought until they felt the crew chief violently pulling them inside the aircraft onto the floor. All three Americans fell inside the Jolly Green with huge grins on their faces. Enemy rounds began impacting the skin of the Jolly Green, passing through it with little resistance, yet the pilot stood fast in his recovery maintaining his hover.

After receiving the word from the crew chief that everyone was on board and safely inside, the pilot expertly tilted the Jolly Green's nose down slightly and headed back to Phu Bai with its cargo of wounded gallant Special Forces soldiers. As the big chopper cleared the extraction area, the A1-Es rolled in one last time, dropping their remaining cans of napalm onto the extraction site itself. What a beautiful sight: two cans of napalm fell from under each wing, floating gracefully down through the jungle, exploding upon impact.

The SAR-2 commander had two sets of Phantom F-4s standing by to deliver the coup-de-gras. Once the A1-Es dropped their final ordinance, the Phantoms mopped up with Mark 82s, more napalm and additional CBU canisters, saturating about a 400-square meter area. If, by chance, there had been any enemy survivors prior to the Phantoms' arrival, they were most likely no longer be living.

As the men aboard the Jolly Green began to look around the fuselage, they couldn't help but notice the massive amount of enemy bullet holes in the skin of the aircraft. This helicopter had been pounded with enemy fire. Woody and the PJ were frantically working on Horton's foot. Everyone became more aware of his own wounds, as the adrenaline levels subsided and body systems began to return to a somewhat normal state. Wes' thoughts suddenly turned to RT Python's severe situation. Having refused extraction until the Bright Light was safe; the small Special Forces recon team was almost assuredly still battling it out, if they hadn't all been killed. Wes couldn't help but think, *"Why do sane men place themselves in deadly situations in order to support their brothers-in-arms?"*

Wes wondered if RT Python would live to tell the story? As he looked through the port hole outside the Jolly Green he saw two A1-E Sky Raiders flying alongside, still faithfully supporting the Jolly Green even though they had no ordnance left. Regardless of the situation, American soldiers no matter what branch always came to the aid of one another, even if it meant dying in the process.

# CHAPTER 24 (A-SHAU)

Aircraft could be heard off to the northwest as the sun crested the A-Shau Valley's eastern mountain range. Occasionally, we were able to get a glimpse of the OV-10 before it disappeared against the cloudless sky.

The members of RT Python were all tremendously relieved that the SAR mission was underway. The Jolly Green and his escort of two sets of A1-Es would be assisting in the extraction of the Bright Light team. As soon as they were all safely on their way to Phu Bai, Jim would request our extraction as well. We as a fighting unit were on our last leg. Although our morale remained elevated, we were running out of ammunition, pained by extended hunger coupled with being mentally and physically worn out. The pain from our wounds was growing in intensity with each second that passed.

As the morning cool air thinned, the sun began to cast its heats of heat down upon us. The ground we occupied didn't look anything like it had when we'd first inserted. As a result of the gallons of blood that had been spilled here within the last 55 hours, the earth was discolored and smelled putrid. Rotting human flesh and organs were scattered as far as the eye could see. The ground was covered with battle scars; blackened, dug out areas where rockets, grenades and other munitions had exploded, leaving gaping holes in the earth.

Momentarily glancing down at my hands and what little of my body I could see, I noticed that I was covered with a mixture of red clay dirt, blood, sweat and gunpowder. Beads of sweat were already forming on my brow as I looked around at the brave men still defending our perimeter. Stress and physical fatigue was etched into each one of our faces. We'd repeatedly experienced the terrible burden of combat, the strain of waiting for each new assault to begin, the pressure of close quarter combat, the tension of not knowing how many or from where our enemies would attack, and the stress that results from having gone without sleep for so long.

When you wrap all this strain with exhaustion and our continuous consumption of dextroamphetamines, it was easy to conclude that we were nowhere near battle alert or the battle ready unit we should be. In fact, we were wrung out, operating in a daze. We were simply going through the motions as we'd been trained to, without conscious thought.

The OV-10 off to the north of us was quickly joined by the Jolly Green and two sets of A1-E Sky Raiders. It was breathtaking to see the escorts on either side of the huge helicopter. Two A1-E's at his 3:00 and two at his 9:00 o-clock positions, flying in perfect unison. With any luck, the Bright Light would soon be rescued from the hell that they had been enduring. Hopefully, they would make it back safely to Da Nang and begin drinking beer and telling tales in the Recon Company Club.

Breaking away from my daydream, I began to hear running noises, lots of them. As I peered over the edge of the hill into the jungle below, I picked up movement. The NVA were charging out of the tree line as quickly as they could, coming up the hillside towards us. Just as I screamed, "Here they come," the jungle came alive with NVA soldiers making their final ground assault against the defenders of the tiny hilltop. Enemy troops poured from the tree line like a large herd of buffalo stampeding. Where had all these men come from? How had they survived all of the heavy air fire brought against them during the previous night? There were hundreds of them, determined to reach the top of the mountain and finish us off.

Surely, they were reinforcements from another NVA unit somewhere down in the valley. Enemy soldier after soldier boldly faced death as they charged forth from within the tree line? Without hesitation we opened up with everything we had. The initial volley was violent and vicious.

Jim was looking over my shoulder down the hill, as he made a call to Covey:

Covey 224, this is Whisky Zulu, over.

Whisky Zulu, this is Covey 224, over.

Covey 224, this is Whisky Zulu, we are under heavy ground assault from an estimated regimental size unit or larger. I don't think we are going to be able to hold them off this time, there are just too many of them. I'm declaring a Prairie Fire. I repeat, I'm declaring a Prairie Fire, over.

Whisky Zulu, this is Covey 224, over.

Covey 224, this is Whisky Zulu, over.

Whisky Zulu, this is Covey 224, I'll be at your location in two mikes, and will be bringing one set of Hobos with me. I'm also calling in two sets of Cobras to assist, once they get on station from the launch site, I'll turn them over to you for support. Over.

Covey 224, this is Whisky Zulu, if you don't get the assets here real quick, you might as well cross us off the game card. We'll try and hold out as long as we can, out.

Jim tried to instill confidence in me over the chaos, explaining that Covey and a set of Hobos were on their way. While I sincerely appreciated his efforts, I knew from the sheer number of enemy troops advancing below us, combined with my previous battle experience, that there wouldn't be much left of us when the rescue arrived. Wave after wave of NVA soldiers streamed forward, hell bent on overrunning us. Charlie was going to finish what he'd started or die trying. No more sniper fire, no more probing of our perimeter; this was for all of the marbles. They were going to deliver the final blow using massive amounts of soldiers no matter what the cost.

Enemy hand grenades, B-40s and bullets filled the air from every direction. No longer did we fire short-controlled bursts at the NVA, we now pulled our triggers to the rear of the M-60 machine guns and fired until the barrels melted, at which point, we put in another barrel and started again. As the last round from my magazine emptied, without missing a beat, I quickly reached into my ammo pouch and began throwing mini-grenades into the advancing assault as rapidly as possible. Within seconds, the enemy had reached our final defenses.

We blew the remainder of our claymore mines down into the maddening rush of troops, tearing gaping holes in their ranks. Amazingly, these vacancies we had blown in their lines were immediately refilled by other enemy soldiers who had been a little farther down the hill prior to the blasts. Enemy bodies, equipment and weapons flew through the air as my grenades detonated amongst them. Enemy soldiers were literally climbing over piles of their fellow NVA who were killed earlier in previous battles or during this assault they were conducting now.

Some of the dead had only recently been killed. However, countless others had been killed much earlier and their carcasses were bloated and rotting from the hot humid Asia sun and unbearable humidity. This didn't seem to phase the advancing troops in the least; they just kept coming. They were on a mission and nothing was going to stop them this time. Out of the corner of my eye, I saw three squads of enemy soldiers running up the ravine. If they got into our perimeter, it would be over. Quickly, I slapped Jung on the shoulder and pointed in that direction. Without wasting a moment, he swung his M-60 around, engaging the assault unit.

Jung never once relieved his trigger pressure as the automatic weapon spitting hot tracers and 7.62mm machine gun rounds into the advancing enemy element. As he fired, I watched round after round go in one side of their uniforms and exit out the other side, impacting the dirt mound behind them. Blood, tissue and body parts were flung in every direction as Jung's deadly fire continuously penetrated the soldiers' bodies. They fell like bowling pins, dead before they hit the ravine floor.

As Jung methodically negotiated the enemy targets, I took care of our front. Each time I pulled the trigger of my CAR-15, an enemy soldier fell to the ground. And yet they kept coming. Without warning, the ground suddenly erupted down the slopes to my left and right, flinging men, weapons, dirt, rocks, trees and debris around the battlefield with the force of a hurricane. We continued to fire as our enemies in front of us exploded or simply vanished. Flesh, bones and tissue were being plastered all over us. It was as if a massive ball of smoke, fire and molten lead rolled through the assault enemy troops.

Stunned, I looked into the sky for an explanation. Sure enough, one of the US Air Force's finest; an A1-E Sky Raider was diving in on our position with his 20mm cannon roaring like a dragon. Large, heavy metal projectiles slammed into the advancing NVA soldiers. Our air support had finally arrived. Thank God! I witnessed the once fast-moving assault force temporarily halt, looking skyward as they stared death in the face. Some of the survivors began to run back down the hill, plowing into their own soldiers in a panic.

But, they just couldn't run fast enough. As soon as Hobo 03 pulled up from his initial gun run, Hobo 04 was hot on his heels, continuing the death run. There would be no relief for the NVA.

In what appeared to be slow motion, I watched enemy soldiers begin to pop over the rim of the firebase, and knew with surety that all was lost and it was time to die. Upon acceptance of the inevitable, again an inner calmness came over my mind, heart and spirit. Confidently, I jumped from my foxhole to meet the enemy as they crested the hill. Firing at the war hounds that had just killed one of our Little People, my aim was perfect.

The first group of rounds hit the gloating NVA bastard on the right side of his face, blowing it through the back of his head. The second fell from four chest wounds and number three sank to his knees after being hit in the pelvic area. He lay screaming in agony while I calmly changed magazines and walked over to him. Looking into his eyes, pointing my weapon in his face I pulled the trigger, sending three rounds into his head. The concussion from my bullets did the rest.

Jim was engaged in close quarters combat at our command post. Hell, every one of us was firing at anything that moved. We'd all come to the realization that we were dead men walking anyway; so we might as well go out in a blaze of glory. The A1-Es rolled in on the advancing enemy the full length of the outskirts of our perimeter again, dropping CBU bombs this time. Hobo 03 rolled into the eastern half and Hobo 04 took the western portion then lining up for a pass at the north and south portions of the hillside.

Turning swiftly to my left, I saw an enemy soldier standing on the rim of the hilltop, pointing a B-40 directly at me. As I lunged for the ground, I pulled the trigger on my CAR-15, knocking the lone gunner backward off the hilltop. Just as he pulled the trigger on his B-40 weapons system he fell backward. The projectile shot past me heading off onto another portion of the perimeter. I looked quickly to see where the round had detonated just in time to see; in slow motion four NVA soldiers take the brunt of the B-40 rocket. The four NVA were there one second and the next, they were gone. Evidently, the round hit one of them in the chest, exploding violently then disintegrating each man that stood on either side of him. Nothing remained of the four except bloodstains on the ground.

Having been knocked to the ground from a rocket explosion, Jim was struggling to get back on his feet. As I moved toward him, he turned his weapon on me and fired. What I didn't know was, as I ran toward him, he saw two NVA soldiers at arm's length away, preparing to bayonet me from the back. Jim's rounds picked the men up off their feet and hurled them back about four feet. With sincerity, I nodded my thanks to Jim for his lifesaving actions. Call it skill, or a combination of luck and skill, but so far as soon as the NVA had crested the hill, this small Special Forces recon team had either killed or wounded every one of them. Someone was definitely looking after us.

Just after I spotted a massive number of NVA soldiers steadily charging toward us, an enemy B-40 exploded viciously slamming me to the ground. At that very instant, a body flew over my head, at first, I assumed it was one of ours, but later learned it was an enemy soldier killed by his own friendly fire. Another B-40 exploded directly into one of our Little People's fighting positions, blowing someone high into the air. To my horror, I saw that it was. It was our baby-son, little BS. He looked like a large piece of paper floating off the side of the hilltop down into the advancing NVA soldiers.

Without hesitation or even being aware of my own actions and response, I ran across the top of the hill top then charged down the hill to retrieve our baby-son. All the while I was advancing towards BS I was looking at his motionless body lying on the ground in front of me; I couldn't tell if he was alive or dead. Somewhere deep inside me, I felt a mental and physical rage overtake me as I continued to close the distance to retrieve him. NVA soldiers rapidly advanced toward me from the front, left and right. I calmly raised my CAR-15 and methodically negotiated each target. It was as if I had a shield protecting me from their bullets as they fired.

How and why I was not cut in half by the tremendous hail of fire, only God knows. Next, I fired a short burst of 5.56mm at two charging soldiers, decapitating one of them instantly. Three more NVA came at me from farther down the slope. As my bullets impacted their bodies, dust from their uniforms puffed into the air and they fell backward, sprawling along the hillside lying motionless.

Returning my attention back to where I last saw BS, I watched helplessly as an NVA soldier stood over him, pointed his SKS at his head and then pulled the trigger. Little BS's head bounced violently about four inches into the air and fell limply back to the ground. It was at that point that I lost it entirely. I was no longer afraid or even concerned about who or what was around me. I was enraged, insane temporarily losing track of my faculties as I focused all my attention and anger on getting Baby-son's body back to our site, and killing as many of those little bastards as I could before they killed me.

I'd had enough of this one-sided war; the NVA constantly hiding when we came to fight them, only showing up when we least expected it. It was pay back time, and I believed I was just the Special Forces soldier to deliver the tab. As the NVA soldier stood proudly over the body of our little baby-son, he turned his head and looked at me and smiled a cruel smile, knowing full well he'd killed our 15-year old child. Sliding and falling down from the slippery side of the hillside, I positioned my CAR-15 to my right side, underneath my armpit and fired a full-automatic volley at the gloating bastard. One round hit his throat, one went through his chest and the other blew his arm off. The last thing the low-life child killer saw as I turned his lights out was BS's face.

My fallen little buddy was now only five feet away as I continued to slide down the hill towards him, reloading my weapon in the process. Just as

I was about to reach for him, an explosion followed by concussion tossed me into the air. I didn't know if I was hit or not and really didn't care. My only concern was getting the little guy's body back up to the top of the hill where he belonged, with us.

For some unknown reason, the battle around me seemed to stop momentarily while I reached down and turned the blood-covered body of our baby-son over on his back so I could lift him onto my shoulder. With his eyes glazed over, he looked at me and softly said, "Trung Si, I think maybe B.S. die now." Detecting motion out of the corner of my eye, I turned to see an NVA soldier trying to impale me with his bayonet. Standing upright, I simply raised the barrel of my weapon extending my arm and let him run into it. He lunged at me, ducking his head as he thrust his bayonet forward and I pulled the trigger, sending the rounds into the top of his pith helmet. His lifeless figure fell immediately to the ground, knocking my feet out from under me as he fell.

With my CAR-15 still in hand, I reached down and pulled the body of BS onto my left shoulder in a fireman's carry, turned and began to negotiate the climb back up the hillside. As I climbed, the extra weight caused me to trip, falling face-first to the ground. Quickly, I regained my feet and continued to climb. As I repeatedly stumbled over dead NVA bodies, I felt my strength quickly dwindling. Just as I was able to see the rim of the hilltop, BS and I were thrown back down the hill by an explosion. Instant pain shot through my right shoulder and the back of my legs. A tremendous stinging and burning sensation quickly erupted throughout my body. I remember impacting the ground with BS still on my back, grunting loudly as my body was hammered to the ground.

Oblivious to the fact that I'd been hit again, I pulled BS back onto my shoulder and started my upward climb once again. Before I made much progress, three more NVA soldiers maneuvered against me. Tossing BS aside onto the ground, my weapon exploded, as if under its own power, sending all three down the hill of this battle-torn slope. The adrenaline pumping within my veins numbed my pain and freed my mind. Two objectives were crystal clear to me: 1) get BS to the top of the hill, 2) kill or maim as many of these slant-eyed maggots as I could on the way up.

Raising my head looking up at the hillside I saw Jim and two of the

Little People totally exposed to enemy fire, providing me cover fire as I struggled to reach the top. I remember feeling concussions from enemy B-40s detonating around me, pressing hard against my internal organs as they detonated. Covey 224 had been watching my retrieval from above. He'd seen how many times I'd been hindered from reaching the top of the slope and decided to do something about it. He rolled in from behind me and fired 17-pound rockets off to my right flank, providing me cover as I climbed.

Round after round was launched from the attacking Covey, as I painfully climbed over enemy bodies and massive battlefield debris with BS still on my back my strength dwindling with each step I took. I was only-steps away from reaching the top when an explosion from behind me hurled me up and on top of the tiny bloodstained firebase. Lying motionless for a moment then regaining my senses, I stood up and ran to my rucksack, dragged it back to where my little Baby-Son lay dying.

I quickly opened up the top of my rucksack and pulled out a 1000 cc bag of D5W fluid replacement and a cutters set (IV Tube). I was no longer concerned with the fighting around me all I wanted to do was save the life of this 15-year old child. I rolled BS onto his back, extended the cutter set and connected it to the D5W, reaching underneath his head to make him more comfortable. It was then that I felt a large gapping hole where his skull should have been.

Reality hit me; this innocent young boy was already dead he just didn't know it yet. As I removed my hand from the back of his head, dark black blood intermixed with brain matter came with it. There was no need for an IV. BS would be dead in a matter of seconds.

An A1-E Sky Raider roared twenty feet over the hilltop above us, waving at me through his cockpit as he flew past. I cradled BS in my arms as he began to cry and call for his mother in Vietnamese. Through rambling words, not all of which made any sense, he asked me if he had been a good soldier. He kept repeating the same phrases over and over as I held him in my arms. How he was forming words at all with half his head gone was beyond me.

Finally, the raspy, deep inhale of life-giving air was followed by the familiar sounds of air passing the larynx. BS had gone into chain strokes, better known as the death rattle. I held him close to my chest as he gasped for air four or five more times, followed by the raspy rattle. After a few moments, the last bit of life left him.

Since there was nothing more I could do for him, I left his tiny body and moved from position to position, my heart broken. Revenge building within me that brought more anger raging within me as I silently grieved.

The heavy ground fighting continued throughout the perimeter. Everyone was covered in blood, filling our nostrils with a stench that most of us would never be able to forget. Suddenly, I realized that the attack had stopped. The NVA had retreated back into the jungle. Staggering to the command post, I angrily kicked dead NVA bodies out of my way then painfully knelt beside Jim. Without realizing I was next to him, Jim began talking to Covey:

> Covey 224, this is Whisky Zulu, over.
>
> Whisky Zulu, this is Covey 224, over.
>
> Covey 224, this is Whisky Zulu. You and the Hobos have saved our ass. I know that we wouldn't have made it if it hadn't been for you. I think that the NVA are regrouping and preparing for another assault. I know that we don't have the ammunition or strength to fight on. Did you get The Bright Light team out, over?
>
> Whisky Zulu, this is Covey 224 no sweat babe, my pleasure. I'll pass on your thanks to the Hobos. That's affirmative the Bright Light is out and on its way back to the hospital, then to the launch site, over.
>
> Covey 224, this is Whisky Zulu I want my team and myself out of here now. Has the extraction package launched yet, over?
>
> Whisky Zulu, this is Covey 224, that's ah roger. The package is on its way and should be here within 10 minutes. The Hobos are Winchester, but said they are

going to continue to hang around and orbit above you to keep the bad guys off, if they can, over.

Covey 224, this is Whisky Zulu, be advised the main assault has been turned back but intermittent fire fights are still going on down here. They're shooting at us from within the tree line, over.

Whisky Zulu, this is Covey 224, thanks for the update. I'll brief the slicks as they fly into your location. You just hang tight and I'll have you out of there in no time flat, out.

Jim lowed the handset, looked over his shoulder at me and reported, "The extraction slicks are on their way, should be here in about 10 minutes. Get the boys ready. We'll send out the dead first. I want you on the first bird out to accompany them to the morgue so they don't get lost in the shuffle. I'll put the seriously wounded on the second slick and I'll come out on the last bird."

I didn't respond, just reached into my pocket and fished for cigarettes. Lighting up two cigarettes, I handed one to Jim and left the other in my mouth. I stood erect and slowly started toward the first foxhole to relay the information on the extraction and prepare the boys to get off this Godforsaken hill.

My movements were sluggish as I staggered across the blood-covered ground. I was physically unstable and staggered like a drunk from foxhole to foxhole, counting off the men and giving them direction on which aircraft they would be lifted out on. As I moved, I took a quick inventory on the amount of ammunition we had remaining. I was somewhat surprised to learn that we only had 300 rounds of M60 machine gun ammo left for the three guns. Those of us who were still standing had three magazines (60 rounds) a piece and one or two hand grenades each.

The shooting around the perimeter had stopped. The only sounds I could hear were wounded men in severe pain and mental agony within our own perimeter. I could see our extraction package orbiting off to the east as they received instructions from Covey 224. The bodies of dead NVA still lay where they fell mangled, cluttering the hilltop from their last attack. I directed a couple of the Little People to assist me in dragging some of them off the crest of the hilltop to make room for the incoming slicks.

After a large portion of the enemy soldiers' bodies were cleared away, I moved little BS toward the center of our perimeter and waited patiently with the dead at my feet. Staring off into the direction of the inbound choppers, I took a drag from my cigarette and knelt down by BS's dead body. Jim caught my attention as he gestured wildly while talking to Covey:

Whisky Zulu, this is Covey 224, over.

Covey 224, this is Whisky Zulu, over.

Whisky Zulu, I'm going to have the gunships come in and fire up the surrounding slopes and tree line before I send in Slick #1, over.

Covey, this is Whisky Zulu, that's a good copy, over.

In the distance, we saw the Cobras break away from the orbiting flight formation and begin their movement toward our position. At first, it looked like there was only one set of Cobras, but as they drew closer, we saw two sets. They were upon us in no time at all, and went to work on the slopes and tree lines encircling the firebase. It felt tremendously reassuring to know that we had air support. Drawing closer, the Cobras opened up on both of our flanks with their mini-guns, following up with 40mm and 17 pound rockets. They were prepping the surrounding areas for the inbound UH-1 helicopters. As the Cobra gunfire flew down from the sky, their rounds impacted the bodies of the dead NVA, bouncing them around in a ghastly last deadly dance.

Jim motioned to me that Slick #1 was on short final. I was to get ready to load the dead and accompany them out. Slick #1 was being escorted into our Landing Zone by a set of Cobras, flying on either side of him as he closed the distance to the LZ. Just as he approached the hilltop, the door gunners opened fire wildly into the surrounding jungles. Had there been any enemy fire, no one could have detected it.

In a sudden rush forward, the helicopter reared in on the Landing Zone its nose up with the intensity of a wild stallion and its tail rotor almost striking the ground. Then it quickly leveled off, resting its skids on the hilltop. With rotor blades turning at maximum RPMs, the chopper rested, momentarily waiting to receive its cargo. Loose red dust rose briskly around the entire area, temporarily obscuring the view of all of us on the ground.

As I slowly got to my feet, my rifle dangled around my neck I bent over to pick up the dead body of our Baby Son. As I reached for him, another set of hands was there to assist. The crew chief from the UH-1 helped me place our dead into the helicopter. Within two minutes, we had loaded with all of our fallen brothers as I crawled in to escort them back to their final destination before their last journey home.

Positioning myself out of the right door of the helicopter, I prepared to fire at any NVA soldier that might appear. The pilot built up torque and lifted the chopper skyward off the hilltop diving down into the A Shau Valley. Again, the red clay dust flew in every direction as the skids of the UH-1 helicopter left the ground leaping skyward.

As we vacated the firebase, I pulled my legs back into the aircraft and rested my back against the door well. We quickly gained altitude and speed. As I rested, I searched my fatigues for cigarettes and found that I was out. The pack was empty. The peter pilot handed me a Marlboro and I nodded my head in thanks and gratitude. Leaning back towards the Peter Pilot I tried trying desperately to evade the fast rushing air coming through the open doors. I tried four times to light the cigarette before I finally succeeded.

The UH-1 continued to climb into the slowly cooling altitude of the Asian sky. With every passing second, we left the firebase farther behind. The once dense hot air began to thin out and cool down, refreshing my blood-covered neck and face. With my back now against the transmission wall, I stared out of the right door as we went into an orbit, waiting for the rest of the extraction package to catch up with us. The crew chief handed me a headset and I turned toward him slightly shaking my head; I didn't want it. He simply laid the headset beside me and returned his attention back to his duties. The cigarette tasted good. The smoke that filled my lungs was actually cooler when I exhaled than the air that circulated around me.

I sat motionless, eyes closed. I could feel the gentle vibration of the helicopter against my back and legs. Slowly, I opened my eyes to find that I was sitting in the blood of my fallen teammates. Dark blood made its way across the floor of the chopper in the direction of the open door. Ever so slowly, it began to blow out and away from the aircraft, baptizing the jungle below.

The gray faces of the dead were calm with their half opened eyes staring off into infinity where the dead wait. There was no sign of life left in them, only the blackness of death displayed on their faces. Soon, the rest of the extraction package was united, along with the gunships. Within minutes, we would be back on the ground in Phu Bai. Yet, I had the heart-wrenching duty of flying to the morgue to deposit our dead, making sure that Graves Registration knew who they were, where they came from and where their final destination would be.

Surrounded by dead recon men, I began to search my soul for an answer on how my life and the lives of my fellow recon brothers had changed so dramatically from being patriots and servants to our government to be transformed into self-made tools of retribution, vengeance, violence and reprisal.

How many metamorphoses had occurred? I no longer adhered to the laws of humanity or the dignity and values of a soldier. I had become a calloused cool-headed executioner and eradicator of human beings. I knew without a doubt that I was now a predator, and an assassin if called upon to perform that duty. No longer did I fight for my country, I now fought for my brothers of the sword and myself.

Life no longer held meaning. I had become a self-made warring crusader and killing machine. Little did I know that these past few days of combat would haunt me for the remainder of my life? Unconsciously, over the course of many years I would experience drastic emotional ups and downs, introversion, and lack of trust, negativism, and inability to express my feeling to my loved ones and subconscious self-destructive thought patterns for years to come.

I searched my soul for the reason I had been spared from the fate of those lying dead around me. Why had I been allowed to walk away from the Valley of Death when so many had been denied that privilege? I thought about how I had killed hundreds of NVA soldiers without even an inkling of remorse or regret. The only physical emotion I had was anger and an overwhelming desire to return to the hilltop and kill more of those little bastards even through I was physically and mentally exhausted.

No longer did I fight out of duty or because it was my mission. I had passed over into the realm of receiving pleasure and a euphoric high for achieving revenge for my brothers whom I loved. My inter most thoughts were interrupted by a tap on my shoulder startling me. The crew chief was offering me another of his cigarettes he had lit. I looked into his eyes, seeing fear, inexperience and confusion staring back at me. Realizing that he was trying to be friendly, I took the cigarette.

Without any facial emotion, I took a big draw, feeling the cool smoke go deep into my lungs. All of the glory and honor that I had come to Vietnam in search of had vanished. My eyes no longer were capable of filling with tears. Now, they only filled with hate, rage and a need to return to the jungle as quickly as possible to continue my revenge.

As the air pressed violently against my blood-covered fatigues, I remembered that an officer had once written about Napoleon's Two Armies. The story went that one of his armies was pretty, shiny and always presentable to the public and other armies. This pretty, shiny army was shown for prestige and moral of the troops while Napoleon's staff worried about his bowl movement and comfort.

Then, there was Napoleon's Second Army. This was his secret army that no one knew existed. These secret soldiers would go anywhere, anytime and attempt the impossible to provide Napoleon with intelligence about his enemies. They would gather intelligence far behind enemy lines, gallantly fighting and silently dying in forbidden places, never to be remembered. You see, their very presence and actions were totally disavowed by Napoleon and his staff.

We the Special Forces, Special Operations soldiers of MACV-SOG were our government's Second Army. We were assigned to do the impossible for the ungrateful and to die alone and forgotten. Both Special Operations and our mission were denied and disavowed in our own country as well.

I now know why men who have been to war together yearn to reunite. They want to tell stories or look at old pictures; they want to laugh or weep together. Comrades gather together because they long to be with the men who once stood shoulder to shoulder with them, who bore true witness to standing beside them no matter what the cost, men who suffered and sacrificed together, who were also stripped of their humanity by an ungrateful Nation.

Someone once wrote. I did not pick the men that fought with me. They were delivered by fate and the military. But, I know them in a way that I know no other men. I have never given anyone the trust that I awarded them. They were willing to guard something more precious than life. They would have carried my reputation, the memory of me. It was part of the bargain we all made, the reason we were so willing to die for one another (author unknown).

As we continue to trudge along high above the clouds pressing towards Phu Bai my mind begins to recall the four phases of life that I read about some time back, I don't remember who the author was. But, who ever wrote it sure had his or her act together.

Phase I, The beginning ages 0-18, childhood, learning, wishing, hoping and dreaming of success in life and glory to ones country and self not really knowing the outcome, the pain that will accompany that self made glory or what physical and mental terrifying sacrifices it will have taken to get there. Individual immaturity and childish assumption on how to make it work for ones self then abruptly and surprisingly learning the bitter truth.

Phase II, The second quarter of you life ages 19-40 getting your glory, praise and a mental monument to yourself followed by the reality of the pains of war that accompany life and life's mysterious and unannounced ups-and-downs. At this stage of one's life the physical and mental anguish having participated in and watching life slip away during combat has become a daily accepted fact and acceptance of life and death.

The constant suffering, sacrifice, personal feelings or invincibility against any harm. You continue to play the mental game of "its no big deal" I did it for an ungrateful country. Regret and/or anger are common place and confusing to ones self because deep down in your sole you know the truth of your feelings.

There is no lying or machismo, only reality. We're always asking why was I spared and why am I continually being punished from an unknown source when I have done so much.

Phase III, The third quarter of our life ages 41-60 memories good and bad primarily the latter of what you have done wrong with the short period of time that you've been here. Wishing you could turn back the pages of your life and re-do those areas that weigh heavy on your spirit, heart and mind.

But the reality is once that page of your life is turned there's no reviewing or having the ability to do it over. Terrible, torturous, regrettable memories of war you wish you could erase from your past and/or praying they had never occurred or come about.

Then lastly the closing of life Phase IV, the final phase as you mentally prepare for death, you sit or lay isolated and forgotten by your loved ones and what you think that you have accomplished in life. Attempting frantically to rationalize to yourself, your shameful historical past only to ask yourself and humanity, "Was it worth all the pain, regret, personal sacrifice, revenge and insanity I put myself through?"

Questioning yourself over-and-over never coming to common ground or a final conclusion until that last life giving breath you hold in your lungs escapes from your tired, withering, aged body. Was it all really worth it? (The author of these phases of life is unknown?)

As long as I have memory, I will think of them all, every day. I'm sure that when I leave this world, my last thoughts will be of my family and my comrades – such great gallant men and faithful warriors and was it really worth it? We the Secret Soldiers of the Second Army!

Last night as I lay on my pillow; I heard my dog tags say:
Don't be blue, old fellow

I'm with you night and day.

If death should ever part us, don't feel sad and
blue. I'll be there to take your place

I'll go home for you.

I know my dog tags are faithful. They go
where e'er I roam. But I will do my

Darndest, to beat those dog tags home.


Author PFC S.G. Leach Jr. (France 1944)

# CHAPTER 25

Headquarters Department of Army Washington, DC 19 March 1976

General Orders No. 6, Section II -

The President of the United States of America, authorized by Act of Congress, July 25, 1963, has awarded the Distinguished Service Cross to

## STAFF SERGEANT LESLIE A. CHAPMAN

## UNITED STATES ARMY

Staff Sergeant Leslie A. Chapman distinguished himself by extraordinary heroism in Vietnam while serving as a member of Reconnaissance Team Python, during the period 16 through 18 February 1971. On 16 February 1971, Reconnaissance Team "Python" was inserted deep into enemy territory to set up surveillance and road blocks against North Vietnamese units operating against allied units at Khe Sahn. Intelligence of the area was reliable but it was believed that a large concentration of enemy forces would be moving under cover of darkness. At 0230 hours, 17 February, Reconnaissance Team Python was probed by an estimated twenty North Vietnamese, nine of whom were killed. At this time heavy enemy troop movement was observed and reported from the Reconnaissance Team's vantage point. During the daylight hours of 18 February, Reconnaissance Team Python came under increasing enemy fire but refused extraction and continued to direct air strikes in an attempt to extract survivors of a helicopter crash which occurred 16 February. At 2330 hours, 17

February, the Reconnaissance Team was attacked on all sides by a numerically superior force and only after hours of heavy fighting were they able to repulse the enemy attack. At 0400 hours, 18 February, the enemy renewed their attacks, concentrating on the East side of the position. The eastern portion of the position was in danger of being overrun when Sergeant Chapman began employing a 60 MM mortar as a direct fire weapon with devastating results. Although wounded, Sergeant Chapman continually exposed himself to enemy fire in his effort to bolster the eastern perimeter. Gunships firing within ten meters of the Reconnaissance Team's defensive position were employed. Shortly after daybreak on 18 February, Sergeant Chapman discovered approximately a squad of enemy soldiers attempting to flank the Reconnaissance Team's position, Sergeant Chapman organized a defensive party of four and began to maneuver to intercept and ambush the enemy element. After the successful ambush had been executed, Sergeant Chapman fell back and reestablished a fighting position. The enemy element continued the attack and was met by a counterattack initiated by Sergeant Chapman. Under Sergeant Chapman's leadership the defenders succeeded in routing the enemy element. At 0830 hours, the enemy launched a massive attack on the Reconnaissance Team's position and succeeded in gaining high ground above the Reconnaissance Teams position. During the assault a B-40 rocket exploded, throwing one of the indigenous soldiers several yards down the slope into the midst of advancing enemy troops. Sergeant Chapman, with complete disregard for his own safety, charged down the slope into the enemy's position killing four of them in close combat. Recovering the wounded soldier he began to negotiate his way back to the reconnaissance Teams position. Although wounded again himself, and knocked down by exploding grenades he managed to carry the soldier back to the position where he administered first aid. During this time he was continually exposed to heavy automatic weapons fire, grenades, rockets and small arms fire. After successfully repulsing the enemy attack the Reconnaissance Team was extracted and credited with 42 enemies killed and assisted in the destruction of 350 killed by air. Sergeant Chapman's extraordinary heroism in the face of overwhelming odds reflects great credit upon him, his unit and the United States Army.

# CHAPTER 26

By virtue of the authority vested in me as President of the United States and as Commander OF THE Armed Forces of the United States, I have today awarded

## THE PREDSIDENTIAL UNIT CITATION (ARMY) FOR EXTRAORDINARY HEROISM, TO THE STUDIES AND OBSERVATION GROUP, MILITARY ASSISTANCE COMMAND, VIETNAM

The studies and Observation Group is cited for extraordinary heroism, great combat achievement and unwavering fidelity, while executing unheralded top secret missions deep behind enemy lines across Southeast Asia. Incorporating volunteers from all branches of the Armed Forces, and especially, U.S. Army Special Forces, SOG's ground, air and sea units fought officially denied actions which contributed immeasurably to the American war effort in Vietnam. MACV-SOG reconnaissance teams composed of Special Forces soldiers and indigenous personnel penetrated the enemy's most dangerous redoubts in the jungled Laotian wilderness and the sanctuaries of eastern Cambodia. Pursued by human trackers and even bloodhounds, these small teams outmaneuvered, outfought and overran their numerically superior force to uncover key enemy facilities, rescue downed pilots, plant wiretaps, mines and electronic sensors capture valuable enemy prisoners, ambush convoys, discover and assess targets for B-52 strikes, and inflict casualties all in greater proportions to their own losses. When enemy counter-measures became dangerously effective, SOG operators innovated their own counters, from high altitude parachuting and unusual explosive devices, to tactics as old as the French and Indian War. Fighting alongside their Montagnards, Chinese Nungs, Cambodians and Vietnamese allies, Special Forces-led Hatchet Forces companies and platoons staged daring raids against key enemy facilities in Laos and Cambodia, overran major munitions and supply stockpiles, and blocked enemy highways to choke off the flow of supplies to South Vietnam. SOG's cross border operations proved an effective economy-of-force, compelling the North Vietnamese Army to divert 50,000 soldiers to rear area security duties, far from the battlefields of South Vietnam. Support these hazardous mission were SOG's own U.S. and South Vietnamese Air Force transport and helicopter squadrons, along with USAF Forward Air Controllers and helicopter units of the U.S. Army and U.S. Marine Corps. These courageous aviators, saving lives by selflessly rising their own. SOG's Vietnamese naval surface forces – instructed and advised by U.S. Navy Seals – boldly raided North Vietnam's coast and won surface victories against the North Vietnamese Navy, while indigenous agent teams penetrated the very heartland of North Vietnam. Despite casualties that sometimes became universal, SOG's operators never wavered, but fought throughout the war with the fame flair, fidelity and intrepidity that distinguished SOG from its beginning. The Studies and Observations Group's combat prowess, martial skills and unacknowledged sacrifices save many American lives, and provide a paragon for America's future special operations forces.

Awarded at Fort Bragg North Carolina on April 4, 2001

# CHAPTER 27

## MACV-SOG-CCN (Personnel Roster, June 1971

| Name | Rank | MOS | Recon Team/Support | |
|------|------|-----|--------------------|---|
| Bellfi, Donnie | LTC/Inf | 31542 | Commander | |
| Elliott, Kent M. | Maj/Inf | 31542 | XO | |
| Guarding, Harold B. | Maj/Inf | 31542 | | |
| Lesene, Edward R. | Maj/Inf | 31542 | MLT-3 | |
| Meloy, John N. | Maj/Inf | 31543 | | |
| Arnold, Wiley R. | Cpt/Inf | 31542 | | |
| BluDau, Colin E. | Cpt/Inf | 71542 | | |
| Butler, James E. | Cpt/Inf | 31542 | Recon Company | |
| Care, Donald G. | Cpt/Inf | 31542 | | |
| Cavallefo, Joseph Jr. | Cpt/Inf | 31542 | | |

| Name | Rank | MOS | Recon Team/Support | |
|------|------|-----|--------------------|---|
| Danahy, Paul A. Jr. | Cpt/Inf | 31542 | | |
| Delk, Luchis | Cpt/Inf | 31542 | Recon Company | |
| Dunaway, John R. | Cpt/Inf | 31542 | Recon Company | |
| Kemmemer, Larry C. | Cpt/Inf | 31542 | Recon Company | |
| Manes, Larry T. | Cpt/Inf | 31542 | Recon Company Cmdr. | |
| Messinger, Keith J. Jr. | Cpt/Inf | 31542 | Recon Company | |
| Sandness, Stephen G. | Cpt/SigC | 0101D | | |
| Slatton, James W. | Cpt/Inf | 31542 | | |
| Sterling, William R. | Cpt/Inf | 31542 | Recon Company | |
| Taylor, Michael E. | Cpt/Inf | 31542 | MLT-3 | |
| Underwood, William J. | Cpt/Inf | 31542 | | |
| Valerski, John A. | Cpt/CE | 31331 | Recon Company | |
| Viseur, Charler B. | Cpt/Inf | 31542 | | |
| Wang, Jon B. | Cpt/MC | 33150 | CCN Surgeon | |
| Watson, (Doc) Ronald L. | Cpt/Inf | 31542 | Recon Company | |
| Wunderlick, Frederick C. | Cpt/Inf | 31542 | Recon Company | |

| Name | Rank | MOS | Recon Team/Support | |
|---|---|---|---|---|
| Dobbs, William E. | 1LT/Inf | 31542 | | |
| Dunnam, Gary L. | 1LT/Inf | 71542 | Recon Company | |
| Falterman, Monroe L. Jr. | 1LT/Inf | 31542 | | |
| Hagen, Loren D. (KIA) | 1LT/Inf | 31331 | Recon Company | MOH |
| Entrican, Danny | 1LT/Inf | 31542 | Recon Company | |
| Michel, Stephen | 1LT/Inf | 71542 | | |
| Oxx, Lawrence M. Jr. | 1LT/Inf | 31542 | Recon Company | |
| Rohen, Gary J. | 1LT/MSC | 33506 | | |
| Walbridge, John H. | 1LT/Inf | 31542 | Recon Company | |
| Wilson, Kesene N. | 1LT/Inf | 31542 | | |
| *Attached Officers* | | | | |
| Utley, Tom W. Jr. | 1LT/ USAF | 2524 | | |
| Vatis, Martin D. | Maj/USAF | 1435H | | |
| Rodriguez, Adrian A. | SGM/E9 | 11G5S | CCN Command CSM | |
| Waugh, William D. | SGM/E9 | 11F5S | Recon Company SGM | |
| West, Donald F. | SGM/E9 | 11F5S | TOC | KIA |
| Austria, Louis | MSG/E8 | 11F5S | S-4 | |

| Name | Rank | MOS | Recon Team/Support | |
|------|------|-----|--------------------|--|
| Baldwin, Howard S. | MSG/E8 | 11F5S | TOC | |
| Budrow, Kimber O. | MSG/E8 | 11F5S | MLT-2 NCOIC | |
| Comerford, Steven W. | MSG/E8 | 11F5S | Recon Company | |
| Dover, Clarence N. | MSG/E8 | 11F5S | MLT-1 | |
| Foster, Willie J. | MSG/E8 | 91Z5S | Chase Medic | |
| Gilbreth, Doner | MSG/E8 | 11F5S | S-2 | |
| Hartshorn, Robert O. | 1SG/E8 | 11G5S | 1st Sergeant | |
| Mullis, Lawrence M. | MSG/E8 | 27120 | ALO | |
| Nelson, David L. | 1SG/E8 | 95B5S | 1st Sergenat Hqs Co | |
| Quiroga, Nemorig J | MSG/E8 | 31Z5S | Commo | |
| Rozanski, Janusz | MSG/E8 | 11F5S | Company 1St Sergeant | |
| Villanueva, Vincent | MSG/E8 | 11F5S | MLT-1 | |
| Weber, Frank F. | MSG/E8 | 11F5S | TOC | |
| Anderson, Kenneth M. | SFC/E7 | 11B4S | MLT-1 | |
| Bath, James O. | SFC/E7 | 11F4S | Recon Company | |
| Bolton, Robert L. | SFC/E7 | 11B4S | Recon Company | |

| Name | Rank | MOS | Recon Team/Support | |
|------|------|-----|--------------------|--|
| Brieley, George W. Jr. | SFC/E7 | 11C4S | Company B | |
| Brown, Walter Jr. | SFC/E7 | 11B4S | TOC | |
| Cheney, David | SFC/E7 | 12B4S | MLT-2 Covey | |
| Dailey, Franklin T. | SFC/E7 | 11B4S | Recon Company | |
| Dalley, Richard J. | SFC/E7 | 11B4S | Training | |
| Fernandez, William M. | SFC/E7 | 11F4S | MLT-1 | KIA |
| Frey, David F. | SFC/E7 | 11B4S | Company A | |
| Freeman, Donald E. | SFC/E7 | 11B4S | S-4 | |
| Hall, Richard N. | SFC/E7 | 11B4S | ALO | |
| Heflin, Richard B. | SFC/E7 | 11B4S | Company C | |
| Hernandez, Samuel D. | SFC/E7 | 11C4S | Recon Company | |
| James, Richard D. Jr. | SFC/E7 | 91B4S | Dispensary | |
| Johns, Gerald A. | SFC/E7 | 11C4S | Recon Company | |
| Jones, Ola C. | SFC/E7 | 05B4S | Commo | |
| Jones, Thomas A. III | SFC/E7 | 11F4S | TOC | |
| Kramer, Philip | SFC/E7 | 11F4S | MLT-2 | |

| Name | Rank | MOS | Recon Team/Support | |
|------|------|-----|--------------------|--|
| Ku, George M. | SFC/E7 | 11B4S | Club | |
| Lane, Alfred S. | SFC/E7 | 11F4S | TOC | |
| Leonard, William F. | SFC/E7 | 11F4S | TOC | |
| Long, Jack Jr. | SFC/E7 | 11C4S | The Phantom Shitter | |
| Loya, Raymond P. | SFC/E7 | 11B4S | Recon Club Manager | |
| Lynch, William R. | SFC/E7 | 12B4S | Co C | |
| Mills, Audley D. | SFC/E7 | 11B4S | Sct | |
| O'Daniel, Lloyd E. | SFC/E7 | 11B4S | OPS | |
| Richard, John R. | SFC/E7 | 11F4S | S-1 | |
| Smith, Michael V. | SFC/E7 | 11B4S | Recon Company | |
| Stedman, Gary M. | SFC/E7 | 12B4S | Recon Company | |
| Stockman, Gene W. | SFC/E7 | 71L4S | S-1 | |
| Taylor, James | SFC/E7 | 76Y40 | S-4 | |
| Turner, James E. | SFC/E7 | 05B4S | Commo | |
| Van Meter, Billy N. | SFC/E7 | 11F4S | Company B | |
| Ward, Allan T. | SFC/E7 | 11B4S | MLT-2 | |

| Name | Rank | MOS | Recon Team/Support | |
|------|------|-----|--------------------|---|
| Wells, Lewis H. | SFC/E7 | 11B4S | Recon Company | |
| Wesley, Charles F. | SFC/E7 | 11C4S | Recon Company | |
| Whitener, James A. | SFC/E7 | 91B4S | Dispensary | |
| Ziblinski, Herry J. | SFC/E7 | 05B4S | MLT-1 | |
| Adams, Frederick G. | SSG/E6 | 05B4S | Recon Company | |
| Adams, Lloyd (Snake) | SSG/E6 | 05B4S | Recon Company | |
| Anderson, Douglas | SSG/E6 | 11B4S | MLT-1 | |
| Arnett, Russell | SSG/E6 | 05B4S | Commo | |
| Ashton, Sweed | SSG/E6 | 11B4S | Recon Company | |
| Bargewell, Eldon | SSG/E6 | 11B4S | Recon Company | |
| Bingham, Klaus | SSG/E6 | 12B4S | Recon Company | KIA |
| Bingham, Oran L. | SSG/E6 | 12B4S | Recon Company | KIA |
| Doner, Horace L. | SSG/E6 | 05C4S | MLT | |
| Brasier, Larry | SSG/E6 | 05B4S | Recon Company | |
| Buts, Kenneth D. | SSG/E6 | 11B4S | Company C | |
| Castillo, Robert J. | SSG/E6 | C5B4S | Recon Company | |

| Name | Rank | MOS | Recon Team/Support | |
|---|---|---|---|---|
| Castro, Guardalup N. | SSG/E6 | 12B4S | S-4 | |
| Chaffee, Colin L. | SSG/E6 | 11C4S | Recon Company | |
| Chapman, Leslie A. | SSG/E6 | 11B4S | Recon Company | |
| Christiansen, Myron B. | SSG/E6 | 05B4S | MLT | |
| Cook, Robert E. | SSG/E6 | 11C4S | Recon Company | |
| Coon, James D. | SSG/E6 | 63C4P | S-4 | |
| Cottrell, George A. Jr. | SSG/E6 | 11B4S | Recon Company | |
| Danzer, Charles W. | SSG/E6 | 11F4S | Recon Company | |
| Daugherty, David D. | SSG/E6 | 05B4S | Recon Company | |
| Doran, Ronald L. | SSG/E6 | 11B4S | Recon Company | |
| Olia, Johnny W. | SSG/E6 | 05B4S | Recon Company | |
| Elliott, Paul D. | SSG/E6 | 73Y4S | MLT | |
| Frisbie, William L. | SSG/E6 | 11F4S | AST | |
| Fry, Ronald L. | SSG/E6 | 11F4S | MLT | |
| Gast, Noel | SSG/E6 | 95B3S | Recon Company | |
| Gary, Rupus T. | SSF/E6 | 11C4S | Isolation | |

| Name | Rank | MOS | Recon Team/Support | |
|---|---|---|---|---|
| George, Gordon S. | SSG/E6 | 11B4S | Commo | |
| Gipson, Charles | SSG/E6 | 11C4S | Recon Company | |
| Graham, Troy | SSG/E6 | 11B4S | MP | |
| Hamlet, Donald W. | SSG/E6 | 05B4S | R&U | |
| Heminger, Patrick J. | SSG/E6 | 11F4S | Recon Company | |
| Hink, Stephen G. | SSG/E6 | 11B4S | S-4 | |
| Holmes, Kenneth | SSG/E6 | 11C4S | Recon Company | |
| Houser, John H. Jr. | SSG/E6 | 11B4S | Recon Company | |
| Hughes, Jackson I. | SSG/E6 | 05B4S | Commo | |
| Hutchesson, Arnold R. | SSG/E6 | 11B4S | Company A | |
| Jay, Charles D. | SSG/E6 | 11C4S | Recon Company | |
| Johnson, Jimmie R. | SSG/E6 | 11F5S | Recon Company | |
| Jung, Gustav P. | SSG/E6 | 11B4S | Unk | |
| Kirby, Stanley, B. | SSG/E6 | 05B4S | Commo | |
| Krempa, William J. | SSG/E6 | 05B4S | Recon Company | |
| Lauck, Ronald W. | SSG/E6 | 76Y4S | S-4 | |

| Name | Rank | MOS | Recon Team/Support | |
|------|------|-----|--------------------|--|
| Lanton, Richard A. | SSG/E6 | 05B4P | Commo | |
| Leavister, John | SSG/E6 | 11C4S | Recon Company | |
| Luttrell, James M. | SSG/E6 | 11B4S | Recon Company | KIA |
| Marble, Robert S. | SSG/E6 | 05B4S | Commo | |
| Martin, Walter | SSG/E6 | 11C4S | Unk | |
| Maynard, Julius | SSG/E6 | 11F4S | TOC | |
| McCoy, Albert | SSG/E6 | 05B4S | Recon Company | KIA |
| McWhorter, Dennis R. | SSG/E6 | 05B4S | Commo | |
| Murphy, Don (Sluggo) | SSG/E6 | 11B4S | Recon Company | |
| Queen, Gary | SSG/E6 | 11C4S | Recon Company | KIA |
| Robinson, David | SSG/E6 | 11B4S | Recon Company | |
| Thompson, Jessie | SSG/E6 | 11B4S | Recon Company | |
| Walton, Lewis C. | SSG/E6 | 11F4S | Recon Company | KIA |
| Andersen, Tony | SGT/E5 | 11B4S | Recon Company | |
| Beiber | SGT/E5 | 11C4S | Recon Company | |
| Berg, Bruce A | SGT/E5 | 05B4S | Recon Company | KIA |

| Name | Rank | MOS | Recon Team/Support | |
|---|---|---|---|---|
| Busler, Charlie | SP5/E5 | 11B4P | Recon Company | |
| Campbell, Jessie | SGT/E5 | 11B4S | Recon Company | |
| Cavianni, Jon | SGT/E5 | 11B4S | Recon Company | MOH |
| Davidson, Ronald | SGT/E5 | 11B4S | Recon Company | |
| Dehnke, Dale | SGT/E5 | 11B4S | Recon Company | KIA |
| Frovary, Ray | SGT/E5 | 11B4S | Recon Company | |
| Haynes | SGT/E5 | 11C4S | Recon Company | |
| Hendricks, Rick | SGT/E5 | 11B4S | Recon Company | |
| Hollingworth, David | SP5/E5 | 11B4S | Recon Company | KIA |
| Jay, Charlie | SGT/E5 | 11C4S | Recon Company | |
| Kelly, Don | SGT/E5 | 11B4S | Recon Company | |
| Lloyd, Allen R. | SGT/E5 | 11B4S | Recon Company | KIA |
| McGlothren, Lemuel D. | SGT/E5 | 11B4S | Recon Company | |
| Pope, Roger | SGT/E5 | 11B4S | Recon Company | |
| Robinson, Robbie | SGT/E5 | 11C4S | Recon Company | |
| Sinton, | SGT/E5 | 11B4S | Recon Company | |

| Name | Rank | MOS | Recon Team/Support | |
|------|------|-----|--------------------|---|
| Strohlein, Madison A. | SGT/E5 | 05B4S | Recon Company | MIA |
| Thomas, Jessie | SGT/E5 | 11C4S | Recon Company | |
| Waters, Mud Hole | SGT/E5 | 11B4S | Recon Company | |

# CHAPTER 28

MACV-SOG-CCN Recon Teams –

Definitions     10 – Team Leader

11 – Assistant Team Leader

12 – Team Member

| RT ADDER | RT ALASKA | RT ANACONDA |
|---|---|---|
| 10 - SP/5 Busler | 10 - 1LT Entricon | 10 – SSG Daugherty |
| 11 - SGT Scott M. | 11 – SP5 Hollingworth | 11 – SSG Bingham O. |
| 12 – SGT Jesperson | 12 – SGT Spaulding | 12 – SFC Ward |
| RT ASP | RT BUSHMASTER | RT CONNECTICUTT |
| 10 – Cpt Delk | 10 – SSG Robinson D. | 10 – SSG Smith A. |
| 11 – SSG Bingham K. | 11 – SSG Bargewell | 11 – SSG Morris |
| 12 – SSG Luttrell | 12 – SGT Smith | 12 – SSG Vance |

| RT CRUSADER | RT INDIGO | RT INTRUDER |
|---|---|---|
| 10 – SGT Dehnke | 10 – SSG Carnes | 10 – 1LT Waldridge |
| 11 – SGT Scott S. | 11 – 1LT Dunnam | 11 – SGT Robinson R. |
| 12 – SGT Kelley | 12 – 1LT Rohen | 12 – 1LT Oxx |
| RT KANSAS | RT KRAIT | RT LOUISIANA |
| 10 – 1LT Hagen | 10 - SGT Hendrick | 10 - 1LT Hanson |
| 11 – SSG Cottrell | 11 – SGT Reese | 11 – SGT Frovarp |
| 12 – SGT Anderson | 12 – Adams | 12 – SSG Leavister |
| RT MAMBA | RT NORTH CAROLINA | RT OKLAHOMA |
| 10 – 2LT Deluca | 10 – CPT Valerski | 10 – SGT Landers |
| 11 – SGT Pope | 11 – SSG Doran | 11 – SGT Boyd |
| 12 – SGT Montgomery | 12 – 1LT Hadley | 12 – SSG Hamlet |
| RT PYTHON | RT RATTLER | RT RHODE ISLAND |
| 10 – Cpt Butler | 10 – SSG Ashton | 10 – CPT Sterling |
| 11 – SSG Chapman | 11 – Beiber | 11 – SFC Ku |
| 12 – SSG Owles | 12 – Vacant | 12 – 1LT Wilson |

| RT SIDEWINDER | RT VIPER | RT FLORIDA |
|---|---|---|
| 10 – Cpt Lemasters | 10 – SSG Heminger | 10 - SFC Hernandes |
| 11 – SGT Hynes | 11 – SGT Jay | 11 - SGT Sinton |
| 12 – Vacant | 12 – SSG Murphy | 12 - SFC Wells |

| RT GEORGIA | | |
|---|---|---|
| 10 – Sgt Thomas | | |
| 11 – SGT Kuse | | |

CPSIA information can be obtained at www.ICGtesting.com
Printed in the USA
245357LV00002B/70/P